Glory and B*llocks

COLIN BROWN is the author of the acclaimed *Whitehall: The Street that Shaped a Nation*. Formerly political editor of the *Sunday Telegraph* and the *Independent on Sunday*, deputy political editor of the *Independent* and Parliamentary correspondent for the *Guardian*, he covered breaking news in Downing Street and Westminster for over thirty years. He lives in London.

ALSO BY COLIN BROWN

Whitehall: The Street that Shaped a Nation

Fighting Talk: The Biography of John Prescott

GLORY
AND B*LLOCKS

The Truth behind Ten Defining Events
in British History

COLIN BROWN

ONEWORLD

A Oneworld Book

Published by Oneworld Publications 2013

Reprinted in 2013, 2014

Copyright © Colin Brown 2012, 2013

This book was first published as *Real Britannia* in 2012

The moral right of Colin Brown to be identified as the Author
of this work has been asserted by him in accordance with the
Copyright, Designs and Patents Act 1988

ISBN 978-1-85168-992-7
Ebook ISBN 978-1-78074-443-8

Illustration credits on p. 315
Designed and typeset by Tetragon, London
Cover design by Stuart Polson
Printed and bound by CPI Group (UK) Ltd, Croydon, CR0 4YY

Oneworld Publications
10 Bloomsbury Street,
London WC1B 3SR, England

Stay up to date with the latest books,
special offers, and exclusive content from
Oneworld with our monthly newsletter

Sign up on our website
www.oneworld-publications.com

CONTENTS

To my sister, Lilian (1931–2009),
who made all things possible

Ten years

The idea for this book started with a blunder by David Cameron. In the midst of the events to mark the seventieth anniversary of the Battle of Britain, the Prime Minister said Britain was a 'junior partner' to the United States in 1940. In fact, Britain was alone when it faced the might of Hitler's Third Reich in 1940. It was not until the attack on Pearl Harbor by Japanese forces, on 7 December 1941, that America entered the Second World War.

When Cameron attempted to repair the damage, he stumbled into another controversy. Interviewed on the BBC Radio 4 *Today* programme, Cameron said: 'Nineteen-forty, to me, is the proudest year of British history bar none. We stood on our own against the Nazi tyranny. Let me absolutely put that on the record. It is the proudest year in all of British history.'[1]

Many would have agreed with him. Churchill himself, when asked by Dorothy, the wife of Lord Moran, his physician, which year of his life he would have chosen to relive, did not hesitate. He replied: 'Nineteen-forty every time, every time...'[2]

It therefore came as a surprise to me that Cameron's seemingly unexceptional remarks provoked an even greater controversy. Suddenly the nation was engaged in a debate: what was Britain's proudest year? Everyone seemed to have a different answer. A YouGov poll in 2010 showed the question sharply divided the nation, between men and women, Conservative and Labour voters. Women tended to opt for years of social or democratic advance – 1833, and the Abolition of Slavery; 1928, when the Suffragettes finally secured votes for women on the same terms as men; and 1948, the year when the National Health Service was born. Men opted for years of military victories: 1415, and the Battle of Azincourt; 1588, with the defeat of the Spanish Armada; 1815, when Wellington met Napoleon at the Battle of Waterloo; and 1982, the victory over Argentina in the Falklands War. The popular favourite in the poll, with the support of twenty-nine per cent of the public was, indeed, 1940. It was the runaway winner among Conservatives (39%), men (38%) and middle-class electors (32%).

This led to a heated debate on BBC *Newsnight* between two histor- ians, Antony Beevor and Kate Williams. Beevor supported Cameron. 'The reason for 1940 is not just a question of national survival,' he said. 'It was a moment of great moral and physical courage which had a tre- mendous effect on the whole of the course of the Second World War. If Churchill had agreed to negotiation as Halifax and one or two others wanted, Hitler would have achieved all of his objectives. That chance of fighting back, with America coming into the war, would have been lost.' Williams disagreed strongly. 'My top choice would be the abolition of slavery because in the Second World War, we were against the aggressor, we were fighting back. With the abolition of the slave trade in 1807 and the abolition of slavery in 1833, we were leading the world. The Govern- ment was doing something that didn't help Britain – Britain made so much money from the slave trade but by responding to the popular swell, people who believed in the rights of their fellow men, we led the world. I really think that was their proudest moment.'[3]

Members of the public pitched in. Some suggested 1966 – the last time England won the World Cup. Another popular choice was 1953, the year when the Union Jack was raised for the first time on Everest by Edmund Hillary, a New Zealander, and Sherpa Tenzing almost on the same day that the Coronation of Queen Elizabeth II took place. But 1953 was also the year in which the England football team were humbled by Ferenc Puskas and Hungary, 6–3, at the 'Empire Wembley Stadium', as it was proudly known then.

Like David Cameron, I had a sketchy understanding about some of the great landmark years in our history, and I therefore decided to find out more about them. I approached the question as I would any political investigation at Westminster or Downing Street, going back to the original sources where I could, challenging the accepted truths, trying to sift fact from fiction, myth from reality. The results were surprising.

I discovered that, contrary to popular belief, the longbow was not responsible for the English (and Welsh) victory at Azincourt; that Queen Elizabeth I's great Armada speech at Tilbury was probably an enormous exercise in spin; and that some who campaigned alongside Wilberforce for the abolition of the slave trade saw him as a hindrance rather than a hero of change. As I reflect in the Postscript, I was also reminded strongly how important that strip of sea between Dover and Calais really is. I was also surprised to find that, despite that natural fortress, we have been successfully invaded at least twice since 1066 – in 1216 as well as in 1688.

My investigations took me to some unexpected places, including climbing out of a window to stand as close as I could to Churchill's secret balcony high up on the White Cliffs of Dover; a Thames-side fort dwarfed by a container port and a power station (an overlooked gem I would recommend anyone to visit); and the picturesque tourist port of Brixham, in Devon, where the Loyal Orange Lodges march every year around the harbour to mark Britain's forgotten Dutch invasion (though it must make the tourists wonder whether they have landed in Belfast). It also took me to unspoiled Azincourt, in Northern France, on St Crispin's Day – and to a charming museum dedicated to French humiliation; as well as to the wealthy Brussels commuter town of Waterloo, where I found a dilapidated farm that was once witness to heroism. If this account encourages more to cover similar ground, it will be worth it.

I also experienced a 'hairs-on-the-back-of-the-neck' moment when I felt I was touching history, such as the time at the Women's Library in London's East End when I held the return ticket to Epsom bought by suffragette Emily Davison before she fell under the King's horse at the 1913 Derby; reading a scrap of paper in the British Library that contained (I am convinced) a scribbled note of Queen Elizabeth I's famous Armada speech; and seeing the north gate at Hougoumont, where the 'bravest of the brave' turned the battle. I met many wonderful people (I apologize in advance if I have omitted many from the Acknowledgements) who help to keep our history alive in museums around the country, including at Brixham and Wilberforce's house in Hull.

But there were also times when I was dismayed by the way that we try to teach our island story today. None more so than the day I went to the National Maritime Museum (NMM) in Greenwich to find out how Elizabeth's piratical captains such as Drake defeated the Dons of the Spanish Armada. I was met at the shiny new entrance (with wave effects) by a notice telling visitors: 'The collection of two million objects have been arranged into groups to represent six different emotions – anticipation, love, sadness, pride, aggression and joy'.

History as six emotions? I found funeral mugs for Admiral Lord Nelson are arranged under 'sadness'. Other items of Nelsonia are displayed under 'love' because they came from the house in Merton, south London, that he shared with his mistress, Emma Hamilton. This seems to me to be treating history as soap opera.

The main gallery at the NMM is dedicated to the Atlantic: slavery, trade, empire. Visitors are told: 'This gallery is about the movement of people, goods and ideas across and around the Atlantic Ocean from the seventeenth century to the nineteenth century. The connections created by these movements changed the lives of people on three continents, profoundly affecting their cultures and societies and shaping the world we live in today.' Yes, I thought, but what about the 'movement of people' up the English Channel in August 1588?

There was a brilliant exhibition at the NMM in 1988 to coincide with the fourth centenary of the defeat of the Spanish Armada, and the research department is excellent. But I drew a blank expression when I asked an attendant: 'Where is the Armada gallery?' That is because there isn't one. There is no coherent display to show how England defeated the Spanish Armada. Nor could I find much about Nelson's campaigns at sea, which literally allowed Britannia to rule the waves in the nineteenth century, but then they were mostly around the Mediterranean. It could be argued that one glaring omission in this book is 1805, the year of Trafalgar, which finally ended the threat of an invasion of England by Napoleon. It seemed to me (and obviously, the pollsters) that 1815 was the more decisive year, for it ended the Napoleonic wars, and largely set the scene for modern Europe.

I asked the NMM whether they were under the spell of *pc world*, the world of political correctness. I was sent the museum's mission statement, patiently explaining that maritime history now is presented in its 'social, political and cultural contexts'. 'This process,' continued the NMM, 'has brought a renewed intellectual energy and excitement to maritime history, which the Museum has both welcomed and actively supported.' I felt like screaming: yes, but what about the battles?

The museum is currently in the middle of a major renewal of all its maritime galleries. By 2020, there will be six permanent galleries covering the Royal Navy (two galleries); maritime trade; exploration; migration; and one combining London, Greenwich and the Thames, which will span the period from Tudor London to today. At the time of writing, Nelson and his precious uniform holed by the bullet that killed him is consigned to a corner of its Maritime London gallery, presumably on the grounds that he lived at Merton and visited the Admiralty in Whitehall or perhaps because his tomb is at St Paul's.

When I first came to London over thirty years ago, there was an entire gallery devoted to Nelson and his battles (although a neon screen raised the question: 'Nelson – a hero?'). There were also mock gun ports where kids could play at firing broadsides. Not any more. There is a great deal of space at the NMM devoted to teaching visitors about climate change and its effects on the oceans of the world, and the Atlantic gallery focuses on the 'social, political and cultural context' of mass migration brought about by trade. This is all very laudable but it seems to me we are in danger of treating Britain's military victories against the Dutch, the Spanish and the French like a punch-up on a drunken night out which we would prefer to forget. There is little to show how a fighting Man o' War was operated. For that, you may be better off reading the Aubrey-Maturin sagas by Patrick O'Brian or travelling to the NMM collection in Portsmouth to see Nelson's flagship, the *Victory*.

Nigel Rigby, head of research, assured me that this will be put right: 'Two new naval galleries, *Navy, Nation, Nelson*, will indeed open in June 2013, and you will not be surprised to hear from the title that Nelson's Trafalgar uniform jacket will be among the superb collection of objects that have been selected for display,' he reported. 'The gallery runs from the Glorious Revolution to the end of the Napoleonic wars and is structured around two interwoven stories: the first concerns the perils, customs and skills that made the Royal Navy, in many ways, a world apart; the second relates to the dazzling richness that nonetheless marked the relationship of navy and nation.' Whether that includes the great sea engagements, we will have to wait and see.

As I researched the Battle of Waterloo, there were reports that the bi-centenary celebrations in 2015 are being kept relatively low-key in London to avoid upsetting the French. It would not be the first time diplomacy has intervened in a national anniversary. Even when that modern-day Boadicea, Margaret Thatcher, was in power, the tercentenary celebrations for the overthrow of the Catholic King James II were played down because the Government was seeking to avoid exacerbating the Troubles. It turned out its fears were well founded. An IRA hit team was rumbled as it scouted out an assassination attempt on an innocent businessman whose only crime was to chair the committee for the celebrations. But that is exceptional.

Research into Britain's 'proudest' year inevitably raised the question: what is Britishness?

Gordon Brown, the former Labour Prime Minister, struggled with the issue when he was in power. He even introduced a US-style citizenship test, though we have not embraced pride in our nationhood like the Americans, and probably never will. More recently, the outspoken historian David Starkey expressed exasperation with our reluctance to celebrate our national heritage for fear of upsetting others. 'A nation cannot exist without a common core of values,' he said on BBC *Question Time* in March 2012. 'We are trying this extraordinary experiment of being a nation without nationalism.'

Churchill, a member of a great political and military dynasty and the author of several great histories, understood the power of our past. When he delivered his famous speech to the House of Commons on 18 June 1940, he would have been acutely conscious that he was speaking on 'Waterloo Day', the anniversary of Wellington's great victory over Napoleon in 1815. 'If we fail, then the whole world, including the United States, including all that we have known and cared for, will sink into the abyss of a new dark age made more sinister, and perhaps more protracted, by the lights of perverted science. Let us therefore brace ourselves to our duties, and so bear ourselves, that if the British Empire and its Commonwealth last for a thousand years, men will still say, this was their finest hour,' he said.

Our natural diffidence can lead us to play down our role in world history. I was reminded of this when talking to a Norwegian while I was researching this book. He told me: 'The history of Britain is the history of the world. Had it not been for the British I would be speaking German today.'

Taking pride in our past is not jingoistic. This book examines our role in the slave trade, as well as our part in ending it. It also questions whether it is right, in the twenty-first century, still to have legislation on the statute book that discriminates against Catholics. As a nation, we are changing. We should not romanticize our past, but nor should we forget it. This is an attempt to show us as we really are.

COLIN BROWN

Glory and B*llocks

ONE

1215

*'All the things which the king
valued too highly in the world'*

<small>LANGHAM POND, RUNNYMEDE:</small>
How King John and the barons may have seen the old Thames.

King John was ill. He was riding at the head of his small mobile force of armed horsemen with his guts in torment and his bowels turning to water. Behind him, his baggage train struggled to keep up, but John needed to get to his first stop on his route, Swineshead Abbey. And to do that, he had to cross to the north bank of the Wash, the great bite out of the Norfolk coast where the sea rushes in across the marshes at high tide.

The route was difficult at the best of times, as the King picked his way across the mudflats where the dunlin pecked at molluscs in the sucking mud, and oystercatchers gave their shrill, wild cries. But this was the worst of times for King John. It was October, the weather was turning foul and he was in a hurry.

He was engaged in a debilitating civil war with his barons, and was in hostile country. He had ridden from a loyalist stronghold at Newark down to Lynn, where he had ordered supplies from the Continent to keep up the war, but he had contracted a terrible bout of dysentery while he had been there, probably from something he had eaten. Now it was consuming him.

Dysentery – known then by its painfully explicit medieval name of the 'bloody flux' – was all too common in Europe in the thirteenth century. John's eldest brother Henry (who would have inherited the Crown before his older brother Richard I) died of the disease in 1183 after campaigning against Richard in a family feud in France. Today, in developed countries, dysentery is generally a mild illness and not fatal. The symptoms normally begin to arise within three days, disappearing after a week, but amoebic strains of the disease, once in the bloodstream, can attack the liver, triggering fever, delirium and death. The only treatment before the development of antibiotics was to stop dehydration by drinking water mixed with alcohol (to kill the bugs in the water). King John desperately needed rest, and medical help.

Barring his way was the Wellstream, the tidal river that covered the mudflats at high tide. He could have gone by a longer route, down to Wisbech and a crossing where the river narrowed, and sent his baggage train on the more direct route across the Wash. This is the theory that was firmly held by academics until the mid-1960s, when it was challenged persuasively by the medieval historian Sir James Clarke Holt. Professor Holt argued that in the hostile Fenlands of East Anglia John was highly unlikely to have separated from his baggage train and its precious cargo. 'The King, especially, was unlikely to let such of his regalia, money and precious movables as he had with him, far from his sight'.[1]

I found evidence to support Holt's theory in a nineteenth-century Ordnance Survey map. It shows that a route across the Wash was still in use as a tidal highway as late as 1824. The date is significant – this was just a few years before the land here was finally drained, and the waters were then held back behind protective banks. With the draining, all signs of the medieval tracks across the Wellstream were wiped out. The track on the OS map is clearly marked across the salt marshes, a dotted line stretching from Cross Keys (still the name of a local village) to the Sutton bank, where a modern bridge on the A17 crosses the River Welland. The label reads 'Wash Way', the name that John would have known for the medieval route across the mudflats.

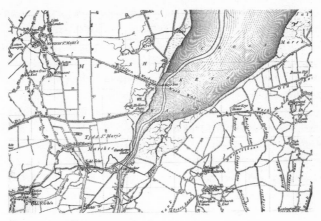

ORDNANCE SURVEY MAP, 1824:
The old path across the Wash, before the land was drained.

He had been told that low tide was at around 11.15 a.m., and he should have waited for a guide. But John was notoriously impatient and, given the fact that he was suffering from dysentery, it is fair to assume he could not wait. The way was probably staked out with poles or branches, but the sea began to run in rivulets across the mud, covering the quicksand.

What happened next has caused controversy for eight centuries, largely because we have to depend on the accounts of monks – the only chroniclers of the time – who had a vested interest in depicting King John, still seen by many clerics in England as an enemy of the Church, being crushed by the forces of God. The monks report that, as King John and his bodyguards kicked their horses on across the salt marsh, the wheels of the baggage train, following behind them, became stuck in quicksand. There were frantic efforts to rescue the laden carts, but they were sinking fast, and nothing could stop them from going down. All that was left was for the horses and men to struggle to break themselves free, so that they would not be swallowed up by the sucking sands.

Ralph, a monk at Coggeshall Abbey, in Essex, wrote that the King lost 'his Chapel with his relics and some of his pack-horses with divers household goods at the Wellstream and many of his familia [household] were drowned in the waters of the sea and sucked into the quicksand there, because they had set out incautiously and hastily before the tide had receded'. Ralph may have seen the religious relics as being of greater value than more earthly riches. Roger of Wendover, from St Albans Abbey, wrote that King John had lost his 'treasures and precious vessels and all the other things which he cherished with special care; for the ground was opened in the midst of the waves, and bottomless whirlpools engulfed everything, together with men and horses so that not a single foot soldier got away to bear tidings of the disaster to the king'.

Roger today would be a tabloid journalist. Yet, he was not exaggerating the deadly speed with which the sea can come in. The mudflats remain dangerous, even with modern technology to guide us, as was seen in 2004 when thirty cockle-pickers, mostly immigrants from China, were caught by a rising tide in Morecambe Bay, on the Lancashire and Cumbrian coast, and eighteen were drowned.

A generation after King John lost his treasure, the tale was embroidered by yet another chronicler, the monk Matthew Paris, who recorded that the quicksand swallowed up 'the packhorses bearing his booty and loot, and all his treasure and household effects. For the ground opened in the midst of the waves and the sand which is called quick sucked in everything – horses and men, weapons, tents, victuals and all the things which the King valued too highly in the world – apart from his life.'

Whatever the extent of John's losses, it is almost certain they included his grandmother Matilda's regalia – the great crown, the gold wand with a dove and the sword of Tristram – which she had worn as Empress of Germany. He is known to have been in possession of her Crown Jewels, and they were never heard of again. His own Crown Jewels may have gone down into the sands of the Wash as well. John was a collector of jewellery, and his treasures were minutely recorded by his clerks in 'patent rolls' of parchment which survive. They list gold and silver goblets, flagons, basins, candelabra, phylacteries – amulets or charms – pendants and jewel-encrusted belts. His regalia, precious silver plate and jewelled cups were missing from the inventories when his son was crowned as his successor a few months later. Whatever their value, the scribes were clear that the impact of the loss on John was fatal. Ralph, the Coggeshall monk, recorded that it had hastened John's death. Shakespeare underlines the political impact in his telling of the life of King John:

> I'll tell thee, Hubert, half my power this night
> Passing these flats, are taken by the tide,
> These Lincoln washes have devoured them

~(?~

John had been counting on using some of his treasure to raise money to continue his fight. With the baggage train, John's last hopes of defeating his enemies sank too. His resistance had finished. In a week, he would be dead.

He retreated to Wisbech to recover; letters pinpoint his arrival there on 12 October. The next day, he covered the forty difficult miles to Swineshead Abbey, crossing more streams and marshes, and spent the night there before riding nineteen miles to Sleaford. John rested overnight at Sleaford, then struggled on to the Bishop of Lincoln's castle at Newark.

A storm blew up during the early hours of 18 October, and messengers struggled against the howling wind to bring letters for the King; they were from some of the rebels, who wanted to return to his banner, but he was too ill to read them. The King was failing. Abbot Adam of Croxton Abbey, a renowned herbal practitioner, was summoned to the castle to act as his doctor and confessor. On his deathbed, John dictated his will and asked to be buried 'in the church of St Mary and St Wolfstan' at Worcester Cathedral. The codicil still survives in the cathedral library.

During the early hours of 19 October, a week after the loss of his treasure in the Wash, John died. In a practice common at the time, Abbot Adam cut out his heart and buried it in the abbey church at Croxton, near Croxton Kerrial, Leicestershire. His intestines were interred on the nearby Windmill Hill, west of the fishponds in Croxton Park, which is all that is left of the ancient abbey. In his sweeping BBC television series, *The History of Britain*, Simon Schama said it showed that, as in life, John 'died gutless'.

As he had requested, John's armed mercenaries solemnly carried his body, minus his troubled guts, across the country to Worcester Cathedral, and then laid it before the altar of St Wulfstan. He was placed in a tomb surmounted with the effigies of St Wulfstan and St Oswald flanking the King's own image. In 1797, John's tomb was opened and the remains were measured, confirming he was just over five feet six inches tall, an inch below the average height for the time. The King's body had been covered in a robe of red crimson damask and the remains of a sword and scabbard lay by his side.

His death sparked a brushfire of medieval conspiracy theories, chief among them that a Catholic monk, based at Swineshead Abbey, had murdered the King by putting poison from a toad in a mug of ale. It was claimed the monk was outraged at overhearing the King threaten to raise the price of bread in retribution for the barons' rebellion. It was also claimed John had died through his own gluttony – by consuming a 'surfeit of peaches'. If so, it must be the only recorded case of killer peaches in British history. Some experts on the flawed King, including the venerable W.L. Warren, believe it is more probable that John contracted his illness during his two-day stay at Lynn. The most likely cause of his death: food poisoning from something he ate there. He was fond of a local medieval delicacy, elvers, or eels, but as these were usually cooked, it may have been the local shellfish, oysters, that were his silent assassins.

It is possible he was murdered by poison. There was a good motive. Barely a year earlier, on 15 June 1215, King John had sealed an agreement with the barons by the Thames at Runnymede, near his castle at Windsor. It was intended to bring to an end a bitter power struggle over his alleged abuse of his powers as a monarch, and would become known as the Great Charter, in Latin *Magna Carta*. But he had repudiated its contents almost before his seal was dry. It was that duplicity which caused his final conflict with his barons. As with Cromwell and Charles I four centuries later, some barons decided that John could no longer be trusted and had to die. John's greatest contribution to our island's history was his timely death at the age of forty-nine.

Had John lived, it is unlikely the world would have heard about the Great Charter. Having repudiated it, he would have ensured that it was buried. Now that his body was safely laid to rest in Worcester Cathedral, the most powerful man in England, William Marshal, made sure the terms laid out in his Great Charter were honoured by John's nine-year-old son once he was crowned Henry III. Sagacious, brave and loyal Marshal, at sixty-nine, crowned a lifetime of service to the House of Angevin as the Protector of England. It is Marshal we have to thank, more than anyone else, for ensuring that Magna Carta lived, and was promulgated in county towns all over young King Henry's kingdom.

Magna Carta is now regarded as one of the great pillars of the (unwritten) British constitution, guaranteeing all citizens basic rights that today we take for granted, including a fair trial by a jury of ordinary people, under the due process of law. At least. that is what the Great Charter is said to mean. But that is just one of the many enduring myths surrounding King John's grubby deal with the barons. And there is more to come.

In the summer of 2015, we will mark the eight-hundredth anniversary of the Great Charter. The leaders of the Western world, headed, I would guess, by the President of the United States, will be arriving in a procession of black limos at the National Trust car park in Runnymede to pour out more fine words about the meaning of Magna Carta as the foundation stone of modern democracy.

It was on the water meadows, now hemmed in by suburbia, between the Staines reservoirs and Windsor Castle, that John's deal with the barons was finally sealed. The bucolic acres at Runnymede moved Kipling to verse:

> At Runnymede, at Runnymede,
> What say the reeds at Runnymede?
> The lissom reeds that give and take,
> That bend so far, but never break,
> They keep the sleepy Thames awake
> With tales of John at Runnymede.

They are still the most famous water meadows in the world but if John (or Kipling) came back today, he might need earplugs. The 188 acres that make up Runnymede, near Windsor, are under the flight path of Heathrow's Terminal 5; the rustling sound of the wind through the reeds mingles with the distant whoosh of the traffic at Junction 13 on the M25, one of the busiest motorways in Europe. The meandering Thames is lined with the motor cruisers of the gin-and-tonic set, and the banks are dotted with grand Edwardian villas. John would have had to take his life in his hands, crossing the busy A308, to reach the parkland where the barons camped. At the Staines end of the meadows, where the barons staked out their pavilions, I can hear the distinctive high-pitched whine of bankers' Ferraris being tuned at a sports-car dealership. Runnymede is surrounded by expensive commuter property these days. Even so, there is something noble about this corner of England, particularly at Langham Pond.

This stretch of water, with Kipling's susurrating reeds, was once an oxbow of the old Thames river complex, and it has since been named a Site of Special Scientific Interest because of the wildlife it supports. In summer, the meadows are rich with ox-eye daisies and buttercups. Dragonflies flit among the rushes, as if time has stood still. A green woodpecker flaps into the trees as I walk with Nigel Boden, the National Trust's countryside manager, through the water meadows, past a herd of red old-breed Sussex bullocks, which graze in some of the fields. 'There still is a sense of place here,' he tells me. 'Even though we have Heathrow Airport and the background noise, you can still get away from all of that. At Runnymede you can take time out and reflect on the history.'

It is a miracle the meadows have survived intact for these eight hundred years. They were used as a racecourse for more than a century, and they could have disappeared completely under executive dormer bungalows and interwar villas if Lloyd George had had his way. The Liberal Prime Minister thought nothing of selling honours for cash, and was ready to sell Runnymede, regardless of its importance, to raise money for the cash-strapped coalition Government in the 1920s. An unnamed spin doctor for the Commissioners of Woods and Forests tried to minimize the historic status of Lot 8 in the Government sale. Defending the sale of the property, he told the *Daily Express* in August 1921: 'The land offered for sale is not Runnymede Island in the Thames where Magna Carta was signed.' This was untrue. But then I discovered that the story of Magna Carta is surrounded by spin, myths and mendacity. Even its date is not strictly accurate.

The document was never 'signed' by John – it was only sealed. Nor did the barons gather on an island in the Thames; this was a myth born of a misunderstanding. For generations, it was believed that, in 1215, the Thames flowed on both sides of the land at Ankerwyke, where lakes and Wraysbury reservoir lie today.

The deal with the barons was indeed negotiated on the meadows where Lloyd George's houses were to be built. It was actually written into the document. 'Given in the meadow that is called Runnymede between Windsor and Staines, 15 June,' the contract concludes, setting it down for all to see.

A public outcry halted the auction. Cara, Lady Fairhaven, the daughter of an American industrialist who was a principal in John D. Rockefeller's Standard Oil, purchased the land in 1929 to preserve it for the nation and as a memorial to her late husband, Urban H. Broughton, a former civil engineer and Tory MP whom she met when he was installing the sewage system for her father in her hometown of Fairhaven, Massachusetts. He had died that year of pneumonia. In 1931, Lady Fairhaven gifted the land to the National Trust, after making a few improvements. She commissioned the fashionable architect Sir Edwin Lutyens, the creator of 'typically' English country homes for the rich, and the colonial centre of New Delhi – to design twin lodges at the Windsor entrance to the park. These were built to accommodate public toilets, sell refreshments, and provide an office and a park-keeper's cottage, now taken over by the National Trust for its offices.

America has a big presence at Runnymede. A short stroll from the car park at the Magna Carta Tea Rooms, a classical Greek temple was set up among the trees by the American Bar Association in 1957 as a memorial to the charter. An inscription says: 'To commemorate Magna Carta, symbol of Freedom Under Law'.

As I stroll around the park, I find I am actually walking on American soil. To mark the seven-hundred and fiftieth anniversary of the Great Charter in 1965, Queen Elizabeth II bestowed three acres of Crown land at Runnymede to the American nation for a memorial to President John F. Kennedy, who had been assassinated less than two years before. It was a public sharing of grief probably not matched in England until the death of Diana, Princess of Wales. The Kennedy memorial is fittingly plain: a massive white slab of stone lying under the trees on the hillside. At the ceremony, it was unveiled by the President's still grieving widow, Jackie Kennedy, and the Queen. The memorial carries a quotation from JFK's inaugural address: 'Let every nation know, whether it wishes us well or ill, that we shall pay any price, bear any burden, meet any hardship, support any friend or oppose any foe, in order to assure the survival and success of liberty.'

Americans probably value Magna Carta more than the British. The founders of the rebel nation incorporated its ideas into their constitution, most especially in the Bill of Rights, which they saw as a way to hold back the tyranny of kings over common folk. The 'founding fathers' gleefully exploited the charter's limits on the rights of one king, John, as a way to assert their independence from another, George III. What is surprising is not that America went along with this conceit, but that the fiction has lasted so long.

Indeed, the US Supreme Court, the highest arbiter of law in the land, has ruled that the rights enumerated in the US constitution have their origins in Magna Carta. And so it should not be surprising that when President Barack Obama addressed the joint Houses of Parliament in Westminster in 2011, he claimed special interest in Magna Carta, nearly co-opting it as more American than British: 'Magna Carta, the Bill of

Rights, habeas corpus, trial by jury and English common law find their most famous expression in the American Declaration of Independence.' The principles of freedom and justice, which each successive US administration has tried to export to the rest of the world, at the sharp end of a missile when necessary, are traced back to Magna Carta with great pride.

Both King John and the barons would be surprised to hear that their agreement has such a lofty legacy. Magna Carta, in truth, was a shabby deal reached between a gang of landowners who did not wish to see their privileged life destroyed, and a weak king with his back against the wall.

Perhaps that is why the British are notoriously blasé about the Great Charter. Magna Carta does not warrant a mention in Shakespeare's play *The Life and Death of King John*, though the loss of his treasure does (the Bard knew a good story when he heard it). A 2008 You-Gov poll showed forty-five per cent of the British public do not even know what Magna Carta is. The Conservative MP Eleanor Laing, on introducing a bill to make 15 June 2015 a bank holiday, Magna Carta Day, noted with 'pity' that Magna Carta is in the syllabus for schools in Germany but not in England. (Conveniently, the anniversary would place the bank holiday in what passes for the high summer in England – though whether this would ensure greater appreciation of liberty or merely provide a day off in the rain is an entirely different question.) Galton and Simpson, the scriptwriters for the television comedy actor Tony Hancock, summed up the national ignorance in an episode of *Hancock's Half Hour* in 1959. Galton and Simpson's courtroom sketch had Hancock ask his fellow jury members: 'Magna Carta – did she die in vain?'

Most people today know John as the evil prince in the Robin Hood tales who used the Sheriff of Nottingham to screw the peasants (both literally and figuratively) while his noble brother, King Richard the Lionheart, was away at the Crusades. The Victorians embroidered the tales of chivalry and totally embraced the romance of *La Coeur de Lion*; he was their ideal national hero, a handsome man in armour in an era when missionary zeal, Gothic arts, romance and chivalry were all the rage. (Charles Barry's mock-Gothic Palace of Westminster is the apotheosis of that style.) In 1860, the Victorians even went so far as to erect an heroic bronze equestrian statue of Richard I, battle sword raised, outside the Houses of Parliament.*

The Victorians poured more scorn (and worse) over the head of the sullied John, while polishing the image of their glistening hero. And thus they wilfully ignored the truth about Richard: far from being dedicated to England, he only spent six months of his reign in the kingdom, spoke French not English, and squeezed as much money as he could from his people to finance the Crusades. He once even said he would have sold London, if he could have found a buyer. Richard set 'new standards in royal rapacity', according to the historian Geoffrey Hindley.[2] His spending was 'a major cause of the grievances in the build-up to Magna Carta'. But King John went further; he extracted more money in taxes from England during his ten-year reign than had any previous king in any previous decade – including his brother Richard.

John undoubtedly got a bad press from the monkish chroniclers of his day because of his seizure of Church assets. Tudor historians portrayed John in the mould of Henry VIII, who defied the Pope but was destroyed by traitors around him. A colourful defence of John was written as early as 1865, at the height of the Victorian fashion for John-bashing, but it made little impact. The author, William Chadwick, said he wanted to cast off 'the immense guano piles of slander and caricature, bigotries and prejudices that have for centuries lain upon his illustrious memory'.

For the most part, the guano stuck.

There have been fresh attempts to rehabilitate John's reputation. More recently, he has been lauded as a good administrator and record-keeper (no wonder modern historians rate him).

There is plenty of evidence, however, that John was the black-hearted villain of English folklore. He turned duplicity into an art form. John ruled by a combination of extortion and blackmail, and used every trick of the feudal law book to keep the barons in his grip. He was prepared to take hostages from his barons' families, to secure loyalty. At one point, he imprisoned the wife of Hugh Neville, a forester, to bring her husband to heel; at Christmas 1204, the King's clerks noted that she offered to

---

* In 2011, a campaign was launched on the Government's e-petition website to have Richard's statue removed, because of the injustices he meted out to Muslims during his reign – three thousand were slaughtered outside the walls of the city of Acre alone. But the legend is hard to dent. In its first days, the petition collected a mere seven signatures.

pay 'the lord king two hundred chickens that she might lie one night with her husband'.[3] He is said to have extracted the teeth of a Jewish financier, Abraham of Bristol, until Abraham gave up ten thousand marks to his lord.[4]

This may have been one of Roger of Wendover's tabloid tales, but John certainly extracted punitive taxes from the estates of his most troublesome nobles, if not their teeth, as a ploy to keep them in debt to the Crown for life. Under feudal law, John grabbed money from widows of tenants who wanted to remarry, or if they wanted to remain single.

John at times behaved like Rowan Atkinson's fictional villain, Black-adder, devising schemes that were so cunning, he forgot how they worked. He expected to be cheated, and invented ingenious codes for his jailors to frustrate his enemies; he formulated a plan to stop them sending false orders for the release of hostages, but forgot the ciphers himself; he instructed one of his castellans not to release any prisoners unless his orders were accompanied by three named members of his household, but then had to write to the keeper of the castle saying: 'we do not well recollect who those three were...'[5]

Below the misery of the squeezed landocracy, the tenants and serfs suffered more. He declared huge tracts of land as forest, thereby seizing absolute control of all the game within it. England was not a happy country under John, said the chroniclers.

It is hardly surprising that John was two-faced – he was taught 'treachery pays' from childhood. The Plantagenets, the English branch of the Angevin Empire, were as dysfunctional as any modern-day Mafia family. John shared the personal traits of the Angevins: spite, pettiness and a total lack of anger management. His father, Henry II, was so enraged on one occasion that he thrashed around the floor, stuffing straw from his mattress into his mouth. In another fit of anger, Henry notoriously appeared to call for the murder of Thomas à Becket, a former ally until he became the Archbishop of Canterbury. The murder in the cathedral made Thomas a martyr and a saint – his shrine is still visited – and turned Henry into a monster.

During his lifetime, Henry gave lands in France to John's elder brothers to administer, leaving John without a kingdom of his own. For this, John was ridiculed by the French as Jean 'Sans Terre' (John Lackland). The son learned well from the father, and also inherited his fits of rage. As a young prince, John would become 'hardly recognisable' when he was angry. 'Rage contorted his brow, his burning eyes glittered, bluish spots discoloured the pink of his cheeks' and his hands 'sawed the air', according to the chronicler Richard of Devizes.[6]

John's mother, the powerful Eleanor of Aquitaine, the only woman to have been both Queen of France and Queen of England, was eleven years older than Henry. She became so outraged by the King's infidelity, she sought revenge by encouraging her sons to go to war against their father for control of her ancestral estates in France. For this, Henry imprisoned Eleanor in various abbeys in England for sixteen years. Eventually, Richard joined forces with the French King Philip II to defeat his father in France and seize the Crown, and Eleanor was freed.

John, the runt of the family, inherited the throne in April 1199 when Richard died during the siege of the castle of Châlus, near Limoges. It was a typically foolhardy show of courage for the Lionheart – he defied the defenders to hit him with their crossbows, and one did, in the arm near the neck; Richard died in agony after gangrene set in. His heart was buried at Rouen Cathedral, but his body is entombed at the Plantagenets' Fontevraud Abbey, Anjou, where his mother, Eleanor, ended her life as a nun.

The barons were just as sinister as this royal 'devil's brood'. They ran their counties from castle strongholds as their personal fiefdoms, a law unto themselves. The right-wing historian David Starkey acidly noted in his TV series *Monarchy*: 'Nowadays, such thuggish disorder tends to come from those at the bottom of the pile. Then it came from the top.'

The 'thuggery at the top' mostly came down to money. The barons complained that King John had taxed them beyond the bounds of accepted custom. A major bone of contention was the feudal tax called 'scutage', which was paid by reluctant landowners in lieu of sending knights on active military service abroad for the King. John and Richard's father, Henry II, had imposed eight demands for scutage over thirty-four years, as he defended his claims to the embattled estates in France. The haemorrhaging of French estates continued after John took the throne. As he lost more estates and his finances dwindled, John imposed scutage, beyond the bounds of accepted custom, at double or treble the old rate of one mark per knight, and more often than his father. In his seventeen years on the throne, John imposed scutage eleven times.[7] He hoped to regain his lost lands in France, and needed to hire mercenary forces to do so.

Scutage was not the only means for extracting wealth from the land. John used other feudal taxes, such as the succession tax, a levy on access to an inheritance, to squeeze more and more money out of the barons. He demanded the enormous sum of £6666 (equivalent to around £3.5 million today) from Nicholas de Stuteville to gain access to his inheritance of land; to pay it, de Stuteville had to surrender his Yorkshire estates at Knaresborough and Boroughbridge to the King.

John's despotic breach of 'custom' lay at the root of their grievances. Like many today faced with hard times, the barons looked to an earlier golden age for inspiration, and relief. In his BBC television series *The Story of England*, Michael Wood relates how they pillaged the past for customs to buttress their case, reaching beyond the Norman Conquest. The barons resurrected the Anglo-Saxon concept of 'fairness' or 'fair play' – an attribute that has since become so imbued in the national psyche that it is ranked among the defining traits of 'Britishness', alongside a propensity for queuing and drinking tea in a crisis.

In addition to Anglo-Saxon 'fair play', the barons found support in a politically astute ally: Stephen Langton, the Archbishop of Canterbury. But then, Langton had a vested interest in seeing that King John's tyrannical tendencies were held in check. The King had objected to Pope Innocent III's appointment of Langton, and as retribution, the pontiff had, in 1209, excommunicated John. It was a power struggle that foreshadowed the later clash between Rome and Henry VIII, which, of course, eventually led to the formation of the breakaway Church of England, with Henry as its head.

John's misfortune was that with Innocent, he was taking on one of the most powerful popes in history. In 1213, the King was forced into an extraordinary retreat, when he surrendered his kingdom to Rome and leased it back in return for a promise to pay a papal tribute of one thousand marks a year (£666 in the thirteenth century), plus compensation for the riches he had seized from the Church. In doing so, John literally became a 'serf' of the Pope, for which he was quickly denounced as a traitor, but the tactic succeeded in maintaining him in power – he had effectively placed himself under the Pope's protection. John also promised the Pope that he would go on a Crusade, like his brother Richard.

This turn of events led to Langton's election as Archbishop of Canterbury. It should be said that Langton was clearly not convinced by John's conversion. While King John was making his obeisance to the Pope, Langton held a secret conclave with some of the barons after a service at St Paul's. That scribbling monk, Roger of Wendover, recorded that Langton informed the barons that a coronation charter agreed by Henry I promising the restoration of the law of King Edward 'has now been found by which you can if you will, recover your lost liberties and your former condition'. This was music to their ears. Wendover added: 'He had a document placed before them and had it read out… They rejoiced with exceeding great joy and all swore in the archbishop's presence that when the time was ripe they would fight for these liberties even unto death.'[8]

Wendover was speaking of the Charter of Liberties, which promised, in vague terms, the restoration of the fair laws of Edward the Confessor, one of the last of the Anglo-Saxon kings. The charter also involved several concessions on reliefs and wardship, marriage and debts to the Crown, all of which were soundly among the barons' list of complaints. Henry I had issued it to gain support after seizing the Crown from his older brother Robert. He may never have intended to honour it, but it was good enough for the barons.

The breaking point came in 1214, after King John returned from France. John and his European allies had suffered a devastating defeat to King Philip of France during the pitched battle of Bouvines. John's hopes of regaining his lucrative French estates had been destroyed; the defeat also increased his need for money. He was furious that his barons had failed to join him in the campaign, and he was determined to exact his revenge – through taxes.

A group of truculent northern barons, including the Lord of Alnwick, Eustace de Vesci, claimed that their feudal responsibilities did not extend to service abroad; they also refused to pay more scutage to make up for John's failed French adventure. John insisted, rightly, that scutage had been paid in lieu of foreign service to his father and his illustrious brother Richard. The barons, led by the nobles of the eastern counties and London – the hothead Robert FitzWalter, Lord of Dunmow; Geoffrey de Mandeville, Earl of Essex and Robert de Vere, Earl of Oxford – were unbowed. FitzWalter and de Vesci, who had both plotted to kill John in 1212, put out stories of how the despotic King lusted after their women; it was intended to gain wider support for their cause among the main body of one hundred neutral barons, with a clear warning that this could happen to others unless John was cut down to size. They demanded a charter from John to reinstate the Charter of Liberties.

John, cunning as ever, shrewdly played for time through the winter of 1214. On the side, he sent for mercenaries from Poitou, as insurance. Then on 4 March, he played his trump card – he took his vows as a Crusader. Not only did it give him the protection of the Pope, under ecclesiastical law, but it also gave him a Crusader's respite from meeting his secular obligations for three years. The rebels responded on 3 May by renouncing their homage and fealty to John. It was a declaration of civil war.

The campaign began well for John, who had made conciliatory noises to win over wavering barons, but the rebels seized London, attracting more young nobles to their cause, though their fathers stayed loyal to the King. The stalemate paved the way for the squalid deal at Runnymede.

The water meadows by the Thames were a convenient half-way point for the King, who arrived from his stronghold at Windsor Castle and the bridge at Staines, which the mounted barons crossed in force on their journey from London. The boggy ground was also chosen because it provided security for the leaders of the two armies, who did not trust each other. The heavy, wet terrain made it difficult for either side to mount a surprise attack on horseback. There is no reliable eye-witness account of how the King or his camp at Runnymede looked; today our picture of how the barons gave their chivalric obeisance to John is largely guesswork and Victorian spin.

It is likely that the King's pavilions were planted on the meadows, and they would have served as the site of the final negotiations, which according to the treaty itself took place on 15 June. But even the date was misleading. Like a modern summit, there were public appearances, but the hard work went on behind the scenes. The King arrived at Runnymede on 10 June to meet the rebel leaders and committed himself to a draft list of their demands, which survives today as the 'Articles of the Barons'. It is likely that covert negotiations were thrashed out between Archbishop Langton and William Marshal, who is now rightly seen as one of the most outstanding statesmen in English history. Marshal was loyal to the Crown, but determined to reach a compromise with the barons. After John's death, Marshal became king in all but name because John's son was still only nine: he was praised by Langton as 'the greatest knight that ever lived'. He died in 1219 in his seventy-second year. He is buried at Temple Church, built for the Knights Templar near Fleet Street, London.

The King and the barons only came together on 15 June to agree formally to the document's terms by the Thames, but this was no more than a 'sealing' ceremony, like modern-day politicians appearing for a photo opportunity at a summit. John and the barons then handed the agreement over to their bureaucrats to work out the fine print. It took at least four more days to agree the wording of the copies of Magna Carta that were sent out under the King's great red wax seal to be read in market squares across the country. A truer date for Magna Carta would be 19 June, when the barons ceremoniously each bowed the knee and renewed their oaths of 'fealty' (feudal allegiance like a vassal) to the King. But the charter continued to evolve – which is why not all of the early copies that survive are identical, word for word.

A total of seventeen copies of Magna Carta are known to exist in the world, but only four copies dated from 1215 have survived, and these are all in England: two at the British Library, including one that was lodged by Stephen Langton in the archives of the diocese of Canterbury; one survives in the archive of Lincoln Cathedral, which is on show in Lincoln Castle; and the best-preserved copy held at the Chapter House at Salisbury Cathedral. This copy was taken to Salisbury by Elias of Dereham, who was steward to Archbishop Langton, and was at the centre of the discussions between the King and the barons. He was entrusted with delivering ten of the thirteen copies, one of which was given to the original cathedral at Old Sarum. Elias later became a Canon of Old Sarum, before masterminding the building of the present Salisbury Cathedral – which is probably how that copy came to be housed in the cathedral archives.[9] The British Library's priceless Magna Carta is on show in the Room of Treasures, as it should be. It sits alongside far more magnificent documents, such as the illuminated Lindisfarne Gospels of AD 680; a first folio of Shakespeare's collected plays of 1623; a sumptuously illustrated medieval manuscript given as a wedding present to Margaret of Anjou and Henry VI; and the seventh-century St Cuthbert Gospel, which survived in the coffin of the saint – the oldest book in Europe.

I call on Claire Breay, Curator of Medieval Manuscripts, to see the copy of the Great Charter on display at the British Library. Away from the cacophony of the Euston Road, it sits in a darkened room, past all the other manuscripts out on show; a bullet-proof glass screen protects it, but the case looks as though it could withstand an armour-piercing shell. Breay tells me that, despite the riches on display around the library, most visitors want to see Magna Carta, although she admits few visitors really know what it contains. 'It's just so iconic.'

At my first glance, the charter does not inspire awe. It is not illuminated, like the early manuscript nearby showing King John hunting deer with hounds. Its lettering is not gilded, to indicate its royal or precious extraction.

Inscribed in medieval Latin in a small hand, the words run across the page and are often so abbreviated, they are difficult to decipher, even by experts. The sentences are not broken down into clauses, as one might expect from a legal document of global significance. The King's scribes scribbled out the contents, much like they were composing a long wish list at the barons' dictation. 'Oh, and another thing – no scutage without representation.'

It is written on parchment, made from sheepskin soaked in a bath of lime. The skin would then be stretched on a frame, to dry under tension, and scraped with a lunular, a crescent-shaped knife, to produce a smooth writing surface.

To apply the King's red wax seal, which is now missing, a chancery official, known as a spigurnel, used a small wooden press to clamp together two circles of beeswax and resin with imprints on both sides, across the cords for attaching it to the document.[10] John's great seal measured about four inches in diameter, and a mobile sealing machine was probably brought to the field at Runnymede to handle the task.

We are speaking in whispers, as though in a hallowed place. And in a way, we are. Breay explains that both of the British Library's copies of Magna Carta come from the seventeenth-century library of the bibliophile Sir Robert Cotton. One copy is said to have been discovered in a London tailor's shop, then given to Cotton by Humphrey Wyems, of the Inner Temple in London, on 1 January 1629. The second was found among the records of Dover Castle and sent to Cotton by Sir Edward Dering in 1630. This was probably the copy sent to the Baron of the Cinque Ports in 1215. Sadly, it was badly damaged in 1731, a century after Cotton's death, in a fire at Ashburnham House, Westminster, where Cotton's collection was then kept. It is virtually unreadable, having suffered fire damage that has left holes in the parchment.

The more I learn about Magna Carta's story, the more I come to sense why this frankly scruffy scrap of parchment should inspire awe. It is partly due to its antiquity. It is amazing that this document, which John's clerks handled, has survived eight centuries intact. But it is also awesome for its inferred meaning – rightly or wrongly – for all free men (and women) today.

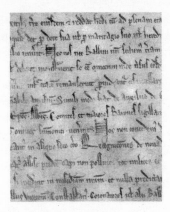

THE COTTON MAGNA CARTA:
A detail from one of Sir Robert Cotton's two parchment copies.

It starts with an open-handed welcome from the King to his enemies, the band of rebel barons: 'John, by the grace of God King of England, Lord of Ireland, Duke of Normandy and Aquitaine, and Count of Anjou, to his archbishops, bishops, abbots, earls, barons, justices, foresters, sheriffs, stewards, servants, and to all his officials and loyal subjects, Greeting.'

Anyone looking for high ideals in Magna Carta must dig deep into its sixty-three clauses. Its first clause is a guarantee of freedom from royal interference to the Church; Stephen Langton, the Archbishop of Canterbury, clearly used his role as the go-between to give priority to his own demands:

> First, that we have granted to God, and by this present charter have confirmed for us and our heirs in perpetuity, that the English Church shall be free, and shall have its rights undiminished, and its liberties unimpaired. That we wish this so to be observed, appears from the fact that of our own free will, before the outbreak of the present dispute between us and our barons, we granted and confirmed by charter the freedom of the Church's elections – a right reckoned to be of the greatest necessity and importance to it – and caused this to be confirmed by Pope Innocent III. This freedom we shall observe ourselves, and desire to be observed in good faith by our heirs in perpetuity

It then descends into a feudal shopping list of barons' demands. These include relief from John's overbearing interference in property rights and inheritance law. Henceforward, an heir who is under age shall have his inheritance without tax or fine when he becomes of age; further, 'no widow shall be forced to marry so long as she wishes to live without a husband, provided that she gives security not to marry without our' – the King's – 'consent'. While they were about it, the barons also laid down some principles for feudal weights and measures (let there be one measure for wine throughout our kingdom, and one measure for ale, and one measure for corn… and one width for cloths whether dyed, russet or halbergert). The charter ranges across royal abuses of feudal customs; the removal of fish weirs to improve navigation; the treatment of debts owed to Jewish moneylenders ('if anyone dies indebted to the Jews, his wife shall have her dower and pay nothing of that debt'); and the hated scutage tax, which could no longer be extracted without the consent of the barons (the first declaration of no taxation without representation). The historian Simon Schama called the list the 'barons' bellyaches'.

Only three of the original clauses are still law: the first defending the freedom and rights of the English Church to elect its own clergy without the interference of the King; another confirming rights on London as a trading centre; and the clause containing Articles 39 and 40 that are at the crux of Magna Carta and have made it the most famous legal document in history:

> ARTICLE 39: No free man shall be seized or detained in prison, or deprived of his freehold, or outlawed or banished, or in any way molested; and we will not go against him, nor send against him, unless by the lawful judgement of his peers or by the law of the land.

> ARTICLE 40: To no one will we sell, to no one deny or delay right or justice.

Those words laid down one of the supreme principles of justice and liberty: a right to the rule of law. They meant that for the first time the King was subject to law, not above it.

These words have been hailed as the birth of civil liberties. Experts at the US National Archive say it was a late edit in the wording of the clause, from 'baron' to 'free man', that made its statements so universal and lasting. However, this interpretation ignores the uncomfortable fact

that 'freemen' in medieval England were privileged men. Magna Carta cut out the mass of people at the bottom of the pile – the peasants, known as villeins. Neither the barons nor John thought they were laying down inalienable rights for posterity. The articles that have made Magna Carta famous were not given any special emphasis; they were just two demands made by the barons in a very long list of grievances.

Perhaps the most radical clause of all allows the barons to set up a commission of twenty-five barons to hold John to the terms of his contract. Its members included the hated ringleaders of the rebellion, such as the firebrand Robert FitzWalter of Dunmow Castle, Essex, whom John had once exiled for plotting to assassinate him.

It was so unlikely and out of character for John to agree to such terms, the barons should have smelled a rat. Perhaps they did. It did not matter to John. It was all an elaborate sham. John had no intention of honouring the treaty: he immediately sent messengers to his powerful ally in Rome, Pope Innocent III, telling the pontiff that he had been forced against his will to agree to the charter.

In a masterpiece of deceit, John secretly told Innocent that, as he was officially the serf of the Pope, he did not hold the legal authority to agree to the contract with the barons without the Holy Father's consent. In spite of the guarantees Magna Carta contained concerning the freedom of the Church, the Pope immediately came down on John's side.

Innocent repudiated the Great Charter in a thundering letter bearing the papal seal, known as a bull. Though John secretly had no intention of fulfilling his pledge to go on a Crusade, the Pope declared that anyone who stood in John's way was worse than the Saracens. 'Even if the King were remiss or lukewarm about the Crusade, we would not allow such great wickedness to go unchecked, for by God's grace, we know how to punish and we can punish such shameless presumption,' said Innocent.

Magna Carta, said the Pope, was 'an agreement which is not only shameful and base but also illegal and unjust'. He threatened to excommunicate anyone upholding it, and to have their lands laid 'under interdict, with the sentences solemnly published throughout England every Sunday and feast day with the tolling of bells and candles extinguished until... they humbly return to his service'.[11] Astonishingly, the Pope's letter bearing the seal of Rome also survives to this day, and is in another display case, alongside Magna Carta, at the British Library.

How John expected to get away with this subterfuge is unclear. The barons were unlikely to give in to threats, even from the Pope. They responded to the threat of excommunication by declaring war on John and his despotic rule. This time, it would be civil war to the death.

The barons' war was a series of vicious, and sometimes brutal, sieges. Rebels who surrendered the fortress in the strategically important town of Rochester, in Kent, to King John had their feet cut off.

The rebels responded to John's campaign by inviting Prince Louis of France, son of King Philip, to invade near Dover with a powerful army of knights. With the barons' contrivance, it was the first successful invasion of its kind since 1066, though it is now almost entirely forgotten. John rode with his force to Kent to oppose the invaders, but – typical of the man – was afraid to strike when he had the chance, and retreated.

Two-thirds of the barons had gone over to Prince Louis, but the barons and the French invaders soon began to fall out over the spoils of war. As the war dragged on into 1216, the pendulum swung in John's favour. John had recently had some important rebel defections back to his banner, including William, the son of his loyal ally Sir William Marshal, the most respected knight in the country, and William Longespee, the Earl of Salisbury, who was an illegitimate son of Henry II. Sensing the barons were cracking, John had gone on the offensive.

He had raised the siege of Lincoln where the redoubtable castellan, Dame Nicola de la Haye, held out against the rebels. Then he had ridden to Lynn on the Norfolk coast, a rich trading port and principal gateway to the Netherlands and Scandinavia.

John was carrying large amounts of gold and precious jewels with which he could finance the war and pay his hired men. He had drawn the riches from safe houses and abbeys where they had previously been kept secure. Lynn was a loyalist stronghold of the King, and his arrival no doubt caused a great excuse for banqueting during his short stay. The records show the citizens of Lynn 'feasted him well'.[12] Having despatched letters during his stay, which help fix the dates of his visit, the King rode out of Lynn at the head of his army on 11 October. That is how he came to be riding across the Wash that fateful day.

King John's death brought about an almost immediate end to the war with the barons. Royalists in the West Country acted quickly to crown his young son, Henry III, in the abbey church at Gloucester on 28 October 1216. The rebels rallied around the boy king after his advisers, who included William Marshal as the King's protector and regent, shrewdly reissued the Charter of Liberties in his name. Professor W.L. Warren, one of the pre-eminent experts on King John, put it simply: 'It is the supreme irony of Magna Carta that, after being demanded by the rebels and killed by the Pope, it should have been brought back to life as a royalist manifesto.'[13]

But, like Humpty Dumpty in *Alice Through the Looking Glass*, Magna Carta has come to mean whatever we choose it to mean.

Since 1215, Magna Carta has been used to defend liberty whenever it has been threatened. When Eleanor Roosevelt launched the UN Universal Declaration of Human Rights sixty years ago, she described it as 'a Magna Carta for all mankind'. The Great Charter has even been invoked by the Indigenous peoples who inhabit the jungles of South and Central America to defend their rights against the destruction of their common land by national government and corporate grabs for oil.[14] These are all well-meaning invocations, but they stretch the actual meaning of the damaged parchments of Magna Carta to breaking point. Roosevelt's words may be grand, but Magna Carta was not a Medieval Human Rights Act.

The legal scope of Magna Carta has been distorted to cover individual rights, which was never the intention of the barons, still less that of King John. This is partly due to the machinations of Sir Edward Coke, the Lord Chief Justice and the outstanding (and overbearing) legal expert of the sixteenth century, who used Magna Carta as a weapon to challenge Charles I's belief in the divine right of kings. Coke insisted that Magna Carta made the King subject to the law. He selectively took the Great Charter's general principles and made them more specific, drafting the Petition of Right of 1628. This document, one of the treasures held in the Parliamentary archives at Westminster, set out limits to the power of the King, including on levying taxes without Parliamentary consent, imprisoning citizens without cause and billeting of soldiers in private houses. It is one of four documents – along with the Great Charter, the 1689 Bill of Rights (see Chapter Four), and the Habeas Corpus Act of 1679 (the right of a prisoner to be produced in court to avoid unlawful detention) – that underpin the rights of all British citizens. Magna Carta had protected the civil liberties of the medieval élite, but Coke ingeniously asserted that it guaranteed individual rights to everyone, of every station.

Then, Coke exported this view to the fledgling American colonies, where law was being made anew. Under his direction, Magna Carta was incorporated into James I's royal charter for the colony of Jamestown, in

Virginia, the first successful English settlement in America. Echoing the words of the Great Charter, Jamestown's charter declared 'the persons which shall dwell within the colonies shall have all Liberties as if they had been abiding and born within this our realm of England'. Subsequently, similar language was embedded in the charters for Massachusetts (1629), Maryland (1632), Maine (1639), Connecticut (1662) and Rhode Island (1663). William Penn incorporated parts of Magna Carta in the laws of Pennsylvania.

When, on the eve of the American Revolution, Massachusetts adopted its own government seal, the medallion carried a militiaman on one side and Magna Carta on the other. Just as the barons had opposed John's scutage, when the colonists declared their independence, they claimed they were resisting an oppressive tax, the 'Stamp Tax'. Their battle cry, 'No taxation without representation', seemed to be a direct descendant of Coke's argument. The American ideas of individual liberty may have been based on a myth but they were exported back to Europe, igniting revolution in France.

The American founding fathers, including Thomas Jefferson, were most definitely familiar with Coke's works: they embedded his philosophy in what are universally considered to be the most famous lines of the Declaration of Independence: 'We hold these truths to be self-evident, that all Men are created equal, that they are endowed by their Creator with certain unalienable Rights, that among these are Life, Liberty and the Pursuit of Happiness.' From these words, a potent American myth was born, that Magna Carta guaranteed 'due process of law' to all citizens. But Magna Carta never refers to 'due process' – far from it.

The phrase 'due process of law' appears for the first time in a statute of Edward III dated 1354, referring to the liberty of the subject. 'No man of what estate or condition that he be, shall be put out of land or tenement, nor taken, nor imprisoned, nor disinherited, nor put to death, without being brought in answer by due process of law,' the statute reads. The first chapter of this statute refers to Magna Carta and says it should be 'kept and maintained in all points'. There is a clear echo of this provision in the Bill of Rights of the US constitution, of which the Fifth Amendment declares: 'No person shall... be deprived of life, liberty, or property, without due process of law.' The US constitution therefore owes more to Edward III and his 1354 statute than to King John and Magna Carta. The aura surrounding Magna Carta is too established now to be dispelled by such quibbles, however.

On 18 December 2007, an American philanthropist, David Ruben-stein, paid $21.3 million for a copy of Magna Carta at a Sotheby's auction in New York City. Rubenstein is managing director of the Carlyle Group, an equity firm whose board has included a former president (George H.W. Bush), a former prime minister (John Major) and numerous US Government officials (Secretary of State James Baker, Secretary of Defense Frank Carlucci and Securities and Exchange Chairman Arthur Levitt). The copy of Magna Carta that Rubinstein purchased bears the great seal of Edward I, not John, and dates from 1297; it is especially important because it appears to be the first version of the charter's text to be incorporated into statute. For five hundred years it was preserved by the Brudenell family, which included James Thomas Brudenell, the Seventh Earl of Cardigan, the blundering cavalry officer who led the charge of the Light Brigade. It was first sold in 1984 to the foundation set up by Texas businessman and one-time presidential hopeful H. Ross Perot, and it remains the only copy in private hands in the world.*

Rubinstein described Magna Carta as 'the most significant document in Western history' and believed 'it was very important that the Magna Carta stay in the United States'. He has generously loaned it to the US National Archives in Washington, DC, on a permanent basis. More millions of dollars were spent in 2011 on its meticulous conservation. Odd holes in the stretched and scraped sheep skin that make up the parchment needed to be filled in, before it could be reframed and tucked safely into an airtight case. The British Library has also considered reframing its copies and placing them into airtight cases in advance of the 2015 anniversary, but unlike the US conservators, the library's specialists prefer to leave the holes in their fire-damaged copy intact. The plan depends on getting the finance – a chancy proposition in Austerity Britain.

In the comfortable view of history spun by Whig historians such as Macaulay and, later, Winston Churchill, the legal rights bestowed by Magna Carta were part of a continuous thread of civilizing rights against despotism that Britain exported across the globe, along with democracy and drains. Claire Breay, my guide at the British Library, says: 'Despite all the claims which have been made for it since, the charter was not intended to be the cornerstone of English democracy, still less the foundation of a code of human rights.'[15] Professor Warren reinforces this view: 'It is, in fact, a Charter of Liberties not a Charter of Liberty, concerned to

---

* Perot made a tidy profit on the document's sale – he had bought it for $1.5 million – which the foundation says will be used for charitable purposes.

secure practical reforms which would protect the upper classes against an over-mighty ruler in current matters of grievance, not to enunciate abstract "rights of man".'[16]

In England, Magna Carta was not the end of the struggle – the uprising of Simon de Montfort in the second barons' war against John's successor, King Henry III; the English civil war of 1642–9 culminating in the execution of King Charles I; and the Glorious Revolution of 1688 all stand as testimony to that. Some, like Margaret Thatcher, expressed fears that despite Magna Carta, our hard-won rights have been surrendered to the European Union, making us vassals of Brussels as we were of the Papacy of Rome in King John's day. Indeed, medieval historian Geoffrey Hindley, an expert on King John and Magna Carta, agrees with Lady Thatcher. 'We have surrendered our sovereignty to Europe,' he told me.

When it comes time to celebrate the eight-hundredth anniversary, Magna Carta is certain to be held out as the bastion of 'Britishness' by those who fear our national identity is at risk. But the rights of ordinary citizens against the power of the ruling classes also may resurface at Runnymede. I discovered some alarm at rumours of a multimillion-pound visitor and interpretation centre being built on these 'sacred' acres to mark the event. 'We don't want to turn the meadows into a medieval theme park,' said one local resident. The Scots and Welsh are also likely to complain that Magna Carta is essentially an English creation, and a special day off work has no relevance for them, especially after devolution.

The Americans have 4 July to celebrate their taking of independence. Perhaps 15 June would be a fitting date to commemorate the basic right of fairness that is seen as one of the enduring qualities of 'Britishness'.

Of what relevance is Magna Carta to the rest of us, the peasants, today? Over the centuries, most of the document has been repealed or become obsolete. Even the 'universal' rights bestowed by Magna Carta are based on a myth, so why is it so important? The late Lord Bingham, a former Master of the Rolls and one of Britain's most senior judges interpreting the law, neatly resolved this contradiction: 'The significance of Magna Carta lay not only in what it actually said but, perhaps to an even greater extent, in what later generations claimed and believed it had said. Sometimes the myth is more important than the actuality.'[17]

The rights we believe are protected in Magna Carta – and too often take for granted – are continually under threat, even today. In the aftermath of the 7/7 terrorist bombings of London, the Labour Government sought to extend the period for which a suspect may be detained without making a charge of criminal act to forty-two days, despite the long-standing Article 39, which says that 'no free man shall be seized or imprisoned' without a fair trial. The opponents who invoked Magna Carta included Kenneth Clarke, who was then on the opposition benches. Clarke was later appointed the Justice Secretary in the Conservative–Liberal Democrat Coalition Government, and continued to champion the charter, though he harboured no illusions about it. During a visit to Runnymede to announce the 2015 celebrations, he said: 'Magna Carta could be represented as an eight-hundred-year-old quarrel between an autocratic king… and a set of barons who represented no one but themselves and their own local and class interests.'

Clarke, a lawyer by trade, made it clear he would fight for the spirit of Magna Carta to be upheld, regardless of who he upset. That applied both to the inquiry he set up into Britain's 'complacent compliance' in the alleged ill-treatment of detainees at Guantanamo Bay, and his wider review of anti-terrorism legislation. 'We have to make sure we don't get so panicked by terrorism or puritanical about other people and how they conduct their lives that we start passing laws which deny people their liberty,' he declared.[18] In October 2011, he again invoked the Great Charter to oppose plans by Prime Minister David Cameron and Theresa May, the Home Secretary, to repeal the Human Rights Act. 'The British are great believers in human rights. We invented the idea. It goes back to Magna Carta,' he said.[19] Then in September 2012, Clarke became Minister without Portfolio.

Clarke is typical of the brave souls who have made sure that Magna Carta has survived attacks on it over the past eight centuries, not without risk to themselves. Whether King John intended it to be so, Magna Carta is a living document, worth far more than the things he valued in his day. The spirit (though not the letter) of Magna Carta is present in the most awkward – sometimes vexing – decisions by our judges, for example the refusal to extradite alleged terrorists for trial abroad. The independence of the judiciary from the diktat of political leaders is guaranteed by later legislation, but its root lies in Magna Carta. King John's Great Charter can be a thorn in the side of democracy, but it is a necessary thorn.

As long as the United Kingdom survives as a free, independent country, this shabby little treaty sealed in the meadows at Runnymede by a king and his barons for the basest of motives will remain a shining landmark for most people. As a nation, we may not know much about its contents, but the granting of the basic right of liberty under the law has shaped Britain and its descendants for nearly a millennium.

As Sir Winston Churchill, in his *History of the English-Speaking Peoples*, grandly declared: 'When the long tally is added, it will be seen that the British nation and the English-speaking world owe far more to the vices of John than to the labours of virtuous sovereigns.'

And what of the thing King John valued in his day – his missing treasure? Nobody has ever found the horde of jewels and silver plate, though there have been many attempts to dig it up, including hiring a 'dowser' to divine the spot with a couple of pieces of wire with a documentary film crew as witness. This is the last, tantalizing mystery surrounding Magna Carta.

I followed John's fateful ride along the A17, which is still the most direct route between King's Lynn and Newark. The route was nominated by the *Daily Telegraph* in 2001 as one of ten 'great drives' in England, though in summer it is congested with holidaymakers' cars and caravans heading from the Midlands to the Norfolk Broads or the resorts of Hunstanton, Cromer and Great Yarmouth. It strikes straight as an arrow across the Fens; breathtaking skyscapes are punctuated by the spires of medieval churches, standing like raised fists against the clouds.

At harvest time, I set out to trace John's painful final ride, but in a 4×4. (If King John had had a Range Rover, we would never have heard of Magna Carta.) The landscape seems huge, without end, but I am held up by an enormous tractor towing a vast trailer, jammed to the rim with a euromountain of sugar beet grown on the rich farmland reclaimed from the sea. Everywhere there are banks and dykes, and fields stretching to the horizon below the raised level of the road.

There is no sign that John ever passed this way, apart from a fold in the land called King John Bank, created after the sea was held back and the wetlands were drained. The track where he crossed the marshes has been lost under the tarmac, now miles from the sea, but there is still a navigable river where the A17 crosses the Fosdyke Bridge. This is all that is left of the treacherous Wellstream, tamed now into little more than a canal, with a modest yachting marina, but this crossing could be the spot where King John's treasure lies buried.

A farmer, now retired, told me there are quicksands not far below the surface if you dig in these parts. 'I had a dead sheep and six barrels that just sank in minutes,' he said. This is not simply local lore. While trying to find the old causeway that John would have used across the Wash, a university team found evidence of the quicksands. I was tempted to dig for King John's 'buried treasure', but I discovered I would need quite a long spade. The researchers found that the medieval levels are now fifty feet below the fields.

There will be speeches and high-blown rhetoric at Runnymede in 2015 but for me, a more fitting way to mark the eight-hundredth anniversary of King John's most undervalued treasure, Magna Carta, would be an organized hunt for his Crown Jewels. The money-grabbing monarch would appreciate that.

TWO

1415

'And Crispin Crispian shall ne'er go by,
From this day to the ending of the world,
But we in it shall be remember'd'

RUE HENRY V, AZINCOURT:
At the actual front line of battle, with reproduction English archers.

It is cold and wet as I arrive in the pretty village of Azincourt on St Crispin's Day, just as it was when Henry V and his bedraggled army arrived here almost six hundred years ago, on 25 October 1415, to do battle against an overwhelming French force, and won.

The sun is milky grey behind darkening rain clouds which lumber slowly over the trees on a westerly wind. Water is lying in the fields among the shoots of winter wheat, and mud oozes underfoot.

I had to scrape the ice off my car windscreen before I set out. St Crispin's Day this year has fallen on the first day of the autumn half-term, and the cross-Channel ferry is packed with groups of kids who roar around the passenger decks of the *Pride of Kent* like an army of Hobbits intent on pillaging the chocolatiers of France.

Henry V boasted, in Shakespeare's timeless prose, that the Feast Day of St Crispin and St Crispian would be remembered 'to the ending of the world':

> This day is called the feast of Crispian:
> He that outlives this day, and comes safe home,
> Will stand a tip-toe when the day is named,
> And rouse him at the name of Crispian.
> He that shall live this day, and see old age,
> Will yearly on the vigil feast his neighbours,
> And say 'To-morrow is Saint Crispian'[1]

Today, the only feast my fellow passengers are interested in is the full English breakfast that comes with a complimentary voucher in the P&O Food Court. Later, sipping tea, the commanders of the half-term invasion consult their maps, plotting their campaigns through the countryside to avoid the toll roads and the hellish Périphérique around Paris.

As the ferry docks at Calais, the invaders run to their MPVs like they are in the Le Mans twenty-four-hour race. They thump off the ferry ramp

HENRY V:
In all his piety and glory, late sixteenth century.

at Calais in their seven-seater people carriers giving hardly a glance at the scene of England's most famous victory against the French in the Pas-de-Calais on their hellish 850-kilometre drive to the Dordogne in a day. I quickly leave all the holiday traffic behind when I turn off the A26 for Fruges on the D928 and go in search of the real Henry V.

It was Henry himself who was responsible for the first piece of spin put out about his piety. The rare portrait we have of the King shows him as he wished to be seen after his coronation at Westminster Abbey on 9 April 1413. It is a profile (possibly designed to hide an unsightly scar caused by an arrow wound in his face); he is young, handsome and carries an air of wisdom. Yet, we are intended to take most note of his brown hair, shaved back in the tonsorial style of a priest. He has become Henry the Pious. Later, Shakespeare anointed the image, turning Henry from 'Prince Hal', the yobbish rake surrounded by drunken soaks like Falstaff, into the warrior-king, the Henry who could rally greatness from his followers, and who, against all odds, defeated the French at Azincourt because God was on 'our' side. Thanks largely to the playwright, a ruthless autocrat has been transformed over the past six hundred years into a national hero, to be wheeled out like a saint to give us deliverance whenever Britain is under threat. In our post-Iraq, post-Blair, post-spin era, however, Henry's image inevitably has been subject to revision. He is now more likely to be reviled than revered, particularly among professional historians. In 2010, Henry was tried for war crimes at a mock trial by members of the US Supreme Court in Washington, DC for ordering the murder of his prisoners at Azincourt. He was found guilty.

As Felipe Fernández-Armesto, author of the magisterial *1492*, puts it: 'Henry's kingship was tainted. His usurping dynasty had no right to the crown. His victories were triumphs of hype, stained by the blood of war-crimes. His piety was remarkable, especially in his zeal for burning heretics, but a saint he ain't.'[2]

Our 'saints' perhaps tell us much about the state of our 'faith' in national heroes, as do their fallings from grace.

~∂~

Azincourt – to use the French spelling – is a mere forty-eight miles from Calais, but for Henry it was a world away. I appear to be the only one heading in its direction as we plunge off the ferry and head for the autoroutes. Instructed by the assertive lady on my SatNav, after half an hour of driving from the port, I leave behind the MPVs packed with families and the juggernauts that all seem to be in the red livery of Norbert Dentressangle. Soon I slide into a quiet world of D-roads that, to my relief, do not require me to fumble in my jeans for euros to pay the tolls.

I pass through charming red-brick villages and roll south through gentle hills until I hit the queues into Fruges, a strung-out market town on a hill. It may be quite picturesque on most days, but it is not so today. The rain is starting to fall, and the market stalls that usually fill the square to make Fruges *intéressant* have been replaced by the dodgems of a travelling fairground. At its heart is a crossroads with the main north–south highway that links Rouen to Dunkirk, the A928. It is a bottleneck at the best of times, and today roadworks are delaying everyone in all directions. Even my SatNav girlfriend seems to sigh with relief when, at last, I get the green light for the long pull up the hill on the south side of the town; it ends in a plateau of windmills. She tells me to go on for four kilometres.

This area was once famous for coal; now they produce power from windfarms. Windmills sprout like Triffids above the more traditional lines of poplars, their propellers turning briskly in the breeze. 'Turn left in two hundred yards,' my SatNav dominatrix insists. She need not have bothered. At the junction, a cardboard knight clad in cardboard armour points the way to the *emplacement antique de bataille d'Azincourt.* I pass a few more bucolic villages of red pantiled barns and farmhouses built of the white stone of the region, and then I spot another knight in armour peeping over a hedge; he is clearly French, as he carries a blue shield with gold fleurs-de-lis; this was traditionally the French royal coat of arms, which Henry V also insisted on using to stamp his claim on his French possessions, including Calais. Nearby, I come across a wooden knight in a surcoat bearing a quartered emblem of three lions and fleurs-de-lis. He is standing sword drawn, bareheaded and belligerent: King Harry.

The leitmotif of Azincourt, though, is archers, not medieval knights in armour. Archers are big in Azincourt. There is a Rue des Archers. The mayor, with an eye on the tourist trade, which brings far more visitors from Britain in the summer, has authorized the placing of wooden cut-outs of archers all around the town. They jump out of the hedgerows and two archers hold up the sign for the car park for the visitor centre in the heart of the old village, where I stop. The *Centre Historique Médiéval* is in the Rue Charles VI, although the French King was actually unable to lead his forces into battle because of his mental instability and never appeared at Azincourt. Unashamedly, the centre is dedicated to preserving the memory of France's most humiliating defeat by the English (and the Welsh). Even the centre's shape reawakens the shuddering, almost mythological memory (at least for the French) of the English and Welsh archers. The glass entrance porch is bow-shaped with six wooden spines, which look as though they are longbows being pulled back to the straining point.

I pay €7.50 and collect my ticket under the entrance's six longbows, before I am ushered into a darkened room just as the Azincourt 'show' is starting. It begins with a tableau with two life-size tournament tents representing the opposing camps on the eve of battle. It is night-time; a spotlight illuminates a figure in the entrance to a candy-striped tournament tent – a life-sized model of 'Harry in the night'. His face moves creepily in projected computer animation, as we hear Shakespeare's lines comparing the eager French with the fearful English: 'The confident and over-lusty French / Do the low-rated English play at dice; / And chide the cripple, tardy-gaited night, / Who, like a foul and ugly witch, doth limp / So tediously away.'[3] It is true; the French nobles did gamble over dice on the eve of the battle for the capture of those English knights who carried the highest ransom on their heads. 'Worthless' archers were represented by a blank face on the dice.

Already feeling a bit anxious at what awaits us in the next room, I shuffle next door with a handful of other visitors to find that a panoramic relief map of the battlefield has been laid out on a table. We sit on raised benches that give us a bird's-eye view of how the thin line of England held out against the massed ranks of the French.

A French family – father with a beard, mother in jeans, son about ten – watch mutely as the story unfolds. In furious sound and vision, with blood-curdling clips from old movies of the battle and spotlights highlighting movements on the battlefield we see how, against all the odds, a force of twenty thousand French were slaughtered by the English force, a quarter of their number. If the family was left in any doubt about the crushing nature of the defeat, we are told the English victory at Azincourt led to an upsurge in 'English nationalism' across La Manche. The show ends with portraits of the great English leaders who followed in Henry V's footsteps. Their faces briefly flash up on a big screen – Elizabeth I, Oliver Cromwell and Sir Winston Churchill. They do not include the 'Iron Lady', Margaret

Thatcher. It seems the handbaggings in Europe are too fresh in the memory for that.

The doors open on our darkened world and the French family leaves looking downcast. Deep down, I suppose I should have an urge to strike the air with a fist and shout 'Eng-e-land'. But the spirit of *entente cordiale* is so strong in Azincourt today, I walk out of the darkened theatre into the October sunlight feeling a bit embarrassed, inclined to apologize for the carnage.

On the way out, I try to engage the young girl behind the counter in the Azincourt gift shop. I say that the film was 'a bit triumphalist – for the English, I mean'.

'We know…' she says with a shrug and the hint of a Gallic smile. She gives me my receipt for three postcards of Henry striking an attitude of triumph.

'It was all a long time ago,' I offer.

'*Oui*,' she nods before bagging up a souvenir brochure of Azincourt.

The French can take credit for accepting their defeat in 1415 *sur le menton* but it is good for business. It is estimated that eighty per cent of the thirty-two thousand tourists who visit Azincourt each year are British. Even so, it is difficult to imagine that the English would ever have created a square in London to celebrate French seamanship if Villeneuve had defeated Nelson at the Battle of Trafalgar.

The Azincourt museum next door is full of items related to the battle, including suits of armour and weapons, and I am invited to have a go. I try lifting a mace. I can just about lift it but it is so heavy, I cannot imagine swinging it around for long. No wonder the French men-at-arms were too exhausted to fight by the time they reached the English lines. And it was not only the men. The museum, in a converted barn, is dominated by a full-sized model of a horse in body armour. The heavy horses contributed to the defeat by churning up the field of battle before an arrow had been fired.

The most telling item, however, is minute. It is in a glass case, and it was found on the battlefield. It is a small spur shaped like a merman. A little note describes it as '15th century, bronze, decorated'. Closer inspection shows that the spur has the face of a man, and the body of what looks like a fish. This spur once graced the armoured heel of a French man-at-arms, possibly one of the many French noblemen who died that day. It was probably worth more in 1415 than a month's earnings for a lowly English archer – muster rolls show archers were paid six pence a day – but death that day was a great leveller.

Leaving the museum, I drive to a corner of the battlefield, where an orientation table has been set up to help identify the points of interest. I arrive as three elderly Englishmen, wrapped up against the wintry weather, are returning to the warmth of a Volvo estate. 'Not many French about, are there!' says one, in a green Barbour wet-weather jacket with binoculars hanging from his neck and who is clearly their leader; he reminds me of Foggy Dewhurst, the bossy character in the television series *Last of the Summer Wine*.

Foggy is right. There are battle re-enactments in the summer, but there is no sign of the French family from the museum or any of the locals celebrating St Crispin's Day on the battlefield at Azincourt today. The only restaurant in the village, the Charles VI, is firmly shut.

We are by a memorial where the D104 joins the little road into Maisoncelle, the village where the English and Welsh archers slept rough overnight while their lords, the knights in armour, found what comfort they could in farm buildings. Henry V did not spend the night in a tournament tent; he wisely stayed in a cottage, leaving his men to shelter as best they could in barns or under hedgerows from the rain and the cold. It would have taken a superhuman effort for me not to desert from Henry's army on a day like today.

The battlefield is the most unchanged site of its kind in Europe. I drive just over a mile south-west along the D104 towards another crossroads where the two forces crashed into each other. I pass trees near the village of Tramecourt on the right; they are all that is left of the woods that hemmed in the French on their left flank. At the junction with Rue Henri V, I am greeted by a line of brightly painted wooden archers in the midst of the flat arable farmland. They look almost comical in their tunics of red and yellow and Lincoln green, arching their bows towards the winter wheat like a crude piece of Disneyland planted in the Nord-Pas-de-Calais. However, their aim is deadly serious, for this was the line where the bowmen met the French; and that day in October 1415, it was piled high with bodies.

Rue Henri V is an old track, linking the villages of Tramecourt and Azincourt. It crosses the road north-east to Calais that Henry's army would have followed on the march from their landing spot on the coast. Near the crossroads, just off the main road, an odd-looking clump of trees conceals a crucifix of iron. That cross marks the mass grave where some of the six thousand French dead were interred after the battle.

~↶~

We all learned the history in school lessons. It was the longbow that brought about the French defeat, as it had been before in the Hundred Years War.

At Crécy, nine thousand English troops had defeated a French force of thirty-five thousand, and all agreed that the battle had been won with the firepower of the English longbow. The longbow undoubtedly was formidable when used properly. In England, men were required by law to practise with the weapon. The bow required skill and great power to draw the bowstring back, which is why France and other European powers tended to prefer the crossbow – it required little strength and not much skill, apart from an ability to aim and shoot, much like a gun. It could be used by the unskilled men-at-arms, called to war at command.

At Azincourt, the English were vastly outnumbered again, possibly by as many as four or five to one, though there are still disputes about the exact numbers. And for centuries, it has been thought that the longbow won Azincourt for the English, once again. But you only have to scrape the surface of the grey, cloying mud of Azincourt's fields to discover that much of what we know about the battle, and of Henry V, is Shakespearean legend.*

Some facts surrounding Henry are not in dispute. Henry was a born leader, although he had not been born to rule. His father, Henry Boling-broke, had forced Richard II to surrender the Crown of England in 1399 when Bolingbroke reclaimed the Lancashire estates that Richard had confiscated from him during exile. When he was crowned, Bolingbroke styled himself as Henry IV and established the red-rose dynasty of the House of Lancaster, a branch of the Plantagenets. His son, Henry, was born in Monmouth, Wales, on 15 September 1386.

The adult Henry V was tall, about six feet three inches, and slim; after he became king, he was invariably clean-shaven, showing off his ruddy complexion and a battle scar on his right cheek where an arrow had stuck in his face during the Battle of Shrewsbury in 1403 when he was sixteen, supporting his father against Harry Hotspur. His scar provided a lasting lesson for young Henry in the power of the longbow that day. His sharp, pointed nose was balanced by soft hazel eyes that, as one chronicler put it, 'flashed from the mildness of a dove's to the brilliance of a lion's', depending on his mood. It was in the theatres of Elizabeth I that the Henry V we

---

* Anne Curry, Professor of Medieval History at Southampton University, says: 'I never tire of watching stage or film versions of *Henry V*, even if they are inaccurate.'

know today was truly born, and the dissolute, womanizing young Hal of *Henry IV, Part I* was cast aside, along with his old boozy friends, once the Crown, which he wanted so urgently, fell into his hands. It did so, at last, after his father's death on 20 March 1413, when Henry was twenty-five.

Quickly, Henry V set his sights on the recovery of the English possessions taken in France by his great-grandfather, Edward III, at the start of the Hundred Years War. He planned his campaign meticulously over the years. While he talked peace with France, he raised taxes and pawned the Crown Jewels to finance war, including a vast fleet of around fifteen hundred ships that could carry twelve thousand men from across England's counties and the land of his birth, Wales. He set off for France in August 1415, as recorded by the Elizabethan poet Michael Drayton in his famous ballad that opens with the lines: 'Fair stood the wind for France / When we our sails advance'.

When Henry arrived with his troops on the French coast, he was full of optimism. Most especially, he was confident in the rightness of his claim to the French throne, which was then occupied by the intermittently mad-as-a-hare King Charles VI, who sometimes believed he was made of glass. (He was probably suffering from what would be diagnosed today as schizophrenia.) But Henry's bold enterprise immediately ran into difficulties. First, he failed in his efforts to force the town of Harfleur, then the country's principal northern seaport, into surrender. It took a month-long siege before the town's elders finally capitulated, on 22 September. By that time, Henry's army had been seriously debilitated by dysentery caused by eating the local shellfish and the exhaustion of the fight. Some in his camp were forced to return across the Channel to England.

He had intended to make a *chevauchée*, a punitive raid, to plunder Bordeaux but was now facing a dilemma. He too could return to England, but to sail home with no more than the keys to one French port would have been seen as a military blunder; further, it risked weakening the unsteady grip that the House of Lancaster had on the Crown. Against the advice of his marshals, he decided to leave around fifteen hundred men, including a thousand archers, to defend Harfleur and advance north along the coast with the remaining nine thousand of his men for Calais, then still an English possession. To military historians today, this is an inexplicable tactic, but Henry's contemporary chroniclers say he wanted to demonstrate that he could march across France with impunity; this would prove that he was the rightful heir, before God, to the nation's throne. In truth, he probably also wanted to emulate Edward III, who had won that famous victory against the French at Crécy. Henry's drive to Calais followed in his great-grandfather's footsteps, declaring that the Somme and Normandy were still 'his' land.

It went badly from the outset. The English came under attack within hours of leaving Harfleur. The harrying by the French continued unabated, like the mosquitoes by the rivers. A French guidebook to Azincourt says: 'The march of the English turned into eighteen days of martyrdom, being constantly attacked by the French army.' It is an exaggeration to say it was 'martyrdom' – in fact, Henry lost very few of his men on the march – but the French harassed the English at every turn as they tried to cross the network of rivers that cut through the Somme region like veins.

The opposing forces played cat and mouse across the marshy, misty region around the Somme for the next week. Henry's army proceeded as fast as it could towards the safety of Calais. On 23 October, they crossed the River Authie before marching through the Picardy town of Frévent within thirty miles of the port. The next obstacle was the crossing of the River Ternoise. On Thursday, 24 October, the Duke of York's scouts rode ahead to find French forces trying to destroy a bridge across the River Ternoise at the town of Blangy to the north of Henry's main battle group. Edward, who was to die the next day in the Battle of Azincourt, fought off the French and secured the crossing, but after scaling the next hill, his scouts spurred their horses back breathlessly to report seeing a terrifying sight. Beyond the village of Maisoncelle, they saw the French cavalry and thousands of men-at-arms spreading across the valley from the east 'like a swarm of countless locusts'. The French had crossed the river further upstream at Saint-Pol and had set their trap for the English on the main road to Calais in the fields between the woods on a plateau near the castle of Azincourt. When he was told they had at last encountered the main French army, Henry V knew that he had no escape. He galloped forward to see for himself the size of the force that faced him, and it would have been daunting, even for a king so sure of having God on his side as Henry V. He saw a vast forest of spears, horses and men in armour with banners flying, assembling in the narrow space between the woods of Tramecourt and Azincourt to bar his way to Calais. Henry returned to his dispirited army, which had halted just south of Azincourt at the village of Maisoncelle to steel their nerve for the battle that would surely come in the morning.

~ℓ~

Late on 24 October 1415, Henry approached the rolling fields of Azin-court with his rag-tag army comprised of about five thousand archers and one thousand men-at-arms. They were almost worn out by exhaustion. Some had travelled on horseback, but most were weakened by their forced march of eighteen days across almost 250 miles of hostile territory including the energy-sapping, boggy marshes of the Somme. They were starving, soaked by torrential rains, cold; some were barefoot, while others had discarded their breeches after repeated bouts of dysentery.[4] They were in no condition to fight. As they looked across to the three villages that formed a triangle – Azincourt, Tramecourt and Maisoncelle – on the looming plateau thousands of knights on horseback and men-at-arms spread across the fields like ripe corn, their French banners waving and trumpets sounding as if they were at a tournament. Indeed, that is how some of the French nobility saw it; they had come to annihilate the English and gain revenge for their forefathers for the disgrace suffered at the Battle of Crécy seventy years before.

Dawn broke cold and miserably wet on St Crispin's Day, and Henry rode out on a small white horse so that the men could see that, despite the odds, he was with them, and if necessary, would die with them. They were soaking wet from the overnight rain, to add to their many discomforts of hunger, exhaustion and dysentery. The bowmen, who had grabbed what sleep they could in the fields and hedgerows around Maisoncelle, had little armour apart from leather to deflect the blows of the French knights' battle swords. Some had jacks – jerkins with small iron plates sewn in between two layers of felt or canvas – to protect the body, and an open-faced helmet, though many wore caps made of boiled leather or osier – wicker – with an iron cross on top to stop a sword slicing through the skull, while others had aventails, hoods of chain-mail. They wore hose and those who still had them wore light shoes, which would prove a life-saver in the coming hours. They kept their bowstrings dry in pouches or under their hats.

The archers were acutely conscious that the French knights were eager to wreak revenge on them for the humiliation inflicted with the longbow at Crécy, and by Edward, the Black Prince, the eldest son of Edward III, at Poitiers in 1356 – the second of the three great victories over the French in the Hundred Years War. The bowmen, never suspecting that Azincourt would be the third in that trio of triumphs, had spent the early hours before the battle cleansing their souls of their sins ready to meet their deaths and then sharpening the short swords and daggers they would use when they ran out of arrows.

It was noticed that Henry was not wearing spurs as he walked in armour among his men; this signalled he intended to fight on foot like them. There is little doubt he rallied his sodden army with a series of speeches before they went to die for him. It is likely he told them of the rightness of his claim to the French throne and his determination to gain victory or die trying, for he would not be ransomed.

Shakespeare, writing in 1599, gave Henry V the stirring words that have echoed down the centuries to inspire both Elizabeth I and Churchill when Britain again faced overwhelming odds against a foreign enemy:

> We few, we happy few, we band of brothers;
> For he to-day that sheds his blood with me
> Shall be my brother; be he ne'er so vile,
> This day shall gentle his condition:
> And gentlemen in England now a-bed
> Shall think themselves accursed they were not here[5]

Other chroniclers put it more prosaically. Henry, according to the French reports, reminded his archers that the English nobles would expect to be spared if they were captured in return for ransom according to the rules of chivalry, but the bowmen of England (and Wales) were viewed as worthless by the French, and could expect to be put to the sword, or at best have their bowstring fingers cut off. This had the desired effect. The archers reacted with defiance; legend has it that the archers insolently waved their fingers in a V-sign at the French, and that the 'two fingered' salute, still a potent insult after six hundred years, has its origins at Azincourt. Indeed, there is documentary evidence to suggest that the legend may be true. Jean le Fevre, who fought on the English side, noted: 'the French had boasted that if any English archers were captured, they would cut off the three fingers of their right hand so that neither man nor horse would ever again be killed by their arrows'.

Henry stood in the centre of the English line, marked out by his own royal standard and the fluttering banners of St George, St Edward and the Trinity. He wore the royal surcoat of blue and red quartered arms, bearing the three lions of Aquitaine and the French quartered lilies, the fleurs-de-lis embellishing his claim to the French throne, over his armour, and a gold crown on his helmet. Drayton said it was lit by diamonds that sparkled like fire. Even allowing for poetic licence, Henry was a highly visible presence at the southern end of the battlefield near Maisoncelle, and a marked prize for the French nobles. He was surrounded by his men-at-arms but the Duke of York and his men stood on the right, barring the way to the King.

In addition to the whinnying of the horses and the pounding of the drummers and the shouts of orders, the English lines were filled with the sound of hammers as the archers hammered sharpened stakes into the ground at a forty-five-degree angle to protect them from the opening charge by the French cavalry. The Elizabethan poet Michael Drayton said they were 'pointed by iron and of five foote long'. This hedge of spears also allowed the nimble archers, untroubled by the weight of armour, the freedom to move in and out of the defensive line to shoot and retreat at will.

Their longbows were cut from a single piece of yew, about six feet long, and fashioned so the heartwood was in the belly, facing the archer, to resist compression, while the sapwood was on the back; together, this gave maximum spring in the shaft to propel the arrows at a velocity of two hundred feet per second. The arrows were thirty inches long, fletched with goose feathers and tipped with pointed bodkins, which could penetrate leather jackets and mail, or barbed broad-heads, which could kill by slicing through flesh. They could rain down death on an army at three hundred yards, and at one hundred and eighty yards they could hit an individual target; at sixty yards they were lethal. The medieval archer drew the bowstring to the side of his face, an effort that required up to one hundred and sixty pounds of pulling power, but it was achieved largely through technique rather than brute strength. Even so, they developed enormous muscles in their arms and upper bodies. Skeletons found on the sunken wreck of Henry VIII's flagship, the *Mary Rose*, show unusually enlarged left arms, evidence that they were once bowmen. Arrows came in sheaves of twelve and the archers would carry at least two sheaves, which they would stick, tip down, in the mud, so that they could be plucked up quickly and shot in rapid succession. The bulk of Henry's archers were positioned in blocks of more than a thousand, on the wings of the English lines of men in armour, so that they could hit the enemy in a crossfire as they attacked. Protected by their barrier of stakes, they waited.

By 11 a.m., the French had still refused to attack; they had time on their side and were waiting for more nobles to join them in the rout of the English. The French had put aside the civil war which had raged between the Armagnacs and the Burgundians and united against the English under the command of three royal dukes: Charles of Orléans, John of Bourbon and John of Alençon, with executive control handed to two experienced military men, John d'Albret, the Constable of France, and John le Maingre, the marshal known as Boucicaut.

With the benefit of hindsight, these war-worn French commanders could not have picked worse ground on which to fight the English. At Tramecourt and Azincourt, the open fields were hemmed in on either side by dense woods, which made it impossible for the cavalry to out-flank the archers on Henry's flanks. The trees also squeezed the wide 'battles' of French men-at-arms into a funnel that would have disastrous consequences.

The two sides stood about a thousand paces apart. Confident in their coming victory, the French sent a herald to ask the English King what ransom he would pay for his freedom; he contemptuously dismissed the offer to *parlez*. Henry, with the agreement of his council, now took the gamble of his life. He ordered his banners forward, and launched an attack on the French. His forces went forward slowly, so that everyone could keep up, but it caught the French off-guard.

Some of the French cavalry and nobles, who had been waiting for over three hours, had left the line when Henry ordered the advance. The English archers were forced to uproot their defensive pikes and run forward until they were a longbow shot from the French, about three hundred paces. There they hammered the stakes into the ground for a second time, and waited for the signal to fire.

Henry, having dismounted, marched in heavy armour on foot with his troops about seven hundred paces to a point near to the farm track between Tramecourt and Azincourt, now Rue Henri V, where they stopped. This was the front line where the two forces of men in armour would crash into each other like bull rhinos in the rutting season, in a pitched battle. Henry remained conspicuous in the centre, in his silken surcoat with its English lions and French fleurs-de-lis. A 'battle' of around five hundred men-at-arms led by the Duke of York held the ground on his right and Lord Camoys commanded another five hundred men-at-arms on his left. Henry carried a heavy broadsword with a cruciform hilt, and a decorated dagger on his hip known as a *misericord* because its blade could release souls. The English knights and men-at-arms carried broadswords, maces for smashing skulls and the murderous pole-axe, combining a spear with an axehead about five feet long. Henry could have worn a basinet, a more protective helmet with a visor, but opted for an open helm with a crown around it, so he could be easily recognized.

Sir Thomas Erpingham, a veteran at the advanced age of fifty-eight, rode out in front of the English lines with his guard and gave the signal for the archers to fire by throwing his baton into the sky. Before it fell to earth, thousands of arrows were already arcing towards the French lines.

Firing around ten arrows per minute, the archers were able to let loose an almost unbelievable storm of seventy thousand arrows at the French massed ranks in just sixty seconds and an awesome barrage of three hundred and fifty thousand arrows in five minutes. A French record describes being on the receiving end as like enduring 'a terrifying hail of arrow shot'.

The French remembered hearing a shout of 'nestroque' or 'now strike' before the arrows rained down on them. A great cry of 'St George!' rose up from the English ranks.

With men and horses already dying in agony from the rain of arrows, the French cavalry went into the attack as their men-at-arms began slogging through the mud on foot towards the English, but instead of their flanking move, the mounted knights were forced by the woods on their flanks to charge straight at the archers and on to their stakes. A French knight, William de Saveuse, who bravely led the charge on the English left, saw his mounted force broken on the archers' spikes. The archers may have stood in front of the spikes to conceal them until it was too late for the cavalry to halt. Horses, trained to overcome fear, ran on to them, and were impaled, throwing their riders over their heads to be killed on the ground. The archers fired at the unprotected horses, which were more vulnerable than their riders in armour, bringing more men to the ground and leaving panic-stricken and riderless battle-horses to cause mayhem among the advancing line of French men-at-arms. Most of the men in armour, however, survived the hailstorm of arrows to engage with the English front line. Arrows may have penetrated eye-holes and air vents in even the finest of the suits of armour, and sent horses into a frenzy, causing more chaos among the knights, but despite the terror, the truth is the hail of arrows killed few French men-at-arms.

The longbow was a fearsome weapon when used against massed ranks, but ballistic studies at the Royal Armouries in Leeds using an identical bodkin tip to one found on the battlefield showed it could go through iron plate, but it could not penetrate the latest development in the medieval arms race: steel plate. Tests replicated by the experts of Southampton

University's laboratories show that when shot against a two-millimetre-thick mild steel plate, a needle bodkin merely buckled, even though the test plate was softer than some of the more advanced armour.

So what did bring about the disaster for the French? The answer lies in the arrogance of the nobles, the weather and the landscape at Azincourt. The French had a carefully laid battle plan, written days before Azincourt, and a partially burnt fragment still survives. About five and a half thousand French archers and crossbowmen standing in the second rank were to open the French attack while the cavalry outflanked the archers and cut them to shreds. A spearhead force of men-at-arms, led by the battle-hardened Boucicaut, would then smash into the English lines like a devastating battering ram and, with the English lines beginning to crack under the assault, the main battle of up to eight thousand men-at-arms led by the young Duke of Orléans with the Constable of France, d'Albret, and the Dukes of Brittany and Alençon would follow up to overwhelm the English. A third battle would be led by the Duke of Bar and the Counts of Nevers, Charolais and Vaudemont to mop up any remaining resistance. The battle plan would have worked with a finely marshalled group of officers, but without their King on the battlefield, the French lacked an effective general to lead them. Once the French nobles had the scent of war in their nostrils, they ignored the advice of their better-trained professional commanders and pushed forward to be in the front line, forcing the French crossbowmen to the rear. With no clear direction, the French assault dissolved into chaos.

The topography of the battlefield, coupled with the woods at Tramecourt and Azincourt, played a major part in the French catastrophe. The battlefield appears broadly flat at first glance, but for the French knights clad in armour, with their visors down, it must have been like walking on the slippery side of a barrel. The land falls away towards Azincourt and the Tramecourt flanks, forcing the French into a narrow front as they moved slowly forward. The trees of the two woods on either side of the battlefield also hemmed them in. The French lines were about twelve hundred yards wide but were reduced to nine hundred yards by the time they reached the English front line.

A sophisticated computer model, created by Dr Keith Still, an expert in crowd analysis, shows vividly what happened. 'If you look at the worst disasters, you can see every element combining in this environment,' he explained.[6] As the moving mass of French men-at-arms in the first battle marched on foot towards the English lines, they were crushed together and, like a football crowd stampeding towards an exit, they began falling over one another in the mud; the panic became worse, as line after line of men in armour fell over those who had fallen in front. Those who were able to remain standing found themselves so tightly squeezed together when they approached Henry's lines, they could not swing their swords. 'Their vanguard, composed of about five thousand men, found itself at first so tightly packed that those who were in the third rank could scarcely use their swords,' a French monk recorded at the time.

To make the French position worse, the ploughed, sodden field in front of the French lines had been turned into a quagmire by their own cavalry, who had chosen to exercise their horses there on the eve of battle. Now the mud played its part. Indeed, according to Andrew Palmer, Professor of Engineering at the University of Cambridge, Azincourt's soil is particularly prone to creating suction when wet.[7]

The troops never expected to get bogged down in mud. Graeme Rimer, Academic Director at the Royal Armouries in Leeds, told me that, despite weighing up to thirty pounds, a suit of armour of the period still enabled men-at-arms to manoeuvre surprisingly well – an 'interpreter' wearing replica armour for the Armouries' studies even managed to do somersaults. As the French marched forward on the day of battle, however, the real men in armour would have been quickly exhausted; the suction created between the solid plate of steel and the oozing mud meant that raising a boot became the equivalent of lifting a fifteen-pound bag of sugar, according to laboratory tests. When they sometimes managed to free their feet from the mud, they would slip and topple to the ground.

Further, as the French advanced in their heavy suits of armour, their visors were drawn down to avoid being hit by arrows in the eyes – as a result, they had little room to breathe. Leeds University and the Royal Armouries at Leeds carried out tests with the help of four enactment volunteers clad in full armour and placed on a treadmill. The volunteers were aged thirty to thirty-four and used up energy twice as fast as men without armour, reducing their pace to 1.7 metres a second. For a fifty-five-year-old, the maximum walking speed would have been cut to 1.4 metres a second[8] – and many of the French nobles were veterans. The researchers also found the breast and back plates of the medieval armour hampered respiration even more: instead of being able to take long, deep breaths while they worked up a sweat, the volunteers were forced to take frequent, shallow breaths, and this too used up more energy.[9] 'By the time they reached the English front line, they would have been exhausted,' Graham Askew of Leeds University put it simply.

The French would have become quickly confused in these conditions. Historian Juliet Barker said: 'With visor down, the basinet was like a diver's helmet, but without the manufactured air supply: it plunged the wearer into a disorientating and isolating artificial darkness.'[10]

Once they began slipping and falling in their heavy armour, the French were as good as dead. Unable to get up, they were easy meat for the archers who, clad in cloth shoes or barefoot, were able to skip through the mud, to despatch the flower of the French aristocracy. The English archers abandoned their bows, to which they had been born, and turned to their 'bollock' daggers – so named by the archers because of the hand guard of two balls – to slit the throats of the French knights, or hammers to smash their skulls, or pikes to drive through the visors of their helmets into their skulls. The proud archers were, in reality, butchers. Blood ran thick in the mud, turning the front line into a charnel house.

One of Henry's clerics witnessed the carnage from the rear with the other wailing priests. In the *Gesta Henrici Quinti* (*The Deeds of Henry V*), he wrote: 'For when some of them, killed when battle was first joined, fell at the front, so great was the undisciplined violence and pressure of the mass of men behind them that the living fell on top of the dead, and others falling on top of the living were killed as well.'

Soon the bodies of the helpless French men in armour were piled high, and some were crushed and suffocated in the mud underneath their friends, killed by the sheer weight of more and more bodies pushing relentlessly forward. Boucicault was pulled out alive from under a pile of bodies when the fighting ended. He was taken captive.

Still, some French knights managed to hack their way through the Duke of York's guards, killing ninety of them along with the Duke, Henry's cousin, before striking for the King. In vicious hand-to-hand fighting, with two-handed swords scything through limbs and clanging against metal, the melee kept moving closer towards Henry until he too was forced to fight for his life. English knights – Sir John Mortimer, Sir Richard Kyghley of Lancashire and Sir John Skidmore of Herefordshire, among them – fell to the French attackers, along with the Earl of Suffolk. The King's brother, Humphrey, Duke of Gloucester, fell backwards, wounded in the groin, and Henry stood over him, hoping to save his life. In the frenzy of fighting to get at the King, a French axe sliced a gold fleurette from Henry's crown but the King survived the blow and led a furious fight-back. The Duke of Alençon, who came close to killing the King, fell to his knees to surrender to Henry himself and removed his helmet in a chivalric act of submission, at which a berserk English fighter smashed his skull with an axe.[11] The killing turned into a rout, as the French forces in the rear, horrified by the carnage at the front, began a retreat. Then the rout turned into a massacre as the archers continued their butchery in the mud. 'No one was captured. Many were killed. The English were increasingly eager to kill for it seemed there was no hope of safety except in victory,' said one eye-witness. 'They killed those near them and then those who followed.'

After more than two hours of fighting, it dawned on Henry and his followers that the day was theirs, but the next act was to tarnish his victory for ever. Despite the killing spree, the English had captured hundreds of French prisoners, who were held under light guard behind their lines. But now Henry was told that a local knight, Isambart d'Azincourt, had led a raid of peasants on the English baggage train at the rear of the English lines near Maisoncelle, stealing valuables including a crown. The King was furious at the breach of the rules of war, but simultaneously a counter-attack launched by the French Counts of Marle and Fauquembergues caused him to panic for the first time.

Henry feared that the hundreds of French prisoners could reverse his victory, if they managed to grab the weapons still on the field of battle. Anticipating a massed counter-attack by the French, he ordered his knights to kill all the prisoners, except the most prominent nobles who would carry the highest ransoms. It was shocking, even for those who had the rage of battle still burning in their nostrils.

Henry's men-at-arms were appalled at his order, not least because it meant giving up the prospect of riches through their ransoms, and refused to carry it out. But the King was adamant and the job of murdering the prisoners was given to an esquire with two hundred archers, who systematically set about cutting the throats of the Frenchmen who had surrendered. They were 'cut in pieces, heads and faces' with daggers jabbed through the visors of their helmets, and some were burned alive in a hut where they were being held. In all, about fifteen hundred French knights survived the massacre after being taken prisoner, but it is estimated that the French King lost one third of his nobles, including the Dukes of Alençon, Bar and Brabant along with ninety-two barons, nine counts and six hundred knights, mostly followers of the Duke of Orléans, whose faction was decimated by Azincourt. Charles, Duke of Orléans, was captured and remained in England for the next twenty-four years. There was no counter-attack, and as the rain continued to fall the next day, Henry and his army marched to Calais, praising God that they had won with the loss of only about five hundred men. Henry did not return to England until 16 November, and then did so as a conquering hero, with a victory procession through London.

Victory at Azincourt was being spun into a rich tapestry of myths by Henry's chroniclers within months of his return to England. The main contemporary account of his victory, the *Gesta Henrici Quinti*, was written to build support for a second invasion of Normandy in 1417.

The first myth was about numbers. Henry's historians exaggerated the scale of his 'miraculous' victory at Azincourt, to show that Henry must have had God on his side. And the dispute about the size of the opposing force still rages today. The author of the *Gesta* said the French had at least twenty-five thousand men, and Henry had around five thousand. Westmoreland, in Shakespeare's *Henry V*, puts the French total at 'three score thousand' – sixty thousand men. Historians Juliet Barker and the late Richard Holmes stick with the traditional view that the French had up to twenty-five thousand men and outnumbered the English by four to one and possibly six to one. Otherwise, Barker says, it makes 'a nonsense' of the eye-witness accounts.[12] Professor Anne Curry, the most radical of Henry V's modern sceptics, insists the French force numbered twelve thousand at the absolute maximum, while Henry had around nine thousand men.[13] This would put a completely different complexion on Henry's victory; it would explode the Shakespearean melodrama, and most of the historical accounts, as complete bunkum.

The wide discrepancy between the eye-witness accounts and the modern evidence may be caused by the disparity between the numbers of men-at-arms on both sides. If you ignore the archers, as chroniclers of the time were apt to do, Henry's small force of one thousand knights in armour was outnumbered by the French men-at-arms by ten to one or more.

The second myth was about the longbow. English victory was secured by a remarkable feat of arms, but there is much compelling evidence to show it was the archers' 'bollock daggers', axes and hammers that inflicted the damage, not the longbow.

The mythical power of the English longbow suits the narratives of both sides. For the French, it explains how the flower of their nobility could be defeated by a horde of peasants from across the Channel. For the English, the longbow is the essential ingredient that made the miracle possible, like the slingshot in the biblical story of David and Goliath, or the Spitfire in the Battle of Britain: a simple weapon that helped the plucky English underdogs beat a far more powerful enemy.

Finally, there is the myth of Henry V himself. Victory at Azincourt changed everything in Henry's lifetime. He returned a hero, with his grip on the throne of England strengthened and his hold on his disputed possessions in Northern France consolidated. The death of so many French nobles paved the way for Henry to conquer Normandy within four years of Azincourt. It gave the English control of large swathes of France, including Paris, for a generation. Under the Treaty of Troyes in 1420, Henry was made Regent of France, and he married King Charles VI's daughter, Catherine of Valois; the King's son, the *Dauphin* Charles, was disinherited from the French Crown. Catherine produced an heir to the House of Lancaster when she gave birth to their only son, later crowned Henry VI, but Henry V never achieved his greatest ambition: the French Crown.

On 31 August 1422, Henry V died of dysentery. He was still campaigning in France. Even in death, the fables surrounding the King were embroidered to encourage national hero worship. He was buried at Westminster Abbey with a dented crown – possibly the one damaged at Azincourt – placed on his tomb. He was granted a special place of honour near the tomb of his hero, Edward III. Here, he had joined the club of the immortals.

Henry's gains were not to last. The old French King, Charles the Mad, may have been periodically insane, but he outlasted Henry V by almost a year. Bizarrely, they were both succeeded by child kings. Joan of Arc inspired the French under Charles VII to reclaim his inheritance and throw out the English. By 1453, with the appearance of powerful siege guns to destroy Henry's fortresses in France, nothing was left of England's continental empire apart from Calais, which was to fall to the French in 1558 under Mary Tudor, who said that when she died they would find 'Calais' inscribed on her heart. For all the signs of *entente cordiale* in Azincourt today, the battle left animosity between the two countries for five centuries until a greater threat – the Kaiser's army – faced France.

The Azincourt campaign was an exercise in hubris. He need never have led his men to near destruction in Northern France. He was single-minded, stubborn and ruthless, when he needed to be. He was, after all, the son of a usurper; the Crown never sat easily on his head. Before Azincourt, he had his old friend Sir John Oldcastle – the model for Shakespeare's Falstaff and a non-conformist, reformationist Lollard – burned at the stake (for the crime of leading a *coup d'état* after his escape, rather than for heresy). Henry never freed his captured French marshal, Boucicaut, the internationally renowned exemplar of chivalry, who died, still in captivity, in 1421 at Methley Hall in Yorkshire. Yet, the King could be magnanimous to potential enemies when he chose, for example restoring privileges to Richard II's heir, Edmund Mortimer. He could also switch from being an amiable monarch to a haughty autocrat when circumstances required it. On balance, he may be judged a flawed human being, but there can be no doubt he was indeed a truly great warrior-king.

His spirit has been invoked whenever Britain has been in peril. Henry VIII used *The First English Life of King Henry the Fifth* to bolster support for a planned invasion of France. Nelson echoed Shakespeare's *Henry V* when he called his captains his 'band of brothers' on the eve of the Battle of the Nile. Sir Winston Churchill employed the rhetoric of *Henry V* when he praised 'the Few' after the Battle of Britain. Churchill, who knew the power of image-makers, also encouraged Sir Laurence Olivier to make his wartime propaganda film with its stirring, definitive portrayal of Shakespeare's Hal to stiffen the sinews of British public opinion for the D-Day landings in 1944. In 1954, historian K.B. McFarlane hailed Henry V as 'the greatest man that ever ruled England'. That may be over the top, but Henry's image still carries the power to inspire. More recently, Colonel Tim Collins was widely praised for using the tone of Shakespeare's Azincourt speech when he sought to inspire his troops, the First Battalion of the Royal Irish Regiment, before going into battle in Iraq.

The truth about Henry V and his victory at Azincourt in 1415 may not be entirely edifying, as the show trial in 2010 found, but Hal's lasting legacy as a great war leader is enduring and, when we are threatened, still capable of inspiring pride in our past.

THREE

1588

'The heart and stomach of a king, and of a king of England too'

OFF THE COAST OF DOVER:
The Invincible Armada in the Channel.

The oars dipped into the water, the lion and the dragon pennants caught the breeze and the Queen's royal barge pulled away from Whitehall stairs. As the barge sliced downriver on the ebb tide, the rambling Palace of Whitehall and its twinkling heraldic beasts were left far behind. It was the early morning of Thursday, 18 August 1588.*

Elizabeth had stepped on board her barge in good spirits in spite of the peril she faced. Powered by the royal bargemen beating time with their thirteen-foot oars, and accompanied by her ladies-in-waiting, her flotilla of barges looked and sounded like a waterborne pageant rather than a queen going to rally her troops against the invasion by the Spanish Armada. There were banners flying, and her richly costumed heralds

---

* 8 August by the old calendar. All dates listed herein follow the new calendar.

made blasts on their trumpets announcing her passage down the Thames. It was just the show of confidence that Londoners needed.

The threat of a Spanish invasion had spread panic through the city. Foreigners had been attacked at random by mobs and members of the ten-thousand-strong London militia, the so-called trained bands, who roamed the streets looking for papists and spies. Heightened tensions in the city led to faction-fighting between foreign camps including a bloody battle with knives and swords in Southwark, south of London Bridge, between servants of the Catholic French ambassador and the Huguenot Henry of Navarre. 'The English hate us Spaniards worse than they hate the Devil,' complained one Catholic. Every householder was expected to have a bucket to fight the fires, if the city with its warrens of wooden houses and shops was attacked.

Elizabeth therefore made a reassuring spectacle for the people cheering from the ramshackle buildings perched on London Bridge and the houses packed along the waterfront. The bells of the churches rang out to welcome the progress of the Queen and her retinue in their gilded barges. Their speed quickened under London Bridge, which was like shooting the rapids as the river squeezed between the central arches, and still more barges streamed by. One barge carried her cousin, Henry Carey, Lord Hunsdon, with the Honourable Band of Gentlemen Pensioners, resplendent in half-armour and plumed helmets. Hunsdon was the son of Mary Boleyn, and had been put in charge of Elizabeth's bodyguard of two thousand troops in the capital. Another barge was filled with the Queen's Bodyguard of the Yeomen of the Guard in their red and gold tunics, while further barges carried the Queen's musicians and more members of her household.

Further downstream, as her barge slid past the Traitor's Gate at the Tower of London, her cheerfulness must have been chilled by reminders of the crises that had plagued her turbulent life: the little green on the hill where her mother, Anne Boleyn, had been beheaded by her father, Henry VIII; and the short flight of mossy steps, where Elizabeth had once arrived as a prisoner of her own Catholic half-sister, Mary.

Now she faced the greatest crisis of her life. She was travelling downriver – the easiest form of transport in Elizabethan London – to deliver a speech to her troops, who were gathering to repel the Dons, at a fort on the river at Tilbury near the mouth of the estuary. It was a speech of defiance against the Catholic King Philip II of Spain and the Armada he had sent to overthrow her. It would prove that the Queen of England was every bit Henry VIII's daughter. It was courageous, spirited and truly imperious and would become the most famous speech of her long reign; it would be recalled down the centuries as the moment when Britain faced a foreign invader and won.

Her high spirits may have been because she was already aware that the danger had passed. There are modern claims that, by the time she arrived at Tilbury, her officers knew or suspected that the Armada had already been defeated and that her appearance was a masterpiece of spin; a fact that continues to be twisted into a victor's historical fiction.

'Like so many of Elizabeth's actions,' the historian Neil Hanson suggests, 'the Tilbury appearance had been pure theatre, mere show, and the speech to her forces that has echoed down the ages was a sham, delivered after the danger had passed.'[1] Historian Susan Frye, who has led the academic charge at the 'myth' of Elizabeth at Tilbury, has cast doubts on the authenticity of her great Tilbury speech. 'No reliable eyewitness account exists of what Elizabeth I wore or said,' she wrote.[2]

Elizabeth loved theatricality, masques and pageants and the theatre; she encouraged Shakespeare and the other great playwrights of the Elizabethan age. She had inherited the Tudor passion for Whitehall masques from her parents (her mother made her debut at court performing in a masque as a damsel in distress), and every year presided over extravagant pageants in the tiltyard at Whitehall for her succession day and her birthday (a tradition maintained today with the Trooping of the Colour for the official birthday of Queen Elizabeth II). Her court appearance, caked in white make-up to cover her wrinkles, a red wig to conceal her grey stubble and gorgeous pearl-encrusted costumes to enhance her majesty, was a daily theatrical show. But was her appearance at Tilbury an elaborate *coup de théâtre*? Was Elizabeth guilty of pulling off a masterpiece of spin that would make her the heroine of the age? Did she know that, as her barge sailed majestically down the Thames to her rendezvous with history, the Spanish Armada had already been scattered by her piratical captains and the Protestant wind? For, between the climax of the battles at sea and her journey to Tilbury, there were ten days. Ten crucial days when her captains already knew that the threat of the Armada had been blown away.

TILBURY POWER STATION, ESSEX:
The fort's causeway, with the chimneys dominating the horizon.

I have to go to Tilbury for the answers. It took five hours for the royal bargemen to row Elizabeth to Tilbury Fort, even with an ebb tide. It's less than an hour by car from central London. Driving towards Basildon on the A13, I turn right for the signs saying Tilbury Port and head towards the scrubby fields and light industrial estates that hug the estuary. The first thing I see when I get close to Tilbury is a towering pair of chimneys. They punctuate the skyline like an Essex wave, a rude two-fingered salute to the rest of the world from the county that has turned Chav life into the art form known as *TOWIE*. They are the smokestacks of the Tilbury coal-fired power-generating station, one of the biggest of its kind in the South of England, supplying heating and light to a million people including the residents of the semi-detached 1970s housing estates that cluster around the docks. There is a small road sign for the historic fort, but my eye is pulled right by the sight of a massive structure like a warehouse on steroids. It is Tilbury's international container and liner port. I drive past canyons of containers, and the huge cranes that lift them on and off the container ships that come to this port from around the world.

There is an old weatherboarded pub on the left, looking like something out of a Dickens novel; that is not entirely surprising, as Dickens knew the area around the Thames with the intimacy of a local. He was fascinated by the prison hulks – old sailing ships with their masts removed – that were moored at Tilbury in the nineteenth century; it was on the bleak mudflats on the south bank of the river not very far from here that Dickens set Magwitch's escape at the opening of *Great*

Expectations. This part of the Thames estuary lives up to the pub's name. It is called the World's End.

Even in the sixteenth century, the marshland at Tilbury had a reputation for being unlovely, as the 'backside' of Tudor London. The stagnant marshes here were known long before the Norman Conquest as Thurrock, a name derived, according to the Thurrock council website, from the Saxon word for the bottom of a boat where bilge water collected, or a 'dung heap in a field'. I get the message. Daniel Defoe, traveller and writer, who is supposed to have stayed in a thatched cottage by the traffic lights in Chadwell St Mary, described the whole shore near Tilbury as 'being low and spread with marshes' and 'unhealthy ground'.

Coming across Tilbury Fort is like seeing a gem set in mud. It is largely forgotten, apart from those like me who come here in search of Elizabeth. It has somehow survived in the shadow of the two giants, the container port to the west and the power station to the east, because of its strategic importance on the river. The riverbank has been built up since Elizabeth's barge arrived here, but there are wooden posts in the mud where the jetty must have been. It is tantalizing to imagine her barge mooring here.

There is a remarkably elegant watergate at the entrance to the fort topped with the royal coat of arms of Charles II. Inside the fort, which is run by English Heritage, I turn left to the old guardroom, which now houses the souvenir shop where staff sell the admission tickets. A line of bolt-action rifles stands in the corner, as though the sentries have just gone for their tiffin break. I appear to be the only visitor.

A cheerful woman in an English Heritage fleece informs me: 'It's mostly Americans who come here. We tell them they have to go to West Tilbury. Queen Elizabeth didn't make her speech here.'

This is disappointing news. I buy a copy of the official guide to the fort and go in search of Elizabeth again. As I walk across the cobbled square, I read the fort was built in 1539 by Henry VIII, who aimed to repel a threat from Charles V of Spain. The original Tudor fort built by Henry was simple: a D-shaped squat tower with cannon below, in enclosed chambers known as casements, and more cannon above, on the roof. It was one of five forts built along the river by the King, who understood the strategic importance of this stretch of the Thames as the gateway to London; he ordered another bastion to be erected on the opposite bank at Gravesend, so that gunners could catch approaching enemy warships in a crossfire. That was never needed. Perhaps the deterrence was enough.

Charles V was not only the head of the Holy Roman Empire and the most powerful Catholic leader in Europe; he was also the nephew of Catherine of Aragon, Henry's first wife, and he had a family score to settle. Catherine had been humiliated when Henry had annulled their marriage, making their daughter Mary a bastard, so that he could marry the ambitious and coquettish Anne Boleyn. The Pope had excommunicated Henry and effectively declared war on the breakaway English Crown.

The Spanish threat would come from the river, just as Elizabeth feared it would in 1588.

I stand on the north wall and look through one of the embrasures across the moat to a perfect replica of a wooden lift-bridge across the causeway. It looks as though it has been there since Elizabeth's day. The ferry road went through the blockhouse at Tilbury in 1588, and you can see the steeple of West Tilbury church peeping above the treeline on the hill in the distance, just as Elizabeth must have seen it. This is the closest I have come to sensing the presence of the Queen around the old fort.

The fort is larger than the blockhouse in Elizabeth's day. It was turned into a formidable fortress with a wide zig-zag moat and huge bastion walls in 1670 for Charles II. He ordered it to be strengthened as a precaution after a Dutch squadron raided the Medway and sank the flagship, the *Royal Charles,* at Chatham harbour thus exposing the English naval defences to red-faced humiliation. The fort was used as a gaol for 268 prisoners captured at Culloden in Bonnie Prince Charlie's Jacobite rebellion in 1746. After that, its fortunes rose and fell with the tide of events, as successive threats of invasion came and went. Magazines for holding nineteen thousand barrels of gunpowder were added in the eighteenth century, with complex arrangements, including blast-proof walls and copper-lined doors, for limiting the risk of an explosion. It remained in use as an ammunition store until after the Second World War. It last saw action as an anti-aircraft ops centre and witnessed the embarkation of tanks and troops for the D-Day landings from the Tilbury docks. Guns still guard the river from the thick walls of the bastion and look across the Thames, but these days they are just for show. The fort was decommissioned in 1950 and declared an historic monument.

Crossing the cobbled parade ground where redcoats marched and were flogged, I am brought back to the present with a jolt by the throbbing of the turbine-powered screws of a container ship. It goes gliding by, its enormous funnel towering over Charles II's gatehouse.

I stand on the immense walls and take a last look across the Thames to the Kent bank, eight hundred yards away, before leaving the fort. The town pier and the pubs that cluster round this stretch of the river at Gravesend on the Kent shore are clearly visible. There was a gun tower on the Gravesend side but that has gone now, swallowed up in the modern town, though the footings survive.

An ancient Tilbury-to-Gravesend ferry service used to cross the river at this point until 1963 when the Dartford Tunnel opened. Romans would have used the ferry to ride north along Ermine Street to York, or, if they were heading home, to ride south across Kent for Dover and Gaul (France). Gravesend still has strategic importance for the river. It is the headquarters of the Port of London Authority's control centre, which provides pilots for helping ships to navigate up the estuary.

Back in the car, I drive inland towards West Tilbury in search of Elizabeth once more. I drive up Fort Road, where her carriage was greeted by her soldiers lowering their bills and halberds – poles with blades and spikes on the end – as she passed by. At the top of the hill, there is a clue; it is called Gun Hill. This is where Robert Dudley, the Earl of Leicester, based his military camp but he was not one to rough it in a tent. He had a pavilion on the ridge, which he described to the Queen as 'yor pore Lyuetenants caby', giving him a dramatic vista over the distant Thames. Leicester and his senior officers, including his headstrong stepson, the Earl of Essex, entertained Elizabeth at this spot.

The field where Leicester's camp stood remained unchanged for centuries. Aerial photographs taken by the RAF showed rectangular features that could have been the drainage trenches surrounding Leicester's pavilion, but in the late twentieth century the field was plundered for gravel quarrying. The site now looks like a very large bomb has hit it; this corner of the plateau has sunk about six feet and is now covered in rough grass.

Could this shabby patch of Essex scrubland be the place where Elizabeth made one of the most famous speeches in the English language? Local historians believe she delivered her speech on the plain near a windmill, a quarter of a mile to the north of St James's Church, West Tilbury. There is no sign of a windmill but the church – a landmark even in Elizabeth's day – is still here. I discover to my amazement that it has been deconsecrated and converted into a private house, though you would not know it from the outside. The fields beyond the village green are largely unchanged, and in summer still grow the corn that was trampled underfoot by the thousands of soldiers laying on the show for their Queen. This is the place I have come to find. This is one of the most famous sites in English history. Yet, there is not a clue that Elizabeth was ever here. Anywhere else in the world, there would be an Elizabethan theme park on the site and an Armada interpretation centre but there is no plaque, pub sign or even 'Bess's Bed and Breakfast'. I leave thinking that perhaps that is for the best.

There is one house nearby that has a tale to tell, however. The Earl of Leicester arranged for the Queen to stay overnight at a local country mansion. There has been some dispute about exactly which hall it was, but it is almost certain to have been Saffron Garden, owned by a local Justice of the Peace, Edward Rich, among the farm fields in nearby Horndon-on-the-Hill, where the Queen could sleep comfortably. John Gerard in his 'Herball' of 1597 wrote of the 'pimpernell or burnett rose which grows plentifully in a field as you go from a village in Essex called Graies unto Horndon-on-the-Hill'.[3] The farmhouse was named after the saffron crocus, used in the yellow dye for cloth, which grew all around it. The Grade II listed sixteenth-century farmhouse still stands in the middle of fields at the end of a farm track, ignored by the busy commuter traffic on the A13 to Basildon and Southend. The two-storey house is T-shaped, timber-framed, plastered and painted white. Upstairs a stone fireplace was uncovered in 1914 with the coat of arms of the Rich family, including a shield topped by a helmet and a dragon, ending doubts that this was indeed the house of Mr Rich, and the house in which Elizabeth stayed overnight. In the public library at Grays there is a pamphlet called *Queen Elizabeth Slept Here* by the local history society, which also found Elizabeth as elusive as a ghost. I have to continue the search for her in the archives.

There is a remarkable Elizabethan map in the British Library showing the 'pricked line' of the flotilla's progress through all the bends in the river from Whitehall to 'Tilburie forte'.[4] It was drawn within weeks of her visit by her Royal Surveyor, Robert Adams, and clearly shows a royal barge with a small flotilla arriving here and troops lining the route along the 'causey' (causeway) to the camp up Tilbury Hill. The Adams map also shows that the river was defended at this point by a blockade of boats moored across the river to halt an attack on the city by Spanish galleons.

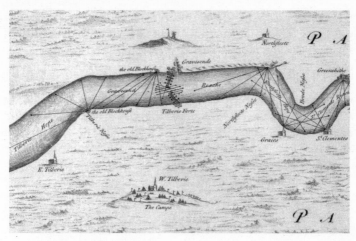

THE RIVER THAMES AT TILBURY:
Detail from the Thamesis Descriptio, drawn by the Queen's surveyor shortly after her visit.

It was a long pull to Tilbury and it would have been warm work in August despite the stormy weather. Rounding Northfleet Hope, the final bend in the river before Tilbury, the Queen would have had a clear view of the 'bridge' of cargo boats and flat-bottomed barges that formed the barrier across the river. They had been secured from the Tilbury bank to the Gravesend shore with forty anchors, chains and ropes. It is clearly shown in Adams's map with lines of fire from the guns stationed on the 'bridge' and the two bastions at the forts on opposite sides of the river. In the centre of the barrier, there was an elaborate mechanism to allow it to open for friendly vessels to pass through. An earlier attempt to block the river by an Italian engineer, Federigo Gianibelli, with a boom of 120 ships' masts bound by a nine-inch rope, broke up on the first flood tide. Designed by Peter Pette, the master shipwright in Deptford, south London, its replacement was strong enough to allow troops to cross from one bank to another, depending on where the Dons landed.[5]

As it happened, the Duke of Parma was planning to land his troops at Margate Bay on the North Kent coast before marching on London, so Leicester's troops would have had need of their wobbly bridge of boats if the Armada had succeeded.

Elizabeth's arrival at Tilbury was described by two eye-witnesses, a poet and a penny pamphleteer. As a result, we know she was met at the little jetty at around noon by her one-time lover Robert Dudley, the Earl of Leicester, whom she had appointed to head her army, and Robert Devereux, the Earl of Essex. Auburn-haired and handsome, Essex had quickly become her court favourite – she called him her 'wild horse', but he proved untamable. Just twenty-three, Devereux had been appointed by Elizabeth as a Knight of the Garter and her Master of Horse at Leicester's instigation. Leicester had held the influential post for nearly thirty years and clearly wished to keep it in the family. Court gossip murmured that Devereux, Dudley's stepson, was actually Dudley's illegitimate son and that he was now also Elizabeth's lover, an inheritance of sorts. But he fatally lacked Dudley's courtly manners and common sense.

Leicester was ageing and ill, suffering with stomach cancer that would kill him within a month. Leicester refused to let his infirmity stop him from receiving the Queen with fanfare. Flying banners, cheering troops, more trumpets and thundering gun salutes awaited her as she stepped ashore.

The Elizabethan writer James Aske, who was there – possibly as a soldier – described the scene in his epic poem *Elizabetha Triumphans*:

> She thence some-way still marching kinglike-on,
> The Cannons at the Block-house were discharg'd:
> The Drums do sound, the Phiphes do yeeld their notes,
> And Ensignes are displayd through-out the Campe.

After some courtly words of welcome, Leicester and the Earl of Essex escorted the Queen to a lavishly decorated four-wheeled coach. Aske said its sides were 'beset with Emmerods, / And Diamonds with sparkling Rubies red, / In chequer-wise by strange invention, / With curious knots embrodered with golde'. With the use of a magnifying glass on the Adams map it is possible to count thirty-four fluttering banners along the line of the causeway to Tilbury Hill with dots for the soldiers.[6] In fact, there were two thousand soldiers lining her route. The troops 'coutch their pikes and bowe their ensigns down' as the Queen passed by in Aske's account 'in token of their loyall beared hearts, / To her alone, and none but only she'.

Leicester, knowing the Queen's love of pageant, carefully choreographed the procession to please her. On the way to his camp – probably by a lower track to the church and the village green, which was less steep than Gun Hill – they were met by a 'troup of brave and war-like horssemen' led by Sir Roger Williams, who had just come back from another garrison at Dover, their horses stamping their feet and foaming at their champing bits. Five hundred horsemen then led the carriage on its way north towards the camp on Tilbury Hill. Elizabeth had wanted to go to Dover to appear in front of her forces on the South Downs and presumably yell her defiance against the Dons as the Armada sailed by, but Leicester persuaded her to join him at Tilbury instead.

Thomas Deloney, the tabloid journalist of his day, bears out Aske's remarks about the men kneeling as she passed. Deloney was a Norwich silk weaver and writer of popular ballads who published his own more downmarket eye-witness account, *The Queen's Intent to See Tilbury Camp*, for circulation in cheap pamphlets. Deloney says the Queen wore a plume of feathers in her hair and bade her subjects, including Leicester, 'Lord bless you all, my friends, but do not kneel so much to me.'

This carries the authentic sound of Elizabeth, who liked to appear modest when it suited her, but Leicester could not help himself. He doted on the Queen, and was keen to ensure that nothing went awry on this grand occasion.

Sir Francis Walsingham, Elizabeth's principal secretary and intelligence chief, was worried about a Catholic assassination attempt on the Queen. After all, the Spanish had arranged for a Catholic fanatic to assassinate the Protestant leader of Flanders, the Prince of Orange, in his own home in Delft only a couple of years before, and Pope Pius V in 1570 had issued a papal bull encouraging Catholics to kill the rebel Queen, like a *fatwa* against her life. It was renewed by Pius's successor, Pope Sixtus V. Thousands of printed copies of his papal bull calling upon her subjects to depose her were put on board the ships of the Armada for distribution when they landed.

Walsingham knew from his intelligence sources that Catholic agents were in Britain intent on helping the Spanish to victory. Killing the Queen would be one sure way of achieving it. Having her marching around in front of eight thousand armed men – some of whom could have been Catholic assassins – must have been a nightmare for the old man.

As one of his measures to counter the threat of assassination, Walsingham had persuaded Elizabeth for her own safety to leave the royal palace in Richmond, where she normally spent her summers away from the stink of the Thames in London, to stay at St James's Palace in Whitehall a mile away from the river, and much easier to protect with soldiers than the

Thames-side Palace of Whitehall created by her father. She was protected by a bodyguard of two thousand men under Lord Hunsdon, reinforced by the ten thousand trained bands of the city of London.

Elizabeth would refer to Walsingham's fears of assassination by one of her own soldiers in her Tilbury speech. Leicester brushed Walsingham's worries aside, however, and penned a note to Elizabeth promising 'you shall, dear lady, behold as good, as loyal and as able men as any Christian prince can show you'. He added: 'Good sweet Queen, alter not your purpose if God give you health. The lodging prepared for Your Majesty is a proper, sweet, cleanly house, the camp within a little mile of it, and your person as sure as at St James's.' He was exaggerating the closeness of the 'cleanly house' – Saffron Garden is about three miles from the site of his camp – but it did the trick. She accepted his invitation.

Elizabeth, even in old-age, with her teeth blackened, her face white with lead powder and her hair replaced by red wigs, liked to be showered with elaborate compliments on her beauty. She enjoyed her flirtations with the men at court, to none of whom she would surrender herself or her throne. But there could be no doubting the sincerity of Leicester's words when, as he guaranteed her safety at Tilbury, he called her the 'most dainty and sacred thing we have in this world to care for; a man must tremble when he thinks of it'.

Dudley and Elizabeth had known each other since childhood. They had grown up together, and at one time Dudley had openly nursed the ambition of marrying the Virgin Queen. She had nicknames for all her principal courtiers, and she called 'Robin' her 'Eyes', but her temper was just as fiery as her father's and she had a stormy relationship with Dudley. She was outraged when, in 1560, Dudley's wife, Amy, was found dead at home after falling down a spiral staircase – outraged not by the death, but by the scandal at court. There were sly whispers that the accident had been engineered by Dudley so that he would be free to marry Elizabeth. Modern conspiracy theorists point out that the one who stood to gain most from this suspicious death was the Queen's Chief Minister, the guileful William Cecil, Lord Burghley, then Secretary of State and later Lord High Treasurer, who was desperate to check Dudley's rise to power, and it certainly had that effect. Elizabeth remained warm towards Leicester, but his ambitions to become her prince consort were destroyed. Frustrated at his failure to win the hand of the Queen, in 1578 Leicester secretly married Lettice Knollys, a court beauty and mother of Robert Devereux. That was bad enough, but it was also without the Queen's permission. The ageing Elizabeth flew into another rage and promptly banished Leicester's new wife from court. She called Leicester a traitor.

Leicester further infuriated the Queen after being entrusted with English forces in the Netherlands. During the 1570s, he had built a close bond with William of Orange and Leicester had pressed Elizabeth to allow him to go with a force to the aid of William against the thirty-thousand-strong Spanish occupying army under the Duke of Parma. The Queen resisted but changed her mind for strategic reasons after the Dutch prince was assassinated. Leicester had not seen active service since his tenure in Mary Tudor's army against the French three decades earlier, and it was a mark of her fondness for him that she put him at the head of eight thousand troops in the Netherlands. She changed her mind again, though, and ordered him not to attack Parma's forces, and to carry out defensive manoeuvres. She was so keen to avoid provoking war with Spain that when she secretly negotiated a treaty with the Dutch to commit British forces to Holland against Spain, she refused the honorary title of Governor-General of the Netherlands because this title was in the gift of King Philip II. She knew accepting it would upset the Spanish. She was therefore furious with Leicester in 1586 when she learned that he had accepted the title in Flanders. He compounded his error with military failures on the ground, and proved too incompetent to unite his forces with the Dutch. In the autumn of 1587, he was summoned back to Britain in bad odour and banished from her court at Christmas, which pained him deeply.

After the turn of the year, with the threat of the war against Spain becoming unavoidable, and with both Leicester and the Queen in advanced middle age, Elizabeth relented. Confronted by the greatest peril she had ever faced, the Queen summoned her loyal Leicester back to court, and, despite any lingering doubts about his military competence, put him in charge of her army as the Queen's Lieutenant and Captain General.

There were other more experienced military commanders, such as 'Black Jack' Norreys and Sir Roger Williams, veterans of the Flanders campaign, who could look after the army for their chief. The Earl of Leicester at fifty-six was no longer the flashy young blade who had once captivated Elizabeth at Whitehall Palace. Still, the Armada crisis enabled him to play the role of valiant knight for his beloved Queen one last time. Leicester bade her to come to Tilbury to 'comfort' his troops.

Leicester's main problem was recruitment. Elizabethan England had no standing army. The country's defences were made up of county regiments organized by the knights of the shires, who provided the weapons, horses and regiments of local men aged between eighteen and sixty. They were formed into militias known as trained bands. Every town and village was expected to contribute, though many men had no training and only makeshift weapons cobbled together from the tools of the fields.

Elizabeth's most senior ministers were expected to muster troops in their own counties to meet the Spanish threat in 1588. Sir Francis Walsingham, now fifty-six, had pledged to don armour and lead a force of fifty lancers, ten carabineers and two hundred foot soldiers into battle. It was perhaps just as well for Britain that his services were never needed in this respect.

The trigger for the invasion had been the execution of Mary, Queen of Scots the year before. Elizabeth, who had been subjected to religious persecution by her Catholic half-sister, Mary, when she was in her early twenties, had sought to avoid religious tension during her own reign. She firmly remained a Protestant, but declared: 'I have no desire to make windows into men's souls.' Mary had enacted a brutal suppression of Protestants, burning more than three hundred at the stake, which alienated her people and earned her lasting infamy as 'Bloody Mary'. Elizabeth had no intention of making the same mistake.

She had instead sought a conciliatory middle way. She brokered a religious settlement that provided a Protestant liturgy but retained the vestments of Catholicism, cleverly resisted Puritan pressure to crack down on English Catholics and popery. Her statecraft paid off. The Queen's fairness to her subjects, regardless of their religion, ensured that most English Catholics were prepared to ignore the Pope's call to arms. They would rather fight for their Queen and country. As Robert Cecil, the twenty-five-year-old son and protégé in statecraft of her adviser William Cecil, wrote: 'It is a comfort to see how great magnanimity Her Majesty shows, who is not a whit dismayed.'

This somewhat ambiguous stance had helped to consolidate the Queen's hold on the nation, even in the most troubled times. Elizabeth was well aware that, while she remained unmarried and without an heir, she was vulnerable to plots. But when the Catholic Mary Stuart fled from Scotland to seek refuge in England, Elizabeth was confronted with a dilemma – as long as Mary lived, she would represent a threat. Mary had been imprisoned for twenty years when Walsingham, anxious to snuff out the threat as the warlike rhetoric from Spain increased, set a trap. The resourceful intelligence chief used an agent to encourage Mary to smuggle notes out to her supporters hidden inside a secret chamber in a beer barrel. He had broken the code used by Mary to write notes to her supporters, and when he uncovered a plot to overthrow Elizabeth, Walsingham allowed the correspondence to continue. He added a postscript to one of her notes, asking for the names of the plotters. When he got the reply he wanted, he snapped the trap shut. He captured the ringleaders, led by the twenty-five-year-old Catholic son of a local landowner, Anthony Babington. Babington and his co-conspirators were arrested, tortured and executed by being hung, drawn and quartered. Mary was found guilty of treason and Elizabeth, after agonies of indecision, signed her death warrant. Paralysed by doubts, she ordered that the death warrant should not be carried out without her instructions, but Cecil was determined not to let her back out; he called a secret meeting of her council and secured their support for her warrant to be despatched to Fotheringhay Castle in Northamptonshire where Mary was being held. Mary was beheaded on 4 February 1587, in the Great Hall at Fotheringhay, clutching a crucifix and wearing a scarlet petticoat as a martyr to her faith.

As Elizabeth had feared, the execution of the Catholic Queen was the catalyst for action by Spain. Armed with the Pope's denunciation of Elizabeth, King Philip of Spain decided to attack England. Philip had been married to Mary Tudor, Elizabeth's Catholic half-sister, until her death without an heir, and he had courted Elizabeth after she succeeded Mary but had been rebuffed. Now he intended to take by force what he had failed to gain through diplomacy from the heretic Queen of England in the name of the Roman Catholic Church. There were good political reasons for war: England posed a threat to Spain's control of the Netherlands, and Elizabeth's piratical captains such as Sir Francis Drake had become a thorn in his side by plundering Spanish treasure ships loaded with gold from the Spanish Main, the colonies in the New World.

The Spanish King began assembling the greatest fleet the world had ever seen. It comprised 130 ships, twenty thousand troops, a siege-train, field guns, small arms of all kinds, gunpowder, lead for musket balls and 180 Catholic priests for converting the population, by force if necessary. Santa Cruz, the elderly Spanish admiral who was to lead the Armada, took to his bed and died and the less experienced Duke of Medina Sidonia, despite his protests that he was ill-suited to the task, was put in charge of the fleet with detailed instructions for the conduct of the Armada from King Philip II himself. Philip's plan was for Medina Sidonia to rendezvous with the Duke of Parma, waiting in Flanders with seventeen thousand of his men and barges to transport them. Parma could not move without the Armada to protect the barges, which were vulnerable to attack by Dutch 'fly boats', fast attack craft that sailed along the coast, and the English fleet.

Walsingham had no need for spies to gain intelligence on the Armada. Reports on the fleet appeared in the press across Europe. From the number of cannon balls (123,790) to the weight of biscuits, bacon and cheese aboard the ships, all the details were published in Lisbon, Madrid, Rome, Paris, then Delft and Cologne. Strategic information was included too: the line of battle was given with the roster of officers assigned. The first line would be made up of twenty galleons in two squadrons, ten from Portugal, ten from Castile, as well as four *galleasses* from Naples. A second line included forty heavily armed merchant ships divided into four squadrons, each assisted by thirty-four lighter, faster ships for scouting and carrying despatches. This line would be followed by a slow squadron of twenty-three *urcas*, hulks and supply vessels, and four Portuguese galleys. It was called *La felicissima armada* – 'the most fortunate fleet' – but soon became known as *La Invencible* (the 'Invincible' Armada).

Elizabeth's response was typical of the woman – she vacillated. While preparing for war, she secretly negotiated with the Duke of Parma for peace as late as the first week of July 1588. Her behaviour exasperated her commanders. Only one could speak to her bluntly – her cousin, Charles Howard, Baron of Effingham. The Queen had appointed Lord Howard as Lord High Admiral because her more celebrated buccaneer captains were eager for war – too eager, in Elizabeth's cautious view. Howard was one of her most trusted advisers and courtly, but could speak to her frankly as others dared not do – he had been one of the commissioners who had found Mary, Queen of Scots guilty of treason, and had warned Elizabeth that her procrastination over implementing the death warrant was alienating her people and her council. She saw in Howard someone with a safe pair of hands to take charge of the fleet. Now he exclaimed in a letter to her: 'For the love of Christ Madam, awake thoroughly and see the villainous treasons around you, against Your Majesty and your realm, and draw your forces round about you like a mighty prince to defend you. Truly, Madam, if you do so, there is no cause to fear. If you do not, there will be danger.'

Elizabeth's naval power was the ace in her hand. It was led by a pack of daring seamen for whom the term swashbuckling could have been invented: Sir Francis Drake, Sir Walter Raleigh and Admiral Sir John Hawkins. They were all accomplished, fearless captains with a profound knowledge of the sea, and a long history of infuriating the Dons with their raids on Spanish ships and ports.

Drake, a favourite of the Queen, had to settle for being Howard's Vice-Admiral, but he was in effect the executive commander of the fleet. Drake was feared by the Spanish, and rightly so. He was the first Englishman to circumnavigate the globe – it took three years and he returned laden with Spanish gold.

The Queen had been one of the investors in Drake's voyage and was rewarded with a share of his fortune equal to a whole year of Parliamentary taxation. She had him knighted on board the *Golden Hind* on his return in 1580 as a reward. She also presented him with a glittering 'star jewel' and a golden cup, with a bowl made from a coconut he had brought back, topped by a model of his ship (both on display in the National Maritime Museum).

El Draque, as he was known in Lisbon, destroyed thirty-seven ships in Cadiz harbour in a pre-emptive strike on the Spanish fleet in 1587. It delayed for a year Philip's invasion plan, which he called the 'Enterprise of England', but Drake was realistic. He said he had merely 'singed the King of Spain's beard'. Drake now pressed Elizabeth to allow him and the other captains to attack the Spanish fleet before it left harbour at Lisbon, but Elizabeth resisted. She wanted to avoid the costly expense of war until the arrival of the Armada left her with no option but to fight. She had become notorious among her ministers for penny-pinching, and insisted on leaving her main fleet in Plymouth manned only by a skeleton crew to save money.

Raleigh, aged thirty-six, handsome, headstrong and courageous, was just the sort of man to throw down his cape for his Queen to walk over, and just the sort of man Elizabeth loved to surround herself with at court. Sir Walter had a broad Devon accent and was so much of a seadog Elizabeth called him 'Water'. An outstanding miniature by Nicholas Hilliard, now in the National Portrait Gallery, shows why she was so attracted to Raleigh, and why he caused such jealousy among the other blades in her court including the Earl of Essex. Painted around 1585, the portrait shows Raleigh with sharp eyes and elegantly trimmed beard. It captures the intelligence and machismo that made him, according to a court rival, 'the best hated man in the world'. He was always ready for a bit of action and a quick profit, particularly if the occasion put him against Catholic Spain. His mercenary anti-papist passion eventually proved his undoing when the political climate shifted with the ascendancy of the Stuarts – James I, who succeeded Elizabeth, ordered Raleigh to be beheaded on 29 October 1618, unjustly in the view of many, for attacking a Spanish outpost in Venezuela in his search for the mythical golden city of El Dorado. He popularized tobacco in Elizabeth's court, and after his execution in Old Palace Yard, Westminster, a tobacco box was found in his cell inscribed: 'It was my companion at that most miserable time.'

Raleigh was only in England in 1588 because he was home seeking supplies for a failed attempt to set up a colony in Roanoke Island, which would become part of North Carolina. He could not return to America because his ship had been impounded. Elizabeth needed all the British ships she could muster to fight the Armada and in 1587 he had 'sold' his ship, the *Ark Raleigh*, to the navy for £5000. He did not receive a penny for it, however. The Queen – ever careful with her coffers – took it as a reduction in the sum she said Raleigh owed the Crown. The ship had two gun decks, and became Howard's flagship as *Ark Royal*, beginning the long line of Royal Navy warships bearing that name to the present day.

Hawkins, at fifty-five, had his most daring exploits at sea behind him, but Elizabeth owed her great victory to his management skills. Hawkins had made his fortune pioneering the slave trade 'triangle' between Britain, Africa and the Americas. During his first voyage to the Caribbean, he had commandeered a Portuguese ship and sold its slaves for a profit – an act that led the Spanish to ban English ships from making port at their colonies in the West Indies. He was also a brilliant naval administrator and, after being appointed Treasurer of the Royal Navy in 1577, he engaged in a range of radical changes in English ship design that gave the English fleet the edge over the Spanish fleet. He developed longer, less top-heavy warships that could sail closer to the wind and fire longer, more devastating broadsides at the enemy.

Largely due to the innovations introduced by Hawkins, the English fleet, comprising a total of about 150 ships, was the most technologically advanced in the world. The Spanish galleons were designed for winning sea battles by boarding the enemy. They had tall 'castles' fore and aft, so they could carry more men for close-quarter actions. They were ideal for sailing the steady trade winds between Spain and the Americas, but in the stormy winds of the English Channel they were top heavy and tended to roll.

The Spanish ships proved difficult to sink, even after being hit by a barrage of English cannon balls, but they were no match for Elizabeth's agile small ships. Sir William Wynter, a rival of Hawkins, had complemented the advances in ship design with improvements in artillery, replacing iron guns with longer brass cannon which could throw a nine-pound or eighteen-pound ball more accurately and further, over a thousand yards. This changed the dynamics of naval warfare for ever. Instead of closing to grapple with the enemy, yardarm to yardarm, like the Spanish, Elizabeth's captains could stand off and hammer the Spanish ships from a distance with long-range cannon fire, raking the decks, smashing holes in their hulls, bringing down spars, tearing holes in sails, snapping masts, reducing fighting ships to unsailable hulks. Naval tactics shifted profoundly from 'man killing' to 'ship killing'.

The Duke of Medina Sidonia was well aware of the superiority of the English warships, and so had conceived a spectacular defensive strategy to protect the King's Armada: the half-moon crescent. By sailing in a closely packed half-moon formation, with the most powerful galleons stationed on the crescent's outer 'horns' and the merchant vessels clustered in the centre arc, the Spanish fleet could envelop any English ships that made a frontal assault.

On 30 July, two months after leaving Lisbon harbour, the crews of the Armada sighted Lizard Point in Cornwall and a curious spectacle – they saw fires springing up along the headlands. Fire beacons had been placed around the whole south coast of England, from Land's End to London, as an Elizabethan early-warning system of the Armada's arrival.

The English crews sprang into action, and panic spread in the towns along the south coast at the sight of the foreign invaders. Philip's 'invincible' Armada had been knocked about by a storm on leaving Lisbon and delayed for weeks at Corunna, Spain. Had it made faster progress, Medina Sidonia would have discovered that, not for the first time, the English fleet was unready, and England's defences on land were dangerously weak.

When he got to Tilbury, Leicester was appalled at the state of the defences at Henry VIII's old bastion. The numbers of men he had been promised had failed to materialize and he wrote despairing letters to

Walsingham in frustration at trying to muster the Queen's forces alone, saying he had been left to 'cook, cater and hunt' for his army while Sir John Norreys and Sir Roger Williams were off inspecting the troops on the south coast. In a letter written shortly before Elizabeth's arrival at Tilbury, Leicester complained: 'If you saw how weakly I am assisted, you would be sorry to think that we here should be the front against the enemy, that is so mighty, if he should land here.'

Tilbury Fort was in a worse state than the army. 'There is not a plat-form to carry the least piece of artillery,' Leicester moaned. Instead of troops, there were cattle grazing the ditches that surrounded the stinking, muddy marshes.

Leicester had been wise to select the more solid ground on the plateau around Tilbury Hill for his camp. From this vantage point, he could view the broad vistas of the Thames snaking east to the sea where the Armada would come, with Tilbury Fort in the foreground and the rolling hills of Kent in the distance. Burning beacons stretching down to Dover would give him early warning if the Spaniards landed in Kent. Then there would be a scramble to get his troops across the bridge of barges to the Kent bank.

There are still disputes about the number of men Leicester mustered at Tilbury. Sceptics suggest he had no more than eight thousand men at Tilbury – nowhere near enough to halt the Duke of Parma's army. Pay records indicate that he was authorized to assemble sixteen thousand five hundred foot soldiers and over one thousand horsemen. A battle plan held in the National Archives shows eleven thousand men assembled in the military review that was staged for the Queen; this included twelve hundred horsemen, thirteen hundred archers and more than two thousand pikemen. It is interesting to note the decline of the longbow in the years since Azincourt – nearly half of Leicester's army carried some sort of early firearm: nearly five thousand men carried a caliver, a short musket fired from the chest, and there were three hundred musketeers. This was still not enough to do battle against Parma, but the county of Kent had mustered a force of eight thousand men, and it is estimated that before the invaders reached London the combined forces in the South of England would have amounted to forty-seven thousand plus seventeen thousand men arriving from other counties.[7]

Queen Elizabeth, escorted by Leicester and his commanders, toured the camp in heat and dust, greeted by the thump of drums, fifes and the cheers of troops with, no doubt, some coarse bragging of what they would do to the Spaniards. After reviewing her troops and visiting all corners of the camp, the Queen, according to James Aske, returned to her glittering coach and was taken to the 'cleanly house', Saffron Garden. With Elizabeth safely delivered, her cavalry escort turned back to the camp. Hundreds of her foot soldiers were left to guard the Queen overnight.

In the evening, she was visited at Saffron Garden by Leicester and the youthful, wayward Earl of Essex. 'The courtiers talke is of the warlike show they sawe that day within the royall campe,' Aske reported. There was praise for the discipline of the men and their well-equipped 'comely' appearance. 'Thus with this talke, Time hasted fast away.'

The next morning, Elizabeth set out for the camp to review her troops on a flat hilltop, a quarter of a mile north of West Tilbury church. It was the perfect theatrical setting for a pageant that would please the Elizabethan mind, with commanding views of the Thames to the south and east, and a rising valley bluff to the north, creating an amphitheatre for their war games.[8]

In a brilliant stroke of showmanship, the Queen appeared before her men on horseback and in armour, carrying a field marshal's baton. Tradition has her dressed in a white velvet jacket under a silver cuirass, riding a white horse and carrying a silver truncheon with gold chasing, transforming the middle-aged woman into the embodiment of the warrior Virgin Queen for whom a Spanish invasion would be like rape. There is no reliable evidence for her outfit but the scene has passed into historical folklore, thanks to the writing of Deloney and Aske, who compared the 'Amazonian' Queen to a constellation of gods and goddesses, including Mars, Aurora, Bellona and Dido:

> Then came the Queen on prancing steed, attired like an angel bright,
> And eight brave footmen at their feet, whose jerkins were most rich in
> sight;
> Her ladies, likewise of great honour most sumptuously did wait upon her,
> With pearls and diamonds brave adorned and in costly cauls
> [netted caps] of gold;
> Her guards, in scarlet, then rid after with bows and arrows, stout and bold.

Elizabeth was a skilled horsewoman, but a page led her horse as she went down among her soldiers, flanked by Leicester and the Earl of Essex. The Earl of Ormonde walked ahead carrying the Sword of State. The Queen was bareheaded, with pearls in her hair; another page followed carrying a cushion on which sat her silver helmet adorned with white plumes. The spontaneous cheering and stamping from her troops was like thunder and Elizabeth said she felt she was 'in the midst and heat of battle'. Seated on her horse, she watched, delighted, as Leicester's strongest battalions gave a demonstration of how they would attack the Dons.

First came four squadrons of horsemen, each about three hundred strong with calivermen at their side carrying their firearms. Then came three wide lines of musketeers, of about one hundred each. Behind them were the three main blocks of troops, the two on the wings consisting of about a thousand pikemen, billmen and archers, with two thousand in the centre. They were flanked by more archers and calivermen. In the rear were more files of calivermen, and the main contingent of over three hundred archers in the centre.[9]

Aske said the troops stirred clouds of dust as they made their mock attacks. The thousands marching to and fro filled the air 'with such a sodaine smoake / As Jupiter did feare least Terra was / New set on fire by heate'. The drums, fifes and trumpets added to the cacophony of the mock battle, enough to thrill the Queen. Elizabeth watched the spectacle 'with joy to see the men keep their rankes'.

When it was over, she rode her horse along the lines of troops, inspecting the men. Sir John Norreys led the vanguard and Leicester's brother-in-law, Sir William Knollys, brought up the rearguard. Both had served in the Netherlands under Leicester. 'The warlike army then stood still / and drummers left their dubbing sound, / Because it was our Prince's will / to ride about the army round,' wrote Deloney. Aske observed that at the end of the pageant, the troops lowered their pikes and lances, 'and all yield reverence to her sacred self'.

Elizabeth addressed her troops at the end of the pageant with the speech for which Tilbury is remembered today. Deloney and Aske's accounts differ, except in one particular – they both say that she offered to fight alongside her men. As improbable as that seems today, it was the key to the creation of the central myth surrounding Elizabeth's long reign: she needed no husband because she was wedded to England and – despite being a 'feeble' woman – she was prepared to sacrifice herself for her country. In Aske's version, Elizabeth said she would fight alongside them like the Roman goddess of war, Bellona, and promised that they would be rewarded (there were grumbles about pay): 'the meanest man who shall deserve a mite, a mountain shall for his deserts receive'. Deloney also recorded Elizabeth, using the royal 'we', saying she would lead them in battle: 'But if our enimies doe assaile you, / Never let your stomackes faile you. / For in the midst of all your troupe, / *We our selves* will be in place; / To be your joy, your guide and comfort, / even before our enimies face!'

There are other versions of the speech, which have fuelled suggestions that the speech we know today is a fiction invented by the Queen and her advisers, such as Walsingham and Leicester, to fix her place in history as the heroine of the Armada year. One of these versions is inscribed in faded lettering on a panel in St Faith's Church, Gaywood, near King's Lynn in Norfolk. The words, which can barely be made out today, appear under a painting, *Elizabeth at Tilbury*, dated 1588:

> It may be they will challenge my [sexe] For that I am a woman so may charge [their] mo[uld] for that they ar but [men] whose breath is in theire nostrells and if God doe not charge England with the sinnes of England we shall not neede to feare what Rome or Spayne can doe against us

In 1612, William Leigh, in his sermon 'Quene Elizabeth, Paraleld in Her Princely Vertues', offered another version:

> Come on now, my companions at arms, and fellow soldiers, in the field, now for the Lord, for your Queen, and for the Kingdom. For what are these proud Philistines, that they should revile the host of the living God? I have been your Prince in peace, so will I be in war; neither will I bid you go and fight, but come and let us fight the battle of the Lord. The enemy perhaps may challenge my sex for that I am a woman, so may I likewise charge their mould for that they are but men, whose breath is in their nostrils, and if God do not charge England with the sins of England, little do I fear their force… *Si deus nobiscum quis contra nos?* [If God is with us, who can be against us?]

Although Leigh's version was made public twenty-four years after the event, Leigh was there, and this repeats some of the imagery that we know from the most famous version, such as Elizabeth's reference to her own sex, suggesting that Leigh's account is more accurate.

Any journalist who has covered prime ministerial visits to the war zones in Iraq and Afghanistan can testify, however, that political leaders often deliver different versions of the same speech over a two-day visit. As one who has frequently covered such events, I find it unsurprising that several versions of Elizabeth's remarks have been attributed to her. That should not mean that they were not delivered. She clearly made several pep talks to her men at Tilbury during Thursday and Friday, 18 and 19 August.

The most familiar version comes from a letter to the Duke of Buckingham by Dr Leonel Sharpe, who had been Leicester's chaplain and was in attendance at Tilbury on the day of the mock battle. It was published in *Cabala: Mysteries of State* in 1654, a collection of letters of ministers to James I and Charles I.

Sceptics say the speech is too perfect.* They suggest the copy of the speech we have come to believe was Elizabeth's was created years after her death by Sharpe, who was an anti-Catholic fanatic. His letter was written sometime after 1623, when the Duke undertook a foreign mission with the future Charles I, to the royal houses of Spain and France to seek a Catholic wife.[10] Historian Susan Frye suggests Sharpe was keen to stop a Spanish marriage taking place, and, in warning Buckingham of the danger, drew a strong parallel between the Spanish actions of 1588 and those of 1623: 'While they were treating of peace in 88, they did even then invade us. I pray God they have not used this treatie of marriage to as bad a purpose.'[11] She adds that 'his account of the events preceding Elizabeth's speech is a series of fictions' that casts serious doubts on the veracity of his account of the speech.

But does Sharpe's readiness to spread anti-Catholic propaganda mean Sharpe's version of the speech is invented too? I don't think so. And I think I have seen the evidence to dispute that. Elizabeth had requested Leicester to circulate the speech among the troops the next day, and he ordered Sharpe to do it. 'She made an excellent Oration to her armie,' Sharpe told Buckingham, 'which the next day after her departure, I was

---

* The famous words are so powerful, it is easy to see why there has been a parade of actresses queuing up to deliver them, including Helen Mirren, Gwyneth Paltrow, Cate Blanchett and Glenda Jackson, who had the political nous – she is now a Labour MP – to deliver a definitive portrayal of the canny, clever, fiery Elizabeth. The only problem with Jackson's performance is that the BBC production has two soldiers in the crowd speaking over her best lines.

commanded to redeliver to all the Army together to keep a Public Fast.'

I go to the British Library to read another copy of the speech that provides support for Sharpe's claim. It is very similar to the text that we know as Elizabeth's Tilbury oration. It is tucked within a book of manuscripts, and the curators are happy to show it to me. I am astonished to be able to handle it, without white gloves.

It looks like an insignificant scrap of paper; it could be nothing more than a shopping list. The handwriting is in English and in ink; it is written on a page about half-A4 in size, and has been folded like a letter. It is collected into a book of early manuscripts from the library assembled by Robert Harley, now known as the Harleian collection at the British Library. There is a note scribbled in another hand on the back (when it was bought by a collector of manuscripts – possibly Harley himself): 'The Queen's Speech bought of Mrs G. Cauls, landlady.'

The text is almost identical to the version in the *Cabala* collection, but there are some small differences; capital letters are left out, as if it was written in haste – possibly as it was being delivered. There are a couple of errors ('butt' should be 'not'); and it is full of Elizabethan abbreviations, such as 'ye', which I have left out:

> My loving people, we have been persuaded by some that are careful of my safety to take heed how I committed my self to armed multitudes for fear of treachery. But I tell you that I would not desire to live to distrust my faithful and loving people. Let tyrants fear I have so behaved my self that under god I have placed my chiefest strength and safeguard in the loyal hearts and goodwill of my subjects. Wherefor I am come amongst you at this [time] butt [not] for my recreation and pleasure being resolved in the midst and heat of the battle to live and die amongst you all, to lay down for my god and for my kingdom and for my people, mine honour and my body even in ye dust. I know I have ye body butt of a weak and feeble woman, but I have ye heart and stomach of a king, and of a king of England too. And take foul scorn that Parma or any prince of Europe should dare to invade the borders of my realm: to which rather than any dishonor shall grow by me, I myself will venture my royal blood, I myself will be your general, judge and rewards of your virtue in the field. I know that already for your forwardness you have deserved rewards and Crowns [money], and I assure you in the word of a prince you shall not fail of them. In the meantime, my Lieutenant general shall be in my stead than

whom never prince commanded a more noble or worthy subject. Not
doubting but your concord in the camp and your valour in the field
and your obedience to my self and my general, we shall shortly have
a famous victory over these enemies of my god, and my kingdom. [12]

The note is neither dated, nor signed, but historian Janet Green, when
working at the British Library on a humanities fellowship, had it checked
by a handwriting expert with other known examples of Sharpe's handwriting. She confirmed that this handwriting is almost certainly Sharpe's
own. He has written on it: 'Gathered by on ye heard itt and was commanded to utter it to ye whole army ye next day, to send itt gathered to
the Queen herself.'[13]

Could this be a contemporaneous note that Sharpe wrote of the
Queen's speech either as she delivered it, or while it was still fresh in his
mind, a few hours after she made it? I think this is almost certainly the
case, and it was this hurriedly made copy that Sharpe must have drawn
on for his letter to Buckingham and printed later in the *Cabala*. It is the
best piece of evidence we have that Elizabeth did deliver the words we
know today as her Tilbury speech.

Holding it, I have one of those 'hairs-on-the-back-of-the-neck' mo-
ments that I had not anticipated when I began my investigation. It carries
the authentic voice of Elizabeth, according to experts such as Green, both
in its rhetorical style and structure. About 250 words, it takes two and a
half minutes to deliver, ideal for addressing troops in the open. She had
a fine education and was accomplished in Latin and the use of rhetoric.
The style of the speech is pure Elizabeth – she ties each thought to the
preceding one, employing doublets ('weak and feeble woman'), paired
synonyms and clever imagery. She was fond of quoting the Psalms and
there are echoes of Psalm 7:4–5 in her speech: 'lay mine honour in the
dust'.

After delivering her speech, the Queen proceeded to Leicester's
pavilion where she was entertained by her officers over lunch. There she
heard reports (which turned out to be false) that Parma would sail for
England with his invasion force on the next tide.

The chroniclers say the Queen's blood was up; she told Leicester,
Walsingham and the other senior officers assembled at the lunch that
she had no intention of going back on her word to her troops; she would
stay and fight Parma and the Spanish invaders whenever they arrived. It
was only with difficulty, according to the chroniclers, that Leicester and

the others persuaded her that Parma would not come out of Calais until he had more certain news about the Spanish fleet. It was time for her to return to the capital.

Yet, her entire performance at Tilbury may all have been just a sham. On 17 August, the day before she set out from Westminster steps, Walsingham received intelligence from Lord Henry Seymour, the naval commander of the 'narrow seas squadron', aboard the *Rainbow*, which had taken part in a great sea battle off the Flanders coast at Gravelines near Dunkirk, saying: 'The Duke of Parma has withdrawn his sea forces to Bruges and Dixmude'. Such a withdrawal not only made a mockery of the Queen's pretence to stay and fight Parma. It also signalled there was absolutely no risk of invasion any longer.

As Elizabeth left Whitehall on 18 August, the ships of Howard's grand fleet, whipped by the tail of a north-easter, came scudding into the safety of the bays of Harwich and Margate with the news that the Spanish Armada had been last seen fleeing north for the coast of Scotland.

Margate is some fifty miles from the Tilbury camp – a day's ride with a change of horses. Walsingham must have heard these reports before Elizabeth left the camp to return to London the next day. Her offer to stay and fight the Spanish, therefore, was mere posturing, part of the heroic pageant that, in truth, Tilbury represents.

There was a heavy downpour as she set out for London on the royal barge, according to Aske, who described it romantically as Nature's 'tears' at her departure. The weather was so bad that her flotilla was forced to land at Erith, on the Kent side of the Thames, about fourteen miles east of Whitehall. Elizabeth spent the night nearby before travelling on Saturday, 21 August to St James's Palace to plan the victory celebrations.

By the time she returned to London, the first reports that the Armada had been defeated had reached the city. The streets were crowded with people shouting for joy. The Queen announced that next St Elizabeth's Day, 19 November, would, like the day of her accession, be a public holiday, with three days of festivities, pageants, cock-fighting, bear-baiting, dancing, plays and tableaux.

From the outset, it had been no easy victory. Howard and his captains were surprised by how well ordered the Spanish fleet had been. At a signal from Medina Sidonia's flagship, the Dons had manoeuvred into their distinctive crescent. They had then fought a series of running battles along the English Channel, watched by fascinated onlookers from the clifftops all along the south coast of England. Never before had such a spectator sport gripped the nation.

On 2 August, in the first serious engagement off Portland Bill, Howard sailed a single line ahead against the northern landward tip of the Spanish crescent and targeted Medina Sidonia's flagship, the *San Martín*. Heralding the shape of things to come, during the ten-hour attack the English fired broadsides of five hundred rounds compared to only eighty by the *San Martín* and all from one side of the ship. Despite their rapid fire, the English could not sink the biggest galleons but crucially, their better sailing abilities gave Howard the weather gauge, enabling his ships to sail upwind, turn and bear down at will on the Armada.

On Saturday, 6 August, Medina Sidonia reached the Calais Roads for his rendezvous with Parma with the Armada largely intact, but he was appalled to discover that Parma was not ready to come out of Dunkirk and his only vessels were barges. Anchoring the Armada left it vulnerable to the threat it feared most – fire ships. Rumours had spread across Europe that the English had a secret weapon – the 'hellburners' – burning ships packed with explosives that could devastate an area a mile wide, sowing death and destruction when they blew up.

Their nightmare came out of the dark at about midnight on 7 August, on a freshening southerly breeze. The Spanish crews were horrified to see eight tall ships, flames licking up their rigging, floating towards them, bright against the night. Flames were flying in fountains, but as the ships bore down on the Armada, the roar of flame was drowned by the booms as their double-shotted guns, white hot with fire, exploded. Medina Sidonia stayed calm and slipped his anchors to sail out of harm's way, but many of his captains, fearing 'hellburners' about to explode among their moored ships, panicked; they cut their anchors and ran before the wind. In fact, the fire ships were not 'hellburners' laden with barrels of gunpowder (which was in short supply in the English fleet), and none caused any serious damage, but it did not matter. The Armada had scattered in terror and confusion and by daylight, Medina Sidonia could see only five of his galleons. Even so, the makeshift Spanish commander still managed to reform his fleet into its crescent shape and take on the English.

An hour after sunrise on 8 August, he engaged the English fleet in a bitter action at the Battle of Gravelines. Intense fighting, as the English fired killing broadsides and the Spanish made repeated attempts to board, went on until 4 p.m. First Drake, in the *Revenge*, attacked the *San Martín*, then Sir Martin Frobisher in the *Triumph* and Hawkins in the *Victory* as they moved in for the kill. With daylight fading, and the English running out of cannon shot and powder, the fighting was finally halted by a violent squall.

This timetable shows the Armada was scattered a full ten days before Elizabeth had left Whitehall. With an intelligence chief as wily as Walsingham by her side, it is almost inconceivable that she did not know its fate before she delivered her speech at Tilbury ten days later.

During the night of 8–9 August, gales swept through the Channel. The 'Protestant wind', as it was later called by Elizabethan chroniclers, made it impossible for Medina Sidonia's lumbering Spanish galleons to turn back and keep his rendezvous with Parma. He had no alternative but to sail north around Scotland and Ireland, making his way for home. On 12 August, Howard gave up the chase up the east coast of England; the last time his crews saw what remained of the Armada, it was running north-north-east beyond the Firth of Forth, near Edinburgh, towards the northern reaches of Scotland.

I find it hard to believe that Walsingham – Elizabeth's resourceful spymaster – was not aware of the Armada's defeat, even allowing for the communications difficulties of the time. Does that mean Elizabeth and her senior ministers were guilty of a cover-up to keep the nation on the alert? It seems likely, though there is no document that I have seen in the archives than can prove it definitively. 'The Queen and the Privy Council were probably apprised of the victory off Gravelines... by August 10. Though the threat of invasion was greatly reduced, they kept this news to themselves,' asserted a 1997 biography of Sir John Norreys, commander of the forces on the South Downs.[14]

Elizabeth's speech at Tilbury, and her review of her troops, appears to have been all part of an elaborate pageant to create a gigantic heroic myth that has lasted to this day.

But that is not the whole story. Despite the ten-day lacuna, the intelligence reports reaching Walsingham from the English captains were inconclusive and confused – Drake had written from on board his ship that though great damage had been inflicted on the Armada, he could not be sure the Spanish would not return. Most of the reports complained that penny-pinching on shot and powder had prevented Howard's fleet from delivering a decisive blow.

Around 10 August – two days after the fire ships scattered the Spanish fleet – Hawkins sent news of the action to Walsingham with a plea of the utmost urgency for more shot and powder. It is not clear when Walsingham received it, but it is almost certain that, carried by a fast ship back to London, the letter would have been in Walsingham's hands before Elizabeth set out for Tilbury on 18 August. After apologizing for his rough handwriting (it was done 'in haste and bad weather'), Hawkins tells Walsingham the fire ships have wrecked Medina Sidonia's hopes of meeting Parma and taking on water with more supplies. 'My Lord Admyrall [Howard] with fyring of ships, determined to remove them, as he did and put them to the seas.'

That ended any immediate threat of England being invaded by Parma, though Hawkins stresses the Armada is still a threat: 'this fleet is here and very forcible and must be wayted upon with all our force which is littell ynoughe'. England would be at risk, he adds, if the fleet is not re-supplied: 'ther would be an Infinite qua[n]tity of powder and shot pvided and continuallye sent abord, wthout the wch great hasarde may growe to our Country for this is the greatest and strongest cobinacon to my understanding, that ever was gathered in Chistendome.' [15]

Significantly, Hawkins does not claim victory. On the contrary, he ended his letter with a warning: 'The Spaniards take ther course for Schotland, my Lo[rd] dothe follow them. I doubt not wth gods favour, but we shall impeache ther landing, ther must be order for vituall, and mony powder and shot to be sent after us.'

Sir Thomas Fenner, captain of the *Nonpariel*, writes separately to Walsingham on 14 August: 'God has stricken the enemy with a wonderful fear.' But again, Fenner impresses on Walsingham that more shot is needed to defeat the Spanish: 'The Spanish fleet was followed up the Eastern coast but [the English fleet] had to return to port to relieve the wants of water and provisions. The want of powder, shot and victuals has caused us many problems.' [16]

The written evidence is overwhelming: Walsingham must have known that the threat of an imminent Spanish invasion had passed when Elizabeth arrived at Tilbury on 18 August. But he could not be sure it would not return.

A letter written by Walsingham on 18 August to the Lord Chancellor, Sir Christopher Hatton, provides clear evidence that he believed the Spanish 'disease' was not dead. Bemoaning the Queen's cost-cutting that had left her fleet short of cannon balls, he ruefully observed: 'So our half-doing doth breed dishonor and leaves the disease uncured.'

Walsingham was not aware until some days afterwards that as London began to celebrate, cold Atlantic storms ripped into the Armada. Even so, most of the damaged ships limped home to Spain. It is estimated that twenty-four Spanish ships came to grief on the rocky coasts of Scotland and Ireland, where many of those who survived drowning in the wrecks were given shelter and eventually helped to escape. Of the 130 ships that sailed proudly from Lisbon, about eighty returned to Spain; thousands of men lost their lives.

Jubilation in England was unrestrained, once the scale of the defeat of the Spanish became known: church bells rang out around the kingdom; London rejoiced that God was a Protestant, and on Elizabeth's side.

The Queen organized another great pageant of thanksgiving with a parade and a service at St Paul's Cathedral. She rode to the old church through the City in a chariot, drawn by two white horses like the Goddess of Victory, preceded by the Garter King of Arms, the Mayor of London, the Lord Great Chamberlain, the Earl Marshal of England and a ceremonial sword. Outside the great West Door, she halted the procession, stepped down and knelt to the ground to give a very public prayer of thanks to God. A poem attributed to Elizabeth I was sung: 'he made the wynds and waters rise, / To scatter all myne enemyes.'[17]

Commemorative medals were struck bearing the inscription: 'He blew with His winds and they were scattered.' At a cost of £1582, Lord Howard commissioned six immense tapestries, each fourteen feet high and up to twenty-eight feet in length, to adorn his manor in Chelsea. They told the story of the victory, from the first sighting of the Spanish fleet off the Lizard to the triumph of the fire ships at Calais. They were eventually sold to King James I at a profit of £100 and hung in the House of Lords, but were lost when the building burned down in the nineteenth century.

Through the fire of the Armada, Elizabeth was transmuted from a vulnerable spinster presiding over a fractious country into *Gloriana*, the heroine of Spenser's *Faerie Queene*. The poet had been introduced to the Queen at court by his friend, Raleigh, and there he gave her a flattering extract from his epic verse. The lines linked Elizabeth to the legendary King Arthur, an association in which Gloriana truly gloried. She granted the poet a pension of £50 a year as reward for his flattery.

This was the 'Golden Age' of Good Queen Bess. Never before had she been so revered. Even Pope Sixtus V, who saw the Armada as a Crusade, was in awe, declaring only half in jest: 'What a valiant woman – she braves the two greatest kings by land and sea. A pity we cannot marry, she and I, for our children would have ruled the world!'

There was one great sadness for Elizabeth, however. Leicester died at his house in Oxfordshire on 4 September 1588. On his deathbed, Leicester wrote Elizabeth an affectionate letter. It would be his last:

> I most humbly beseech your Majesty to pardon your poor old servant to be thus bold in sending to know how my gracious lady doth, and what ease of her late pain she finds, being the chiefest thing in the world I do pray for, for her to have good health and long life. For my own poor case, I continue still your medicine and find that [it] amends much better than any other thing that hath been given me… Your Majesty's most faithful and obedient servant, R. Leicester. Even as I had writ thus much, I received Your Majesty's token by Young Tracey.

Elizabeth treasured it. She wrote 'His Last letter' on it, and kept it in a coffer until her own death in 1603.

The iconic image of the Armada year, 1588, is not a picture of the famous Spanish crescent, a tactical map or military plan. We do not think of, say, the Battle of Gravelines where Howard's and Drake's ships mauled the Spanish or of the fire ships that were sent into the anchorage at Calais to spread terror. Instead we see Elizabeth as Gloriana on her throne, resplendent in a dress dripping with pearls – a sign of her chastity – resting her right hand on a globe of the world. Her fingers play over the Americas, perhaps remembering Raleigh's attempt to conquer the colony of Virginia for a second time only the year before. Behind her, on the left, as if through a window, we are given a view of the English fire ships threatening the Spanish galleons; through another window we see the Armada wrecked beneath the northern cliffs. This is the *Armada Portrait* of Elizabeth I.

ELIZABETH I, THE ARMADA PORTRAIT:
Painted by George Gower, circa 1590.

Three versions of the *Armada Portrait* are known to have been painted. The most complete version is held by Woburn Abbey; at some point in the past, the version at the National Portrait Gallery was cut down to a more traditional vertical format, with the scenes of the ships in the background cropped and painted out – as if to say that only the Queen is important. A third version in private hands is said to have been a copy commissioned by Drake in honour of his Queen.

The Elizabethan use of imagery was powerful but misleading. Victory over the Armada did not mean that England ruled the waves. England failed to destroy Spain as a naval power; the Armada was not entirely wrecked, but nearly two-thirds of Medina Sidonia's warships returned to Spain – indeed, there were recriminations against Howard for failing to sink more Spanish galleons (a charge that completely misunderstood the strength of the Spanish wooden ships). An expedition to invade Portugal, led by Drake and Norreys, within twelve months of the defeat of the Armada proved a complete failure. Over the next fifteen years, more treasure from the New World reached Spain than in any other similar period in the country's history.

The defeat of Philip's 'invincible' fleet may have encouraged Protestants in Europe but the victory for Elizabeth was at home. It enabled her to reign unchallenged for another fifteen years until her death over an

England that remained Protestant and independent. But more than that, the defiant nature of her victory over a foreign invader consolidated the sense of nationhood among the English people and continued to inspire leaders in Britain for centuries afterwards.

There can be little doubt that the Queen's dramatic appearance as *Gloriana* at Tilbury – with more ham than Hamlet – was designed to enhance the image of Elizabeth as the saviour of the nation, and it worked. Hazel Forsyth, Curator of Archaeology at the London Museum, told me: 'I think there is some element of truth in that. I think it was politically expedient for her to join her forces. It helped her reinforce her dynastic authority.'[18]

Even the doubters accept that the Tilbury speech that was immediately circulated around the country has had a profound and lasting effect on how we see Elizabeth – and thus England – today. 'Whether or not Elizabeth actually gave this speech, Elizabeth at Tilbury has become a myth of nationalist sentiment as useful to seventeenth-century nationalists as to those historians who experienced World War II,' says Professor Frye. The Queen's review of the troops, she adds, proved 'a brilliant stroke which grew more brilliant in the succeeding weeks, years and centuries because it provided a moment through which generations could cast Elizabeth I as the powerful political icon she remains'.

Elizabeth was a genius at public relations for her own age. She needed to be, to survive the forty-five years of her long reign. Towards the end, with the population growing sharply from three million to four million, poverty increased and her Government responded by creating the first state support for the poor, to damp down the threat of rebellion or food riots. She dealt decisively with direct threats – even her favourite, the Earl of Essex, went to the block after raising a rebellion against her – but she was a consummate politician. She was acutely aware, particularly as a woman, that she could only rule with the consent of her people. She was careful to placate her Parliament – in her last address to Parliament in 1601, known as her 'Golden Speech', she said: 'There is no jewel, be it of never so high a price, which I set before this jewel; I mean your love.'

Elizabeth helped to create a Britain that is recognizable today as an independent nation, fierce in its defence of its identity. The defeat of the Spanish Armada in 1588 was truly one of the great landmarks of Britain's history. If her speech was a sham, I cannot help asking: so what?

FOUR

1688

'What happened in 1688 was not a glorious revolution.
It was a plot by some people... to replace a Catholic king with another king
more acceptable to those who organized the plot'

BRIXHAM HARBOUR, DEVON:
The Orange Parade.

The snare drums rattle like gunfire, the big bass drum booms out and the concertinas strike up the jaunty, rollicking tune of 'The Sash'.

Colonel Sanderson's Memorial Concertina Band (it comes from Liverpool and is not to be confused with the KFC colonel) leads the march with a rolling swagger to the thump of the big bass drum past the statue of William of Orange who stands aloof on his plinth by the harbour wall.

A steward in a bowler hat is at the head of the march with a colour guard carrying the flags of the Union and St George. They are followed by around five hundred men and women wearing orange sashes, and in the centre are two small children dressed as King Billy and Queen Mary II.

It could be a scene from Belfast, but this is the fishing port of Brixham in the soft underbelly of the Devon coast that calls itself the English Riviera. They are here because almost 323 years ago to the day, the Protestant Prince William of the Dutch house of Orange landed in Brixham with his mainly Dutch invasion force on 5 November 1688 to oust James II, a Catholic, from the throne of England.

Brixham today is more interested in tourism than Protestantism. The harbour with fish and chip shops and souvenir stores full of holiday tat is firmly dedicated to relaxation rather than revolution. There is even a Catholic church near the harbour (the Church of Our Lady founded in 1883).

For most of us, the arrival of the Prince of Orange with a force of twenty-one thousand men is Britain's forgotten invasion.[1] It has been carefully brushed underneath the national carpet. It is no longer the done thing in polite company to beat the drum for the man responsible for putting down the Catholics at the Battle of the Boyne, especially after the historic Good Friday Agreement ended years of sectarian war in Northern Ireland. Unless, it seems, you belong to an Orange Lodge, and you feel the need to reassert your Loyalist tradition.

Each year on a Saturday as close to the anniversary as possible, a small army of Orange Lodge members invade the port to show the rest of us that they have not forgotten. They march around the town just as William must have done at the head of his army, with fife and drum, to celebrate the landing that delivered England from Popery in a largely bloodless coup that became known as the 'Glorious Revolution'.

Before the bands become visible, tourists are puzzled and look to the sky as the distant rumble of the drums increases. Perhaps it is coming on to rain. I am standing outside the Carousel Amusement Arcade, which is playing 'My Darling Clementine' incessantly on a loop, and then spy some banners and Union flags marching down from Berry Head past the Ernie Lister Bar, named after a local character.

A few minutes later, they burst from Fore Street by the Blue Anchor pub as if someone has turned up the volume. Drums rattle and boom and concertinas blast out their jaunty tune.

Rigged out in black uniforms with orange sashes, the concertina band and the Orange marchers wheel left at the Taste of Devon fudge and ice-cream bar on the corner and into the Strand overlooking the yachts sinking into the mud in the harbour.

The statue of King Billy stands on the harbour wall, sandwiched between the bus shelter and the whelk stall, now shuttered because it is the end of the season. The Victorians erected the statue in 1888 by the wall for the bicentenary of William's landing in Brixham. He appears to have his nose in the air, but that is because he has had a municipal nose job after losing part of it to stone-throwing vandals some years ago.

On the base of the statue is a plaque chiselled: 'William Prince of Orange, afterwards William III King of Britain and Ireland Landed near this Spot 5th November 1688. "The liberties of England, the Protestant Religion, I will maintain".' This ungrammatical message was flown in letters three feet high from William's frigate, *Brielle*, alongside his flag, displaying the arms of Nassau quartered with those of England.

Three small boys sit on the plinth, ignoring the marchers. They are eating fish and chips in paper wrappers from the Golden fish bar across the road, where it says you can 'sit in for £4.95'. A seagull uses King William's head as a perch to eye the boys and their discarded fish bits.

KING WILLIAM III:
With guest for takeaway.

The band temporarily halts. The boys with the fish and chips clear off, and the children playing William and Mary move in. They lay a wreath on the statue where their predecessors had been sitting. The band moves on past a shop selling traditional Cornish pasties (although we are still in Devon), and the following marchers give 'The Sash' the full-throat treatment. Some spectators on the street, including a man near me with an Ulster accent, join in:

> Sure I'm an Ulster Orangeman, from Erin's isle I came,
> To see my British brethren all of honour and of fame,
> And to tell them of my forefathers who fought in days of yore,
> That I might have the right to wear, the sash my father wore!

It drowns out 'My Darling Clementine'. Beyond a new trendy restaurant, the Old Market House, the big bass drum booms out and the marchers wheel right and string past another bit of the William of Orange story – a modest monument that contains a slab of the mottled rock on which the Prince is reputed to have stepped when first coming ashore in Brixham bay.

Brixham was little more than a row of fishermen's cottages then, with no harbour. Today it is one of the biggest fishing ports in the South of England and it is a multimillion-pound business. The Orange marchers stop and gather for a brief service outside the grey doors of the new Brixham fish market at the end of the harbour wall, part of a £20 million revamp of the town.

The soft October light makes the Orange banners and the orange silk sashes that their fathers wore stand out against the gloomy grey sky. The banners say they are the LOLs (Loyal Orange Lodges) of Bristol, Plymouth and Liverpool. A big man stands in front of me with bare knees, going blue with cold. He is wearing an anorak and an orange sash with a kilt, showing Orange support is still strong north of the border.

Brother Nicholas Baker, the Worshipful District Master, reminds the Lodge members gathered around with their banners, as if they needed it, that William's landing was 'a pivotal moment in British history'. He says: 'The Glorious Revolution established many of those liberties we enjoy today and became the cornerstone of the British constitution.'

He runs through the list – most especially, the Bill of Rights, which he says 'established in law modern Parliamentary democracy and a constitutional monarchy, sovereignty through Parliament, the freedom to march, the freedom to demonstrate and the freedom of speech'. These freedoms were fought for in two World Wars, he adds. He does not mention the Act of Settlement, which introduced the freedom of Protestants to bar Catholics from the Throne of England for ever.

The service is conducted by the Worshipful Brother Ian McFarland, district chaplain of the Plymouth Loyal Orange Lodge No. 64. We sing 'Abide with Me', the moving hymn written in 1847 by the local vicar, the Rev. Henry Francis Lyte, as he watched the sun going down over Tor Bay. I've sung it at Cup Finals, where it has become the football anthem, but never like this before. It is 'Abide with Me' with a beatbox backing, rapped out by the snare drums and the concertinas.

With his back to the grey doors of the fish dock, Brother McFarland prays for the deliverance from darkness of those who follow 'false religions'. He is not specific, but we can guess who he means. After the service, we disperse. A rainbow has opened up over the harbour.

Some have travelled hundreds of miles to be here, and judging by their accents, a strong contingent has come from Northern Ireland to parade their colours around the town. But there is the burr of West Country voices too, though few appear to be from Brixham. I ask a cheerful Liverpudlian who is fiercely proud of his Orange Lodge why they come all this way. Is it bigotry? He smiles and replies with disarming honesty: 'They say it's bigotry. Yeah, well, maybe, in a little way it is.' Jimmy pauses, then adds: 'But it is part of our heritage. The whole point of the Orange institution is that it is a religious organization.'

I ask Jimmy about the reports in that morning's newspapers from the Commonwealth Heads of Government Conference in Perth, Australia. David Cameron, the Prime Minister, has got approval to change the Act of Settlement. For the first time in three hundred years, it would allow members of the Royal Family who marry a Roman Catholic to be eligible to succeed to the throne. Jimmy is not too happy.

'I am loyal to Queen and country because the Crown is a Protestant Crown, regardless of how many cultures live in Britain,' he says. 'My fear is that if you change that law, it is the first step back to Rome. It has always been Rome's aim to get this country back, ever since Henry VIII.'

Then he adds: 'This is why we have got to show in the famous words, "We have not gone away".' I suddenly realize where I have heard the 'famous' words before. Jimmy has turned a phrase by the dissident Real IRA on its head.

He is sixty, but the Orangemen and -women who travel down to Brix-ham are by no means a dying breed, though they may feel marginalized.

They are a normal cross-section of British life – young men, out for a good weekend, some with rings through their ears, and young women, including one with hair dyed a vivid red. She must surely be a Liverpool supporter.

John from Liverpool, who wears a bowler hat with his orange sash, says proudly that a new Orange Lodge is opening next year in Cardiff, and they expect to have twenty-two members. 'We haven't had a Lodge in Cardiff since 1913,' he says. With an impish grin, he adds: 'It is going to open on St Patrick's Day.'

William is Brixham's biggest catch, but apart from the statue and the plinth of stone, there are few signs he ever came here. Brixham has its mind on other things. Earlier in the summer, I arrived expecting to find the connection to be exploited everywhere – the King Billy pub, the William of Orange curry house and the William and Mary souvenir rock shop clustered around the harbour. I found one bar over at the posh end of the harbour, by the new marina, named after William III. It is Sir Francis Drake, a Devon boy but not from Brixham, who hogs the limelight. A full-scale replica of his ship the *Golden Hind*, in which he circumnavigated the globe, takes pride of place, and until recently there was a Drakes Pizza place nearby.

I got the impression that the local fishing folk would rather King Billy had landed somewhere else, a bit further down the coast. Plymouth, perhaps. Or Land's End.

I walked up the steep narrow lane between colourful terraced houses to the local Anglican parish church, All Saints, to see whether this corner of Devon was still a hotbed of sectarian Protestantism. The Victorian parish church with its stout tower stands over the town, the kind of landmark William could have used when he was searching for a safe anchorage. It was built in 1815, the same year that Wellington defeated another threat to Protestant England at the Battle of Waterloo. Outside a poster informs visitors this is 'the church of the Rev. Lyte, author of "Abide with Me".' He certainly would have had a fine view of the bay from this perch, high above the harbour, as he composed his hymn.

The entrance porch is up another steep flight of steps. Inside, a number of trawler families are festooning the roof of the nave and the aisles with fishing nets and hanging historic burgees, flags of long-gone sailing trawlers, such as the *Pilgrim* and the *Vigilance*, for the annual Festival of the Sea. They are enthusiastic to talk about their fishing traditions, but politely reticent about the annual invasion of the Orangemen and -women. 'We don't have much to do with them,' says one gnarly fisherman in a blue smock in his strong Devon burr.

A well-spoken lady in an anorak draws me to one side and whispers: 'We don't have anything to do with the Orange March. It's a bit scary.' I didn't find the Orangemen and -women in Brixham scary. They were polite and cheerful. But I know what she means. Religious zealotry strikes a jarring note among the jolly seaside souvenirs around Brixham harbour today.

At the Brixham Heritage Museum, run by a small group of dedicated volunteers, the starring role of King Billy in the town's history is limited to a small display. The museum is squeezed inside the cells and the front desk of the former police station. There is a tableau dedicated to the police inside one of the old station cells; it holds a dummy prisoner, who used to moan until it frightened the children too much. Elsewhere, there is a spotted hyena skull, and odds and ends that have been collected to create a Victorian living room in one old cell. Still, the theme of the museum is the sea. An entire gallery at the back – possibly where the police made their tea – is dedicated to Brixham's fishing past, including what it did in the two World Wars.

What little they have on William of Orange is tucked in a room upstairs. There is a portrait in oils of the Prince of dubious provenance and a cheap print of *William III Landing at Brixham, Torbay* by Jan Wyck. Painted in 1688, it shows the Prince as a dashing horseman in buff-coloured coat on a pure white charger. In the background, troops are disembarking from the ships in Brixham bay and horses are being lowered over the side to swim ashore. The original, measuring six feet by five feet, is held by the National Maritime Museum in Greenwich. But despite its political importance (we are still officially a Protestant country because of that landing), it is not on show there or anywhere else. I checked and was told it was in storage, and the Orange Lodges suspect they know the reason why: these days it's a bit of an embarrassment.

My local Brixham guide, a genial pensioner in a smart blue blazer, was once a leading light in the local chamber of commerce. He has almost single-handedly kept alive the town's business links with the modern House of Orange in the Netherlands. He proudly points to a photograph of the present Prince of Orange, Queen Beatrix's eldest son and heir, Crown Prince Willem-Alexander and his young wife, Crown Princess Máxima. And that is about it.

~(∂~

Three hundred years ago, it was touch and go whether William would land at Brixham at all.

William had planned to land near the mouth of the Humber in Yorkshire, which was known to have strong Protestant sympathies. Hull is still one of the few cities in Britain to have a statue of the Prince of Orange, 'our great deliverer'; it is still delivering relief with the nearby Art Nouveau urinals.

A landing near Hull would have meant a much shorter sea journey for William and his transports, but his scouts reported back to William's flagship that James II had reinforced the local stronghold and was prepared to oppose him.

William wisely ordered a change of plan. At a signal, his entire fleet – the biggest assembled since the Spanish Armada, one hundred years before – tacked south, and sailed unmolested past the Straits of Dover, where it could be seen clearly from the Downs and west, beyond the Isle of Wight, as far as Tor Bay.

In London there was panic. James II had nervously ordered a gilded weather vane to put on top of the Banqueting House in Whitehall so that he could see which way the wind was blowing. The golden flying arrow is still there to this day, largely forgotten as it spins in the wind above the London traffic. As long as the wind blew from the west, he was safe. But the vane showed the wind had changed to blow from the east, which would carry William and his invasion ships to England. James ordered prayers to be said for deliverance from a Protestant wind.

Their prayers were clearly ignored by the Almighty. For five days aboard his flagship, *Brielle*, named after the town where the Dutch independence campaign against the Spanish began, William and his fleet were wafted along by an easterly breeze. But suddenly this propitious Protestant wind threatened to destroy his plans for the invasion of England. William's flagship was engulfed in a thick mist as it approached Tor Bay. The pilot missed his mark and the ships sailed too far west, past the bay's western end. In a break through a dense sea mist, the pilot realized his error. Unless the wind dropped, they could not easily sail back. To go on would have meant fighting their way ashore, as King James II had reinforced the garrison in Plymouth. They were also short of time. The English fleet had got out of port and was racing after the Dutch along the south coast, propelled by the same easterly that had hurried William's fleet from Holland.

William feared his great and daring enterprise was doomed. An officer on board the Prince's ship turned to Gilbert Burnet, a Protestant theologian and historian, and said: 'You may go to prayers, Doctor. All is over.' Burnet's Protestant prayers were quickly answered. The steady easterly wind slackened, then changed direction and began to blow from the south-west. Within a few hours, warmed by the November sun, William and his fleet were able to sail back around Berry Head into Tor Bay, and let the anchor cables run out within hailing distance of the rocky shoreline.

There were a few fishermen's huts on the beach where the farm fields dropped steeply down to the sea, and little else to greet the Dutch invasion of England by William of Orange. William was probably carried ashore, but tradition has it that he stepped from a barge to make land on a big grey rock. It was shortly after noon on 5 November 1688. He had staged the first successful invasion of England since the Norman Conquest (not counting the invasion of Louis of France to support the barons' rebellion against King John in 1216 – see Chapter One).

William immediately called for two horses and rode up the steep hill out of the bay. He was joined by Frederick, Duke of Schomberg, the seventy-two-year-old commander of his army. To their relief they found they could order the landing of the entire invasion force unopposed.

More than twenty thousand men were brought ashore by midnight. It took two days to get the horses on dry land. The wind had dropped, leaving the bay 'like glass', but James's fleet was becalmed for two days off Beachy Head, unable to attack the Dutch fleet when it was most vulnerable. When one of James's ships did reach Tor Bay to see the topsails of the Dutch ships, the fleet was hit by another westerly gale that forced it to run down the coast to shelter in Portsmouth. By then, William was already marching his army through Newton Abbot.

Prince William had good reason to think that he had God on his side. William of Orange was the son of Charles I's daughter Mary, and was now the champion of Protestantism in Europe. He could lay a claim to the English throne in his own right but he had a stronger claim through his wife, also called Mary. She was James II's eldest daughter by his first wife, Anne Hyde, who had died in 1671 and was the next in line for the throne of England, if her father died without an heir. This gave William a double claim to the Crown.

Their wedding in 1677 had been a marriage of political convenience for William, who believed it would consolidate his alliance with England against Catholic France and Spain. James was reluctant at first to give his consent, but was persuaded that marrying his daughter off to one of the great Protestant families of Europe would reassure public opinion at home about his own Catholicism.

As a fifteen-year-old bride used to the frivolous court of her uncle Charles II, Mary was ill-prepared for life with the small, asthmatic, dour Calvinist William, who was eleven years older than her. She is said to have wept throughout the ceremony at Henry VIII's great Tudor Palace of Whitehall. But they eventually became a devoted couple despite his affairs, including a lifelong relationship with her lady-in-waiting, Elizabeth Villiers.

James had inherited the throne after the death of his brother, Charles II, the 'merry monarch' who was scandalously free with his many mistresses. Charles produced at least fourteen illegitimate children, but he had no legitimate heir. He died of a seizure, aged fifty-five, surrounded, as diarist John Evelyn noted with disapproval, by his concubines at Whitehall Palace in February 1685. The only problem was that James was a committed Catholic and not inclined to compromise. He was described by one biographer as 'humourless and so obsessed with his own rightness that he showed virtually no interest in the views of others'.[2]

Despite their misgivings, the Tories in Parliament supported the hereditary right of accession, and James was duly crowned with full pomp and ceremony on St George's Day, February 1685, at the ancient Abbey in Westminster, with the great anthem, *My Heart is Inditing*, by Henry Purcell, Master of the King's Music, ringing in his ears. A sumptuous pictorial guide to the coronation was published as a public relations exercise to promote the King among opinion formers (that is, those who could afford the book). Its lavish illustrations included portraits of loyal retainers holding up a canopy over James in the regal procession from Westminster Hall to the Abbey. One of them is Samuel Pepys, who had given up his secret diary when his eyesight failed and was now a comfortable member of the political establishment, as Baron of the Cinque Ports.

With a willing Parliament and a pacific public, James therefore had everything going for him – if he showed a little humility and guile. However, the Glorious Revolution is a story of remarkable political ineptitude that rendered James II England's last Stuart King.

~()~

James managed to squander the grudging support of his people within three years of inheriting the Crown. Protestant leaders in England had been reluctant to risk having a Catholic put on the throne, fearing a return of the persecution of Protestants practised by the last Catholic monarch, Queen Mary.

They feared the results of another bloody civil war even more, however – it was only thirty-six years since the last blood-letting between Cromwell's 'roundheads' and Royalists ended in the execution of Charles I. James, as a devout Catholic, had already been forced to resign as Lord High Admiral after Parliament passed the Test Act of 1673, barring Catholics from public office.

But at the start of his reign they were acquiescent, even when they were presented with the choice of rebellion. Three months after James's coronation, the Duke of Monmouth, a Protestant pretender and one of the illegitimate sons of Charles II, raised his own flag of rebellion, but at that stage the people stubbornly refused to join in. Monmouth had been born, during Charles's exile in the Netherlands, to Lucy Walter, a voluptuous beauty with tumbling ringlets of dark hair, and one of the Prince's many lovers. Monmouth staked his claim in the belief that England would rise up and support him because of his faith. He might have been a bastard, but he was a Protestant bastard.

The rebellion was a masterpiece of bad timing. Coming only three months after James II had been crowned, the move to depose the King was premature. It was also hopelessly ill prepared.

Monmouth had been Charles II's favourite, and had been spoiled by the King's indulgence, promoted to take charge of the army as the King's Captain General. He was popular and dashing, but insanely headstrong. Monmouth landed at Lyme Regis on the Dorset coast on 24 May 1685 with a pathetically small force – fewer than two hundred men; he was counting on the people.

Almost as soon as he set foot in England, Monmouth blundered. He had failed to gain support for his enterprise in advance with political leaders in London, and alienated many Protestant sympathizers by declaring himself King. By acting without Parliament's approval, he lost all hope of support at Westminster. He also gave James the excuse he needed to charge him and his supporters with treason. He managed to gather about three thousand supporters in the West Country, but after a ham-fisted attempt to mount a surprise night attack on James's forces, his army of naive, ill-equipped farmhands was routed at the Battle of Sedgemoor.

He was captured hiding in a ditch, disguised as a shepherd. He made a sorry plea for his life on his knees to his uncle James, but as he had committed an act of treason by declaring himself the rightful King, James brushed the appeal aside.

Monmouth was beheaded at the Tower of London on 15 July 1685. Even his execution was botched. The axe-man took four blows and finished the bloody job of severing his head with a knife.

The threat of any renewed Protestant uprising was crushed in the notorious 'Bloody Assizes' at Taunton by Judge Jeffreys, who sentenced three hundred of Monmouth's misguided followers to death. A further eight hundred were transported to the West Indies as a public example.

The ease with which Monmouth's rebellion was snuffed out encouraged James to believe that he had God on his side. 'God Almighty be praised by whose blessing that rebellion was suppressed,' he confided to his private devotional diary. The outcome also reinforced his view that the Catholic Church was a force for good, and a bastion against disorder and rebellions.

William, biding his time in Holland, saw it as an example of how not to carry out a coup.

Having overcome the threat to his Crown, James II now overplayed his hand. In November 1685, he asked Parliament to exempt Catholics from the hated Test Act, which had barred him from public office. When Parliament refused, he suspended Parliament. He issued a 'Declaration of Indulgence' promising religious tolerance to Catholics, dismissed Anglican clergymen from Oxford University's Magdalen College who did not support his pro-Catholic policy and formed the widely feared alliance with the despotic Catholic King of France, Louis XIV. Crucially, he alienated his limited support at Westminster in July 1687 by completely dissolving Parliament.

Having lost the support of the Tories, his power base at Westminster, James unnerved the public by bringing in Catholic soldiers from Ireland into England, which the Whig historian Thomas Babington Macaulay said was a 'fatal' mistake. A satirical ballad lampooning the Irish troops in England had become popular among ordinary soldiers. Now many were prepared to whistle 'Lillibullero'.

Ignoring public opinion, James had also commissioned his architect,

Christopher Wren, to build a new Catholic Chapel Royal for his second wife, Mary of Modena, next to the Banqueting House of Whitehall. It was attached to a new Italianate wing of the old Tudor palace, which replaced Henry's famous long Privy gallery, which ran from the river to the roadway.[3] At the chapel's opening on Christmas Eve 1686, Evelyn was shocked by the sight of James II at a Mass with Jesuit priests. He confided to his diary: 'I could not have believed that I should ever have seen such things in the King of England's palace.'

None of this would have provoked the invasion, but on 12 June 1688 James wrote a fateful letter to William of Orange telling him that two days earlier, his wife Mary had given birth to a child at St James's Palace, and that it was a healthy boy:

> The Queen was, God be thanked, safely delivered of a son on Sunday morning, a little before ten. She has been very well ever since but the child was somewhat ill this last night of the wind and some gripes, but is now, blessed be God, very well again and like to have no returns of it, and is a very strong boy. Last night I received yours of the 18th... It is late and I have not time to say more but that you shall find me to be as kind to you as you can expect.[4]

James's Protestant daughter Anne, who lived with her stepmother, helped to spread wild claims that the baby boy was a 'changeling' – there were rumours the baby was brought into the Queen's chamber in a bedpan. But the birth of a legitimate male heir changed everything.

In Holland, William realized that with a son to carry on the Stuart dynasty, his own wife, Mary, would never inherit the Crown, and England would continue to be ruled by a Catholic king for another generation, depriving him of an ally against France and Spain.

Protestant leaders in England were also appalled at that prospect. A group of four peers, a bishop and two former trusted confidants of the King now plotted James's overthrow. They wrote a secret letter, dated 30 June 1688, inviting William to invade with a sufficiently large force so that he might succeed where Monmouth had failed. They were risking their lives in the enterprise, but the gamble paid off: they were later showered with dukedoms and other hereditary titles as a reward and now represent the greatest pillars of the English establishment. The barter enabled six of the signatories to found some of England's grandest houses: Cavendish (later Duke of Devonshire); Talbot (Duke of Shrewsbury); Danby (Marquess of Carmarthen); Lumley (Viscount and Earl of Scarborough); Edward Russell (Earl of Orford) and Henry Sidney (Viscount and Earl of Romney).

Sidney, who had been James II's Groom of the Bedchamber when he was Duke of York, penned the letter. It said:

> The people are so generally dissatisfied with the present conduct of the government in relation to their religion, liberties and properties (all which have been greatly invaded) and they are in such expectation of their prospects being daily worse that Your Highness may be assured there are nineteen parts of twenty of the people through the kingdom who are desirous of a change and who, we believe would willingly contribute to it

It was also signed by Henry Compton, the Bishop of London, who later crowned William at Westminster Abbey.

James II kept up his own correspondence with William, and wrote a deceptively chatty note to him on 17 September 1688. Despite its friendly tone, it carried a thinly veiled threat: he was ready to destroy the Dutch fleet if it came up the Thames in an attempt to repeat the Dutch destruction of the English fleet in the Medway in 1667. 'I intend to go tomorrow to London, and the next day to Chatham to see the condition of the new batteries I have made in the Medway and my ships which are there. The Queen and my son are to be at London on Thursday which is all I shall say but that you shall find me as kind to you as you can expect.'[5] It was to be his last letter to William.

William had left nothing to chance. He assembled a fleet of sixty warships and seven hundred transport ships carrying twenty-one thousand troops, four thousand horses and twenty-one guns. He also carried a smithy, a portable bridge of barges and a printing press that would play a crucial role in winning the hearts and minds of the English people. All he needed was the wind to blow from the east.

James began a forty-hour service of continuous prayer on 28 September for divine deliverance in his Catholic chapel at Whitehall. In a panic, he also took the precaution of reversing some of his pro-Catholic decisions, including issuing a summons to recall Parliament. It was all too late. Evelyn vividly recorded the panic, spreading daily, and how the people – against the wishes of their King – fervently prayed for an easterly wind:

> 28 SEPTEMBER. I went to Lond: where I found the Court in the uttermost consternation upon report of the Pr: of Oranges landing, which put White-hall into so panic a feare, that I could hardly believe it possible to find such a change.

> 16 OCTOB: Hourely dreade on expectation of the Pr: of Oranges Invasion still heightned to that degree, as his Majestie thought fit to recall the Writes of Summons of Parliament; to abrogate the Commission for the dispencing power (but retaining his owne right still to dispense with all Laws) restore the ejected Fellows of Magdalene College Oxon: But in the meane time called over 5,000 Irish, 4,000 Scots; continue to remove protestants and put papists in to Portsmouth and other places of Trust; and retaines Jesuites about him, which gave no satisfaction to the nation, but increasing the universal discontent, brought people to so desperate a passe as with utmost expressions even passionately seeme to long for and desire the landing of that Prince, whom they looked on as their deliverer from popish Tyrannie, praying incessantly for an Easterly Wind.

> 24 OCTOB: The Kings Birth-day, no Gunns from the Tower, as usually: The sunn Eclips'd at its rising: This day signal for the Victory of William the Conqueror against Herold neere Battel in Sussex: The wind (which had hitherto ben West) all this day East, wonderfull expectations of the Dutch fleete.

The timing of his landing could not have been more auspicious. The Fifth of November was already the day on which England celebrated the death of Guy Fawkes and the Catholic Gunpowder Plotters, who had attempted to blow up James I and his court at Parliament. In Newton Abbot the Prince's Declaration was printed off from his mobile press and read out. It justified the invasion and condemned the 'king's counsellors' for illegal acts, claiming there had been a denial of the rights going back to Magna Carta: 'Therefore it is, that we have thought fit to go over into England,

and to carry over with us a force sufficient, by the blessing of God, to defend us from the violence of these evil counsellors.'

There was a carnival atmosphere in the towns of the West Country as William and his army slowly made their way to London by mid-December. His army presented an exotic sight to seventeenth-century eyes, more like a travelling circus than an invasion force, as one witness recorded:

> First rode Macclesfield at the head of two hundred gentlemen, most of English blood, glittering in helmets and cuirasses and mounted on Flemish war horses. Each was attended by a negro, brought from the sugar plantations on the coast of Guiana. The citizens of Exeter, who had never seen so many specimens of the African race, gazed with wonder on those black faces set off by embroidered turbans and white feathers. Then with drawn broad swords came a squadron of Swedish horsemen in black armour and fur cloaks. They were regarded with a strange interest; for it was rumoured that they were natives of a land where the ocean was frozen and where the night lasted through half the year, and that they had themselves slain the huge bears whose skins they wore. Next surrounded by a goodly company of gentlemen and pages, was borne aloft the Prince's banner. On its broad folds the crowd which covered the roofs and filled the windows read with delight that memorable inscription, 'The Protestant religion and the liberties of England.' But the acclamations redoubled when, attended by forty running footmen, the Prince himself appeared.[6]

Prince William wore armour 'on back and breast' and a white plume and was mounted on a white charger. The moment was turned into a painting for posterity by Sir Godfrey Kneller, the German-born painter to the English court. (It was probably commissioned by William III and is in the Royal Collection.)

The invaders split into two columns beyond the beachhead but, after Exeter, reformed into one force as they approached Salisbury. There, William – given good intelligence from his many spies in James II's army – expected to meet James's forces.

James had already turned down an offer of a negotiated peace, saying he would yield nothing more, 'Not one atom'. He had amassed a formidable force of twenty-five thousand men with another seven thousand marching to join them when he rode into camp on 19 November 1688, but he had never commanded an army before and was seized by crippling indecision, conducting pointless reviews and inspections.[7]

About to go to Warminster to inspect the troops with his general, John Churchill, the King's nose began to bleed violently. The bleeding lasted for three days. Then, on 24 November, the Earl of Middleton wrote to Lord Preston with devastating news: Churchill and others at Warminster had defected to William's banner. 'Roger Huett brought news from Warminster that Lord Churchill's Grenadiers went last night over to the enemy… The Duke of Grafton and Lord Churchill are missing, and not doubted but they are gone to the enemy.'[8] One of William's most trusted friends, Hans Willem Bentinck, made First Earl of Portland the following year, scribbled in the margins of his record of the campaign: 'The Duke of Grafton my Lord Churchill Lieut. Gen. and Mr. Barckley [Berkeley] gentleman in the household of the Princess of Denmark and Colonel of a dragoon regiment coming from the King's army came to join him.'[9]

The royal nosebleed is now seen as a symptom of extreme stress, showing that James panicked and suffered a form of nervous breakdown, but at the time, the King wrote in his diary that he saw it as a sign of divine intervention – that God had stopped him going to Warminster, where he may have been murdered at the hands of the traitor Churchill. Churchill left behind a note explaining that he was a Protestant and he could not draw his sword against the Protestant cause.*

Later the same day, 24 November, with growing evidence that the command of his army was disintegrating, James's war council decided to retreat from Salisbury to London. Swearing vengeance on Churchill, the King raced back to London only to find his daughter Anne was missing with her friend, Sarah Churchill, wife of the turncoat. The women had been confined to a corner of the Palace of Whitehall across the road from the riverside palace, in Henry VIII's Tudor cockpit, which had been converted into apartments in Cromwell's day on land that today is near Downing Street, behind the Cabinet Office at 70 Whitehall. After a messenger brought news of Churchill's defection, their guards were doubled and the Princess screamed: 'I will jump out of the window rather than be found here by my father.'

---

* Churchill was rewarded by William with the title of first Duke of Marlborough and became one of England's greatest generals. He was presented by a grateful nation with Blenheim Palace, named after one of his great European victories, and birthplace of his descendant, Sir Winston Churchill.

Anne retired to her bedroom, and at dead of night, dressed in night-gowns and slippers, they managed to escape down the back stairs through a doorway that still leads into Treasury Passage, next door to 10 Downing Street.[10] Compton, the Bishop of London, the Princess's gallant old tutor, helped them to escape. He met the women in a carriage in Whitehall; they climbed aboard to find the Bishop had exchanged his ecclesiastical garb for a buff coat and jackboots and his crook for a sword and pistols in holsters. The Bishop took Sarah and Anne to his official residence in Aldersgate Street until they could be reunited with their husbands.

When he heard of Anne's flight, the King – convinced it was all the work of the Churchills – cried: 'God help me. My own children have forsaken me.'

Facing defeat, the King reluctantly opened negotiations with William, but privately admitted to the French ambassador to London, Paul Barillon, that they were a feint.

> I must send commissioners to my nephew, that I may gain time to ship off my wife and the Prince of Wales. You know the temper of my troops. None but the Irish will stand by me; and the Irish are not in sufficient force to resist the enemy. A Parliament would impose on me conditions which I could not endure. I should be forced to undo all that I have done for Catholics, and to break with the King of France. As soon, therefore, as the Queen and my child are safe, I will leave England and take refuge in Ireland, in Scotland, or with your master.[11]

James's agents, however, now lost their nerve, and refused to obey his order to smuggle his wife and child to France from Portsmouth, which led to an escape attempt that turned into a tragic farce. They returned to St James's Palace, but over a tense and unhappy supper on 9 December – a hundred paces from where his father, Charles I, had been beheaded in 1649 – James decided they should flee, separately. At two o'clock the next morning, the Queen finally escaped across the river, disguised as an Italian laundress, with her child covered up like a bundle of laundry. They went by coach to Gravesend and were taken by ship to France.

The next morning, James made his own escape. He boarded a carriage in the inner court at Whitehall and set course for the horse ferry at Lambeth. As he crossed the Thames to Vauxhall, he flung his great seal of office into the river to avoid it being used to summon Parliament in his name, or to sign his own death warrant. Months later, the seal was dragged to the surface in a fishing net, and the fact that he had discarded it was to count against him. Parliament decided that James had not been overthrown; by abandoning his office, he had abdicated.

His trials were not yet over. Learning of his overthrow, the London mob ran riot, demolishing Catholic chapels and houses, including the Spanish ambassador's house with its rich library. Then James was captured trying to escape by boat when it put in at the little port of Faversham on the North Kent coast. John Evelyn noted on 13 December: 'The King flies to sea... putts in at Feversham for ballast... is rudely detained by the people: comes back to Whitehall.' William and his army now advanced from Windsor – more than a month after landing – to stake his claim to the Crown at St James's Palace. William ordered James to retreat from Whitehall, so that a *parlez* about his surrender could begin. James went to Rochester but returned to Whitehall for Sunday Mass. He dined in public too. After abortive negotiations, he retreated again to Rochester.

William, for good political and personal reasons, had clearly decided against seeking the execution of his father-in-law. Instead, he connived in James's escape. James made a run for it again and this time, with William's support, he was successful. Evelyn recorded that at noon on 18 December, the King took a barge to Gravesend before sailing for France, while the Prince of Orange filled Whitehall with Dutch Guards.

The invasion was over, but there was more bloody business to enact before this extraordinary chapter was finished. James was put up as an honoured guest of Louis XIV in the splendour of his former palace, which Louis had vacated for Versailles. There could be no more sumptuous place of exile, but emboldened by the support of the French King, James would not let go of the English Crown so easily. He landed in Ireland in 1689 with fifteen thousand troops. The invasion of Ireland was to be the stepping-stone to an invasion of Scotland and England, but William met James and his Irish and French troops on the banks of the River Boyne where they were decisively defeated in the battle that is still celebrated by the Orange Lodges each year.

After protracted negotiations with Parliament, in which William insisted on being crowned as king in his own right, on Ash Wednesday, 13 February the Dutchman and his wife were proclaimed, as King William III and Queen Mary II, the first joint monarchs in British history, at that *tour de force* of Italianate Stuart taste, the Banqueting House. There were bonfires, bells were rung and guns were fired in celebration.

Evelyn disparagingly described how, instead of appearing sombre over seizing her father's Crown, and issuing some diplomatic words about the need to succour the nation, Mary had excitedly inspected her new quarters in the Palace – those built for her stepmother – as if she were at a wedding, 'so as seeming to be quite Transported: rose early on the next morning of her arrival and in her undresse before her women were up; went about from roome to roome, to see the Convenience of White-hall: Lay in the same bed and apartment where the late Queene lay: and within a night or two, sate downe to play at Basset as the Queen her predecessor us'd to do... This carriage was censured by many.' Evelyn added: 'She seems to be of a good nature, and that takes nothing to heart whilst the Prince her husband has a thoughtfull Countenance, is wonderfull serious and silent, seems to treate all persons alike gravely: and to be very intent on affaires, both Holland and Ireland and France calling for his care.' Despite his wife's enthusiasm for her new apartments, William refused to live at Whitehall by the river because the damp aggravated his asthma. Instead, they built a modern palace for the couple at Kensington in a style both had been comfortable with in the Netherlands. It was later to become the home of Diana, Princess of Wales.

The old Tudor palace at Whitehall, abandoned and neglected, burned down on 2 January 1698. Evelyn noted it was bitterly cold (that easterly wind again) and a maid – she was Dutch, and had come over with William's entourage – left sheets drying by a charcoal brazier. 'White-hall utterly burnt to the ground, nothing but the walls and ruines left.'[12]

He could have said the same about James II's reign.

The Painted Hall at the former Royal Naval College (previously the navy pensioners' hospital and now Greenwich University) has been used for many Hollywood films. It may now be more famous as the set for the opening sequence of *The Pirates of the Caribbean: On Stranger Tides*; visitors in 2011 gawped open-mouthed at Johnny Depp's Jack Sparrow outfit on temporary loan from Disney in a glass case at the hall's entrance. But it was the painted ceiling that made visitors slack-jawed in the early eighteenth century. And what they were astonished by was a masterwork of pure political spin: an allegorical celebration of the joint accession of King William III and Queen Mary II.

OLD ROYAL NAVAL COLLEGE, GREENWICH:
*William III, Queen Mary II and The Triumph of Liberty
over Tyranny in the lower hall.*

Painted by Sir James Thornhill, who was paid £3 per square yard for his work, the mural was started in 1708, six years after William III's death; it was not completed until 1727. It shows William and Mary enthroned in heaven, with Peace and Liberty triumphing over Tyranny. There is no sign or symbol of James II, but Thornhill's rendition is as crude as the script of a Disney movie in depicting the villain. Lying at William's feet, on his knees and clutching a broken sword is the French King, Louis XIV, who wears a yellow tunic to indicate cowardice and defeat. There is also a tumbled mitre, representing the fallen Catholic Church. This neck-straining spectacle shows the Glorious Revolution of 1688 as a victory for common sense, which established the supremacy of Parliament over the Crown and put Britain back on the path towards a modern constitutional monarchy and Parliamentary democracy.

The overthrow of the Catholic James II was presented by Whig historians as part of the gradual progression of Britain to enlightenment, from Magna Carta to the current day; it was a view sponsored by Macaulay, who pushed the message in his highly readable five-volume *History of England*. Socialist historian A.J.P. Taylor also hailed the Glorious Revolution as 'the foundation of our liberty'. In this cosy narrative, gradual change has saved Britain from violent upheavals such as the French Revolution. It is a comfortable, pipe-and-slippers view of our nation as a place where common sense will prevail, which conveniently forgets the bloodletting of the English Civil War and the beheading of Charles I in 1649.

Margaret Thatcher, then Conservative Prime Minister, put forward that rosy gloss on history in the 1988 Commons debate for the tercentenary of the Glorious Revolution. It had, she said, secured 'tolerance, respect for the law and for the impartial administration of justice, and respect for private property. It also established the tradition that political change should be sought and achieved through Parliament. It was this which saved us from the violent revolutions which shook our continental neighbours and made the revolution of 1688 the first step on the road which, through successive Reform Acts, led to the establishment of universal suffrage and full Parliamentary democracy.' This fable has held for nearly three centuries. But she was speaking before her own hold on power was violently shaken by street riots in London against the poll tax in March 1990, which ultimately led to her downfall.

Tony Benn, then Labour MP for Chesterfield, rejected this version of events: 'What happened in 1688 was not a glorious revolution. It was a plot by some people… to replace a Catholic king with another king more acceptable to those who organized the plot… Nor was 1688 the establishment of our liberties… Are we to welcome a Bill of Rights that says that papists could not sit in either House of Parliament?'

It is difficult to disprove Benn's argument by showing that the overthrow of James II by William III was a 'popular' uprising. In the absence of seventeenth-century opinion polling, there is no conclusive evidence either way to show what the 'man in the street' of Stuart England really thought about the arrival of William III. There were, of course, pockets of Protestant protest, in Hull and in the West Country, in support of William. The eye-witness reports suggest that William's march from Brixham was welcomed by the general public in the towns through which he passed, but behind the colourful show was a serious army.

In fact, William was so disappointed by the failure of more landed gentry to join his banner in the first few days that he threatened to go back to Holland. This gives credence to the claim by the Left that it was a coup by an élite of the landed classes. But that is not the whole story – James alienated Parliament, academics, lawyers and, fatally, the commanders of his army, particularly Churchill, who swung behind William. James also found that juries would not convict those he accused of refusing to obey his pro-Catholic edicts. And we have Evelyn's diary evidence that people prayed for deliverance from their Catholic King with a Protestant wind.

It is hardly unexpected that many ordinary people did not join his army. In the West Country the trials that followed the Monmouth Rebellion were a recent reminder that they could end up on the gibbet if they joined another rebellion that did not succeed.

David Starkey has persuasively argued that William was the first modern monarch. In his own country William was a Stadtholder, a ruler of the Dutch states but not a sovereign. William, acting like a chief executive for England plc, brought over to Britain some of the modern economic innovations which had made the Dutch a great trading nation, such as public borrowing and the creation of the Bank of England. This led to steep growth in Britain's overseas trade and its status as a world power. This was the part of the Revolution that was truly 'Glorious' for Britain. William also brought Britain into a stable alliance with the Protestant Netherlands, enabling him to challenge the power of France and change the balance of power across Northern Europe. In conceding a constitutional monarchy, he stripped away some of the mystery of royalty. He abandoned the practice of touching the sick for the 'King's Evil', or scrofula (a swelling of the lymph glands caused by tuberculosis), a practice that had been revived by Charles II at the Banqueting House in Whitehall.

The coronation of William and Mary was quickly followed by constitutional reforms with a Bill of Rights, curbing the powers of the monarch for ever; the Triennial Act ensuring Parliament was automatically summoned every three years; and the introduction in 1697 of the Civil List, giving Parliament control over the royal expenditure as well as the raising of all revenue for the armed forces. However, as a Commons Library paper points out, the 'Bill of Rights' is a misnomer. It is not like the United States' written constitution, nor does it set out individual rights. It was rushed onto the statute book to give legal force to the removal of James II for misgovernment, and then to settle the line of accession through the descendants of William and Mary, then through Mary's sister Princess Anne and her descendants. The bill was designed to curb future arbitrary behaviour of the monarch, and to guarantee Parliament's powers over the Crown, thereby establishing a constitutional monarchy.[13]

Some provisions of the Bill of Rights are still important – Articles 1 and 2 state that laws should not be dispensed with or suspended (as James did for more than two years) without the consent of Parliament; that Parliament should be frequently summoned with free elections (Charles II had not called Parliament for four years before his death); MPs and peers should be able to speak and act freely in Parliament (the attempt by Charles I to imprison five ringleaders of Parliamentary resistance led to civil war); no armies should be raised and no taxes levied without the authority of Parliament; and (how modern can you get?) cruel and unusual punishment should not be inflicted on those in custody. Other provisions, such as the right to bear arms, are upheld in America but are clearly obsolete in modern Britain.

The most glaring anachronism is its reference to 'preserving of the King's person and government by disabling papists from sitting in either House of Parliament'. This has since been repealed, along with many of the other measures, but some anti-Catholic measures remain on the statute book.

After passing the Bill of Rights, Parliament realized that the settlement for the line of succession was unlikely to last. Mary II died childless in 1694, and William – who was rumoured to be gay – did not remarry. Princess Anne's last surviving child, Prince William, the Duke of Gloucester, died six years later, thus ending the line.

More legislation was necessary to stop the exiled James II or his Catholic son James Francis claiming the Crown. Parliament passed the Act of Settlement in 1701 to ensure the Crown of England went to the Electress Sophia of Hanover, who was the granddaughter of James I and, more importantly, Protestant.

The Act of Settlement made it illegal for a Catholic to take the throne of England, or for an English monarch to marry a Catholic 'for ever'. That was intended to ensure that nothing like the Catholic Stuart reign could occur again.

Three hundred years after William stepped ashore in Brixham, the Act of Settlement reads today like a bigot's charter against the Catholics. For that reason, the anniversary of the invasion in 1988 was deliberately played down by the Government of the day. There was no national bank holiday, no street parties and no orange bunting to celebrate the tercentenary of the Glorious Revolution even though Mrs Thatcher, a die-hard Unionist, was in power. The tercentenary was limited to a couple of royal visits, a debate in both Houses of Parliament and an entirely forgettable (at least by me) exhibition in the Banqueting House, Whitehall.

The late Lord Whitelaw, the Conservative Leader of the Lords, said there was 'no general wish' for national public celebrations, but then he was acutely aware of the dangers of stirring up religious hatred in Ireland. As the Ulster Secretary in the Heath Government, he had opened up a line of contact with the IRA about a possible ceasefire in its sectarian war in 1973.

In 1984, the IRA narrowly missed murdering Mrs Thatcher in the bombing at the Grand Hotel, Brighton. As it happens, it also missed me by about twenty minutes when the hotel's massive chimney stack came down in the bar where I had been drinking with fellow lobby journalists.

Lord Whitelaw knew that a national celebration for William of Orange in 1988 could have cost lives. The late Sir Charles Tidbury, the chairman of the brewers Whitbread, was put on an IRA death list because he accepted the post of chairman of the William and Mary Tercentenary Trust planning the public celebrations for the anniversary of his landing in Brixham.

Tidbury was no great supporter of Mrs Thatcher, but his 'offence' in the eyes of the IRA high command was that he had taken charge of what muted celebrations took place for the Glorious Revolution in 1988. It was no idle threat – two republicans, Pearse McAuley and Nessan Quinlivan, were stopped by officers guarding Tidbury's farmhouse in Hampshire in 1990 and were charged with conspiracy to murder. They escaped from Brixton prison before serving their sentences and are free today because of the Belfast peace agreement.

It was against that background that Queen Elizabeth II and the Duke of Edinburgh sailed to Brixham to mark the anniversary in 1988. The Queen arrived in the Royal Yacht *Britannia* in fog, like William, and unveiled the plaque on the obelisk where William stepped ashore. Specially for the occasion, according to the locals, the William stone was removed from the obelisk and laid on the red carpet up the short flight of steps by the fish quay. It was put there so that the Queen could symbolically repeat history by stepping on the same rock when she came ashore.

Elizabeth II was wary about committing a faux pas when she saw the odd-looking stone lying in her path. 'What is that doing there?' she is said to have asked, before stepping over it.

When the Queen performed the unveiling ceremony on the quayside at Brixham, she may have reflected on the impact that the legacy of 1688 is still having on her own family three centuries later.

In the twentieth century, if Prince Philip, the Duke of Edinburgh, had been a Catholic, Elizabeth would have been barred from the throne. HRH Prince Michael of Kent lost his right of succession because of his marriage to a Roman Catholic. In 2008 Autumn Kelly, baptized as a Catholic, converted to the Church of England before marrying Peter Phillips, enabling him to keep his place in the line of succession.[14] In 2011, it was felt necessary that Catherine Middleton, before she was married to Prince William, should go through a Church of England confirmation service just to underline the fact that she was a Protestant. It was held in secret at St James's Palace, within a few yards of the apartment where James II's son and heir was born in 1688 – the birth that triggered William III's invasion and his overthrow. Had Kate Middleton been a Catholic, the Queen's grandson, the next in line to the throne after the Prince of Wales, could never become William V.

There is no longer any bar to a Catholic becoming Prime Minister – the bar on Catholics in Parliament was repealed by the Roman Catholic Relief Act 1829 – but the former Labour Prime Minister, Tony Blair, felt so uncomfortable at combining his growing attraction to the Church of Rome and his duties (such as approving the appointment of bishops of the established Church of England) he left office before converting to Catholicism. Such blatant religious discrimination is in breach of the European Human Rights Convention. So far no king or queen has had to take a case to the European Court.

Since he could not secure a divorce from Catherine of Aragon, Henry VIII made himself the Supreme Governor of the Church of England after leading the breakaway from the Church of Rome in 1536. Undoing this part of our past is fraught with difficulty. It could unravel the thread of our constitution that makes the monarch the head of the Established Church of England.

Repeated attempts at repeal of the Act of Settlement have been made in the past decade, the last by Labour Prime Minister Gordon Brown, but they foundered on inertia and constitutional complications including the need to consult parts of the Commonwealth where the Queen remains head of state. Even with the approval of the Commonwealth heads of government, it may still require amendments to the Bill of Rights (1689), the Royal Marriages Act (1772), the Coronation Oaths Act (1688), the Crown in Parliament Act (1689), the Accession Declaration Act (1910) and the Act of Union (1707), Article 2 of which specifies that Roman Catholics may not ascend the Throne of the United Kingdom – a daunting job of law-rewriting. As one Anglican group said: 'Tamper with this, and the whole house of cards comes tumbling down.'

David Cameron is committed to making the change, but as the Orange marchers in Brixham showed, he will not do so without a fight.

FIVE

1815

'The success of the battle turned upon closing the gates'

Château d'Hougoumont, Braine-l'Alleud, Belgium:
The south gatehouse.

I am driving into the heart of euroland, and I wish I had taken the Eurostar. The road swings north past Dunkirk, and for the next hundred miles, skirting the ancient Belgian towns of Bruges and Ghent, I am tailgated at seventy miles per hour all the way to Brussels. I am driving through Belgium because – in addition to Aldophe Sax, the inventor of the saxophone; Hercule Poirot; Magritte, the surrealist who painted men in bowler hats; and a green vegetable that smells like damp dogs – Belgium is also famous for the battle that determined the fate of Europe for a hundred years.

Two hundred years ago, my journey would not have been possible. Napoleon had imposed a trade and travel ban on Britain. Britons were bottled up on their small island making 'staycations' *de rigueur*, which is one reason why Byron's epic poem *Childe Harold's Pilgrimage*, based on his own Grand Tour of Europe, was such a hit in England when it was published in 1812. Broadstairs became the Bordeaux of Britain. But then came the Battle of Waterloo, and we were free to explore the Continent on the Grand Tour.

Napoleon and the Duke of Wellington could not have picked a better spot than Waterloo for their epic power struggle. It left future generations with a reminder of what can happen when nations go to war, just eight miles south of Brussels, now the capital of euroland. If Napoleon had won at Waterloo on 18 June 1815, I might be on the Eurostar to the headquarters of a European Union in Paris. The story of the battle is the story of Europe.

It is with some relief that I see the big road signs for Waterloo, and get off the Brussels ring-road, the RO. I find myself driving along country lanes surrounded by rolling countryside. Not much has changed in this gentle landscape since the Duke of Wellington and his army arrived, except for one thing – the Lion Mound.

A monster mound of earth with a lion on top dominates the skyline for miles around. It is as if a green pyramid has been dumped inexplicably in the Belgian landscape, like one of Magritte's green bowler hat jokes. The mound was built in 1826 on the orders of King William of Orange, when Belgium was part of the United Netherlands, to mark the spot where his son, the Prince of Orange, was wounded by a musket ball in the shoulder.

Given that thousands died horrible deaths all around the Prince, it was like building a mountain to a fleabite, and to Wellington, it was sacrilege. Four hundred thousand cubic metres of soil were scraped up into the Mound, flattening two crucial features of his battlefield – the Mont-Saint-Jean ridge and a sunken road. The Duke was furious that by flattening out the contours, the *Butte du Lion* robbed future generations of the chance to see for themselves the tactical genius behind his great victory.

Wellington, who later returned to the battlefield as a tourist with the Prince Regent, was outraged. 'They have altered my field of battle,' he said. He was being uncharacteristically mild, if that is all he really said, though the alterations could have been worse. In 1973, there was a plan to drive a motorway through the battlefield. It was stopped by a spirited protest campaign led by the current Duke of Wellington.

THE LION MOUND:
Where the Prince of Orange was wounded.

The first Duke of Wellington had learned, during his years of hard military campaigning in India, Portugal and Spain, that a ridge with a reverse slope had a double advantage: protection for his infantry from enemy cannon fire, and the element of surprise when they stood up to fire volleys into the enemy ranks at point-blank range. He had scouted out the ground in the weeks preceding the battle while he was dallying in Brussels with his mistress, Lady Frances Wedderburn-Webster, and he had found the ridge he had been looking for near the hamlet of Mont-Saint-Jean, where the Paris road crossed the Charleroi–Brussels road. The ridge stretched from Hougoumont to Papelotte with the crossroads in the centre, a distance of about two and a half miles.

He ordered his surveyors to produce a topographical map of the landscape. The map, now in the Royal Engineers Museum at Chatham in Kent, was captured by the French, and recaptured during the preceding Battle of Quatre Bras. It is one of the most precious relics of the battle, and reveals that the surveyors had little clear idea precisely where Wellington intended to fight. The actual battlefield is in the top right-hand corner of the four-piece map, and the army surveyors must have wasted many days meticulously plotting the rolling hills to the west where the fighting never happened.

Wellington had no doubts about precisely where he wanted to make a stand. The Duke hurriedly ringed the Mont-Saint-Jean ridge in pencil so that his officers understood precisely where he planned to meet Napoleon, and his map still bears his urgent 'O'.

I park by Le Café Wellington on the ridge that Wellington circled with his pencil. It lies under the shadow of the Lion Mound, which today houses a battlefield interpretation centre for tourists. I am here to meet my battlefield guide, Michael Farrar, a former English teacher who lives with his French wife in Waterloo, now a smug commuter town for Brussels bureaucrats. Waterloo is so well off that it boasts an Apple Store; the local Carrefour hypermarket has its own very helpful sommelier.

The town of Waterloo is nearly three miles behind Wellington's front line. The nearest town to the battlefield is Mont-Saint-Jean but, lacking a decent hotel, Wellington commandeered Waterloo's Bodenghien Inn (now the Musée Wellington) as his headquarters. It was here he composed his famous despatch to Lord Bathurst, the Secretary-at-War, after the battle and datelined it: Waterloo.

Had he slept on the field like his men, it would have become known as the Battle of Mont-Sain-Jean. Pubs and roads from London to New Zealand, the railway station on the south bank of the Thames, the bridge across the river, would all have been named Mont-Saint-Jean instead of Waterloo.

Most of the quarter of a million visitors who come to the battlefield at Waterloo each year pay their €12 to watch a film of the conflict, or view the Victorian panorama painting. Then they climb the 226 steps to the top of the *Butte du Lion* for a bird's-eye view of the battlefield, before retiring to Le Café Wellington to contemplate the carnage over *bœuf Wellington* or a Napoleon pizza.

All around this ridge, there were acts of astonishing heroism and sacrifice but none more so than at a farm called Hougoumont, which is why I am here. Hougoumont was on the extreme right of Wellington's lines and down a slope, about a quarter of a mile below the ridge. It was in an exposed position, close to the French lines, and had it fallen, Napoleon would have been able to outflank the allied forces to attack the men he had concealed behind the ridge. My guide is delighted that for a change, he has a customer who wants to see Hougoumont. At least it avoids climbing the steps to the top of the Mound.

Wellington gave the task of defending Hougoumont to a towering Scot, Lieutenant Colonel James Macdonnell of the Coldstream Guards, with support from four light companies of Foot Guards from General

John Byng's Second Brigade stationed on the ridge. The units were chosen because they boasted some of the best sharpshooters in the army. They were stationed there with troops from the Second Nassau Regiment, a company of Hanoverian riflemen and one hundred men from the German Luneburg field-battalion. Macdonnell was ordered to hold Hougoumont at all costs.

Baron Friedrich von Muffling, a fat Prussian officer who had been put on Wellington's staff to improve liaison with Wellington's allied Prussian commander, Gebhard Leberecht von Blücher, asked whether he really expected to hold Hougoumont with fifteen hundred men. 'Ah,' said the Duke. 'You don't know Macdonnell.'[1] In fact, Wellington committed over three thousand five hundred men to the defence of Hougoumont during the day.

The Coldstream Guards arrived at Hougoumont cold and wet, on Saturday afternoon, 17 June 1815, after the retreat from Quatre Bras, the opening skirmish between Napoleon's forces and the two armies commanded by Wellington and Blücher. Napoleon had caught Wellington by surprise – he had been at the Duchess of Richmond's ball in Brussels – and had succeeded in driving a wedge between Wellington's coalition forces and the Prussians, though he failed to inflict a decisive defeat. Macdonnell's men found the farm almost deserted. The château's owner, Chevalier de Louville, and his family had fled but his gardener, Guillaume van Cutsem, and Guillaume's five-year-old daughter were still nervously sheltering in the farmhouse.

There had been a farm at Hougoumont for five centuries. The Knights of Malta established the château by the main Nivelle to Mont-Saint-Jean road in the fourteenth century. It was clearly marked on Wellington's map as a small orange square, and named as 'Goumount'. In fact, the farm formed three sides of a square, surrounded to the south by an elm wood.

Macdonnell set about turning the farm into a fortress. He ordered his riflemen to prepare their defensive positions before the light went. They smashed the red pantiles out from the roof of the great barn that ran down the whole south side of the farm facing the French. Men climbed into the attics to take up firing positions in the rafters.

On the south-east corner of the farm, at right angles to the great barn and facing the wood, stood a huge gatehouse with two large gates. Macdonnell ordered his sharpshooters to take up firing positions from the windows on the first floor and the attic window in the roof. Many of his men were equipped with Baker rifles that were far more accurate than the 'Brown Bess' muskets, which had to be used in volleys at less than one hundred yards to be effective. Baker rifles were muzzle-loaded, but the rifled barrels could spin lead balls, making them more stable in the air. Ballistics tests have shown they could drop French skirmishers at more than three hundred paces before the French got close enough to fire volleys with their old-fashioned muskets.

The gatehouse concealed a small courtyard and the handsome château, attached to a petite chapel with a pretty little spire. A modest house for the farmer formed an L-shape with the gable end of the château, overlooking the farmyard. In the centre of the farmyard was a well for drawing water, with a dovecote for pigeons above it. The scavenging Guards would have made light work of their eggs and their meat before trying to catch some sleep.

On the north side, there was another gateway to a sunken farm track leading up to the ridge. Macdonnell left open the heavy blue wooden doors to the north gate so that carts could keep his units supplied with ammunition.

At the back of the château, there was a walled garden in the formal Flemish style – trim box hedges laid out in geometric patterns.

To the right of the south gatehouse, there was an eight-foot-high brick wall that ran for about two hundred yards, protecting the garden and a large apple orchard. Macdonnell's men hacked out bricks from the long garden wall to act as fireloops, and they laid out timbers from the barns as makeshift fire-steps so they could fire over the wall at the enemy.

The French troops were under the command of General Count Honoré Reille, who gave the honour of taking Hougoumont to Napoleon's youngest brother, Prince Jérôme, aged thirty. He still had something to prove to his older brother, the Emperor: loyalty.

Jérôme Bonaparte had married an American merchant's daughter, Elizabeth Patterson, twelve years earlier without his brother's permission. Napoleon was so incensed he refused to allow Elizabeth into France, although she was pregnant. She gave birth to Jérôme's son, Jérôme Napoleon Bonaparte, on 5 July 1805 at 96 Camberwell Grove, Camberwell, a Georgian town house that still stands on the leafy street in inner-city south London. They would never see each other again.

Napoleon had annulled the marriage and arranged for Jérôme to marry a German princess, making him the King of Westphalia. He now commanded the Sixth Division of eight thousand men.

~ᐧᐧᐧ~

Napoleon's choice of Jérôme to lead the attack at Hougoumont was to prove critical. Jérôme, perhaps because he wanted to impress his father, completely misunderstood or ignored his orders that this was merely a diversion from the main assault, and drew more of Napoleon's forces into a determined day-long attack at the farm, calling upon reinforcements from Comte Maximilien Foy's Ninth Division, General Bachelu's Fifth Division and Kellermann's cavalry corps.

It had rained heavily through the night, causing rivers of water to gush into men's sodden boots, and as dawn broke on Sunday, 18 June, Private Matthew Clay of Wellington's Third Guards, like many soldiers that morning, checked the flintlock of his musket to see if it would still fire. Muskets were notorious for misfiring when it was wet. Clay primed his rifle, opened the frizzen, poured some dry powder into the pan, cocked the hammer and fired at an object he had put on a bank of earth. 'The ball embedded in the bank where I had purposely placed it as a target.' Then he waited.

The French had expected Napoleon to start the battle at around 8 a.m., but Napoleon delayed another three hours. As a former gunnery officer, Napoleon knew that cannon balls would not ricochet in the mud, and would deaden their impact on Wellington's infantry. He wanted to wait until the ground started to dry out. At around 9 a.m., the rain finally stopped and the sun began to break through the storm clouds.

The first shots in the battle were fired by Napoleon's battery of 246 guns in the direction of Château Hougoumont. A British officer took out his pocket watch and noted it was 11.20 a.m. When the guns ceased their pounding of Hougoumont, Jérôme's men marched forward though the fields of waist-high ripening rye, with their boy drummers beating out their incessant message to drive Napoleon's army on. Napoleon was a clever tactician, but he had a simple approach to battle – hard pounding by his guns of the enemy centre followed by a frontal attack by his massed troops – that had seen armies across Europe crack. But the core of Wellington's army was battle-hardened and disciplined. It would not crack so easily.

Over the next eight hours, Macdonnell would earn his reputation for tenacity and valour. As soon as the French skirmishers came into range of the farm through the woods, the defenders opened fire.

Restlessly patrolling the ridge on his chestnut charger, Copenhagen, Wellington directed his telescope at the French columns in blue tunics and shakos – tall peaked caps – as they advanced towards the farm. He ordered Major Bull's horse-drawn battery of guns to open fire at the French with howitzers. They were armed with a secret weapon – shells containing balls – that was the brainchild of an artillery officer, Henry Shrapnel. The shells had been adopted by the British army in 1803, but were still not used by the French. Bull's fusillade caused death and mayhem among the French infantry, and checked their advance for a time, but the shells alone could not stop the waves of Jérôme's attacks.

Jérôme's troops filtered through the woods and tried to storm the gates by sheer weight of numbers, but they were repeatedly beaten back by the furious fire from the farmhouse. They charged through a hedge and a line of apple trees screening the garden wall, but were decimated in a storm of musket and rifle fire. The grassy area in front of the wall – no more than thirty paces wide – became a killing zone as the bodies of the dead and dying piled up.[2]

Some of the Coldstream Guards had been positioned in a cottage garden to pick off a few of the French skirmishers to the south of the farm. Desperately seeking cover in the open ground, they hid behind a haystack near the gatehouse at the south corner. When the French set the hay alight, the Guards pulled back. Ducking musket balls, they bolted through the twin north gates and slammed them shut.

Their retreat left the south side of the farm unprotected, and Colonel Cubières of the First Légère led a charge around the side of the farm towards the north gate on his horse, but he was shot and wounded by snipers positioned in the rafters. Realizing the charge had faltered, a huge French soldier called Legros (nicknamed by his friends *L'Enfonceur*, the Smasher), snatched an axe from a French pioneer soldier and led a squad of men charging after the Guards to the north gate.

The defenders shut the gates and put up a furious fire, but the wall was so high it was difficult to bring the French attackers into their sights without being shot from below. After several failed attempts, Legros used his massive power to smash the gates open. Then he and about thirty Frenchmen, plus a drummer boy, charged into the yard. Macdonnell, fearing the farm was about to fall, led four of his men – Captain Wyndham, Ensigns Gooch and Hervey and Corporal James Graham of the Coldstream Guards – through the melee to close the gates.

Risking their lives, they forced the gates shut, trapping Legros and his followers in the farmyard, where they were shot or clubbed with rifle butts and then hacked to death with swords and bayonets; none but one of the Frenchmen was shown mercy. Private Clay, who was in the thick of the action, wrote in his memoirs that they spared 'no one inside but a drummer boy without his drum, whom I lodged in a stable or outhouse; many of the wounded of both armies were arranged side by side, having no means of carrying them to a place of greater safety'.

Clay also recalled seeing Corporal Graham, a twenty-four-year-old Irishman from Clones, County Monaghan, 'carrying a large piece of wood or trunk of a tree in his arms… with which he was hastening to secure the gates against the renewed attack of the enemy'. As Graham jammed the wood against the gate, a French soldier scaled the top of the gate with the intention of opening it from the inside. Wyndham shouted at Graham, who snatched up his musket from Wyndham and shot the French rifleman dead.

From the ridge, Wellington could see smoke rising from the barns of Hougoumont far over to the right of the battlefield. Focusing with his telescope, he saw flames spreading from the haystack to the barn and leaping across to the roof of the château. The Duke hurriedly scribbled a note to Macdonnell insisting that even the burning ruins were to be defended to the last:

> I see that the fire has communicated itself from the hay stack to the roof of the Château. You must however still keep your men in those parts to which the fire does not reach. Take care that no Men are lost by the falling in of the Roof or floors. After they will have fallen in, occupy the Ruined Walls inside of the Garden, particularly if it should be possible for the Enemy to pass through the Embers to the Inside of the House.

Many of the injured had been laid in the barn and men were still firing among the burning rafters in the roof. Corporal Graham asked Macdonnell for permission to leave his post as flames shot through the roof of the great barn, to drag his injured brother Joseph from the fire. Many were burned alive as the timbers crashed down in flames from the floors above, and guards who had been in the roof fell through the burning floors. Joseph Graham survived for five days before dying from his injuries. James Graham, one of three brothers who had enlisted in 1813, was promoted to sergeant for his bravery after the battle.

Colonel (later Lieutenant General) Sir Alex Woodford of the Coldstream Guards wrote: 'Some officers attempting to penetrate into the stables to rescue some wounded men were obliged to desist from the suffocation of the smoke and several men perished. The flames, as is well known, stopped at the little chapel. The French never, as far as I recollect, got into the garden. They were in the orchard but did not scale the garden walls.'[3]

Two months later, in August 1815, a vicar from Framlington in Suffolk, the Rev. Norcross, was so moved by the tales of heroism at Waterloo that he wrote to Wellington in Paris to offer a pension of £10 a year for life for any soldier he nominated. Wellington passed the letter to Sir John Byng to nominate one of the Guards. Byng chose Graham for his action at Hougoumont; the army sergeant from County Monaghan became famous as the 'Bravest Man in the British Army'. The vicar went bankrupt, however, and his pension ran out after two years. Graham died comfortably but in relative obscurity in his native Ireland, in the Royal Hospital of Kilmainham, aged fifty-four, in 1845.

Hougoumont today appears just as it did in sketches made shortly after the battle. Michael Farrar and I walk past a wood, along a farm track. I can hear the rush of the traffic on the RO, but Hougoumont is quiet. The only danger these days is from the cows in the field, which seem to be giving me a hostile look. Perhaps that is because they are not used to visitors.

I expected Hougoumont to be occupied, with smoke curling from a chimney, a Wellington *café de thé* offering Belgian chocolates, Napoleon farmhouse biscuits and Josephine gâteaux, but Hougoumont looks abandoned.

We walk to the north gate through which the courageous Legros and his followers smashed their way in. The yard where they were killed is unchanged, but the wooden gates have gone, replaced by wire-mesh fencing, which is chained to a gatepost and bolted. We are confronted by a sign pinned to the fence: 'Keep Out'. Beyond it, the farmyard and the farm buildings look deserted and forlorn.

Wellington said after the battle: 'The success of the battle turned upon closing the gates at Hougoumont.' If so, the course of Europe was decided here. Yet right now, it looks forgotten.

The château was left a smouldering ruin after the battle, and was never rebuilt. There are a few great stones left, now overgrown by rough grass. The farmyard, though, remains achingly atmospheric. Peering through the mesh of the steel fence, it is easy to imagine the deafening roar of battle, the shouted orders and the cries and screams of the many men who died on this spot. I feel a prickle of the hairs on the back of my neck; the poignancy of Hougoumont's past hangs in the air like a cold cloud of sadness.

With my guide, I walk around the long red-brick barn that runs the entire length of the south side of the farm. This is where the hayrick caught fire and where Colonel Cubières was shot from his horse.

The track takes us round to the front of the huge gatehouse, the towering main entrance to the farm where the French were cut down in their thousands. All that remains of the wood where Prince Jérôme's *tirailleurs*, or riflemen, kept up their lethal fire on the farm, are three elm trees; two are grey and dying, like Jérôme's men. The gatehouse is still intact. It looks just as it must have done to Jérôme's advancing troops – formidable.

There are pantiles missing from the roof of the barn adjoining the gatehouse, as if they have just been knocked out by Corporal Graham and the Coldstream Guards to give them clear lines of fire down at the attackers. The two great windows in the gatehouse and the attic window where Macdonnell's sharpshooters took up position are still there, but boarded up. It must have been like shooting at apples in a barrel.

The enormous dark blue carriage gates are locked and bolted just as they were throughout the siege. A wall to the right of the gatehouse seems colossal and impossible to scale; it forms a right angle with the gatehouse, like a trap. Men stormed the building with little hope of breaching its defences. The sketch made after the battle shows an open pit near this spot, with bodies being tumbled into it. I look around but can find no marker of a mass grave.

To our right, the long garden wall where hundreds died is still standing, though it is propped up here and there by timbers. Astonishingly, the fireloops that Macdonnell's men hacked out of the wall with their bayonets are intact after two hundred years, still looking out onto the grass where Jérôme's infantry were cut down.

We walk around the north side to see if we can gain entrance through the old orchard, just as Jérôme's men did. We squeeze over a barbed wire fence by a tree and find ourselves in the orchard. It feels like being a child again, hopping over a wall to scrump some apples but the apple trees have gone, and the ground is overgrown with coarse grass.

Jérôme's troops skirted the wall and came this way, only to be cut down among the apple trees before most of them could reach the walls of the formal garden screening the back of the château. The barbed wire I climbed over was put there to keep out the cattle, but they must have found their own way in. The grass where the French attackers died is a minefield of cowpats.

I tiptoe between the cowpats to the long garden wall over to the left, and stoop down to look through a fireloop just as Private Clay and his fellow soldiers would have done. It must have been terrifying to see the charging troops coming at them as they fired their muskets at point-blank range.

In the overgrown orchard there is a solitary obelisk. It stands as a monument to the bravery of the Frenchmen who fell here. It is topped by the imperial eagle proudly carried into battles all over Europe by Napoleon's legions, and it bears a quotation from Napoleon on its base: 'The earth seems proud to carry so many brave men.' Nearby are two overgrown stone slabs, covered in lichen. They are the gravestones of two British soldiers: Captain John Lucie Blackman of the Coldstream Guards, who was killed in the fighting and buried on this spot, and Sergeant Major Cotton, who survived the battle to become a battlefield guide and died in old-age.

Hougoumont was still a working farm with a tenant farmer until a few years ago. Somebody has tried to smarten up the walls around the farmyard with whitewash, but it is discoloured and peeling. More fences prevent intruders like me exploring further; we are barred from the farmyard and its barns.

It seems remarkable, given its importance, that, at the time of my visit at least, Hougoumont is officially out of bounds to visitors. But there is a reason.

Like a miracle, the little chapel that was attached to the château remains standing. The chapel's most prized possession was a priceless fifteenth-century cross with Christ nailed to it. The crucifix was nearly six feet high and still bore the marks of the fire from the siege on Christ's feet. Injured soldiers sheltered beneath it when the barns and the château were in flames all around them. Like the cross, and the chapel, they were untouched by the fire, which truly seemed miraculous. But the cross was stolen in February 2011, which is why the Belgian authorities circled Hougoumont with a steel fence.

Recently the chapel has been painted a brilliant white and its little spire has been painted black. It looks incongruously smart against the dilapidation around it. My guide is polite, but he seems not too happy at the whitewashing of the chapel's rustic red-brick walls. He fears the atmosphere that hangs over Hougoumont could be lost if it is 'over-restored'. 'I like it looking like that,' Farrar tells me as we stand gazing at the farm. 'I don't want them to come and restore it and put a tea room in it.'

Later, looking around Hougoumont as the sun sinks low, he adds: 'It is full of ghosts.' Fourteen thousand French infantry were thrown at Hougoumont's walls, and about eight thousand were killed or injured. The allied losses numbered about fifteen hundred, including 348 Coldstream Guards.

We return to the ridge to scout out the land, as Wellington must have done in the hurried preparations to meet Napoleon's army after the Emperor's escape from exile on the Mediterranean island of Elba. Nearby, a farmer is piling up a pyramid of sugar beet in a perfect thirty-foot-high reproduction of the Lion Mound at the top of the slope. It is part of the European food mountain. Is it what this victory was for?

Napoleon had been back for one hundred days. He had slipped past the Royal Navy and landed at Antibes on the south coast of France. Then he had marched through the mountains to the Alps near Mégève – a route now remembered fondly in Michelin guides as *La Route Napoléon* – before heading north to reclaim Paris. He had gathered supporters as he went. Marshal Michel Ney, his old ally, had been sent to intercept him, but Ney, like his army, had defected to the Emperor. Bonaparte had retaken power in Paris after the Bourbon King, Louis XVIII, had fled to Ghent.

Napoleon Bonaparte was a charismatic and ruthless military leader who had risen through the ranks and proclaimed himself Emperor to impose order after the chaos of the French Revolution, the Reign of Terror, the guillotining of King Louis XVI in 1793 and the creation of the French Republic. With his gift for inspiring loyalty in others and his communication skills (he coined *bons mots* like a Hollywood scriptwriter), he could take Europe by storm today without firing a shot, as a charismatic political leader, a media mogul, or a combination of the two – like Silvio Berlusconi, Italy's former president.

Until the Terror took hold, the Revolution, which drew its inspiration from the founding fathers of America, had been welcomed by some liberal thinkers in England. Paris attracted writers such as Wordsworth and Charles Dickens – an avowed republican – as well as social reformers. Revolutionaries such as George Danton wanted to go further, to chop off the heads of the monarchs of the rest of Europe in the name of the people. France began exporting revolution by declaring war on the Netherlands, Italy and Britain. That led to war across Europe lasting a generation. It ended – or the leaders of Germany, the Netherlands, Belgium and Britain thought it had – when Napoleon had been forced to abdicate after a humiliating retreat from Moscow and the forced roll-back of his forces in the Iberian peninsula in response to the tactics of a brilliant young British general, Arthur Wellesley.

Napoleon had been packed off to Elba, while the European leaders restored to themselves much of the territory he had taken with the 1814 Treaty of Paris. Given his lust for power, it is difficult to see how they believed that Napoleon would be satisfied with occupying a small island patrolled by the Royal Navy. Perhaps it was the power of hope over experience.

The last hope of stopping him now lay in Wellesley. He was the third son of the First Earl of Mornington, from an Anglo-Irish family with an estate in County Meath. Arthur had been an unpromising boy until he bought a commission in the army. While he toiled as a soldier, his older brother Richard had inherited the family title and gone off to rule the Raj as Governor General of India. Arthur had spent a disconsolate time campaigning in the Low Countries under Prince Frederick, the Duke of York, whose indecision inspired the nursery rhyme: 'The grand old Duke of York / He had ten thousand men / He marched them up to the top of the hill / and he marched them down again'. Wellesley said the experience had taught him a great lesson in how not to conduct a war. Arthur's military career took off when he joined his brother in India. The Governor General's patronage put a few more senior officers' noses out of joint, but Wellesley answered his critics with his conduct in the field: he led a series of spectacular victories against the sultan states. It denied the ambitions of the French to occupy part of India, and enabled Britain to tighten its grip on this corner of its Empire.

Wellesley used the experience he gained in India to force Napoleon's armies to retreat from Portugal and Spain and returned home a hero. In 1814, he was ennobled by a grateful nation as the First Duke of Wellington. It seemed as if he would live out his life as a Tory politician, until, that is, Napoleon escaped.

Wellington was attending the postwar talks at Paris and the Congress of Vienna when the news came that 'Boney' had landed in the South of France. Wellington was hurriedly put back in the saddle, as commander of the allied forces of Europe, alongside the separate Prussian army under Gebhard Leberecht von Blücher. Blücher was seventy-two but a tough old warhorse, and he hated the revolutionary French. Wellington and Blücher mustered about one hundred and twenty thousand men, nearly twice the size of Napoleon's army, on the border of Belgium, then part of the United Netherlands, intending to march on Paris.

Napoleon, following a strategy that had succeeded in the past, struck first. His aim was to prevent Wellington and Blücher from uniting their forces and to defeat them separately, and it nearly worked. Wellington admitted later: 'It has been a damn nice thing – the nearest run thing you ever saw.'

Napoleon and Wellington were both aged forty-six. It was the first time they had faced each other in battle, and the Emperor underrated the Duke, despite Wellington's string of victories against Napoleon's generals in Portugal and Spain. When a member of the Emperor's staff praised Wellington at a dinner at Le Caillou, a cottage near the Waterloo battlefield, he snapped back: 'I tell you, Wellington is a bad general, the English are bad troops and this affair is nothing more serious than eating one's breakfast.'

Wellington had a higher opinion of the little Emperor. The Duke regarded Napoleon as a military genius, worth forty thousand troops, and shared his view of the allied army. The Duke privately admitted he had been put in charge of 'an infamous army, very weak and ill-equipped'.[4] But then he was never very complimentary about the Belgians and the Dutch either.

The British still like to pride themselves on 'winning' the Battle of Waterloo, but the overwhelming majority of Wellington's army came from the rest of Europe. The Hanoverians, Nassauers, Dutch Belgians, the King's German Legion and the Duchy of Brunswick fielded forty-three thousand men – sixty-four per cent of Wellington's army. Only 23,991, thirty-five per cent of the total, were British, and it's worth stating outright that many came from Ireland and Scotland. It was a truly European victory. The British contingent comprised fifteen thousand infantry, nearly six thousand cavalry, three thousand artillery soldiers and seventy-eight guns. In all, Wellington had sixty-seven thousand men and 156 guns on the ridge, and was facing a French force of sixty-eight thousand men and 246 guns ranged across the opposing slopes less than a mile away.

Napoleon still excites hero worship in France. His aphorisms, tossed out like coins, included: 'A leader is a dealer in hope', and 'Courage is like love, it must have hope for nourishment'. Napoleon's escape from Elba in February 1815 after three hundred days of exile gave his loyal French supporters the hope that they could rise again to become masters of Europe. It was just like the old glory days, except Napoleon was past his prime. He was running to fat and suffering from piles, which made riding difficult that day.

In stark contrast, Wellington, hawk-like with sharp eyes and a nose like a raptor's beak, seemed to be everywhere on the battlefield.

The Duke was not loved by his men – he called them 'the scum of the earth' – but he was respected. He cut a distinctive figure riding the ridge on Copenhagen with his staff close by. Having slept overnight in Waterloo, he shaved, breakfasted lightly on tea and toast, and, assisted by his valet, dressed in a blue frock coat worn over the gold knotted sash of a Spanish field marshal, with a blue cloak to shield himself from the rain, white buckskin breeches and hessian boots.* At his neck, he wore a white stock or high cravat (a style promoted by the Regency dandy Beau Brummel) and he sported a plain cocked hat with the black cockade of Britain with smaller ones for Spain, Portugal and the Netherlands. Thus, suitably attired as a gentleman going to war, at 7 a.m Wellington rode out to do battle with Napoleon.

In another of his sayings, Napoleon once advised his generals: 'Never interrupt your enemy when he is making a mistake.' Now it was Napoleon who made a series of blunders, which Wellington was happy to exploit.

~✐~

---

* A portrait painted in 1815 to commemorate the battle shows Wellington wearing the soft calf-length leather boots, made to his specification by Hoby of St James's. They became known as Wellington Boots, but he did not wear them at the Battle of Waterloo.

Napoleon's three-hour delay in launching the battle at Waterloo proved a fatal error. In his novel *Les Misérables*, Victor Hugo blamed the weather for Napoleon's defeat at Waterloo: 'Had it not rained on the night of 17–18 June 1815 the future of Europe would have been different… an unseasonably clouded sky sufficed to bring about the collapse of a World.' The great writer was peddling a patriotic French myth to excuse the Emperor for having a bad day. It was not the rain that defeated Napoleon. It was bad judgement. The three hours' delay crucially gave the redoubtable Blücher vital time to come to Wellington's aid before Wellington's line had been broken.

The importance of this delay did not become clear until years after the battle when Lieutenant William Siborne was commissioned to produce a large and detailed model of the battlefield. Siborne, like a good journalist, went back to original sources to build his meticulous model; he wrote to scores of veterans who had served at the battle for their recollections and eye-witness accounts; he spent eight months surveying the battlefield; and he discovered an uncomfortable truth about Wellington's great victory: he owed it to Blücher.

Siborne's model showed Blücher arriving on the field of battle with his Prussian troops earlier than the Duke had admitted in his Waterloo despatch, and with much greater impact, by threatening Napoleon's right wing before the centre had started its retreat. Siborne implied that Wellington had downplayed the impact of Blücher's forty thousand Prussian troops to claim more credit for the victory for himself.

Wellington dismissed Siborne's account as 'mistaken', demanding that the Prussian troops on his model be removed. Siborne insisted his account was accurate. In effect, Siborne was calling Wellington a liar. Wellington had his revenge by ensuring that the Waterloo model was rejected by the War Office, despite being a popular hit and attracting an audience of one hundred thousand when it was put on display at the Egyptian Hall, Piccadilly.

It is now on display at the National Army Museum next to Chelsea Hospital, where Siborne died in 1851, with a copy at the Royal Armouries, Leeds. Wellington had his way: most of the tin Prussian soldiers were removed.

~⟨⟩~

Napoleon made another blunder over the assault on Hougoumont. He never saw its strategic importance; as a result, he failed to advance his guns to blast holes in the walls that would have allowed Jérôme to take the farm.

We drive to the crossroads, and park by a bus shelter under the shade of some tall elm trees. This is where Wellington established his field head-quarters, within sight of Napoleon's battery of heavy twelve-pounders, the guns the Emperor called his 'beautiful daughters'. Their roar could be heard in Dover.

One elm tree from this spot was felled in 1818, and twenty years later it was turned into two chairs, for the Duke and the young Queen Victoria. The land falls gently away behind us on the Brussels side. This is the reverse slope, where Wellington concealed most of his infantry.

To the south and Charleroi, where Napoleon's forces crossed the border from France, the road descends a gentle slope. Not far below the ridge is another farmhouse, La Haye Sainte, which was also bitterly fought over during the battle because it protected Wellington's centre.

About a mile away, the farm fields rise up from a dip in the land to a white farmhouse. This is the inn where Napoleon established his field headquarters. It was called *La Belle Alliance* by its hopeful landlady after she had married her fourth husband. Napoleon's main gun battery was in the field just below the inn. Concealed in a hedge, there is still a raised platform that may have been used by the Emperor to survey the battlefield.

Siborne's account of the battle says: 'The formation of the French lines was scarcely completed when the magnificent and animated spectacle which they presented was heightened in an extraordinary degree by the passing of the Emperor along them, attended by a numerous and brilliant staff. The troops hailed him with loud and fervent acclamations. There was depicted on their brows a deep-rooted confidence in his ability, with such an army, to chain victory to the car in which he had already advanced in triumph to within a few miles of the capital of Belgium.'

It was about 2 p.m. Wellington stationed some riflemen in a sandpit by La Haye Sainte farmhouse; they could clearly see Napoleon saluting his troops as about a third of the French army marched in dark blue packed ranks towards them. It was a petrifying sight for a soldier armed only with a rifle. Wellington's riflemen quickly retreated behind the thin red lines on the ridge.

Wellington was able to study his adversary through his telescope from his own vantage point by the crossroads. In the heat of the battle, one of his gunners asked for permission to target Napoleon, who, in his blue coat, white breeches and bicorne hat, was easy to identify on the opposing hillside. Wellington brushed aside his request. 'It is not the business of commanders to be firing upon each other,' said the Duke. The French batteries had no such concerns. Where the bus stop now stands with a plastic canopy, it was raining cannon balls on Wellington and his staff.

Wellington had never lacked courage, but he seemed to have a charmed life that day. He came through without a scratch, though most of his staff were killed or injured. Sir William de Lancey was killed by a cannon ball that suddenly bounced up and hit him in the back while he was on his horse, speaking to the Duke. Lord FitzRoy Somerset (later Lord Raglan, the doddery commander of British forces in the Crimean War) was hit in the right arm by a musket ball fired from La Haye Sainte, requiring it to be amputated at the elbow; he told the surgeons: 'Don't carry away that arm until I've taken off my ring.'

In one of the last salvoes of the battle, Henry Paget, the Earl of Uxbridge, was hit in the leg by grapeshot that had passed over Wellington's horse. Uxbridge exclaimed: 'By God, sir, I've lost my leg!' to which Wellington replied: 'By God sir, so you have.' This may seem an extraordinarily terse exchange, even for the stiff-upper-lip British, but the two men were on unusually bad terms. Six years earlier, Paget had run off with Lady Charlotte, the wife of Wellington's brother, Henry Wellesley. Despite the obvious difficulties between them, the Earl was put in charge of the whole of the allied cavalry and horse artillery, and had earlier in the day distinguished himself, leading a famous cavalry charge to break d'Erlon's infantry.

Uxbridge cheerfully survived the amputation, telling Wellington's aide-de-camp: 'I've been a beau for forty-seven years and it would not be fair to cut the young men out any longer.' His leg was buried in the garden of the house in Waterloo that was used as a field hospital, and given its own headstone. The 'grave' of Uxbridge's leg and the chair on which he sat to have it amputated were gruesome tourist attractions for many years. A false leg used by Uxbridge, which became a model for the British army, is one of the more bizarre items in the Horse Guards museum in Whitehall.

Only one member of Wellington's staff escaped uninjured, the Hon. Major Henry Percy, who was sent to London by Wellington immediately after the battle with the Duke's report of his victory. The despatch was carried to Downing Street in a ladies' purple velvet handkerchief purse, which had been given to Percy as a keepsake on the eve of the battle by an admirer at the Duchess of Richmond's summer ball.

The ball was one of the more surreal events surrounding the battle. It was held in a coach-house at the rear of the Richmonds' elegant rented town house (now replaced by hideous modern office blocks). Many of the society ladies of Europe flocked to the ball like moths to a flame, enjoying the proximity to the danger of war. They included Lady Caroline Lamb, the wife of William Lamb MP, later Lord Melbourne, who would become Queen Victoria's first Prime Minister. (Lady Caroline had become notorious two years earlier because of her very public and tempestuous affair with the poet Lord Byron.) As Napoleon marched on Brussels, the Gordon Highlanders danced reels and rich and fashionable ladies swirled in their Regency finery to the new craze, the Waltz. Many of the young officers with whom they danced, sipped champagne and flirted would be left dead or injured on the battlefield. As Lady Caroline wrote: 'There never was such a Ball – so fine and so sad. All the young men who appeared there shot dead a few days after.'

The casualties included her own brother, Colonel Sir Frederick Ponsonby, a cavalry officer. He survived after being hacked by sabres, run through by a lance and left for dead, and she nursed him back to health in London.

These days you take your life in your hands by crossing the main Charleroi–Brussels road. We wait for the lights to change and then run for our lives, dodging the juggernauts, and reach the other side with relief. The ridge continues for another mile or so to some trees on the eastern end of the battlefield, where Blücher arrived in the nick of time. The ridge road is closed to traffic because it is being dug up by the local water board, allowing us to walk along it without fear of being mown down.

There are two small standing stones on either side of the track. They look like milestones, but they are key memorials of the battle. One marks the spot where Sir Thomas Picton was killed in a truly heroic action. A Welshman, he was leading the Anglo-Dutch infantry but had seen his Dutch–Belgian infantry panic and fall back; cursing in his usual manner, Picton, on horseback, stood firm. His three thousand men in two thin lines faced an attack by the massed blue ranks of twelve thousand French infantry under d'Erlon, who shouted 'Vive l'Empereur!' as they reached the crest of the hill. Lieutenant General Picton was fifty-seven, and had a premonition he would be killed; he had overslept and had quickly donned his civilian clothes, including a top hat, for the battle. He saw the French suddenly halt and ordered his men to fire a volley; seizing the moment, with the French caught by surprise, he shouted for the charge. As he did so, he was shot through the right temple. He was the highest-ranking British officer to die in the Battle of Waterloo. He became so famous in death that towns in Ontario and New Zealand were named after him.

Nearby, on the opposite side of the track, leaning at an angle after the excavations of the water board, is a memorial stone to the Twenty-seventh Inniskilling Regiment, and the hundreds of men who were cut down on this spot. Its brass plaque is a classic example of British understatement: 'Of the 747 officers and men of the Regiment who joined battle, 493 were killed or wounded. A noble record of endurance.'

It marks one of the most famous parts of the battle when Ney ordered the French cavalry to charge, thinking, wrongly, that Wellington's forces were in retreat. As the French horses thundered over the ridge, the allied infantry formed a series of defensive squares on the plateau. The square, arranged with bayonets pointing out like the spines of a porcupine, was the only way of protecting infantry in the open against the sabres of the cavalry at full gallop, but under sustained cannon fire, they could be ripped apart. It required nerves of iron to stay in formation. An ensign in the First Foot Guards wrote:

> At 4 o'clock our square was a perfect hospital, being full of dead, dy-ing and mutilated soldiers. The charges of cavalry were in appearance very formidable, but in reality a great relief as the artillery could no longer fire on us; the very earth shook under the enormous mass of men and horses. I shall never forget the strange noise our bullets made against the breastplates of the cuirassiers, six or seven thousand in number who attacked us with great fury.[5]

Eleven times the French cavalry charged the squares of red tunics on the plateau and were beaten back, like waves on rocks. The day after the bat-tle, Wellington inspected the field and saw the bodies of the Inniskilling Regiment on the ground, still in square formation.

The climax of the battle came at around 7 p.m. when the thin red line of British infantry above Hougoumont was wavering and Napoleon called up his Imperial Guard to deliver a crushing blow that would lead to a French victory. Wellington had anticipated the move, and ordered Major General Maitland's First Brigade of Guards to form a line four deep to meet them. As they did so, Napoleon's battery opened fire at the lines of red tunics on the ridge. They flung themselves into a ditch and crouched against a bank, where they were hammered by Napoleon's battery of cannon.

Once the bombardment ended, Napoleon's élite guards advanced. When they were yards away, the Foot Guards were ordered to stand up and fire. For the first time in their long history, Napoleon's 'invincible' Imperial Guard faltered.

Captain H.W. Powell of the First Foot Guards gave a vivid eye-witness account:

> Suddenly… as the smoke cleared away a most superb sight opened on us. A close column of grenadiers of la Moyenne Garde, about six thousand strong, led by Marshal Ney were seen ascending the rise *au pas de charge* shouting 'Vive l'Empereur.' They continued to advance till within fifty or sixty paces of our front, when the brigade were ordered to stand up. Whether it was from the sudden and unexpected appearance of a corps so near them, which must have seemed as starting out of the ground, or the tremendously heavy fire we threw into them, *La Garde*, who had never before failed in an attack suddenly stopped. Those who from a distance and more on the flank could see the affair, tell us that the effect of our fire seemed to force the head of the column bodily back. In less than a minute above 300 were down.[6]

Watching from the ridge, Wellington saw that Napoleon's finest troops were cracking. Wellington rode to his men, and shouted: 'Now, Maitland! Now is your time.' Throwing caution to the wind, the Duke stood up in his stirrups as the French veterans faltered and waved his hat in the air, hailing his men: 'Go on. They won't stand. Don't give them time to rally.' It was only when they heard the command for the general advance that the defenders at Hougoumont knew they had survived.

For the Emperor, it was the last throw of the dice. The Prussians swarming in from the east captured his baggage train and ransacked his jewels as he fled to Paris and then the coast. Napoleon tried to escape to America, a revolutionary ally, but was trapped at Rochefort and surren-dered to the Royal Navy rather than go as a prisoner of the Bourbons back to France. He wrote to the Prince Regent seeking protection: 'Your royal Highness… I have ended my political career and come, like Themistocles to seat myself at the hearth of the British people. I put myself under the protection of her laws and address this entreaty to Your Highness as the most powerful, the most steadfast and the most generous of my foes.'

If the Prince knew the name Themistocles (a populist Athenian general who suffered exile but was praised after his death as the saviour of Greece), the reference failed to do the trick. Napoleon was sent into exile again, this time on the much more remote island of St Helena in the South Atlantic. First, though, he became a tourist attraction on a British warship, HMS *Bellerophon*, while it was moored for ten days in the bay at Brixham and Plymouth Sound. At least he was not executed like Ney, who was shot by firing squad for treason in the Jardin de Luxembourg in Paris on 7 December 1815. Napoleon died on 5 May 1821, apparently from stomach cancer though there are persistent reports he was poisoned.

Victory for Wellington was complete although the carnage was appalling. Napoleon had lost twenty-five thousand men in the battle and another eight thousand in the retreat, but Wellington suffered fifteen thousand casualties and Blücher a further seven thousand, leading Wellington to comment: 'Nothing except a battle lost can be half so melancholy as a battle won.'

It was a line he reworked many times, but it was near to the truth.

The day after the battle, piles of bodies were put in pits on the battlefield, or were burned by peasants who covered their mouths and noses with handkerchiefs.[7] It is also estimated that at least twelve thousand horses died at Waterloo, and their carcasses were piled high in huge smoking pyres.

Horses pulling tourist carriages from Brussels shied at the smell of death in the fields at Mont-Saint-Jean. One of the tourists in the following months was Lord Byron. He was disappointed to discover how quickly the fields had been returned to the plough but bought some battlefield souvenirs, soldiers' badges bearing the French eagle and a round musket shot, which he sent to his publisher, John Murray, in St James's. They are still in the publishing house's collection.

Weeks after the battle, the Duke still wept over dinner when the casualty list was raised. He was most moved to discover that his much-liked aide-de-camp Sir Alexander Gordon had died in his cot at the inn where he wrote his despatch, after having his leg amputated without anaesthetic. He wrote to Gordon's brother, Lord Aberdeen, hoping the battle would lead to lasting peace: 'I hope that it may be expected that this last one has been so decisive, as that no doubt remains that our exertions and our individual losses will be rewarded by the early attainment of our just object.'

Victory at Waterloo brought to an end almost twenty-five years of continuous war in Europe. It enabled the nations of Europe who had suffered so much at Napoleon's hands to reaffirm the status quo they had agreed weeks before the Battle of Waterloo at the Congress of Vienna, chaired by the Austrian statesman Metternich. It was a deeply conservative agreement, buttressing the European monarchies. However, the fear that revolution in France could still infect the rest of Europe continued to haunt European capitals, and it led to an over-reaction to try to suppress it.

Nowhere was that more true than in Britain. Wellington had won the war for Europe in Waterloo, but at home, Britain was at war with itself.

This was the glorious age of the Regency. Prince George had launched his Regency in 1811 with a lavish party at Carlton House where the dinner service alone cost £60,000. But many of Wellington's troops who fought at Waterloo and enlisted through poverty returned home to destitution after the battle.

The Enclosure Acts of 1809 forced many off the land by denying them access to farmland, previously held in common ownership for a few cows and a vegetable patch. John Clare, the country poet, witnessed the biggest change to rural life for a thousand years from his mother's cottage in Helpston, Northamptonshire and raged against it in rhyme:

> Thus came enclosure – ruin was its guide
> But freedom's clapping hands enjoyed the sight
> Tho comforts cottage soon was thrust aside
> And workhouse prisons raised upon the scite
> Een nature's dwellings far away from men
> The common heath, became the spoiler's prey
> The rabbit had not where to make his den
> And labour's only cow was drove away[8]

The rural poor were driven into factories, or as Clare says, workhouse prisons in the northern towns. They exchanged impoverished rural cottages for slums and the 'Satanic mills' foreseen by the poet William Blake in Britain's burgeoning industrial cities. They were forced to live in places that could have come from the pages of Charles Dickens's novel *Hard Times* and the home of Mr Gradgrind, Coketown imagined there:

> In the innermost fortifications of that ugly citadel, where Nature was as strongly bricked out as killing airs and gases were bricked in; at the heart of the labyrinth of narrow courts upon courts, and close streets upon streets… where the chimneys, for want of air to make a draught, were built in an immense variety of stunted and crooked shapes… lived a certain Stephen Blackpool.

The population had risen in one decade from 8.9 million to 10.2 million by 1811,[9] and Britain was straining to breaking point under the cost of the Napoleonic wars, which had forced William Pitt to introduce income tax for the first time.

Prince George had delusions of grandeur and aped the lavish imperial style of the Emperor Napoleon. He led the ambitious rebuilding of the capital in the elegant Anglo-Renaissance style we now know as Regency. He encouraged the Government to commission John Nash to replace tenements, slums and shops with Regent Street, sweeping from Regent's Park to his own graceful mini-palace, Carlton House (since demolished).

Britain was a country of two nations: the rich minority who ruled the poor masses. Private wealth also contrasted with public austerity, far greater than the cuts in public expenditure we have seen in recent years. The public purse was so drained that Waterloo Bridge, the official monument to the battle, had to be funded by private subscription.

Waterloo Bridge was opened with great pomp and ceremony in 1817. The Duke of Wellington marched across it to the sound of cannon firing a salute to equal the number of guns seized at Waterloo. But after the bunting came down, travellers were charged a toll of a penny to cross it.

Factory owners grew fat on the trade that war brought, while many workers saw wages fall as new machines such as the Spinning Jenny or Whitney's gin, a cotton rotation machine, did the work of ten labourers or more. Some fought against the poverty, and smashed the new machines that threw weavers out of work overnight. They burned down mills and became known as Luddites (after an eighteenth-century rebel industrial worker), despite risking the death penalty or deportation to Australia. Byron spoke up for them in the House of Lords, but the Government of Lord Liverpool – a man who feared reform would lead to revolution, as in France – opted for repression to keep the lower classes in order.

Vast fortunes made from overseas plantations, coal mines and textile mills were squandered on Regency luxuries by the rich, while for the poor the price of bread went up. Parliament passed the Importation Act in 1815 – the year of Waterloo – to impose a tariff on cheap imports of corn, thus raising the price of bread to protect the profits of British farmers (the landed gentry, who reaped the rewards of their tenant workers).

A natural catastrophe that year made the hardship even worse. The eruption of the Tambora volcano in the Dutch East Indies remains the biggest volcanic eruption in recorded history. It blacked out the sun with its ash, causing a temporary change in the climate and ruined the harvest right across Europe for more than a year. It may have been the cause of the unseasonal rain at Waterloo and was blamed for making 1816 a 'year without a summer'.

There has been plenty of controversy in Britain about the causes of the summer riots in 2011 and the violent protests by students against the introduction of university tuition fees, but they have one direct link to what happened in Britain in the aftermath of Waterloo. They are a reminder that Britain has frequently been disfigured by street riots. At least the students and the inner-city rioters had the vote. In the early nineteenth century, the poor had none. The democratic disconnect between the 'haves' and 'have-nots' in 1815 led to violent riots in the streets. The difference between then and now is that these were food riots – demands for the basic right to eat – by people who were facing starvation.

Britain had become the world's first industrialized country, but its democracy was hopelessly out of date. Many of the mushrooming northern cities did not have a single MP and Henry 'Orator' Hunt, a wealthy farmer and self-appointed champion of the masses, drew huge audiences (eighty thousand people in Birmingham) to hear him call for Parliamentary reform.

The bloated Prince Regent, later George IV, seemed to embody the disregard with which the rich viewed the poor. He was pilloried in the popular press by cartoonists such as James Gillray and George Cruikshank as a lecherous glutton. As he was returning to Buckingham Palace after the State Opening of Parliament, his carriage was surrounded by protesters and one of its windows was broken. It was probably only a stone, but he claimed it was an assassination attempt.

The attack on the Prince and the public disorder gave the Government the excuse to introduce more repressive laws – Habeas Corpus, the right to be freed from unlawful detention, was suspended and the Seditious Meetings Act was passed by Parliament to curb private clubs and societies that might be plotting the overthrow of the Government.

England was a tinder box, and a spark would lead to another tragedy. It came on the hot summer's day of 19 August 1819, when Hunt went to Manchester to address a mass public meeting at St Peter's Field near the centre of the town (near the G-Mex, where the Conservative and Labour parties now hold their annual conferences). His supporters had issued leaflets carrying a cartoon of a white worker on his knees in chains; it was a satire on the famous anti-slavery campaign logo – Britain had declared slavery illegal abroad but was still exploiting it at home. Sixty thousand people attended.

At 1.30 p.m., Hunt marched towards a couple of carts that had been lashed together to form a platform for the hustings (the site is in Windmill Street, across the road from the convention centre, at the glass and concrete rear of the Radisson Edwardian hotel). The band struck up 'See the Conquering Hero Comes' and – to show they were not being seditious – 'God Save the King'.

There was a carnival atmosphere but the Manchester magistrates, fearing revolution, sent in two troops of the local Manchester Yeomanry Cavalry to arrest the ringleaders as Hunt was speaking. They were not regular soldiers: many were tradesmen, and some were said to be drunk.

The militiamen cantered into the square, slashing people with their sabres as they went. Two bands of regular Hussars were called in and were ordered to disperse the crowd while the deputy constable went to arrest Hunt.

Sir John Byng, the soldier who commanded the Guards on Wellington's right wing at Waterloo, was in charge of the Northern Forces but he had no control of his men that day. A total of fifteen protesters were killed and over six hundred and fifty helpless victims were injured in only twenty minutes.

Over two hundred of the victims including women suffered sabre wounds; women were targeted because, dressed in white, they resembled *Marianne*, the figurehead of the French Revolution. A volunteer constable gloated to the crowd in St Peter's Field: 'This is Waterloo for you.' Within a week, the radical *Manchester Observer* newspaper coined the title, 'The Peterloo Massacre'.

The reactionary Lord Liverpool was Britain's Prime Minister from 1812 to 1827. When he suddenly died of a stroke, and George Canning, who replaced him, also died, and Canning's successor, the First Viscount Goderich, resigned, George IV called on Wellington to rescue the country from the crisis. Wellington was the greatest soldier the nation had ever produced but as a natural conservative and authoritarian, the Duke was not well suited to cope with the changes taking place in nineteenth-century Britain.

Wellington was fifty-eight, and rode his old warhorse, Copenhagen, to Downing Street to show the smack of firm government, but the demands for reform were not to be stopped as simply as Napoleon. He conceded Irish emancipation but held the line against wider, more liberal reforms: he was convinced that giving in to mob rule would lead to anarchy, the very collapse of society.

A patrician snob who believed in keeping the lower orders in their place, he vehemently opposed electoral reform. The hero worship for the victor of Waterloo turned to scorn. The mob stoned his windows at Apsley House, his town mansion at Hyde Park Corner, and he had iron shutters fitted to protect them, for which Wellington was ridiculed as 'the Iron Duke'. In 1830, he declared in a debate in the House of Lords that 'as long as he held any station in the government of the country, he should always feel it his duty to resist [reform] measures'. Hopelessly out of touch with public opinion, the saviour of Europe was forced out of office within a month. Sydney Smith wrote: 'Never was any administration so completely and so suddenly destroyed; and, I believe, entirely by the Duke's declaration, made, I suspect, in perfect ignorance of the state of public feeling and opinion.'

Britain teetered on the brink of becoming ungovernable when the Lords held up the reforms. Wellington was again called to form a crisis government, this time by William IV, but could not do so and eventually Wellington, the Lords and the King relented.

The Great Reform Act was passed in 1832. It granted representation in Parliament to the newly wealthy burghers of the northern towns and cities, raising the franchise by sixty per cent though the right to vote was based on property and it was still denied to women.

Wellington lived long enough to be revered as a pillar of the state in his old-age. He died, aged eighty-three, in 1852 at Walmer Castle in

Kent, his official residence as Lord Warden of the Cinque Ports, and was buried next to Lord Nelson in St Paul's Cathedral. His legacy was peace, for a time, on the continent of Europe.

~()~

Wellington's victory at Waterloo did not resolve the European 'problem' for Britain. Indeed, I suspect it encouraged a latent British feeling of superiority towards all foreigners that may well have exacerbated it.

Buoyed by the Royal Navy's dominance of the seas, achieved by Nelson's great victory at Trafalgar in 1805, Britain became the first superpower of the modern world. During the long Victorian era, it adopted a foreign policy posture described at the time as 'splendid Isolation' from Europe.

After Waterloo, Britain cast itself as the 'saviour of Europe', coming to the aid of its tiresome European neighbours only when it really had no other choice, in the Great War of 1914–18 and the Second World War in 1939.

Given this past, it is hardly surprising that Britain never really became a fully paid-up member of the European club in the twentieth century. The British still view the Continent from the wrong end of the telescope. Fog in the Channel is still interpreted as 'Europe cut off from Britain', even after the building of the Channel Tunnel.

The financial crisis surrounding the European single currency in 2011 and 2012 increased the impression in Britain that euroland is a place to be kept at arm's length. Demands for a referendum on Britain's continued membership of the European Union were resisted by political leaders of all the main parties, who clearly fear the popular verdict.

It is likely that when it comes time to mark the bicentenary of the Battle of Waterloo, it will be celebrated with another great European jamboree, with the emphasis on unity rather than our centuries-old Anglo-French rivalry. The current Duke of Wellington is spearheading the British contribution to the party through 'Waterloo 200'. As part of their contribution, the Belgians, who will be hosting the party, are planning to give the main battlefield centre at the Lion Mound a €28 million facelift, with 3-D films and smoke and noise special effects.

That could leave Hougoumont looking down at heel. A charity, Project Hougoumont, was set up in Britain to restore the farm, with generous support from the Belgian authorities of Walloon, but it ran into financial difficulties. It was launched in 2008 by Richard Holmes, the military historian and Wellington expert, to rescue the farm from further decay because of its historic importance. Part of the garden wall at Hougoumont was rebuilt, but much of the farm was still crumbling and the barn walls were still bulging when, sadly, Holmes died in 2011. Work was scheduled to start at Hougoumont in spring 2013 for completion within about a year. Walloon promised to provide most of the funding, but in the middle of a recession, the British were finding it difficult to raise matching resources. Professor Holmes said it would be a shame to see it fall down, but Britain's National Lottery cannot help finance the restoration of Hougoumont because it is on foreign soil. Alice Berkeley of Project Hougoumont told me: 'Hougoumont Farm is not a pretty sight these days... we are just waiting to raise enough money privately to convince the Walloonian authorities that we at Project Hougoumont can produce our share of the costs: about £2 million. Progress is slow.'

There is a monument to Victor Hugo, one of the first to speak about a 'United States of Europe', on the battlefield, near *La Belle Alliance* inn. It is a single column surmounted – in a typical Gallic flourish – by a crowing cock. (Anybody would think they had won the battle.) Oddly, though memorial stones are dotted about the battlefield, there is no great monument to the British at Waterloo.

There is no better place to mark Britain's contribution to the creation of a modern democratic Europe than at Waterloo, and specifically at the little farm at Hougoumont. Surely a few euromillions can be spared from the euromountain in Brussels, and who better to find it than the landlords of euroland, the Belgians?

THE FARM, HOUGOUMONT:
The state of the buildings in 2011.

SIX

1833

'I well remember… a conversation with Mr Pitt
in the open air at the root of an old tree at Holwood'

KESTON VALE, THE WEALD, KENT:
The site of the Wilberforce Oak.

Three young men strolled at ease, enjoying the spring sunshine, through the wooded parkland surrounding William Pitt's country house on 12 May 1787. They were talking about politics. All were in their twenty-seventh year, and at the beginning of long political careers which would place them high among the dominant political figures of the Georgian age. Pitt, known as 'the Younger' because of his father William's own towering political career, had already made his mark as the youngest Prime Minister in British history. Alongside Pitt were his intimate friend William Wilberforce and Pitt's cousin, William Grenville; Grenville would become Prime Minister after Pitt's death. But after this day, Wilberforce would arguably be the most famous of them all.

Holwood House, near the village of Keston in the North Weald of Kent, was a few hours' ride south from Downing Street in Pitt's phaeton, a four-wheeled carriage drawn by two horses, but it was a world away from the stress of office. Pitt's house was small and neat, and stucco-white, making it stand out brightly among the rolling wooded hills. The former hunting lodge had six bedrooms and was comfortable for a bachelor, but it was modest by the standards of the political leaders of the age. Pitt's predecessor, William Cavendish-Bentinck, the Third Duke of Portland, occupied Bulstrode, his family's stately home near Gerrard's Cross in Buckinghamshire, while he was Prime Minister.

A little over three years before, Pitt had become Prime Minister at the age of twenty-four and, as First Lord of the Treasury, he combined the job of running the country with being Chancellor of the Exchequer. It was a formidable challenge, but he had already shown his maturity, and his mettle, in turning a minority government, hounded by the Whigs under the leadership of the brilliant debater Charles James Fox, into a steady and popular administration that would last eight years.

When they came to a ridge beneath a canopy of oak trees, they sat down and Pitt raised an issue that he had been turning over in his mind. That spring Pitt had plenty on his mind. He had rejected a measure he would normally have supported, the repeal of the anti-Catholic Test Acts, which prevented Catholics and dissenting Protestants from holding public office, and he was wrangling with his conscience over it. His main preoccupation would have been familiar to modern Chancellors such as George Osborne in the age of austerity – he had to tackle a massive public debt burden after the costly disaster of the American Revolutionary War; debt interest payments consumed over half of the Government's annual revenues. Pitt raised the duty on the luxuries of the well-to-do, and secured a sinking fund to pay off debt. He was also becoming worried by the growing French influence in the Netherlands, which would soon see Britain dragged into France's revolutionary wars in Europe. In his second term in 1799, he adopted a novel solution to the rising cost of the war against Napoleon – the introduction of income tax.

These pressing issues of state were not foremost in Pitt's thoughts that afternoon, however. Rather, he was alarmed by some intelligence he had gleaned from his allies at the House of Commons: one of his arch rivals was about to take up a bill to abolish the slave trade. His friend Wilberforce – known as 'Wilber' by his family and a few close friends

– had been talking in private about Britain's role in the inhumane traffic for long enough; for Pitt, it was time for some action.

Wilberforce recalled years later: 'I was staying with Pitt at Holwood… and I distinctly remember the very knoll upon which I was sitting, near Pitt and Grenville, when the former said to me, "Wilberforce – why don't you give notice of a motion on the subject of the slave trade? You have already taken great pains to collect evidence and are therefore fully entitled to the credit which doing so will ensure you. Do not lose time, or the ground may be occupied by another."'

In his *Recollections of William Wilberforce*, published in 1865, John Harford, a friend for thirty years, said Wilberforce told him that when Pitt warned 'the ground may be occupied by another' he was referring to Fox. There is further evidence to support this assertion from Fox himself. Wilberforce said that when he tabled the motion to introduce the matter before Parliament, 'Fox said he had himself seriously entertained the idea of bringing the subject before Parliament; but he was pleased to add that, it having got into so much better hands, he should not interfere'. Fox later joined the campaign and helped to bring the abolition of the trade to fruition.

Pitt must have realized an abolition bill would be controversial and occupy the Commons for years ahead, so why did he encourage Wilberforce to take it up?

It was obvious that before long, the demands for action would become irresistible. The calls for abolition had been growing into a moral crusade among radical Evangelicals, Methodists and Quakers; they were now even gaining support in the graceful drawing rooms of polite Georgian society. So, too, some members of the Church of England were beginning to mobilize against the trade. It is doubly shocking, therefore, to find the Church's missionary wing, the Society for the Propagation of the Gospel in Foreign Parts, had lucrative investments in at least one slave plantation in the West Indies – the Codrington plantation in Barbados, where the slaves had their owners' mark, 'Society', branded on their chests with red-hot irons. The Church's justification was that it was rescuing the 'heathen' from their ungodly lives in Africa, but all too soon it was left 'caring' for the souls of the slaves (slaves at the plantation often died within three years of their arrival). The acceptability of such practices was meeting greater moral attack. There had been petitions to Parliament, and a society for the abolition of the slave trade was about to be formed in London.

Pitt's motives for pressing Wilberforce to take up the cause have never been fully explained. Perhaps he was simply tired of hearing his friend droning on about the subject and decided to bring it to a head. Pitt also may well have felt that persuading Wilber to get his teeth into an issue such as the abolition of the slave trade would do him good. Wilberforce had emerged from a bout of depression (today it might be diagnosed as a nervous breakdown) followed by a deep religious conversion; Pitt felt Wilber needed an issue over which to put his Christian beliefs into action and absorb his restless mind.*

Pitt knew he was powerless, even as Prime Minister, to drive an unpopular bill through Parliament, especially against the great vested interests he knew would fight to stop it. These included men such as General Banastre Tarleton, a wounded hero of the war against American independence and an unbending opponent of abolition, who anticipated financial damage to his Liverpool constituency if the trade was ended; and pillars of the establishment as high as the Duke of Clarence, the future William IV, who were convinced that if Britain abolished the slave trade throughout its widening Empire it would hand the commercial advantage to its rivals abroad, such as the French, Spanish, Dutch or Portuguese, all of which traded in slaves.

Pitt innocently may have wanted to avoid his friend being denied the credit for being the first to propose abolition. But I believe he was playing a double game. I suspect the key motive for encouraging Wilberforce to take up his campaign was that Pitt, a shrewd political operator, wanted to prevent it being championed by his greatest political enemy, Fox.

Pitt was a reformer, popularly known as 'Honest Billy', but the Younger Pitt was also a hard-headed politician; he had to be, in a period which had seen eight administrations in the ten years to 1783 when he formed his first Government. All prime ministers, then and now, want control of Parliament, and Pitt must have realized that if Fox took up an anti-slavery bill, it could block up his Parliamentary timetable, perhaps delaying some of his more urgently needed financial measures. However, Pitt clearly felt that with his bosom friend Wilber in charge of the campaign, he could maintain some influence over the progress of the anti-slavery bill, including delays to the legislation, if necessary, which Fox would have resisted.

---

* Wilberforce helped to found the Royal Society for the Prevention of Cruelty to Animals, the National Gallery, the Trustee Savings Bank (the TSB is now part of Lloyds) and a multitude of other good causes.

Sceptics argue that Pitt wanted to block the legislation for the abolition of the slave trade. I believe this is nonsense. Pitt was sympathetic
to the cause against the slave trade; in 1788, he ordered a Privy Council
inquiry into the trade that gave weight to the calls for its abolition. Pitt
also knew, however, that it would be a mistake for his Government at that
stage to take up an abolition bill to spike Fox's guns. It was far simpler to
leave it to an Independent to bring in the measure as a backbench MP.
That could answer the public demand for action without committing his
Government one way or the other.

Before the party system had been established, Pitt had to rely on
winning over independently minded MPs to get his measures through
Parliament, which was worse than herding cats. To gain support for
an issue as controversial as the abolition of slavery, Pitt would face a
Parliamentary nightmare, and he had more than enough to occupy him.
My experience as a political editor is enough to convince me that Pitt
wanted his friend Wilber to take up the abolition campaign to stop Fox
doing so. Wilberforce's role in one of the greatest philanthropic Acts of
Parliament in British history was born out of a political fix by William
Pitt to keep Fox at bay.

Wilberforce answered the case perfectly: he possessed the passion and
the patience to pursue the campaign in Parliament through setbacks and
delays, knowing full well he had Pitt's support and counsel behind the
scenes. The young Prime Minister knew Wilberforce was just the man.

After his religious awakening, Wilberforce had threatened to give up
politics altogether and, having become sickened by gluttony (Pitt was
in the habit of regularly drinking three bottles of port at a sitting, and
there were lavish banquets to attend as an MP) and sin (Wilberforce
gambled at cards at Boodle's and may have once visited a brothel), he had
also threatened to cut himself off from his former friends. Wilberforce
resigned from his clubs – Boodle's, Brooks's, White's and Goosetrees –
sold a racehorse, cut down on his partying and limited his wine intake to
no more than six glasses a day. Pitt, however, persuaded him not to give
up his friends and his seat in the Commons.

At the time of his great personal crisis, Wilberforce also sought the
advice of a charismatic preacher, John Newton. He was as unlikely a priest
as it was possible to imagine, more an old sea-dog than dog-collar wearer.
Newton had spent most of his life at sea, both in the navy after being
press-ganged and serving on slaving ships. He was a former slave-ship
captain himself, but had gradually undergone a conversion to God. It

was only after a stroke that he gave up the sea and sought a new life as a priest. Newton had been accepted into the Church of England – after great difficulty – and had become renowned as an Evangelical preacher and composer of hymns, including 'How Sweet the Name of Jesus Sounds'. He took inspiration from a miraculous deliverance from a storm at sea to write his most famous hymn, 'Amazing Grace':

> Amazing Grace, how sweet the sound,
> That saved a wretch like me.
> I once was lost but now am found,
> Was blind, but now I see

In his old-age, Newton attracted many seeking guidance to the church where he was rector, St Mary Woolnoth, Lombard Street, built in 1727 in the Baroque style by Nicholas Hawksmoor. They included Wilberforce, who had been introduced to Newton by his aunt as a child and had been spellbound by the former sailor's tales of Africa; now Newton became his spiritual mentor. Newton told his troubled young supplicant: 'God has raised you up for the good of the church and the good of the nation. Maintain your friendship with Pitt, continue in Parliament – who knows but for such a time as this God has brought you into public life and has a purpose for you.'

Now Pitt settled on the issue that would give Wilber extra justification for remaining in Parliament: putting his religious convictions into political action. It was the spur Wilberforce needed.

Wilberforce's mind had been weighing the case for abolition long before he and his friends sat down on the ridge at Keston. He had been lobbied to adopt the cause in Parliament a year earlier, when he visited Sir Charles and Lady Middleton, fellow Evangelical Christians, at their home in Barham Court, Teston, in Kent. Sir Charles was an MP and could have taken up the cause himself, but, prompted by his wife, urged Wilberforce – already noted as a persuasive voice in the Commons – to become the spokesman for the abolitionists in Parliament. A former Royal Navy captain, Sir Charles (later Lord Barham, and the head of the Royal Navy in 1805, the year of Trafalgar) had become appalled by the conditions on board when he had recaptured a slave ship that had been taken by the French in the Caribbean. It was infected with the plague, and his ship's surgeon, James Ramsay, later published a book condemning the inhumane conditions of the slave ships and plantations.

Then, only a few days before the three friends met under the oak at Keston, the most dogged activist for abolition, Thomas Clarkson, had called on Wilberforce at his rooms at 4 Old Palace Yard, Westminster (now a grassy plot by Westminster Abbey). Clarkson had left Wilberforce a copy of his celebrated *Essay on the Slavery and Commerce of the Human Species*, which had won Clarkson a prize at Cambridge in 1785. The essay had been written as a Latin test for his tutor, Dr Peter Peckard, the university's Vice-Chancellor, who had been horrified by the case of the *Zong* massacre, in which 133 slaves were chained together and thrown overboard when supplies of fresh water ran low while the ship was in the Caribbean. The incident became public after the owners of the *Zong* made an insurance claim for the 'loss' of their 'cargo' – the slaves. The legal argument turned on whether the claim was justified, and was taken as a straightforward case of property rights, but it led to moral outrage.

Clarkson, having become enthralled by the subject, worked like an investigative journalist, travelling to public houses, drinking dens and low dives on the waterfront of the main slave ports at Bristol, Liverpool and Glasgow, interrogating crewmen off the slave ships and gathering detailed facts about the trade and the inhumane conditions on board, at personal risk to himself. He was attacked by a gang in the Liverpool docks but, being over six feet tall and burly, fought the men off and escaped.

As a founder member of the new abolition committee, Clarkson knew petitions alone would not do. The cause needed a Parliamentary spokesman. He had arranged for Wilberforce to have dinner again, in a few nights' time, with the Middletons, as well as a number of other leading supporters, to persuade him to become their champion.

With Pitt's prompting, Wilber made up his mind. He would take up the cudgels for the cause and he would not lay them down until he was too old and infirm to carry on. Over the next four decades, abolition was to make his name.

The vista that Pitt and his friends enjoyed has been encroached upon by factory units and suburban housing on the southern edge of the middle-class commuter town of Bromley, south London, but oaks still cloak the hillside. I park my car nearby, wondering where the track to Wilberforce's oak starts. There are few signs to show that this footpath – no more than a gap in the bushes by the busy A233 – leads to the remains of one of the most historic oak trees in Britain. I have to dodge a red London bus as I cross the main road from Biggin Hill to Bromley Common, and then I plunge into the bushes. The path is narrow, and even at mid-day it is quite dark under the dense canopy of branches and shrubbery. It is not the sort of footpath I would advise Wilberforce to take at night these days. There is a barbed-wire security fence on my left and glimpses of modern buildings beyond. Pitt's house has long gone, replaced by a gated complex of flats, which each sell for over £1 million.

It is a short walk before the thick scrub and trees give way to an open vale, with oaks as far as the eye can see. This is clearly the spot. There is a fence on the right (under a sapling oak planted in 1969), and the remains of an old oak trunk and a few lifeless limbs which lie on the ground; this is all that is left of the original Wilberforce Oak, which blew down in a storm in 1991 (it is not to be confused with a great old oak that still stands, but appears to be dead, a short way down the hill). A few feet above the path on a grassy bank there is a stone seat, but it is out of bounds behind another fence. It was laid in the shadow of the Wilberforce Oak in 1862 by the historian Lord Stanhope and carries a quotation from Wilberforce's diary recalling the moment that was to change his life, and the lives of countless others:

> At length, I well remember after a conversation with Mr Pitt in the open air at the root of an old tree at Holwood, just above the steep descent into the vale of Keston, I resolved to give notice on a fit oc- casion in the House of Commons of my intention to bring forward the abolition of the slave trade. [1]

The inscription says it is from Wilberforce's diary. It is true he was a prolific diary writer, but this is a popular and enduring myth. In fact, this quota- tion comes from a five-volume hagiographic biography of their father by Robert and Samuel Wilberforce, and was recalled by Wilberforce in old-age for inclusion in the book.

As I stand admiring the view, a few hikers walk by with a dog. They are bound for Downe House, where Charles Darwin lived. These days Darwin's house is a much bigger tourist attraction.* In summer, when the oaks are in leaf, concealing the houses and light warehouses that

---

* The author of *On the Origin of Species* and his devotedly religious wife, Emma, frequently walked to Holwood to admire the parkland with the Wilberforce Oak, half a century after Pitt, Wilberforce and Grenville sat there.

have spread into the vale, there is still an illusion that the view has not changed much, though the roar of traffic from the A233 would make it difficult for Pitt to be heard by Wilberforce today. On this point, I say bring back the phaeton.

Slaving is as old as history, and so are the rebellions against it. Spartacus, who led the slave army against the Roman legions around 71 BCE, was merely the most famous rebel. Old Testament Hebrews were slave owners; Arabs were great slave traders; and several of the founding fathers of America, including George Washington, Thomas Jefferson, James Madison and Benjamin Franklin, had slaves – though Franklin freed his during his lifetime and helped start the Pennsylvania Anti-Slavery Society.

The first blacks arrived in the London Company's colony of Virginia in 1619. Recent research suggests that, apart from providing cheap labour, African slaves were also used in the tobacco plantations of the new colonies because they were naturally more resistant to malaria.[2] By 1807, slavery had been banned in every US state north of the Mason–Dixon line, separating Pennsylvania to the north and Maryland to the south. The resistance in the Southern states to ending slavery was one of the sparks that ignited the American Civil War in 1861.

The 1860 census shows that there were four million slaves in the US when the war began. In contrast, while its ships transported millions of slaves to the colonies, the British Isles had a very small black population, numbered in tens of thousands, mainly limited to the ports. Britain had never sanctioned slavery on home soil – though it had existed, here and there.

The dubious 'credit' for starting the trade in slaves between Africa and America goes to the Portuguese, who set the first slave galleon on its way to the New World in 1444. By the middle of the eighteenth century, Britain, with its naval power, dominated the trade. It operated a slave trade 'triangle' whose sharp angles were defined by economic efficiency – ships loaded with tools, guns and clothes to trade would sail from Bristol, Liverpool or Glasgow to the west coast of Africa; from West African ports, the ships would pick up a cargo of slaves at around £22 per head, then set off to the West Indies or the American colonies, where the human cargo could be sold at £50 a head to plantations, mines and households mainly comprised European settlers; and the ships would return to Britain laden with sugar, tobacco and other goods picked up from the American ports. Unsentimental speculators could more than double their money – investors in the *Ann*, sailing out of Liverpool in 1753, paid £3153 but gained £8000. The accountants in Liverpool and Bristol reckoned the trade brought in between £250,000 and £300,000 a year, equivalent to more than £10 million today. An estimated one hundred thousand slaves a year were transported to the Americas; in all, from the start of slavery by the Portuguese to its end in 1867, eleven million Africans boarded ships to be transported and 9.6 million survived the passage to be sold into slavery.

It was the loss of life on the 'Middle Passage' between Africa and the Caribbean that convinced Wilberforce it was a vile trade that had to be stopped. One Liverpool slave-ship owner, James Penny (after whom Penny Lane is said to be named), told the Privy Council inquiry that he allowed singing and dancing by the slaves on board, and seemed satisfied that the fatality rate on his ships was one in twelve. 'The average allowance of width to a slave is fourteen and two-thirds inches,' Penny reported. Wilberforce was horrified by the evidence. 'As soon as I had arrived thus far in my investigation of the Slave Trade,' he told the Commons, 'I confess to you so enormous, so dreadful, so irremediable did its wickedness appear that my own mind was completely made up for Abolition.'

In 1807, he succeeded in passing the first Act of Parliament onto the statute book to end human trafficking, but it was not until 1833, when Wilberforce was on his deathbed, that slavery itself was abolished throughout the British Empire. Even then, it took another eight years for slaves to be emancipated.

There had been earlier attempts to abolish slavery in some of the new states in America; the first anti-slavery society was set up at the Rising Sun Tavern in Philadelphia. But the seeds of the successful British campaign were sown under that oak tree in Keston.

The red-brick house where William Wilberforce was born is down a narrow lane in the heart of the old Georgian quarter of Kingston upon Hull, in the East Riding of Yorkshire. Its size and its warm exterior come as a pleasant shock among the grey stone buildings. On closer inspection, the building is delightful, with kinks in the floors and eight not-quite-symmetrical sash windows on either side of the grand two-storey entrance. It sits behind an impressive gateway, looking like it has a smile on its face, though today it tells the grim history of slavery and Wilberforce's role in abolishing it.

William's grandfather, also named William, was from old Yorkshire stock that could be traced back to Saxon times. (The family name had originally been Wilberfoss.) He had moved to the town in the early eighteenth century to better himself. He had become mayor after marrying into a Hull trading family, the Thorntons. Sarah and William Wilberforce had two sons, and it was their youngest, Robert, and his wife, Elizabeth Bird, who produced an only son who would end the slave trade in Britain.

When William was born at Wilberforce House on 24 August 1759, it was a place for Yorkshire sweat, toil and profit. Built in the 1660s, it had been the home and business premises of the Thornton and Wilberforce families for the past half-century, with sailing ships moored at the back, three or four deep at a time, alongside narrow landing stages, known in this part of the North-East by their old Norse name, *staiths*. This was Hull's heyday, when it stood as one of the nation's principal ports for trade with the Baltic and Scandinavia, and the family was prospering. William must have got used to the smell and noise of the busy docks as labourers unloaded cargoes of iron ore from Sweden and flax, grain and timber from the Baltic into the family warehouses attached at the back of his home. The walls and the space for the windows are all that is left now of the warehouses, which stood overlooking the staiths and the dock wall off the River Humber.

The boy was sent to the local grammar school in 1767, but the following summer his father died, at the age of forty, when William was only nine. The running of the firm was taken over by Abel Smith, a partner in the firm who married into the family and went on to found two banks that eventually, through many mergers with others, spawned NatWest.

William was sent down to London to a boarding school in Putney, under the protection of an aunt and uncle in Wimbledon, to whom he became very attached. They were friends of George Whitefield, an Evangelical Christian and open-air preacher, one of the leaders of the movement that became known as Methodism.

William's mother, however, would have no truck with Methodists and their Evangelical ways, which were spreading across England like the flu. Mrs Wilberforce ordered her son back to Hull to avoid him becoming infected, and packed him off to the grammar school at Pocklington, a village near York, because the head of his old school in Hull, Joseph Milner, had turned Methodist too. (This must have been a great disappointment to the family; Milner had been appointed by William's grandfather to the post.) William's mother may have been fighting a losing battle. John Wesley, a powerful opponent of slavery, preached across the road from Wilberforce House in the Methodist Chapel in George Yard, now called Gandhi Way. But William was not yet 'serious' about his religion, and enjoyed the theatre and other entertainments that some of the preachers regarded as sinful.

When he went up to St John's College, Cambridge, in 1776, his grandfather had recently died, leaving William, at the age of seventeen, a young man of independent means. With no reason ever to worry about earning a living, he led a hedonistic student lifestyle, gambling and drinking, but it was here he met the more studious Pitt, and formed a bond that was to last for the rest of their lives (despite the strains caused by the French wars, which Wilberforce regarded as a distraction).

Wilberforce left university with little interest in taking over the family firm. Like Pitt, he set his sights on a glittering career at Westminster. Together, they excitedly looked down from the public gallery on the clashes in the Commons chamber between the political stars of their day, particularly when Charles James Fox was involved. Wilberforce spent £8000 in September 1780 encouraging the voters of his hometown, Hull, to elect him as MP. He entered Parliament at the age of twenty-one – a few months before Pitt. The future Prime Minister stood for one of the university seats in Cambridge and lost, but secured another seat in January 1781 to join his friend at Westminster. Wilberforce was not a Party man and remained an Independent, though he was conservative in his views and mostly supported Pitt's Tory administrations.

Wilberforce inherited his aunt and uncle's house, Laurel Grove, in Common Southside, Wimbledon where he entertained Pitt and his friends at drinking parties. 'We will be with you before curfew and expect an early meal with fresh peas and strawberries,' Pitt wrote to him. As two young men with the political world at their feet, they could hardly be blamed for enjoying the sort of wild parties today associated with footballers and reality TV celebrities. Wilber was never po-faced about his faith (to his family, he seemed more at ease after embracing Evangelical Christianity), but with his growing commitment came a conviction that he should cast aside sin and follow 'the strictness and purity of the Christian character'.

Slavery was a far greater sin that was going on under the noses of Georgian society when Wilberforce 'found God'. It was tolerated because it had made Britain and its ports rich. Traders in Bristol, Liverpool, Glasgow and London grew fat on the trade, though most cities prospered from it in some way. The Wilberforce shipping firm never dealt in slaves but the trade's profits came to Hull, all the same. Hull traded in tobacco and sugar that had been grown in slave plantations and James Hamilton, the trader who resided in the houses next door, dealt in tar produced by slaves in the American colonies.

Hull may not seem like a must-see destination, but Wilberforce and an anti-slavery museum, which has been established in Wilberforce House, have put the Yorkshire town on the tourist trail for hundreds of African Americans and Afro-Caribbeans who come to England as part of a search for their roots.

I arrive in Hull with the glib assumption that a museum dedicated to the man credited with the abolition of the slave trade will be uncontroversial. I quickly realize how wrong I can be. Two hundred years after Wilberforce's abolition of human trafficking, emotions are still raw, especially for the families of the victims.

'I took a tour of African American people from New York,' one museum guide tells me as we visit galleries of artefacts from the campaign to end the slave trade. 'They had tears in their eyes because they are the descendants of slaves, and this is part of their history.' For those with more direct links to Britain, particularly those whose families were uprooted from West Africa and forced to work in the former British colonies in the West Indies, the museum sometimes provokes anger at the injustice, which is still going on. When they make the pilgrimage to Hull, some visitors raise the question: when are you going to apologize?

Even Wilberforce, and the role he played in the campaign, is a cause of controversy. 'There is a love–hate relationship with Wilberforce,' says my guide. 'Certain people would not speak to me if I said I worked at the Wilberforce museum because they think he has monopolized the history of the abolition movement. He is seen as part of the establishment, and he took so long to push it through. If you read his 1789 speech and other speeches, you notice how nice he was about the plantation owners.'

In his speech on 12 May, he declared: 'I mean not to accuse any one, but to take the shame upon myself, in common, indeed, with the whole parliament of Great Britain, for having suffered this horrid trade to be carried on under their authority. We are all guilty – we ought all to plead guilty, and not to exculpate ourselves by throwing the blame on others;

and I therefore deprecate every kind of reflection against the various descriptions of people who are more immediately involved in this wretched business.' He clearly pulled his punches in this speech, but in his defence I would say he did so in order to get a hearing from their allies inside Parliament who were trying to frustrate his bill.

In the end, Wilberforce got the credit but the foot soldiers of the abolition campaign are largely forgotten, none more so than Thomas Clarkson. He did the dogged legwork – or to be more precise, his horse did – covering thirty-five thousand miles on horseback in pursuit of evidence against the slave trade that Wilberforce then used in the House of Commons.

Wilberforce was hero-worshipped in his lifetime, buried at Westminster Abbey (the ultimate accolade in Victorian society); he has an American university, the first there established specifically to teach black students, and a multitude of study centres named after him. There are enough marble statues of Wilberforce around the world to rebuild the Parthenon, and his bust sits nobly in that pantheon of heroes of the Victorian age, on the front elevation of the Foreign Office, alongside Drake, Livingstone, Cook and Franklin.

In contrast, there is a modest monument to the memory of Thomas Clarkson, with the inscription 'The Friend of Slaves', near his grave in the village churchyard of St Mary, Playford, in Suffolk. (Playford Hall, where he died still complaining about being written out of the history of abolition, was put up for sale for over £3 million in 2011, but it was offered strictly as a private house rather than as a potential Clarkson museum.) He has a bypass named after him, Thomas Clarkson Way, on the outskirts of Hull, Wilberforce's city. In Wisbech, Clarkson's hometown on the Lincolnshire–Cambridgeshire border, there is a community college named after him; and Clarkson's travelling chest with many drawers for the African goods he said could have produced an alternative trade to slavery is a star attraction at the Wisbech and Fenland Museum. But Wisbech is more famous for its association with King John and his treasure or, more recently, the treasure showered on a local couple who scooped a eurolottery jackpot of over £100 million. In 1996, Clarkson got some of the recognition he deserved, when a memorial plaque to him was put up in the north choir aisle of Westminster

Abbey, but he was still overshadowed by Wilberforce. It is sandwiched between a statue of Wilberforce and one of Sir Stamford Raffles, the founder of Singapore.

Unlike the burly Clarkson, Wilberforce was short, about five feet four inches, and emaciated. A portrait dated 1794, when he was thirty-five, shows him with grey powdered hair. He had a fancy taste in clothes, judging by two of his coats which have survived and are on show in the Wilberforce museum, although they are probably for court dress: one is mauve velvet, which has faded to green; the other, gold silk. Both indicate that Wilberforce was boyishly slender; he might have been called anorexic today. It appears he fasted largely for religious reasons (he also put a stone in his shoe to chafe his worldly pride). He was frequently unwell, with stomach pains brought on by a chronic condition that is thought to have been colitis, inflammation of the colon. He was prescribed laudanum (tincture of opium), which may have contributed to his emaciation and his chronically poor eyesight.

Yet, throughout his life those who knew him testified to his sense of fun and his wit. He was engaging company, and his joyful gift of lifting people's spirits gained him admirers in the Commons, even among his opponents. Perhaps his chief asset was his voice: he possessed a mellifluous voice that was both strong and pleasing to the ear, and gave him a presence that his poor physique might have denied him. He was always singing (mostly hymns) and was known at Westminster as 'the Nightingale'. James Boswell, witnessing Wilberforce speaking at the hustings in York Castle in 1784, was surprised by his powerful voice, recalling years later 'the shrimp swelled into a whale'. Sir Nathaniel Wraxall, in his *Historical Memoirs* of 1815, marvelled that such an ugly, undignified little man could speak with great perspicacity and fluency. He spoke fast, which was difficult for the Parliamentary reporters, but one who heard him said the tones of his voice were 'so distinct and melodious that the most hostile ear hangs on them delighted'.

Wilberforce at first resisted joining the abolition movement because he wanted to maintain his independence. It was not until 26 April 1791 – four years after Clarkson founded the anti-slavery committee in London with eleven others, mostly Quakers – that Wilberforce formally enlisted with four other MPs, including the Whig Charles James Fox.

~ℓ~

DESCRIPTION OF A SLAVE SHIP.

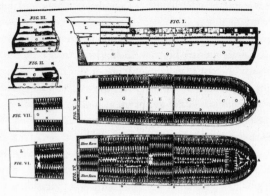

THE BROOKS SLAVE SHIP POSTER:
Illustrating the case for abolition of the slave trade.

There are marks on the wall of an upstairs gallery in Wilberforce House to show visitors the cramped space in which slaves were kept in captivity. For the weeks that it took to make the Middle Passage, they would be manacled by the neck, hand and foot in fetid conditions between decks, given a space six feet high by four feet wide for men and five feet ten inches by one foot four inches for women.

The museum also preserves iconic artefacts of the anti-slavery movement: a poster of the slave ship *Brooks* packed with the torsos of the slaves lying on the decks; a cameo medallion of a kneeling black slave with the inscription 'Am I not a man and a brother?' – the logo of the anti-slavery campaign when it was launched in 1787. The cameo was produced in the thousands by the china manufacturer Josiah Wedgwood, who, in addition to being the supplier of the cream pottery known as Queen's Ware to the newly enriched middle classes of the Industrial Revolution (and which made him a fortune), was also a Unitarian, a grandfather of Charles Darwin and a committed abolitionist. Many women wore the attractive Wedgwood medallion as a brooch or to decorate their hair, as a show of their support for the cause. Some even formed groups and organized a boycott of Caribbean sugar in protest against the slave trade, since they could not become members of the main abolition societies which were reserved for male members only.

The poster of the *Brooks* demonstrates how adept the anti-slavery campaigners became at propaganda. They had to be. They were up against the vested interests in Parliament of a multimillion-pound industry that paid for much of Britain's economic growth, and those vested interests were determined to defend the status quo to the last. Even the Church of England was prepared to defend its slave investments in the West Indies. Speaking in the Lords against one of Wilberforce's many bills (he made several attempts at abolition over the years), the Duke of Clarence declared: 'The proponents of the abolition are either fanatics or hypocrites, and in one of those classes I rank Mr Wilberforce.'

The minutes of the inaugural meeting of the Society for Effecting the Abolition of the Slave Trade are held in a brown leather volume at the British Library. 'At a meeting held for the Purpose of taking the Slave Trade into consideration, it was resolved that the said Trade was both impolitick and unjust,' notes Thomas Clarkson's flowing hand.

It was no accident that the society's first meeting was held in the Quaker bookshop and printing works at 2 George Yard in London's East End. One of the society's founding members was James Phillips, a Quaker and a printer, and the Quaker printing press would come to be the abolitionists' most powerful weapon. They printed a flood of leaflets, posters and petitions. The small corner of the financial district where the shop and printing works once stood now has a suite of smart new offices but there is no blue plaque on their front. Perhaps that should change by the time of the next major anniversary of the emancipation of the slaves, in 2033?

It was at 2 George Yard that thousands of copies of the *Brooks* poster were run off. The initial print run was for seven hundred copies, but it was reprinted thousands of times after that. 'This print seemed to make an instantaneous impression of horror upon all who saw it,' wrote Clarkson. One clergyman compared it to Dante's *Inferno*. Its fame made it a singular piece of evidence for the legislative debate. At a hearing in Whitehall of the Privy Council inquiry into the slave trade set up by the Prime Minister, on 11 February 1788, Wilberforce presented a wooden model of the *Brooks*, now on display at the museum, to illustrate the appalling overcrowding on the ship.

Like much in the anti-slavery story, even the *Brooks* poster is not entirely what it seems. The ship was certainly a slaver. It was built in 1781 and used as a slaver out of Liverpool until 1804. It was first registered by Lloyd's of London as the *Brook* and then the *Brooks*, after the family of its owner, Joseph Brooks, and often spelled incorrectly with an 'e'. The family had been in Liverpool since at least the sixteenth century, and

Joseph himself had been involved in forty-three slave voyages between 1770 and 1790.[3]

The image, which moved many who saw it to oppose the trade, appears to be an architect's drawing of the *Brooks* showing hundreds of black figures crushed together like sardines. It was true that slave ships such as the *Brooks* were packed like that. John Newton, the slave-ship captain turned Evangelist preacher, would testify to that in his memoirs. But the drawing was not actually a plan of the *Brooks*; it depicts another ship, discovered by a branch of the anti-slavery campaign in Plymouth.[4] Clarkson and the leaders of the campaign in London immediately saw the drawing's propaganda value. The Privy Council inquiry had published an alphabetical list of slave ships, with their dimensions – and the *Brooks* was first on that list, putting the ship's name in the news. And so in April 1789, Clarkson and his fellows cleverly labelled the poster as the *Brooks*.[5]

The anti-slavery activists had learned a great deal over two decades. The first blow against the slave trade had been struck in 1772 by Granville Sharp, later the founder chairman of the anti-slavery society. Sharp, a philanthropist, paid for a test case to be tried by the chief judge, Lord Mansfield, arguing successfully that an escaped slave called James Somersett should be freed because slavery had not been legal in England since the twelfth century. The judgement freed Somersett and established that slaves brought to England were free men, but did nothing for those in British colonies abroad. 'We have no slaves at home – then why abroad?' asked the writer William Cowper in 1785. 'Slaves cannot breathe in England; if their lungs receive our air, that moment they are free. They touch our country and their shackles fall. That's noble, and bespeaks a nation proud. And jealous of the blessing. Spread it then, and let it circulate through every vein.'

Wilberforce was no radical; it took him two years to get his campaign in the Commons under way, and he was quickly accused of being too soft on those engaged in the trade – a charge, I discovered, still levelled at him today. One Wilberforce biographer, William Hague, the Conservative Foreign Secretary in the 2010–15 Conservative–Liberal Democrat coalition, knows enough about Parliamentary procedure to absolve him of blame; Hague takes the view, which I share, that Wilberforce had to go cautiously to maintain his own coalitions of support for abolition at Westminster.

Gradually building alliances at Westminster, he continued to press for change, putting forward bill after bill, which all failed to get the necessary votes in the Commons and the Lords. It is no wonder that under this painfully slow process, Wilberforce had agonies of self-doubt and bouts of soul-searching, possibly fuelled by opium, during which he was tempted to give up the campaign.

The breakthrough came as a result of a brainwave by James Stephen, a maritime lawyer and anti-slavery campaigner, who said that as Britain was at war with Napoleonic France, legislation should be passed to stop the French from trading with its colonies. This meant that England, with the most powerful navy in the world after the Battle of Trafalgar of 1805, could intercept ships going to French colonies, including slave transports, effectively ending the trade to the parts of the Caribbean not administered by Britain. Wilberforce took up the idea and, with the backing of Lord Grenville, now Prime Minister, in the Lords, he outmanoeuvred his opponents to push a measure through both Houses. Few could oppose a measure against France while Britain was at war. General Tarleton complained they were coming at the issue of abolition with 'a side wind' – and now the wind was in their sails.

The sudden death of William Pitt on 23 January 1806, at the age of forty-six had robbed Wilberforce of a friend and ally, but Grenville proved himself more decisive. With the aid of Charles James Fox, now Foreign Secretary, abolition's opponents were finally routed, with a vote of 283 to 16 in favour of the Slave Trade Bill. The session had lasted through most of the night on 22–23 February 1807.

Hugely emotional scenes greeted the passing of the bill. Members broke with tradition and gave a tearful Wilberforce three hearty cheers. In the 2006 biographical film *Amazing Grace*, directed by Michael Apted, Wilberforce's wife looks down on him with adoration from the public gallery.* In fact, women were not allowed into the gallery at that time, and had to settle for hearing debates in a cabin in the roof space above the lantern, out of sight of the men below. Wilberforce was among those who believed that women had no place in politics.

---

* Wilberforce was played in the movie by the handsome Ioan Gruffudd of *Fantastic Four* and *Hornblower*. He was portrayed running through gardens in flowing shirts with William Pitt the Younger, played by Benedict Cumberbatch – reminiscent of a romantically soft-focus advert for Cadbury's Flake. There is no evidence that Pitt was gay, though he was a lifelong bachelor.

The victory was certainly owed to Wilberforce's tenacity and the effectiveness of men like Sharp, Clarkson, Wedgwood and Newton as well as black activists such as Olaudah Equiano, who in 1789 had published his renowned memoirs of being a slave. *The Interesting Narrative of the Life of Olaudah Equiano* helped to create an early public groundswell of support. Sharp, Clarkson and Wedgwood were subscribers for the book's first printing; Sharp and Clarkson put themselves down for two copies each. Wilberforce is not listed among the book's early supporters, and indeed there is no hard evidence that Wilberforce and Equiano ever met. Equiano did not live to see the Slave Trade Bill; he died on 31 March 1797, ten years after the meeting in Keston Vale, but ten years before the Act passed the Commons and the Lords.

Timing is everything in politics, and the time was right for a change in the slavery business. There had been riots among the slaves; Haiti had become a slave-run republic, and the economic rationale for importing slave labour was fraying. Cheaper production in Brazil was making Britain's colonial sugar plantations less competitive and less profitable. Cultivation might be extended through an unceasing supply of slaves but that could lead to ruin, via overproduction. After calculating their prospects, the old landed interests in the West Indies swung round in favour of stopping the slave trade.[6]

It was not the end, however. The 1807 Act, for which Britain justly feels proud, abolished the trade; it did not abolish slavery.

A quarter of all Africans who were enslaved were transported across the Atlantic after 1807. In 1808, the British West African Squadron was established to suppress slave trading, which continued in contravention of the law. There were successes. Between 1820 and 1870, Royal Navy patrols seized over fifteen hundred ships and freed a hundred and fifty thousand Africans destined for slavery in the Americas. But there were still injustices too. While Royal Navy personnel were rewarded for each slave released live, few were returned to their homes. Many were put ashore in Sierra Leone, the chaotic colony set up on the west coast of Africa for freed slaves by the idealistic Granville Sharp. Most of the people settled there were from Nova Scotia, and had been freed after the American War of Independence.

Seven long years after Wilberforce's first Act abolishing the slave trade was passed, appalling 'justice' was still being meted out to slaves living under British law. Court records from the British colony of Dominica in the Leeward Islands, now in the National Archives, reveal the horrors from just one month, January 1814: Hector, a runaway, was given one hundred lashes and ordered to be worked in chains for six months – he was one of the lucky ones. John Pierre, a runaway, was hanged, and then his head was cut off and put on a pole, with his body left on a gibbet. Peter, a supporter of a mutiny among twenty 'Negroes', was hanged, his head cut off and put on a pole with his body left on the gibbet as well.[7]

Surveying the horror of these brief accounts, it seems extraordinary that, in the many debates leading to the 1807 vote, Wilberforce the Evangelist told the Commons that it would be 'madness' to give immediate emancipation for slaves until they were ready to manage their own lives as 'happy peasantry' – and he did not suggest that would be any time soon. His speech on 28 February 1805 is among the earliest records of Hansard, the Parliamentary report:

> He [Wilberforce] did not wish to avoid that part of the subject on which the opponents of the abolition dwelt so much; he meant the eventual emancipation of the negroes in the West Indies. He had never concealed that his hope was that such might be the ultimate effect of the abolition of the African importations... but although he felt that the immediate emancipation of the negroes in the West Indies could not be expected, for that before they could be fit to receive freedom it would be madness to attempt to give it to them, yet he owned he looked forwards, and so he hoped did many others, to the time when the negroes in the West Indies should have the full enjoyment of a free, moral, industrious, and happy peasantry.[8]

To be fair to Wilberforce, he was trying to avoid alienating support among Independent MPs, among whom he feared demanding too much, too soon.

Wilberforce was criticized for his caution by the rising generation of abolitionists – campaigners such as Elizabeth Heyrick, leader of a women's anti-slavery society in Leicester, and Sir George Stephen, who accused Wilberforce of being inept, addicted to moderation, compromise and delay. Wilberforce dismissed much of the backlash, particularly the complaints coming from women such as Heyrick. 'For ladies to meet, to publish, to go from house to house stirring up petitions – these appear to me proceedings unsuited to the female character as delineated in Scripture,' he said.

It would take another twenty-six years, until 1833, at which point Wilberforce had been retired from Parliament for eight years, before slavery was outlawed throughout the Empire. By then, Wilberforce had joined forces with the reform-minded Christian campaigner Sir Thomas Buxton, whose candy-like memorial fountain stands in Victoria Gardens by the House of Lords, to bring about an end to slavery across the realm.

Abolition of slavery, rather than merely the trade, required the reform of Parliament itself. The Great Reform Act of 1832 (which I would regard as Britain's proudest political achievement but for its glaring lack of a vote for women) widened the franchise for men and redistributed power across the newly industrialized towns and cities emerging in the North of England. (The first attempt to pass it had led to Wellington's downfall; see Chapter Five.) The new MPs who were swept into office by the reform were ready to vote for change.

Three days before Wilberforce's death on 29 July 1833, at the age of seventy-three, Parliament finally passed the Abolition of Slavery Act. As he lay dying, Wilberforce said: 'Thank God that I have lived to witness a day in which England is willing to give twenty millions sterling for the Abolition of Slavery.'

There was still inequality in treatment between the exploiters and the exploited. The 'twenty millions sterling' for which Wilberforce thanked God – almost forty per cent of the national budget at that time – was paid in compensation to the plantation owners. The Bishop of Exeter and three business partners were paid nearly £13,000 to compensate them for the loss of 665 slaves that year. Nothing was paid to any former slaves.

Further, the emancipation of the slaves was not immediate. The Act came into force in 1834, at which time all slaves over six years of age had to spend four or six years as 'apprentices' before they were truly free.

Even before Wilberforce's death, his central role in the history of the abolition campaign was being established by his sons, Robert and Samuel, in their *Life* of their father. They wrote out several key characters, including Clarkson, and reinforced myths surrounding Wilberforce's actions. The role of the Church of England, which was considered by many activists to be one of the most brutal slave owners in the Caribbean, was quietly set aside. So too were the missionaries who went with slave traders to Africa to convert the people taken as slaves to Christianity under the banner of the Society for the Propagation of the Gospel in Foreign Parts. The thorny question of the Church's stance was given a dignified burial, while the guilt of the nation for its involvement in the slave trade was acknowledged. A plaque at Wilberforce's tomb in Westminster Abbey reads:

> His name will ever be specially identified with those exertions which, by the blessing of God, removed from England the guilt of the African slave trade, and prepared the way for the abolition of slavery in every colony of the Empire: In the prosecution of these objects he relied, not in vain, on God; but in the progress he was called to endure great obloquy and great opposition: He outlived, however, all enmity.

By the time Queen Victoria had taken the throne in 1837, the part played by her nation in exploiting slavery had been sanitized for public consumption. For nearly three hundred years, Britain had enjoyed profits from the trade; an English seaman, Sir John Hawkins, hero of 1588 and Elizabeth I's defeat of the Spanish Armada, had established the 'Triangular Trade'. With Victoria's reign, the Empire reached its zenith and a proud nation placed a statue on the face of the Foreign Office in Whitehall to symbolize its civilizing influence on the rest of the world: a naked figure of a woman and child representing Africa whose manacles have been broken by Britain.

The national self-congratulation about ending slavery has come full circle since then. The two-hundredth anniversary of the 1807 Slave Trade Act was accompanied by a bout of guilt over Britain's historical exploitation of slaves. The Church and Tony Blair, then Labour Prime Minister, both marked the bicentenary by issuing public apologies for Britain's part in the slave trade. That provoked howls of criticism from the Conservative Right. A permanent display on the Atlantic trade at the National Maritime Museum today accuses Britain of using abolition to foster its imperialistic ambitions. 'Promoting legitimate trade, European forms of religion, and government to Africa, paved the way for colonial rule later in the nineteenth century,' the exhibition tells visitors.[9] The display points out that Wilberforce's Act did not even manage to stop the transportation of slaves, a fact that cannot be shrugged off.

The Far Left argues that Wilberforce was a marginal figure in the fight to abolish slavery: it was a revolution brought about by the slaves themselves, like Spartacus against the Romans. That is stretching the truth to breaking point. The campaign was predominantly white, male and middle class, but there were women and blacks involved too, as illustrated by a painting in the National Portrait Gallery, *The Anti-Slavery Society Convention, 1840*, by Benjamin Robert Haydon. The convention was held in June of that year at the Freemason's Tavern in London. Haydon captures Thomas Clarkson making some point with his index finger raised, in full flow as he delivers his speech. He is looking directly at a black man seated in the centre foreground of the packed meeting room. This is Henry Beckford, a delegate from Jamaica and a freed black slave. Beckford has his back turned to the viewer, but ironically his prominence in the painting caused great controversy at the time because of his colour.

A descendant of Henry Beckford, the theologian and writer Robert Beckford is stirring more controversy today. He has put a price on assuaging Britain's guilt over slavery; he says Britain should pay compensation of £7.5 trillion. 'I wouldn't expect that £7.5 trillion to be paid, because it would bankrupt the country, but it provides a measure of how much we contributed to Britain and how much we would be due,' he said.[10]

In spite of the work of Wilberforce and his followers, human trafficking remains a multimillion-pound global enterprise. In July 2012, two members of a Travellers' family in Luton were jailed in the first case of slavery in the UK for two centuries. The husband and wife were prosecuted under the Coroners and Justice Act of 2009 for using forced labour. The judge in his sentencing said: 'In 1834, slavery was abolished in the British Empire. It did not mean that overnight, slavery, servitude and the incidence of forced labour came to an end.'[11]

Often it proves difficult to prosecute modern 'slavers' because cases may fall under the immigration laws, sex crimes, or between the two. There are now calls for Wilberforce's law to be clarified once more. Perhaps the most fitting memorial to him would be a new Slavery Act.

SEVEN

1928

'Deeds not words'

TICKET TO THE DERBY:
Emily Davison's day return to Epsom Racecourse.

Racehorses are galloping at full speed around Tattenham Corner in the Epsom Derby.

This is the last bend before the final straight and the winning post, where thousands of racegoers are cheering in the stands, and King George V and Queen Mary are watching from the Royal Box. There is a roar from the crowds as the horses round the long left turn. Then, a woman ducks under the railings and runs onto the racecourse. In an instant, she is knocked flying by Anmer, a thoroughbred owned by the King. Anmer tumbles on its side and somersaults, unseating its jockey. The horse stands but the rider lies utterly still. Nearby, the woman lies on the turf. She seems more like a heap of rags than a person. The crowd, who a moment before had been cheering, surges towards the turf and surrounds the prone figures.

The time is 3.10 p.m., 4 June 1913. It will be remembered as the moment when a suffragette 'threw herself under the King's horse'. The iconic image of the suffragette being trampled by George V's horse has come to symbolize the bitter struggle that women fought to win the right to vote in Britain. But though the incident was caught in gruesome clarity by British Pathé's hand-cranked cinema cameras filming the Derby, the arguments about what actually happened that day have continued ever since.

The woman at the Derby is Emily Wilding Davison, a leading militant in the Women's Social and Political Union (WSPU), which had been founded in 1903 by the charismatic Emmeline Pankhurst. Four days later, Emily Davison died in hospital of her injuries without regaining consciousness. She was forty years of age.

Cinema audiences were horrified by the silent moving images in the British Pathé film but they also capture a quaint lost world, a moment in history before Britain was changed for ever by the brutality of the First World War. Just as it is today, Derby Day 1913 was not just a race on the flat; it was a social event. A writer at the time said the race collected 'the rank of fashion and the scum and riff-raff'. The thieves and swells, the punters in straw boaters and aristocrats in top hats, the bookies and the hucksters, and the ladies in flamboyant bonnets – they all came together at Epsom Downs. Despite the modernity of the Pathé movie, the scenes – all but the fateful, tragic one – play as though they have been lifted from *The Derby Day*, William Powell Frith's satirical Victorian painting of the festivities.

Stagecoaches and motor cars – a novelty in 1913 – trundle up a dusty track on the centre of the course; a crowd watches two men pummel each other in a makeshift boxing bout; policemen with regulation moustaches hold up glasses of beer for the cameras during an open-air lunchbreak; urchins pause from begging pennies to stare shyly at the lens; and King George V steps down from a horse-drawn carriage, Queen Mary by his side, in front of the exclusive Royal Enclosure. The King is wearing a top hat, but most of the men in the stands are wearing jaunty straw boaters. Many of these men posing for the cameras would be swept away in the tide of war that would hit the Western front of Europe the following year. With them would be buried the Edwardian age of deference and many of its stifling social barriers, including the position of women as second-class citizens.

But the archive footage of Davison's protest does not answer the nagging question: did she mean to commit suicide at the Derby or, like so many other milestones in Britain's history, is that yet another myth, created to assuage our collective guilt over taking too long to right a social wrong?

To discover more about Davison, you have to go to the Women's Library in the East End of London, where most of her archives are kept. It is down a side street, around the corner from Aldgate East tube station, and surrounded by tough blocks of council flats.

Davison would have known the district. In her day, the area around the library would have been a warren of slums, and the narrow streets were frequently visited by the suffragettes, who also fought poverty among the women of London's crime-ridden East End. She had once even considered setting fire to post boxes in Aldgate but decided against it, because the people there were too poor. She firebombed post boxes in Fleet Street instead.

In nearby Limehouse she was arrested, in 1909, for the second time in her life. Davison and her good friend, Mary Leigh, were protesting outside a hall inside which David Lloyd George, the hated Liberal Chancellor of the Exchequer, was making a speech on his radical 'People's Budget'. 'I was busy haranguing the crowd when the police came up and arrested me,' Davison later wrote to a friend. She went on hunger strike in Holloway prison, fasting for 124 hours and losing one and a half stones in weight, before she was freed.

Her protest at the Epsom Derby in 1913 was just the latest and most shocking in a series of militant outrages that appalled polite Edwardian society. At the inquest into Davison's death, the coroner seemed to speak for the nation when he said: 'It is exceedingly sad – so it seems to me – that an educated lady should sacrifice her life in such a way.' Parliament and the Press were united in their conviction that Davison had crossed a line. This was no longer justified protest but 'wicked madness'. The *Morning Post* reported the protest under the headline: SENSATIONAL DERBY – SUFFRAGIST'S MAD ACT. The establishment was convinced the suffragettes had become hysterical in their push for the vote.

As I scan through the microfiche of the original press cuttings of the day, I discover that the *Post*'s 'sensation' was not the injuries to Davison; it was the fact that a 100–1 outsider, Aboyeur, had gone on to win the race after an objection was upheld against the favourite, Craganour, for barging. The paper was also concerned about the King's jockey, Herbert Jones, aged twenty-eight, who had been thrown by Anmer. 'The King,' says the *Post*, 'made immediate inquiries regarding his jockey who had no bones broken.'

Two days later, while recuperating at his home at the King's racing stables at Newmarket, Jones received a telegram from Buckingham Palace. It had been sent by a palace flunkey on behalf of Queen Alexandra, the Queen Mother. 'Queen Alexandra was very sorry indeed to hear of your sad accident caused through the abominable conduct of a brutal lunatic woman. I telegraph now by Her Majesty's command to enquire how you are getting on and to express Her Majesty's sincere hope that you may soon be all right. Wighton Corbyn.'

Jones's psychological wounds went far deeper than his physical ones. No one ever suggested Davison's death was his fault, but Jones attended the funeral and claimed he was haunted by her face for the rest of his life. In 1951, he switched on the gas in his kitchen and took his own life. He was seventy-nine.

Had she lived, Davison would have been prosecuted for injuring the jockey. In the Home Office files, I find a memorandum to the Liberal Home Secretary, Reginald McKenna, which is brutally unfeeling. Mc-Kenna was a banker, and politically out of his depth in dealing with the delicate problem of the suffragettes. The note, written as Davison lay dying, reads: 'The D of PP [Director of Public Prosecutions] says that if Davison recovers, it will be possible to charge her with doing an act calculated to cause grievous bodily harm to the rider of the horse.' One is tempted to ask, what about the horse? Perhaps she should be prosecuted for that too.

Davison remained in a coma for four days after being rushed from the Derby track to Epsom cottage hospital. Efforts were made to relieve the pressure on her brain, but she died on Sunday, 8 June, without regaining consciousness. The death certificate barely conceals the doctor's outrage – 'fracture of the base of the skull caused by being accidentally knocked down by a horse through wilfully rushing onto the race course at Epsom Downs during the progress of a race'. The certificate gives her address as her mother's home in Longhorsley, near Morpeth, Northumberland. It said Davison had 'no occupation' and was unmarried.

The story of Emily Davison's death, and a little of her life, unfolded at the inquest, which was held in the cramped red-brick police court at Epsom on 10 June. None of the original inquest transcripts was kept for posterity, but *The Times* gave a full account of the proceedings the next day.

Emily's half-brother, Jocelyn Davison, a retired naval captain, was called as a family witness and the foreman of the inquest jury went quickly to the point: 'Did you know anything that would lead you to feel that she was abnormal mentally?'

'No. Nothing.'

Suicide was a criminal offence for those who failed in their attempts, and a source of shame for families, no matter the cause, at the time. It was therefore in the family's interests to show that Emily had not committed this unspeakable crime.

The family appointed Thomas Yates to represent them at the inquest. He was a lawyer and the husband of Rose Lamartine Yates, a fellow suffragette and close friend who, with Mary Leigh, had visited Davison's bedside hours before she died. They draped the WSPU colours on the screen and the bedhead before they left.

Encouraged by Yates's gentle questioning, Jocelyn Davison told the jury about Emily's character, describing her 'considerable gifts' as a speaker and writer on women's issues. She had won a BA degree and was devoted to the women's movement, he said.

'Can you form any idea as to why she committed this act?' Yates asked.

Davison replied: 'In my own mind, I am perfectly certain that she had no wish to commit any act to do away with her life and I feel it was entirely an accident...'

'Did she do this by way of protest with a view to calling public attention to the fact that the Government have not done justice to women?'

The coroner for West Surrey, Gilbert H. White, may well have been under orders from the Home Office not to allow his court to be turned into a show trial against the Liberal Prime Minister, Herbert Asquith, and his Government. He intervened, angrily curtailing Yates: 'I cannot allow that. I am not here – and these gentlemen [the jury] will agree with me – to inquire into anything political at all.' The now defunct *Western Times* reported there was 'some applause from the jury at this pronouncement'. Such was the public dislike for the suffragette cause.

Later, Police Sergeant Frank Bunn gave his own eye-witness account. He had been on duty 'on the same side of the course as the lady but some fifteen or twenty yards nearer the winning post'. He described in a matter-of-fact manner how he had seen the woman run out and get knocked down. Immediately after the incident, he had written in his notebook:

> Several horses passed by when a woman, supposed Emily Davison, ran out from under the fence and held her hands up in front of HM King's horse, whereby she was knocked down and rendered unconscious.
>
> Dr Lane of Banstead attended to the woman and directed her removal to the Cottage Hospital, Epsom, where she was taken in a private motor car No LA7959 owned by J B V Faber Esq [a Dutch businessman], Manor House, Ewell, who placed same at disposal of police. Mrs Warburg of 2 Craven Hill, Paddington, rendered great assistance to the injured woman and accompanied her in the motor car to hospital, she formerly having been a nurse.

Sergeant Bunn added: 'The horse which pitched over onto its head stopped on the course and was handed over to Mr George Prince, Egerton House, Newmarket by PS 35 T Lewis. It received slight cuts to the face and body and injury to its off fore hoof. No other personal injury. No expenses incurred by the police.'[1]

In his notes, Bunn listed the items that had been found on Davison. He discovered two suffragette flags, identifiable by their trademark green, white and purple stripes, folded up and pinned to the back of her jacket, on the inside. They were one and a half yards long and three quarters of a yard wide – large enough for the racegoers to see if she had managed to unfurl them. On 'her person', in the police jargon, he found:

> one purse containing three shillings eight pence and three farthings; one return half railway ticket from Epsom Race Course to Victoria No 0315, two postal order counterfoils for two shillings and six pence crossed written in ink thereon, one for E Gore and dated 1/4/13, one insurance ticket dated May 10 1913 on G E railway to and from New Oxford Street, eight half-penny stamps, one key, one helper's pass for Suffragette Summer Festival, Empress Rooms, High Street Kensington for 4th June 1913, one small memo book, one race card, some envelopes and writing paper, one handkerchief

These personal belongings, as well as Davison's private letters, notebooks and files, are secured in boxes at the Women's Library and rarely put on view, even for researchers. But I persuade the archivists to bring them out. I am not allowed to touch the items themselves. They are held in little plastic cases, which will protect and preserve them like ancient treasures.

I lay out Davison's things under the bright lights of the library, feeling as though I'm standing before a body in a post-mortem examination. She suddenly seems close. The small box about the size of a tea tray contains her pathetically small ladies' purse – brown leather with a brass snap clasp. It is just big enough to contain the few coins she was carrying. There is also a collection of her WSPU medals, with their green, white and purple striped ribbons; some bear the bar awarded to those women who had gone on hunger strike.

The suffragettes' famous hunger strikes were a terrible tactic, used against themselves in protest not at their lack of vote, but at their treatment as common criminals. They were demanding 'first-division status' – in effect to be treated as political prisoners. McKenna, the Home Secretary, had conceded this status to Emmeline Pankhurst and her daughter Christabel, but would not extend it to the suffragettes in general. In many ways, McKenna faced the same difficulties with the suffragettes as the Thatcher Government in the 1980s, when IRA prisoners including Bobby Sands went on hunger strike in the Maze prison; then, Sands was allowed to die. McKenna, however, was determined he would not be blamed for causing women's deaths, so he authorized force-feeding of any suffragette inmates who went on hunger strike.

Force-feeding is a torture. 'The doctor gripped my head and began to force the tube down my nostril. It hurt me very much… I immediately commenced to choke and retch and suffocate,' Davison wrote in a letter, describing the horrors of the practice. Once the tube was in place down the throat, a woman warder pushed a funnel into the top of the tube and poured liquid food down it. It was usually mixed with a drug intended to pacify the woman. But that was not the whole horror of it. Emily struggled; the tube often was misguided; and the doctor pushed so hard it cut her throat, or came out through the mouth.

Yet, the most poignant item in the Women's Library collection is a small square of orange cardboard, stamped with the number 0315. It is the return half of Davison's third-class train ticket from Victoria Station to Epsom. It is printed with the letters 'LLB and SC Ry' (London, Brighton and South Coast Railway), 'Epsom Race Course to Victoria, eight shillings and six pence no particular class of carriage guaranteed'.

This stub of cardboard challenges the popular perception that persists today that she killed herself. Why would she have bought a return ticket to Epsom if she had intended to take her life?

The doubts grow. Among the small things that belonged to Davison, there is also the helper's pass for the Suffragette Summer Festival at the Empress Rooms in Kensington High Street. The pass was valid for 2.30 p.m. to 10.30 p.m., 4 June – the day of the Derby. Either Davison had decided to subscribe to the event as a small, final display of commitment to the cause, or she intended to go back to the festival later that day.

The day before the Derby, she had met her friend Mary Leigh at the festival. They had stood before the statue of Joan of Arc that dominated one end of the hall. Davison had saluted St Joan like a soldier about to go into battle. She seemed in high spirits, and told Leigh she would come every day 'except tomorrow – I'm going to the Derby tomorrow'.

'What are you going to do?' asked Mary.

'Ah,' she said, putting her head a little on one side, her eyes smiling. It was a gesture she made when she could not say too much to her friends. 'Look in the evening paper,' she added, 'and you will see something.'

When she left, she went to the WSPU headquarters at Lincoln's Inn House and asked the staff there for two union flags.

'What for?'

'Ah,' she replied. She did the little gesture, with her head on one side. They got the message.

'Perhaps I'd better not ask.'

'No, don't ask me,' she replied.[2]

The jury decided (in the family's favour) that Emily Davison was an accidental martyr. Having heard all the evidence – about her character, her state of mind and her railway ticket – the jury found there was not enough to return a verdict of suicide. Her death was simply a 'misadventure'.

Thomas Yates, the family lawyer, collected Emily's personal possessions after the inquest and gave them to his wife Rose for safekeeping. Later, Rose Yates became responsible for keeping the archives of the suffragette movement as a whole, and that is how Davison's small things came to be in the Women's Library, where the main archive is kept today.

There is a note, in Rose Yates's neat handwriting, attached to Davison's race card, note book, latchkey, purse and her return ticket: 'The race card found on Emily Wilding Davison when she stopped the king's horse at the Derby, 4 June 1913. This evidence won the verdict of misadventure not suicide.' This Epsom race card holds more clues. Half a century later, Mary Richardson, a 'comrade in arms' who once tried to destroy an Old Master in the National Gallery as part of the suffragette campaign, revealed she had been with Davison that day. Davison had used the race card to shield her eyes from the sun. 'A minute before the race started, she raised a paper or some kind of card before her eyes. I was watching her hand. It did not shake. Even when I heard the pounding of horses' hoofs moving closer, I saw she was still smiling. And suddenly she slipped under the rail and out into the middle of the racecourse. It was all over so quickly.'

At the inquest, Police Constable Eady, who was standing on the opposite side of the track to Sergeant Bunn, was asked by the coroner whether it would have been possible for Emily Davison to pick out any particular horse. 'I do not think it would be possible, the way they were bunched together,' he said. This corroborated Bunn's evidence: 'The horses came along in a heap, not strung out at all… It was a close race, and between the first horse and the last there was a distance of only a few yards.' But on this point, they were both quite wrong.

Neither Bunn nor Eady revealed to the inquest jury that as Davison waited for the Derby to start at 3 p.m., she had marked her card for the preceding races. I turn the pages of the card over in the library's files. It still bears the numbers she wrote alongside the runners and riders: she pencilled in a number '1' in the 1.30 p.m. Canterbury Plate alongside Honeywood; in the 2.30 p.m. Juvenile Selling Plate, she noted the first three runners and riders in order of their finishing places. By the time the Derby runners were under starters' orders, Emily had studied the form. She knew the horses, and crucially, by reading the race card, she knew the colours of the riders' silks. She could not miss the jockey wearing the King's colours, even if she only had a split second to spy them: Herbert Jones's silks were of rich red sleeves and a blue body.

I do not believe Bunn or Eady lied under oath, but it was in the interests of the police and the Government to play down Davison's choice of target. The establishment clearly preferred the fiction that Davison was a mad woman, intent on a reckless act of martyrdom, and chose the King's horse by accident. They did not want the public to hear that the true target of her shocking protest for women's suffrage had been the monarchy. This truth was too dangerous. The monarchy was revered in Britain at the time – it was only twelve years since the end of Queen Victoria's 'long and glorious' reign – and any attack on the King (or his horse) was not only unthinkable, it was seditious. Even the suffragettes wanted to avoid that charge.

Had the coroner called for the Pathé film to be shown at the inquest, he would have tended to agree with Bunn's and Eady's accounts that she could not have identified the King's horse in the split second before she was hit. The unedited version is too fast; the race and the collision seem over in an instant. However, if the inquiry jury had had the benefit of modern technology, they may have had a different view. After leaving the Women's Library, I discover an enhanced version of the 1913 Derby film. It has been slowed down and a funereal piano accompanies the events. Frame by frame, one sees a totally different picture of the day, one that flatly contradicts the policemen's evidence. Far from being 'in a heap', as Bunn testified, the horses are strung out as they round Tattenham Corner into the final straight. Davison has been circled in bright yellow, and can be seen running through a gap in the horses.[3] Then, to my amazement, she stands quite calmly, well away from the white rails.

She lets one, two, three horses fly past her, to her right.

She is wearing a jacket over her long Edwardian skirt, with a large bonnet, as though she is attending a garden party.

You can sense she is taking her time to pick her horse.

Anmer is near the back of the field, and on its own. As the horse thunders towards her, she steps firmly towards it and puts up her hands.

Half a ton of thoroughbred racehorse at full gallop smashes into her body. Her hat spirals off to the left. She is sent tumbling, one, two, three times, her body a rag doll, her neck and head hitting the ground with each turn. Judging by the distance between the rail posts, she is thrown at least twenty-four feet.

Even a century later, the film sparks anger – but it's not clear if the anger is always directed at the establishment. Among over five hundred comments posted on YouTube, where the enhanced version is posted, one person simply asks: 'Why?'

The inquest never found a reason for her action, except as a mindless protest. But if she was not trying to kill herself under Anmer's hoofs, what was she trying to do?

There was plenty of evidence from eye-witnesses that she tried to grab the horse's bridle. According to *The Times*, PC Eady told the inquest that after he saw Davison duck under the rails, 'she raised her hands before she was quite upright, facing the other horses which were coming on, and she was then struck by a horse – it seemed to [me] with its front feet'.[4] Bunn testified: 'She threw up her hands in front of the horses and was knocked down.' An unnamed eye-witness said: 'There was a scream and I saw a woman leaping forward and making a grab at the bridle of Anmer, the king's horse.'The press, including *The Times*, interpreted this to mean that Davison was trying to pull the King's horse down, like an Indian brave wrestling a colt to the ground in a Hollywood western. And indeed, the title frame of the Pathé film states, as fact: 'Suffragette killed in attempt to pull down the king's horse.' But it seems unlikely, on the face of it, that a woman standing many hands shorter than the thoroughbreds would imagine that she could bring one down.

There is a further clue to her intentions, but it was not presented to the inquest because it was probably not known to the police. In addition to the two concealed flags, Davison also carried a scarf in the suffragettes' colours, which was wrapped loosely around her waist. After she was hit by the King's horse, the scarf fell onto the churned-up turf, close to where her body came to rest. The scarf was later picked up by the clerk of the course, not by Sergeant Bunn. I think she intended to tie this scarf around Anmer's bridle, so that the horse – the King's horse – would be carrying the suffragette colours across the finishing line.

This would have been a very public petition to the King as he sat in the Royal Enclosure by the winning post, had she succeeded.

There is another, more disturbing question that cannot be answered by Davison's personal effects: was she put up to the action by the Pankhursts?

The *Daily Express* saw a dark hand at work behind Emily Davison's protest, and it twisted Jocelyn Davison's evidence to make its point: 'Miss Davison's half-brother had given evidence showing how his sister's great attainments and brilliant record had withered like Dead Sea fruit under the malignant influence of militancy.' Even the *Manchester Guardian* agreed. In keeping with its liberal traditions, it was sympathetic towards the cause of women's suffrage, but it joined in condemning the protest as 'wicked'. The *Guardian*'s leader writer pointed the finger of blame at the Pankhursts: 'It is a horrible responsibility for those who have used the ascendency of their own attractive personalities to drug the minds of women of splendid intellect and character, like Miss Davison, into the state of diseased emotionalism which has led her to a wicked act.'

There can be little doubt that by referring to the 'attractive personalities', the *Manchester Guardian* writer was referring to the Pankhursts, though he did not name them. Emmeline Pankhurst and her eldest daughter, Christabel, were seen as the beautiful middle-class face of the suffragette movement. The strikingly handsome Pankhurst, often seen in public with her hair swept up, was the WSPU's field marshal, and charismatic, witty and headstrong Christabel was its radical general.

Emmeline Pankhurst was born in Manchester's Moss Side in 1858 when it was a well-to-do address. She had made her mark in London with her husband, Richard, a socialist lawyer, who was twenty-four years her senior. They lived in fashionable Russell Square; she opened a fabric shop and in the evenings they entertained socialist friends; they joined the Independent Labour Party. But the Pankhursts had moved to Manchester when money became tight, and Richard died of a stomach ulcer in 1898.

To support the family, Emmeline Pankhurst took a full-time job as a registrar of births, deaths and marriages. The experience gave her fresh insights into the poverty endured by women in Manchester.

She had been a member of the Society for Women's Suffrage (SWS), which had been founded in 1886 by Millicent Fawcett (after whom the Fawcett Society is named, which still campaigns for women's equality). The 1832 Reform Act had widened the franchise and paved the way for modern democracy, but this milestone in the British constitution had one glaring omission: it failed totally to address the rights of fifty per cent of the population – women. Fawcett was part of the tradition of women seeking change through constitutional means, going back to the early feminists such as Mary Wollstonecraft, the celebrated author of *A Vindication of the Rights of Woman*. These women had been part of the fight against slavery and the slave trade at the turn of the eighteenth century. They were known as 'suffragists', and their tactics were mostly law-abiding.

After a falling out with the SWS, Emmeline was persuaded by Christabel that more direct, militant action was needed. Nothing else would shake men out of their complacency. 'Deeds, not words' was their motto. Emmeline appeared to those around her to be spellbound by her sparkling, determined daughter who, only in her twenties, directed the militant action with her mother's devoted, unflinching support.

The campaign quickly escalated from stone-throwing, window-smashing and mass demonstrations in Parliament to incendiary bombs and personal attacks on ministers. In 1906, the outraged *Daily Mail* branded them 'suffragettes'. It was intended to be a term of derision, but the Pankhursts embraced the name as a badge of pride.

But the Pankhursts were not campaigning for universal women's suffrage; they had dedicated the WSPU to winning votes for women on the same terms as men, who only qualified for the vote if they were over thirty and owned property. It was, in my view, a political blunder – campaigning for votes for rich, propertied women. Nonetheless, they attracted millworkers in the North and poor women from London's East End by the score.

The terms of the campaign led to a lasting rift with some key members of the embryonic Labour Party. Keir Hardie, the Labour leader, supported the Pankhursts unequivocally. Other Labour figures suspected that Emmeline Pankhurst was a closet Tory, seeking votes for predominantly Tory women who owned their own homes or whose husbands owned the property. (I have found it is a suspicion that survives today among Labour MPs.) The Pankhursts' strategy also alienated the Liberal Chancellor, later Prime Minister, David Lloyd George, who was sympathetic and could have been their ally. Lloyd George refused to concede votes for women because he thought it would lead to more support for Conservatives – making Lloyd George a prime target of suffragette attacks. I suspect the loss of support from Labour and the Liberals helped to put back the hopes of winning support for women's votes by a decade, until after the First World War, when their cause became irresistible.

Their militancy may have been justified by the fact that they had no other means of making their voices heard, as they did not have the vote. Parliament therefore was bound to be their main target. 'We were very much at the epicentre,' Mel Unwin, the archivist of the suffragette exhibition at Westminster, told me. 'If they were doing it today, they might be protesting outside St Paul's.' The pioneers for women's suffrage learned one important lesson from their earlier struggle to abolish slavery. 'It showed you can make a difference with something really big,' said Unwin. However, she added, 'They were getting nowhere until you get the suffragettes.'

The escalation of the women's suffrage campaign into direct action may have grabbed the headlines but it split opinion, even in the movement. Today, the Pankhursts and their fellow activists might well be treated as suspects under the Prevention of Terrorism Act, which allows detention without charge and house arrest. Their direct actions shattered Edwardian illusions about women being the 'gentler sex'. The turning point in tactics came in 1905 when Christabel was arrested and sent to Manchester's

Strangeways prison for assaulting a police officer who had approached her after she had heckled the Foreign Secretary, Sir Edward Grey, in Manchester Free Trade Hall. She spat at the officer deliberately, with the aim of being imprisoned. She and a fellow suffragette, Annie Kenney, a millworker, emerged from the prison a few days later as heroines. The episode, and most especially the response, convinced Christabel – like many terrorist leaders since – that it was only by provoking the Government into more repressive acts that women would gain the side of public opinion. She had not anticipated the extent to which greater militancy would test the support of some followers and alienate the press.

Still, the high-profile actions attracted new recruits to the campaign. Emily Wilding Davison was one of them. She joined the WSPU in 1906, at the age of thirty-three, just as the Pankhursts were stepping up their militancy. Davison told friends she had joined because she was upset by the distortions being served up in the press about the women's cause. But like many women, Davison may have truly been won over by the force of Christabel's fiery rhetoric.

The year 1906 also marked a watershed in British politics. The Liberals were returned to power with a landslide victory over the Tories. The new Government had promised radical reform in its electioneering on the stump, including the first foundations of the welfare state – with old-age pensions, national insurance and an early form of sick pay. It was a time of great hope for change, but on the subject of women's votes, the WSPU found the Liberals were just as implacable as the Tories they had defeated. That in turn increased support for more militant action, orchestrated by Christabel Pankhurst.

In February 1906, the Pankhursts called a mass meeting at Caxton Hall to hear the outcome of the King's Speech, setting out the programme of forthcoming legislation. When they learned it did not include a bill to give women the vote, they rallied a mass demonstration to converge on the St Stephen's Hall entrance to the House of Commons where the women could lobby MPs in person. On 9 March, they marched towards Downing Street and demanded to see the new Liberal Prime Minister, Campbell Bannerman. When they arrived at Number Ten, they rapped on the door; two women dashed inside when it was opened.

In April, the Pankhursts and their followers shouted protests from the House of Commons public gallery after Keir Hardie tried to raise the issue of votes for women in the chamber and was blocked by opponents. More disruption of Parliament took place in October, when ten women, including Annie Kenney and the youngest of the Pankhurst sisters, Adela, were arrested for 'using threatening and abusive behaviour' in the Commons. They were jailed and granted first-division status as 'political' prisoners – a concession that was later withdrawn.

In 1907, Emmeline Pankhurst moved back to London with her daughters to be nearer the centre of power. That February, the most violent mass protest took place after a 'Women's Parliament' at Caxton Hall passed a resolution demanding votes for women. Emmeline Pankhurst led a procession of four hundred women to Parliament singing 'Rise up women! For the fight is hard and long' to the tune of 'John Brown's Body'. When they arrived at Westminster Abbey, they were blocked by massed ranks of police. Running battles with the police lasted for several hours. More than fifty women were arrested, including Sylvia Pankhurst, Emmeline's second daughter, aged twenty-four. (Sylvia later became a revolutionary socialist and Hardie's lover.)

A still bigger demonstration came on 21 June 1908, when Hardie, George Bernard Shaw, Mrs Thomas Hardy and Mrs H.G. Wells led a procession through London to Hyde Park, followed by forty bands and thirty thousand people. At the park, the Pankhursts made impassioned pleas for votes for women to the assembled crowd, which was reported to be nearly half a million. The *Daily Chronicle* estimated three hundred thousand people were present; *The Times* put the figure at between a quarter and half a million. The WSPU's own newspaper, *Votes for Women*, claimed: 'it is no exaggeration to say that the number of people present was the largest ever gathered together on one spot at one time in the history of the world'. But like the march of around one million people against the war in Iraq that filed past the Houses of Parliament in February 2003, the mass rally had little impact on ministers.

Having failed to secure change through peaceful means, the WSPU stepped up its militancy instead.

Nothing seemed to be safe; a multitude of places were targeted, though even the most radical women such as Davison drew the line at bombing people. At 5.45 p.m. on 1 March 1912, gangs of marauding women made a co-ordinated attack in the fashionable West End, taking out hammers concealed in their voluminous dresses and smashing plate-glass windows in shops including Burberry, Liberty and Marshall & Snelgrove. 'We started at Marble Arch and then bang went all the windows,' one suffragette proudly recalled in the audio archives of the Women's Library.[5] On other days, they chained themselves to statues in the entrance hall to the House of Commons, breaking off bits that the guides show to tourists today as a point of interest. They also, more bizarrely, broke thirty-eight panes of glass in the Orchid House at Kew Gardens, and burned down the tea bar at Regent's Park. These were hardly male refuges, and it succeeded in outraging the middle classes. A glass case containing some of the Crown Jewels at the Tower of London was also smashed.

It was the misfortune of Britain and the Pankhursts that, just as the WSPU campaign was being stoked up by the fiery Christabel, Herbert Henry Asquith, a visceral opponent of women's suffrage, became Liberal Prime Minister. He took office in 1908 and remained there until 1916.

Asquith took his lead from William Gladstone. Gladstone is revered by Liberal Democrats today as the greatest leader of the nineteenth century. Gladstone – the 'People's William' whose government introduced the secret ballot – was a late convert to Parliamentary reform; this great Liberal was opposed to any sudden shift towards votes for women. Asquith's opposition seems also to have been based on sheer male prejudice against the 'gentler sex'. In 1920, two years after women gained a limited right to vote, Asquith wrote to Hilda Harrison, in the intimate correspondence between the two after her husband was killed in action in 1917 roughly at the same time as his son, that most women were 'ignorant of politics, credulous to the last degree, and flickering with gusts of sentiment, like a candle in the wind'. Asquith and the Pankhursts became locked into a long-term power struggle in which neither side would give way.

As the suffragettes' militancy increased, they took actions that would make many of today's activists, such as the Occupy campaigners and the student rioters, blanch – and Emily Davison was often linked with some of the wilder protests. She firebombed those post boxes on Fleet Street, and elsewhere, and planned to blow up Durham Cathedral with dynamite from a colliery. She was also believed to be responsible for setting a bomb in hallowed Westminster Abbey. It failed to go off properly, but it damaged King Edward I's precious coronation chair holding the ancient Stone of Scone.

She was not alone. A trio of women physically attacked Asquith, an avid golfer, while he was on a putting green. They burned the slogan 'Votes for Women' into the putting greens of golf courses with acid, thus anticipating the tactics used in the anti-Apartheid campaign against the all-white South African cricket tour by Peter Hain, later to become a Labour Cabinet minister.

In her most audacious attack, Davison and her accomplices blew up an empty house being finished for Lloyd George near Walton Heath golf course. They were never caught but Emmeline Pankhurst was tried for incitement after a journalist reported that she had claimed responsibility for the bombing. 'We have blown up Mr Lloyd George's house – we have tried blowing him up to wake up his conscience,' Pankhurst reportedly said. The mother of the movement was handed the harsh sentence, given that no one was injured, of three years in prison; there, she went on hunger strike. By then, Pankhurst was in her mid-fifties, and the repeated trauma of incarceration, hunger-striking and force-feeding could be potentially fatal.

A number of feminists argue that Davison's action at the Derby was planned out of concern for Pankhurst's safety. A protest that caught the eye of the nation might help to ensure that Pankhurst was not killed by the authorities' prison regime. Davison's death would thus be seen as a sacrifice to save Pankhurst's life, or at least to seek revenge, committed by a devoted follower.

The truth is that Davison was no innocent tool of the Pankhursts. When she bought her return ticket for Epsom, Davison was notorious herself. She had become a pest to the authorities at Parliament, being arrested five times in quick succession for protests in the Palace of Westminster. There was a logic to her militancy. Each of her stunts at the Commons was triggered by a fresh insult to women.

In April 1910, Davison hid for over twenty-four hours in a heating duct in the Commons. She was only discovered late on a Sunday afternoon when she needed water. Her aim – though hopelessly naive – had been to break into the chamber to ask Asquith in person why he was reforming Parliament by creating life peers in the House of Lords while he would not allow women a vote for the House of Commons.

In June the same year, she threw two lumps of chalk through the windows of the Crown Office in Old Palace Yard. Messages were tied to the rocks, addressed to 'Mr Asquith': 'Give full facilities to the New Bill for women's suffrage' and 'Indignant womanhood will take this insult, be wise'. Her protest this time was in retaliation for the Prime Minister's statement earlier in the day that the Government was dropping a pledge to support a conciliation bill for women's suffrage. The Parliamentary archives still have the pencilled note from an exasperated policeman who reported the incident to his superior: 'Sir that suffragette found in the air shaft has broken some windows in the Crown Office, Old Palace Yard.'

A few months later, on 18 November 1910, Asquith announced that he was shelving the Women's Suffrage Bill, which would have given the vote to a small minority of women with property. Deprived of the vote and dismissed by the ministers, what else were women supposed to do? Violent protests ensued. Emmeline Pankhurst led a deputation to the Prime Minister, but she was roughly handled by police; it turned into a near riot with hooligans hurling abuse at the suffragettes. Some of the women claimed they had been sexually abused by the police. It became known as Black Friday. Davison was absent that day, but shortly after the riot, a policeman witnessed her throw a hammer through a window between the chamber of the Commons and the division lobby.

Her most celebrated Parliamentary protest was symbolic and entirely peaceful, however. It was staged on the night of 2–3 April 1911, when every resident in England was officially recorded in their place of abode for the mandatory national Census. Dozens of suffragettes broke the law by spoiling their papers. When Davison's Census paper was delivered to her lodgings at Russell Square, she wrote across it: 'As I am a woman and women do not count in the State, I refuse to be counted.' She then decided to boycott the Census by spending the night in the Palace of Westminster to make her point that women demanded a presence in Parliament.

The medieval hall with the greatest hammer-beam roof in the country was built by William Rufus in 1097. It has witnessed coronation feasts for kings and queens, including Anne Boleyn; the inauguration of Oliver Cromwell as Lord Protector; and show trials for enemies of the state, including Thomas More, Guy Fawkes and Charles I before he was be-headed in Whitehall. It has also seen many political protests, but never one quite like Davison's. She sneaked into the Crypt, the small chapel in the south-west corner of the Norman Banqueting Hall, and hid in a broom cupboard. She was discovered by a startled cleaner in the night, and marched off to the nearby Cannon Row police station once more.

She was victorious in one way: having been found in the broom cupboard on Census day, she was officially recorded as residing at the Palace of Westminster. There are two forms registered in her name for that night; her entry at the Commons misspells her name as Davidson. It reads: 'Found hiding in crypt of Westminster hall, since Saturday.'

It wasn't her only night visit. On 26 June 1911, she was found in the Commons at 2.23 a.m. climbing over a three-foot-high railing at the members' staircase. 'This is the same woman who has been found here on former occasions,' Chief Inspector Scantlebury ruefully noted.

The Commons broom cupboard in which Davison hid is under lock and key behind some stout iron railings (they clearly don't want any repetition of her protest), and out of bounds to the general public unless accompanied by an official guide. But in 1999, two Labour MPs with a rebellious streak, Tony Benn and Jeremy Corbyn, sneaked down and turned it into an unofficial shrine to Davison and her role in women's suffrage. It is surely one of the oddest political landmarks in Britain. The brass plaque they screwed onto the back of the door in the cleaner's cupboard says: 'She was a brave suffragette campaigning for votes for women at a time when Parliament denied them that right. In this way, she was able to record her address on the night of the census as being "The House of Commons", thus making her claim to the same political rights as men.' So powerful is the martyrdom image, the plaque goes on to repeat the myth that she deliberately killed herself for the cause: 'Emily Wilding Davison died in June 1913 from injuries sustained when she threw herself under the king's horse at the Derby to draw public attention to the injustice suffered by women. By such means was democracy won for the people of Britain.'

The cupboard is down a flight of steps, at the back of the beautiful subterranean chapel that is still used today for weddings and christenings. It is tucked away to the right of an ornate Arts and Crafts organ. Inside the sturdy wooden door, the cupboard is cramped, about five feet square, with no room to curl up and sleep. When I visited it, there was a broom in one corner, and the space was even more restricted by electricity cables. It is not a comfortable place to spend the night.

Standing in Westminster Hall near the Crypt, Corbyn tells me: 'There was lots of stress and strain between Emily and the Pankhursts, who were more middle class and bourgeois. She was seen as a trouble-maker and as more working class.' As in the past, Emmeline Pankhurst's Tory tendencies are still a source of suspicion on the Left.

As it happens, Davison could count herself just as middle class as Emmeline Pankhurst. Davison was born on 11 October 1872, at Roxburgh House, Vanburgh Park Road, a comfortable middle-class home just off Blackheath, a wealthy suburb of south-east London, still home to rich bankers. The Davisons' house is long gone but when she lived there, the area with its breezy open space overlooking the Thames was favoured by prosperous businessmen because it was out of the smoke and filth of the city.

She spoke with a 'Southern' accent. Her family, however, were Northerners, from the wild country around Morpeth in the North-East of England, and despite being born and brought up in the South, she never lost her family's distinctly stubborn Northern grit.

Her father, Charles Edward Davison, who was from Morpeth, had met his first wife, Sarah, in India, where he was seeking his fortune. They came back to London to raise a family of nine children, but Sarah died at the age of forty-four. Charles did not stay a widower for long; he married a Northumberland girl, Margaret, aged nineteen. Emily was their second child. Soon after Emily's birth, the family moved to a roomy Georgian country home, Gaston House, in Sawbridgeworth on the Essex–Hertfordshire border.

They moved later to central London where Emily was given a good education, first at Kensington High School and later at Royal Holloway College. She was twenty-one when her father died in 1893, and the money suddenly ran out. Emily went North for his funeral, visiting the parish church at Morpeth, St Mary's, for the first time to see him buried in the family grave (where she would be buried twenty years later, after the Derby misadventure). Davison's widowed mother returned to her family roots in a village near Morpeth called Longhorsley, where she ran a shop. But she insisted that her talented daughter complete her education in London.

Davison was forced to seek work as a governess while continuing to study for the final schools exams at Oxford University through Holloway College. She gained a first in English Language and Literature and a BA degree. The pride of the family can be seen in a photograph of the young graduate wearing her university cap and gown – the most often-seen image of Davison, since it was used in the WSPU memorial leaflets at her funeral. It does her no favours. She is holding her rolled degree in both hands like a truncheon, and seems to be looking down her nose at the camera. Her plain face, thin lips turned down at the edges, stares out at us as though she disapproves. In short, it makes her look like a prig.

This can hardly be the same woman who, family friends in Longhorsley recalled, on hearing she had won a degree, had dashed into her mother's shop and grabbed fistfuls of black bullets – humbugs – which she tossed into the air to the joy of the village children. Nor does it sound like the woman who playfully signed herself by her childhood name, Emelye, from the 'fair Emelye' of Chaucer's *Knight's Tale*, in a note to her mother shortly before she died.

The first biography of Emily Davison, written by Gertrude Colmore as an extended obituary in 1913, has been dismissed as hagiography.* But Davison emerges in its pages as a much warmer, more vigorous and humorous woman than this public image suggests. She enjoyed ice skating, playing the piano and singing, though there was a religious zeal about her commitment to the suffragettes' cause. Friends in the movement recall a Bible was always by her side, and she was fond of quoting suitable tracts. She wrote one of her favourite religious slogans on the wall of her prison cell: 'Rebellion against tyrants is obedience to God'.

Some suffragettes saw the movement as part of a crusade against male sexual oppression. They wanted to expose the hypocrisy of Edwardian society, which put women on a pedestal to be worshipped while turning a blind eye to marital rape. Their work coincided with the documentation of abuses that made Charles Dickens's descriptions of low life in London look tame. There were reports that women in London were kidnapped and sold on the Continent as sex slaves. A woman who ran a brothel in Half Moon Street was let off with a fine because the Crown wanted to conceal the names of her influential clients; this, despite appalling evidence that rich and powerful men had indulged their fantasies with children who had been kidnapped and drugged at the woman's hands. Lloyd George excited particular loathing because he was a known womanizer.

In some ways, the movement took on the traits of a sex war. On 10 March 1914, Davison's ally at Epsom, Mary Richardson, used a meat cleaver to slash the *Rokeby Venus* by Velázquez – the Old Master equivalent of a topless photograph of the busty model Jordan. This portrait of a naked woman, reclining on a bed admiring her face in a mirror so that male visitors could admire her bare buttocks, represented to Edwardian feminists everything that was evil in the male-dominated world.

In her book *The Ascent of Woman*, Melanie Phillips says: 'The militants attacked men, masculinity and marriage as the fount of society's ills...

---

* Colmore's novel *Suffragette Sally* came out two years earlier, in 1911, and followed a group of suffragettes – thinly veiled depictions of women in the movement – from the conciliation bill to Black Friday.

It was through sexual relations that men held women in their power both in and out of marriage, wounding and abusing them and keeping them enslaved. The antidote was sexual separatism: celibacy, chastity and lesbianism.'[6]

Davison's sex life remains a tantalizing mystery. Davison showed affection to a number of close friends in the movement. She gave a book of Walt Whitman's poetry to her friend, Mary Leigh, on 29 December 1912. It is inscribed from 'Comrade Davison' to 'Comrade Leigh'. The slim volume, stored at the Women's Library, is heavily lined in the margins in Davison's hand. Key passages are emphasized: 'the dear love of comrades' (triple lined); and 'take this kiss, / I give it especially to you, do not forget me... / Remember my words... / I love you' (single line). Whether this indicates more than comradely love is impossible to tell. A Miss Morrison was described at her funeral as 'Miss Davison's companion'. Research has shown she may have been Edith Morrison, one of the first twenty-four women to become a barrister, though whether there was an intimate relationship is not clear.[7] In any case, there is no evidence that Davison ever had any close male friends.

Her attachments were primarily to the movement. She had surrounded herself with the cult of the martyr, like Joan of Arc, her inspiration, and she was not under the Pankhursts' control. Indeed, by the time of her death, she was regarded by them as a loose cannon. The Pankhursts anticipated that Emily Davison's freelance operations might one day backfire on the WSPU.

Almost exactly a year before the fatal Derby Day stunt, on 25 June 1912, Emily Davison threw herself off a balcony in Holloway prison to protest against the treatment of suffragettes in gaol. The immediate trigger was the Home Office's continued refusal to allow the suffragettes to be treated as first-division political prisoners. They had given Prime Minister Asquith and McKenna, the Home Secretary, a deadline to extend this special status to all of the women imprisoned for the cause; it had expired without response. Most of the suffragettes in the prison went on hunger strike and blockaded themselves in their cells, but one by one, the prison warders smashed open the doors.

Davison was one of the last to be tackled. She wrote an account for the *Suffragette* that was published a week after her death:

A regular siege took place in Holloway. On all sides one heard crow-bars, blocks and wedges being used: men battering on doors with all their might... My turn came... I lay like a log for some time... In my mind was the thought that some desperate protest must be made to put a stop to the hideous torture which was now being our lot. [8]

The warders could not force the door open and when they opened the spy-hole, they found out why. She had used wooden slats from a spare bed to barricade the door. After a long, fruitless tussle, a visiting magistrate ordered a hosepipe to be pushed into the cell through a broken window. Then they set the water jet on her. It was the equivalent of being hit by water cannon, and the treatment lasted for a quarter of an hour. It was later ruled illegal, and Davison was awarded compensation.

Drenched, and weak, she could hold them off no longer; they finally broke open the door. But she was not finished. She chose her moment, escaped the confinement of the female prison warders and threw herself from the balcony of the cell-block.

Her fall was caught in the wire netting suspended over the well between the floors. Having failed, she tried twice more to throw herself to the prison floor from the balconies, eventually knocking herself out.

She later told the Governor of Holloway she did so because she believed 'one big tragedy would save others'.

In a tract called *The Price of Liberty*, also published posthumously, Davison fully embraced the idea of martyrdom, and seemed to foreshadow her own death. She wrote that to make a sacrifice for one's friends was noble, but 'to re-enact the tragedy of Calvary for generations yet unborn, that is the last consummate sacrifice of the Militant'.

In her autobiography, *My Own Story*, Emmeline Pankhurst used Davison's words against her. The blame for Davison's death, she argued, lay squarely on the woman's own shoulders. Pankhurst asserted that – regardless of the inquest verdict – Davison was intent on martyrdom at the Epsom Derby:

> Emily Davison clung to her conviction that one great tragedy, the deliberate throwing into the breach of a human life, would put an end to the intolerable torture of women. And so she threw herself at the King's horse, in full view of the King and Queen and a great multitude of their majesties' subjects.

Pankhurst clearly realized her campaign would be damaged for a generation if it appeared, in the words of the Queen Mother, that she had used a 'brutal madwoman' as a pawn for her own ends. It was in Pankhurst's interests to show that Davison was a martyr, and that she was not mad. It suited her case to assert that Davison had committed suicide, even if it meant rejecting the findings of the inquest jury.

But what if the Pankhursts suggested the protest to Davison?

There were many reports in Morpeth, not reported to the coroner at the inquest, that two days before she left Longhorsley for London, Davison had received a mysterious but important telegram. No one could say from whom it came or what was in it, but locally they were sure it came from someone in 'the movement' and its message left Davison 'depressed and not her usual self'. A cousin later claimed that Emily had informed her mother in confidence after the telegram arrived that she was going to carry out a demonstration at the Epsom Derby and it involved a 'calculated risk'.[9]

Local people in Morpeth say she practised for the race by trying to grab the reins of a running horse at a nearby horse fair.

It was also said that local WSPU activists in the North-East had drawn straws to decide who should carry out this risky stunt, and Davison had picked the short straw; the telegram, it was rumoured in the village, came from 'comrades' in the local branch of the WSPU, urging her to go ahead. This could well be so. The mysterious telegram has never been found, but if she did get her 'marching orders' it was almost certainly not from Emmeline Pankhurst, as Davison was much out of favour with the Pankhursts when she died.

She had given up a teaching career in 1909 to work full-time for the WSPU as a writer and campaign organizer. By 1913, she had lost the WSPU job that she loved. Colmore's sympathetic biography says 'employment by the Union was not compatible with the position of the freelance which she had adopted'. What Colmore meant was that Emily was sacked by the Pankhursts (who were the only authority that mattered in the WSPU) because she refused to obey their orders.

Emmeline Pankhurst has been described by the writer Rebecca West as a 'reed of steel'. Others were more blunt. Her own supporters criticized her for being autocratic. She was ruthless with critics, and even her friends; she expelled the editors of *Votes for Women*, Frederick and Emmeline Pethick-Lawrence, from the WSPU in 1912 when they disagreed with her. But the militants in the North-East branch of the WSPU, including

Davison, are said to have operated like a self-contained cell, independent of control by the Pankhursts in London. The irony was not lost on those around her: while Pankhurst was supposed to be campaigning for democratic rights for women, she ran the WSPU like a dictator.

The Pankhursts may have found it difficult to control Davison while she was alive, but they made full use of her after her death.

Emmeline Pankhurst knew the value of propaganda. She even lied about her own birthdate to enhance her image as a revolutionary – she frequently spoke about the inspiration she drew from being born on 14 July, Bastille Day, but her birth certificate shows she was born a day later.

The Pankhursts gave Davison the martyr's send-off she may have dreamed of. The death was treated with the solemnity of a state funeral by the leaders of the suffrage movement, though some have compared it to a 'mobster's farewell', a swaggering show of strength, putting up two fingers to the authorities. The whole affair was choreographed and colour co-ordinated with consummate skill by Grace Roe, Pankhurst's chief organizer.

On 14 June 1913, Davison made the return journey from Epsom to Victoria Station, for which she had a bought her return ticket, in an oak casket. Her body was accompanied by several of her comrades, who dressed in white to invoke the defiant spirit of Joan of Arc.

At Victoria Station, the coffin – bearing a brass plate etched with Davison's favourite saying, 'Fight on and God will give the victory' – was carefully lifted off the steam train and mounted on a horse-drawn carriage. It was draped with a purple WSPU pall cloth, decorated with two broad prison arrows embroidered in silver, as a tribute to the time she spent incarcerated in gaol for the cause.

Four black horses pulled the funeral carriage, and six suffragettes, including Sylvia Pankhurst, marched alongside dressed in white.

The coffin was preceded by four of Davison's dearest friends, including Mary Leigh, the drum major of the WSPU; Elsie Howey, who was known to dress as Joan of Arc in full armour on horseback at suffragette events; and Vera Holme, a horse-lover who once rode on horseback from a WSPU conference in Caxton Hall, Victoria, half a mile to Parliament to deliver a message to the Prime Minister.[10] These like-minded friends marched behind two banners proclaiming: 'Thoughts have gone forth

VICTORIA STATION, LONDON:
Emily Davison's funeral procession, 14 June 1913.

whose powers can sleep no more! Victory! Victory!' and 'Greater love hath no man than this, that he lay down his life for his friends' – a saying later chiselled onto Davison's monument.

The women in white were followed by women in black carrying bunches of purple irises, and they were succeeded by women carrying red peonies, who were followed by women in white carrying Madonna lilies. The procession included fifty hunger-strikers, some on release because of ill health, and hundreds of women ex-prisoners. Many men also took part, wearing black armbands to show their solidarity. An empty, horse-drawn carriage also made its way with the funeral march. It was intended to carry Emmeline Pankhurst, but she had been arrested by the police. She was on release due to ill health from hunger strikes during her three-year sentence for 'bombing Lloyd George'. Making her way to join the funeral march, the police argued, showed that her health had improved enough to send her back to prison – a re-arrest allowed under the hated so-called Cat and Mouse Act. Without her, the carriage took the journey as a mute protest.

The long slow procession from Victoria Station brought the carriages and motor cars in central London to a standstill.

At St George's Church, Bloomsbury, an estimated six thousand women took part in the service. Brass bands were interspersed among the mourners, so that as the doleful roll of drums and the muffled notes of Chopin's Funeral March faded from one marching band, the theme was picked up by another.

The impact, even before the advent of live television coverage, was huge. More than fifty thousand people turned out on the streets to watch the funeral pass by. The *Daily Herald* noted that as it wound its way through London's 'pleasure district' of Soho, the girls from the sex industry – 'painted women, sisters of the world's sorrow and vice' – stood on tip-toe to see the coffin of the woman who had died fighting for their rights.

The service included the hymn 'Fight the Good Fight' that Davison had sung a few weeks earlier with her family at home in Longhorsley. The coffin was taken to King's Cross Station and then put into a goods van for its final journey to Newcastle and on to Morpeth. It was accompanied once more by her four friends, who kept vigil around the casket in the baggage car as the train rocked its way north.

Huge crowds turned out the next day in Morpeth as Davison was buried in the family grave, where her father had been laid. The site is marked by a large four-sided stone monument with a cross on top and the suffragette slogan 'Deeds not Words'.

Inevitably, the suffragettes were put under surveillance by the Special Branch of the Metropolitan Police. Among those who squeezed into the back of the police court at Epsom for Davison's inquest was Detective Superintendent Quinn, head of the Special Branch. I found documents in the National Archives at Kew revealing that because of the increased threat from the suffragettes, the Home Secretary secretly approved a request for an increase in the Special Branch force.

The Special Branch had been created twenty years earlier, after the Irish Brotherhood launched a terrorist bombing campaign in Whitehall using dynamite. The Fenian attacks occurred just as Scotland Yard was coping with the public panic over the killings of Jack the Ripper.

The authorities may have investigated whether there was a link between the Fenians and the suffragettes, but the two bombs at Lloyd George's house were more like something cooked up in the girls' laboratory at St Trinian's than an Irish nationalist cell. Davison and her accomplices had packed gunpowder into two tins, then lit a couple of candles that touched the fuses when they burned down. Police found the second bomb intact. The candle had been blown out by the blast from the first explosion.

Three years later, Special Branch uncovered the most bizarre plot concocted for the cause of women's suffrage – an attempt to kill Lloyd George with a poison dart fired through a blow pipe as he played golf. One woman was charged for the scheme, Alice Wheeldon from Derby, and was sentenced to ten years. She was freed, but died of Spanish flu in the epidemic of 1919. Later it emerged that the main witness against her was an MI5 agent, an agent provocateur. There is now a campaign to grant her a posthumous pardon.

At the outbreak of the Great War in 1914, Emmeline Pankhurst ordered an end to the suffragette attacks. She now threw herself into the war effort as an ultra-patriot with all the passion she had used to campaign for votes for women. She appeared on recruitment platforms and called for 'War Service For All' – compulsory call-up for men, and war work for women. Her patriotic speeches became more extreme, damning any and all critics as 'pro-German'. Christabel, who had previously taken a break from militant action by going into palatial self-exile in Paris, joined her mother in appealing to English nationalism in such fanatical terms she would have found an echo with Mosley's fascist blackshirts of the 1930s.

The war changed Britain for ever. Women worked as never before. They donned overalls and laboured in armament factories, making shells with high explosives; used heavy machinery; and drove lorries and cars. By the end of the war, few men were prepared to deny that women had earned the right to vote. The Representation of the People Act was easily passed in 1918 to extend the franchise to women for the first time, but even then, Parliament refused to give equality to women.

As Emmeline Pankhurst had wanted, the vote was limited to women of thirty years of age and older who had property; at the same time the vote was given to all men of twenty-one or over. Julie Gottlieb, history lecturer at Sheffield University, said: 'The press played on this fear that the men were going to be swamped by women; they outnumbered the men in the twenty-one-to-thirty age group; that is one of the main reasons that the legislation in 1918 was framed the way it was, to make sure that women were not going to outnumber men in the electorate.'[11]

It took another ten years to persuade Parliament to pass the legislation that finally gave equal voting rights to women and men at twenty-one. By 1928, change in Britain had created a very different society. The age of deference had gone; the age of couldn't-care-less extravagance, the Charleston and a new breed of self-assertive, hedonistic women in short dresses, known as Flappers, had dawned. As a result, the constitutional reform over which so much ink, energy and blood had been spilled was flippantly known as 'the Flapper Vote'.

After the war, Emmeline Pankhurst shocked her daughters by joining the Conservative Party, confirming the suspicions of Labour leaders that she had been a Tory all along. She never gained a seat in the Commons, and died on 14 June 1928. She had been able to vote for a decade herself, but she missed by a fortnight seeing the Representation of the People Act of 1928 come into full effect under the law. She is buried at Brompton Cemetery and a large statue of her stands in the Victoria Gardens, behind the House of Lords, as a testimony to the eventual success of her courageous fight.

Christabel Pankhurst found God, and went on to campaign against 'Male Lust and Venereal Disease' in America. She died there in 1958, aged seventy-seven, and is buried in Santa Monica, California.

Sylvia Pankhurst denounced her mother as a traitor to the cause, and celebrated her revolutionary fervour by having a child out of wedlock. The birth so appalled her mother she reputedly spent a day weeping over the shame. Sylvia's younger sister Adela, estranged from their mother and packed off to Australia where she co-founded the country's Communist Party, for her part took a jaundiced view of the victory for women's votes: 'The real reason for the capitulation of the government was that the war really crushed the old faith in voting and Parliaments among men who had votes.'[12]

There were many ironies in their victory. None of the Pankhursts won a seat. The first woman to be elected, in December 1918 – Countess Constance Markievicz – had never supported the suffragettes. She was an Irish Nationalist and refused to take her seat at Westminster because she believed in Home Rule for Ireland; in fact, she had been to Holloway herself, for her Republican activism, during the campaigning. So, one year later, the first woman to take a seat in the House of Commons was the acerbic high-society American, Lady Nancy Astor. She 'inherited' the seat, Plymouth Sutton, from her husband when he took the hereditary title of Viscount Astor and was disqualified from sitting in the Commons.

Since Lady Astor's arrival in the Commons, male domination of politics has proved stubbornly resistant to change. The House of Commons still retains the atmosphere and some of the culture of a gentleman's club of the Edwardian era; there is a rifle range in the basement, but few facilities for women with babies. It could be said that the Pankhursts' campaign paved the way for the first woman Prime Minister, Margaret Thatcher, in 1979, but more caustic critics say she hardly counts because the Iron Lady acted more like a man with her Cabinet (for more on that, see Chapter Ten). At the 2010 General Election, 143 women MPs were elected but they still make up only twenty-two per cent of the House. In February 2012, some women MPs complained that a draught beer in the Strangers' Bar was an insult to them. It was called 'Top Totty' and boasted a picture of a near-naked woman on the pump. It was quickly removed but the point was made. Westminster is still a man's world.

One hundred years after Emily Davison's death much still needs to be done at every level of British society to make women more equal, but women are now up against a much more difficult foe than men: apathy. Today, the right for which Emily Davison gave her life is taken for granted. Hull West, a seat not far from where she is buried, has the unenviable record for the lowest turnout at the last election; only forty-five per cent of the electorate bothered to show up at the polls.

In the village of Longhorsley, where her mother's stone-built house still stands opposite the Shoulder of Mutton pub, I was told visitors are more likely to ask about fine sausages than Davison. Mr Green, the village butcher, was commended for his sausages in a write-up in the *Sunday Times*. Jane Cotton, who runs Pele Cottage bed and breakfast, reports that no one asks about Davison these days. 'Absolutely no one. They don't seem to realize she lived here.'

Davison is not completely forgotten. Parliament is putting on an exhibition in 2013 to mark the one-hundredth anniversary of her death. Thousands of visitors already troop past a glass case as they make their way to the public gallery of the House of Commons, perhaps little understanding its significance. It contains a faded, fragile silk scarf, with green, white and purple stripes, stained with mud. It is the scarf that Davison was wearing when she fell under the King's horse.

I can't help wondering whether her sacrifice was worth it. Surely it was the social upheaval caused by the First World War, rather than Davison's death, that paved the way for women to get the vote?

The Labour MP Jeremy Corbyn has no doubt that her death made a difference. 'I think she was very brave in doing what she did. I don't know whether she intended to kill herself. But who remembers the prisons minister who locked up Gandhi? Everyone remembers Gandhi, not the minister. Those who step out of the box change history. We owe a lot to Emily Davison.'

EIGHT

1940

*'If we could get out of this jam
by giving up Malta... he would jump at it'*

VIEW OF THE WHITE CLIFFS OF DOVER:
*Hermann Goering, sixth from right, commander of the Luft-
waffe, on the coast of France, 1940.*

Hermann Goering, Commander-in-Chief of the Luftwaffe,
gathered with his senior German officers on 1 July 1940 for
a remarkable photograph. As a snapshot of history, taken by
Joseph Goebbels' propaganda unit, it has few equals. It captures the moment that Britain stood alone against the might of Hitler's Third Reich,
and held its collective breath.

Dressed in greatcoats with peaked caps atop their smart grey uniforms,
the Germans stand on a rough wooden platform on a beach near Calais,
on the north coast of France, and look across the English Channel to
the White Cliffs of Dover. One officer in the centre of the twenty-two
men trains a pair of field glasses on the English coast, twenty-one miles

away. He seems to be straining to see what Churchill's 'Blighty' is really like. His binoculars are aimed almost directly at the Norman Dover Castle, standing proud above the cliffs, which might have given him a false impression of the average Englishman's home.

They look relaxed, like a bunch of gangsters enjoying a break by the sea after their smash-and-grab raid across France; after the *Blitzkrieg*; after the chaotic evacuation of the British army from the beaches at Dunkirk. A few days earlier, Hitler had taken a private tour of some of the landmarks of Paris – the Louvre, L'Opéra, the Eiffel Tower and Les Invalides containing Napoleon's tomb (he spent a long time there).

Goering, sixth from the right, stands out in the crowd because of his bloated figure. He is wearing a grey battle tunic with knee-length jackboots and shining spurs.

He has turned to his left, as if affably engaging in banter about the ease with which his Luftwaffe will crush the Royal Air Force. He is probably boasting, as he frequently did: 'Hitler can leave it to my Luftwaffe boys to bring the drunken warmonger Churchill to his knees.' He – along with the rest of the German high command – is brimming with confidence about the prospects for England's capitulation; as with France, it is inevitable. He might even be planning his orders for a new uniform from the King's tailors in Savile Row, to be placed once London, like Paris, has surrendered to the threat of his Heinkel bombers. Goering, the jovial face of the Nazi Party, had a penchant for outrageous military uniforms: his own officers joked he would wear the uniform of an admiral to take a bath.

Like many of the legends of that tempestuous year, there is more than a hint of spin around the picture. The weather that day was wet – you can see the rain shining on the makeshift stage on which Goering and his band of officers are standing. Visibility was so poor that the White Cliffs of Dover could barely be seen from the French coast. Curators at the Imperial War Museum, where the image is part of the archives, say there are suspicions that Hitler's wartime *spinmeister* had the photograph doctored – the White Cliffs may have been enhanced to 'make the image more dramatic'.

Goebbels was well aware of the potency of the White Cliffs in the background. That wall of chalk – the very fact that it appears to be almost within Goering's grasp, within touching distance of his posing officers – makes it chilling. It was intended to show the world that all that stood between Hitler's Third Reich and the invasion of England was that narrow strip of sea. And Churchill.

The White Cliffs came to symbolize the safety of home to millions of troops fighting abroad, including the Yanks when the Americans finally entered the war. Vera Lynn gave them the hope in 1942 that, when the war was over, 'bluebirds' would be flying over the White Cliffs of Dover again. The song 'The White Cliffs of Dover' has become as British as 'Land of Hope and Glory', but it was clearly penned in America: bluebirds are not a British species – they are American thrushes. No matter. The yearning for home and a return to peace was enough.

Surrender was far from Churchill's mind that day as Goering and his officers posed in front of the 'enhanced' White Cliffs. The Prime Minister told his Chief-of-Staff, General Hastings Ismay (known as 'Pug' because he resembled the snub-nosed breed of dog) to produce a report on the feasibility of 'drenching' the beaches with mustard gas if the Germans invaded.

Churchill's private secretary, Jock Colville, noted in his diary: 'He considers that gas warfare would be justified in such an event. The other day, he said to General Thorne [General Andrew Thorne, commanding forces south of the Thames]: "I have no scruples, except not to do anything dishonourable," and I suppose he does not consider gassing Germans dishonourable.'[1]

VICE-ADMIRAL RAMSAY'S HEADQUARTERS, DOVER:
Churchill looks across the Channel towards occupied France.

Less than a fortnight later, Churchill posed for his own photograph on a vantage point high on the famous cliffs overlooking the Channel. Wearing a pinstriped suit and a tin hat, he looks through a pair of binoculars at the French coast, back to where Goering had stood.

The balcony with an iron railing is part of a warren of tunnels burrowed into the chalk more than a century before, during the Napoleonic wars. They were commandeered by the War Office to create a secret headquarters for military operations in the strategically important Dover Straits. To reach it, the Prime Minister had to squeeze through a window of a 'cabin' in the tunnel used by Vice-Admiral Sir Bertram Home Ramsay as his naval headquarters. Ramsay, like the tunnels, had been brought out of retirement for the war because of his reputation as an organizer. Churchill had decided to visit the tunnels in a gesture of thanks – it was from here that Ramsay masterminded the evacuation of three hundred and thirty thousand British and French troops from Dunkirk. The project was given the snappy codename Operation Dynamo, but that hardly concealed the fact it was a defeat.

Churchill cautioned against turning the evacuation into a victory. 'Wars are not won by evacuations,' he said on 4 June. But it encouraged a die-hard attitude in Britain when hope appeared to have gone; throughout the war, and long after it, the British prided themselves on their 'Dunkirk spirit'.

Today, despite a fall in traffic caused by the Channel Tunnel, the White Cliffs of Dover still stand as the iconic gateway to England for thirteen million visitors each year. Most of them know the country for fish and chips, the Queen and driving on the left, and most of those coming off the ferries at the port at the end of Marine Parade give but a quick glance upwards to the impressive Norman castle on the cliffs, let alone notice the balconies carved into them.

English Heritage runs the castle and the historic tunnels as a tourist attraction. I am taken down the tunnels in the chalk along the steep path that Churchill trod several times in 1940 to Ramsay's headquarters. They still ring with typewriters, the black Bakelite telephones and the sound of bombs, as though Ramsay and his staff are still there, but the authentic sounds of his headquarters are part of a multimedia experience to teach visitors about the war.

Vice-Admiral Ramsay's cabin office, with a desk, a few maps on the wall and a bunk bed, has been cleared to make room for the computers that run the 'secret tunnels' show. The balcony where Churchill stood is

THE VIEW TOWARDS RAMSAY'S CABIN:
The middle 'window', where Churchill stood in 1940.

blocked up and out of bounds. It can be seen if you walk along the Marine Parade and look high up above the Victorian villas, many of which are converted into bed-and-breakfast accommodation frequented primarily by long-haul truck drivers rather than tourists. Churchill's balcony is the middle of the three 'windows' in the cliffs, overgrown and mostly forgotten.

I ask for permission to stand where Churchill surveyed the Channel, and I am allowed, as a special concession, to step out through a window onto a balcony a few feet from Ramsay's cabin.

Stretching my legs across the windowsill, I get a seagull's view of Dover and the Channel. Churchill, who was sixty-five when he became Prime Minister, must have found it a bit of a squeeze, although those around him said he seemed energized by the war. Ferries are plying their way across to Calais, silver in the sunlight filtering through heavy cloud, while twenty tankers and container ships follow the sea lanes that make the Channel one of the busiest watery motorways in the world. Through binoculars I can see the surprisingly high white chalk cliffs of France, along which Goering stood.

Down to the right, I spy on the town of Dover. The beach area has had a makeover with a smart paved section, but the town is not a pretty sight. 'It's taken a beating,' says one of my guides. Dover was shelled during the war by huge German guns on the French coast, and received over two thousand direct hits, but the real damage has been inflicted since the war.

An unsightly dual carriageway bisects the town, an ugly scar cutting the town off from its seafront. Over to the left, a concrete ramp spirals over the port, carrying the heavy lorries up the steep hill out of town into Kent. This monumental traffic ramp turned fairground ride to the clifftop is called the Jubilee Way. The port is to be privatized, and there are fears that Dover could be bought up by – perish the thought – the French. Dame Vera Lynn is backing an alternative plan to save Dover for its people. The battle over Dover rages as fiercely as ever.

The town prides itself on the perfectly preserved castle on the clifftop, but the most prominent landmark from the sea, apart from the chalk cliffs themselves, is a tower block of former council flats: the Gateway. It seems to turn its back on the town. Across the dual carriageway, another concrete block, twelve storeys high, stands like a blackened front tooth on the seafront. It was to be a Swiss-owned hotel, but the guests never came; it was converted into offices but has been empty for a decade. It is surrounded by dereliction. The area was zoned for redevelopment, to be completed by 2014, but since the supermarket chain Asda pulled out, it looks less likely that the blighted city centre is going to get its facelift any day soon.

Dover was never a fashionable watering hole like Brighton, though it tried. The White Cliffs Experience opened with a fanfare in 1991 in an effort to cash in on the town's history. It now houses the local museum and has been renamed the Dover Discovery Centre.

Dover residents don't really blame the council. One local tells me jobs went with the collapse of the Kent coal-mining industry, the switch to air travel and the building of the Channel Tunnel when Margaret Thatcher was in power.

Prince Charles, the Prince of Wales, considered coming out against the building of the 'Chunnel'. At a discreet London restaurant, the heir to the throne sounded out me and a handful of other journalists on whether he should make a speech opposing the building of the tunnel before construction started in 1987. It was not, he said, just the loss of jobs on the ferries that concerned him. That was bad enough but, he added, 'England will no longer be an island.'

Prince Charles was looking at 'this sceptred isle' from a uniquely royal perspective, following the lines of John of Gaunt in Shakespeare's *Richard II*:

> This precious stone set in the silver sea,
> Which serves it in the office of a wall
> Or as a moat defensive to a house,
> Against the envy of less happier lands,
> This blessed plot, this earth, this realm, this England.[2]

Shakespeare had written the play for the court of Elizabeth I only five years after this narrow strip of ocean, combined with English ingenuity on the seas, had seen the Queen's triumph over the Spanish Armada.

I told our future King that a stance against the Chunnel would bring him into direct conflict with Thatcher, the elected Prime Minister; it could have provoked a constitutional row about the interference of the Crown, echoing down from Magna Carta. He never made the speech, and the tunnel – thirty-one miles long and, at its deepest, two hundred and fifty feet beneath the sea – opened in 1994. Though it is exclusively for trains, seventeen million passengers and fifteen million tonnes of freight cross the Channel through it in thirty-five minutes each year.

Dover remains on the front line of another invasion – by asylum seekers and illegal migrants seeking a better life in Britain. 'The council had a duty to house people where they landed, and Dover was expected to put them up,' one resident told me. 'The town is tired.'

Dover and its chalky cliffs have been an important crossing point from the continent of Europe since well before the Romans (the town discovered a Bronze Age boat buried in its midst, and thus boasts that the first cross-Channel ferry is three thousand years old). There had been other invasions, including the Glorious Revolution in 1688, but Churchill, with his expert grasp of history, was keenly aware that he was living through one of the greatest crises Britain had faced for a millennium when the Normans wiped out Anglo-Saxon culture. He feared all that Shakespeare had written about would be lost, that by now we would all be speaking German, living under the heel of the Nazi jackboot and working as slave labour in VW factories.

In 1940, Dover was the front line of the Battle of Britain. The fighting was so intense, in the air and on the sea, that the Dover Straits became known as Hellfire Corner. Film crews keen to get some footage of the war in the late summer of that year had only to take the steam train from Charing Cross. There is graphic footage of German Stuka dive-bombers attacking a convoy of cargo vessels trying to get into port. A cheerful English commentator accompanying the images sounds as if he is covering a game of cricket: 'He's coming in, he's missed... but he's having another go.' A German fighter plane is hit, and goes cartwheeling to destruction across the choppy sea. 'Oh boy! I've never seen anything as good as this.'

Churchill travelled to Dover again on 11 July 1940. He had asked the Director of Navigation at the Admiralty, Captain Morgan, to draw up a list of dates and locations along the south coast when a combination of high water near dawn, on nights with no moon, made it likely that the Germans would launch their invasion. The most likely date, Morgan and his team had reported, was 11 July. So that was the date Churchill picked for his tour of inspection of Ramsay's tunnels.

Most leaders, sensibly, would have avoided personal danger to preserve a grip on power as well as their own skins. But danger was like a magnet for Churchill. It always had been. In the Sudan, as a young soldier, he had taken part in the last great cavalry charge at the Battle of Omdurman, firing his pistol at the hordes of spear-carrying Dervishes. He wrote about it, and it reads like pages ripped from a *Boy's Own* magazine. Later, as a war correspondent during the Boer War, he became famous overnight when he was captured by the Boers and escaped. During his time as Home Secretary, he had been shot at during the Sidney Street siege, when a group of anarchists had been cornered in London's East End in January 1911. It had even been said that a bullet had passed through his top hat. As it could never be proved, this should be best counted as 'near myth'.

For this visit, he had taken a 'comfortable' train to Dover with Jock Colville. They were joined by a few close aides including Duncan Sandys, who was married to Churchill's daughter Diana, and had been wounded in Norway. The old man was looking for excitement, but he was disappointed. Goering's Luftwaffe failed to attack.

There had been a spectacular dogfight in the skies over Dover the day before, when 120 German fighters and bombers attacked a British convoy between Dover and Dungeness. As Colville noted in his diary: 'From the Admiral's room, in the face of the cliff, we looked across the sunlit Channel to France and could scarcely bring ourselves to realise it was enemy territory.' The party went on to Deal on the Kent coast:

It was a glorious evening with excellent visibility and we could see Cap Gris-Nez thirty miles away over an expanse of rolling Kentish Downs. But it was too clear and cloudless for enemy planes and for an aerial spectacle we had to be content with patrols of Spitfires glinting in the sun 10,000 feet above us. Winston was disappointed; the whole object of his journey had really been to see an air-raid!

Churchill's image today is the personification of the British bulldog spirit, the indomitable warrior, and above all the typical true blue Conservative. Nothing could be further from the truth.

Winston Spencer Churchill was born in Blenheim Palace, a scion of one of England's greatest generals, John Churchill, the Duke of Marlborough. His mother, Jennie Jerome, was a rich and beautiful New Yorker, making him half American. But despite his pedigree, Churchill was branded as a turncoat by the establishment, much like the Duke who deserted James II for William of Orange (see Chapter Four). He had ratted on the Conservatives in 1904 by crossing the floor of the Commons to join the Liberal Party, then he had ratted again in 1925 by defecting back to the Tories. As a result, he was regarded by his own side as a reckless maverick, an adventurer. He was not trusted by the Tory high command around the Conservative Prime Minister Neville Chamberlain.

In the 1930s, Churchill had been consigned to the political wilderness. He still had a seat in the Commons as the MP for Epping, but earned his living through journalism. (It was in his blood – his mother's family had owned the *New York Times*.) In his spare time, he enjoyed bricklaying, building walls at his beloved home, Chartwell, in Kent, and oil painting; he did a nice line in splodgy landscapes, some of which have gone on display in the galleries of various grand British homes, including Leighton House museum in London's Holland Park.

The airy sitting room at Chartwell with its views across the rolling hills of the North Weald became a salon for dissidents within the Government. Here, until the war, Churchill maintained a one-man campaign against Chamberlain's policy of appeasement towards Hitler's Germany. He was armed with intelligence from Westminster insiders, a few like-minded Conservative MPs, disgruntled civil servants and experts such as Professor Frederick Lindemann, later Lord Cherwell, who was known as the 'Prof' to the family. Throughout the war, Lindemann would feed Churchill's appetite for knowledge about the latest scientific wizardry.

Churchill would be proved right, but at the time, he was treated by Chamberlain's cronies like an almost extinct volcano, still given to dangerous eruptions but a remnant of a past epoch. And he had been wrong in the past about so much – the disaster at Gallipoli when he was at the Admiralty in the First World War (he was so cast down by the failure of beach landings against the Turks that he volunteered for the trenches in France); the return of sterling to the straitjacket of the gold standard, which made recession in Britain far worse when he was Chancellor of the Exchequer (he rated that the biggest mistake of his life).

Churchill was marching out of step with public opinion when Chamberlain flew back to Heston aerodrome from his talks in Munich with the German Chancellor, Herr Hitler, and announced he had secured Hitler's signature for an agreement that meant 'peace for our time'. Appeasement today is viewed as a dirty word, but that was not so on 30 September 1938. Britain, secure on its island, surrounded by Shakespeare's 'moat', was bitterly aware of the pain that the First World War had wrought, and was desperate for peace on the continent of Europe – almost at any price. Churchill was an obstacle to that peace. My own father, who hailed from the working classes in Liverpool, regarded Churchill as a 'warmonger' – a common view at the time.

Being able to say 'I told you so' gained Churchill little support when he was proved right, in 1939, after Hitler had repudiated his bargain with Chamberlain and invaded Poland. At that point, hostilities became inevitable. Chamberlain, the polite man in the morning coat with the rolled umbrella, accepted that it would be a mistake to keep Churchill in the wilderness as Britain went to war.

The Prime Minister put Churchill in charge of the Royal Navy as First Lord of the Admiralty, the post he had held as a Liberal in the Great War. Navy chiefs sent a signal to the fleet underlining their delight: 'Winston is back!' Churchill set about his new task with characteristic brio, using his old maps in the Admiralty to plot the war against the German U-boats that threatened to strangle the flow of American supplies from across the Atlantic.* He was keen to take the war to the Nazis.

When the Germans invaded Norway, Churchill was the driving force behind landing British troops there to deny the Germans the port of

---

* The maps are still there, but the building has been taken over by the intelligence services and is out of bounds – no special concessions in this case.

Narvik. The port would allow the Germans to ship iron ore to the Ruhr, a vital cog in the German war machine. The operation led to the first British debacle of the Second World War, but it was Chamberlain – uncomfortable in the role of wartime leader – who paid the price.

Towards the end of the famous two-day Norway debate in the Commons on 7–8 May 1940, Leo Amery, one of Churchill's supporters, melodramatically quoted Cromwell's words to the Long Parliament: 'In the name of God, go.' Chamberlain had a majority of eighty-one at the end of the debate, but many Tories abstained or voted against him; even his staunchest supporters, such as the dilettante diarist 'Chips' Channon, described Chamberlain as 'shrunken' and a 'broken man'. When the result was read out, MPs broke out into spontaneous cheering and burst into a chorus of 'Rule Britannia'. Chamberlain, believing he had lost the confidence of the Commons and, more importantly, the country, did the honourable thing and resigned as Prime Minister. Unknown to most people, he was suffering from stomach cancer which was to cause his death in November that year.

In seeking a successor to lead Britain in its hour of need, King George VI and Queen Elizabeth, later the Queen Mother, would have preferred the cool-headed (some said cold) Foreign Secretary, Lord Halifax, to the headstrong Churchill. But the aesthete Halifax (sometimes called the 'Holy Fox' for his love of hunting and his religious piety) was an architect of Chamberlain's appeasement policy, and in May, the King and Queen still favoured appeasement; it was only during the Blitz that George VI and the Queen came to embody the British spirit of resistance. The deciding factor, however, was Labour's refusal to work in a coalition under Halifax.

Halifax had enough self-awareness to acknowledge that he could not hold the country together for war. When R.A. (Rab) Butler, Halifax's loyal junior at the Foreign Office and a staunch member of the pro-appeasement group, went to Halifax's room to try to persuade him to run for the premiership, he found his boss had slipped out to the dentist's – a diplomatic toothache that Butler later said may have changed the course of British history. Butler continued to cause mischief, and his reputation never recovered; he came close to the top but was rejected for the premiership in 1957 and 1963.

Churchill, however, had the common touch, and was the people's popular choice. That made him George VI's belated choice too. Late on 10 May, Colville, a supporter of appeasement who had been with

Chamberlain in Downing Street, reported to 'Chips' Channon and other pro-Chamberlain MPs that he had just come back from Buckingham Palace where 'Winston had kissed hands and was now Premier'. Channon recalled: 'I opened a bottle of Champagne and we four loyal adherents of Mr Chamberlain drank "To the King over the water".'[3]

Churchill was Prime Minister but Chamberlain remained leader of the Conservative Party. That politically significant detail did not seem to bother Churchill unduly. 'I felt as though I were walking with destiny and all my past life had been but a preparation for this hour, and these trials,' he said.

The fate of the whole of Europe was cast like dice on that day. At 5.30 the same morning, Hitler had unleashed the *Blitzkrieg*, lightning war. German armoured divisions under Field Marshal Karl von Rundstedt drove through the supposedly impassable Ardennes forest into France. German stormtroopers captured strategic bridgeheads in the Netherlands and Denmark via parachute landings supported by Goering's bombers.

As Churchill began forming a government of national unity, von Rundstedt's Panzer divisions sidestepped the old-war fixed defences along the Maginot Line, crossed the River Meuse and smashed through the French defences at Sedan. German army group A, commanded by Field Marshal Fedor von Bock, advanced through the Netherlands and Denmark to confront the British army along the Franco-Belgian border. In London, Churchill made Clement Attlee, the Labour leader, his deputy, and included both Chamberlain and Lord Halifax in his coalition Cabinet to lock in those Tories who still supported their policy of appeasement in the face of German aggression. As further reassurance to his Conservative detractors, Churchill kept Halifax as his Foreign Secretary. He also brought in his own cronies, called the 'Insurgents' by Channon. They included Lord Beaverbrook, the rumbustious Canadian proprietor of the *Daily Express*.

Churchill put the 'Beaver' in charge of boosting aircraft production, which the media magnate did while upsetting everyone around him. In many respects it was an extraordinary appointment. Under Beaverbrook's direction, the *Daily Express* had been the most ardent supporter of appeasement in Fleet Street, and an unrelenting critic of Churchill. Noël Coward satirized Beaverbrook's lack of judgement in his wartime film *In*

Which We Serve: a warship, inspired by the exploits of Lord Mountbatten's destroyer HMS *Kelly*, sinks as a copy of the *Daily Express* floats by with the headline 'No War This Year'. Churchill had a cinema fitted out under Admiralty House so he could watch movies during the war; the faded 'cinema' sign can still be seen down a flight of steps to the left of the building's courtyard. The projectionist noted in a little black book (now in the Imperial War Museum) that Churchill said this film was 'One of the finest films I have seen'. Regardless of Churchill's personal opinions, for reasons that were hard to fathom by those around the Prime Minister, Beaverbrook held Churchill in personal thrall.

In France, von Rundstedt's Panzers made unbelievably rapid progress, cutting off the main French army from the British Expeditionary Force. The Germans then swung north in a left hook to reach the coast at Abbeville, a mere ten days after they had crossed the French border. The Danish, Dutch and Belgian Governments tumbled faster than dominoes, leaving the encircled British army with no choice but to retreat. Along the wide corridor leading to Dunkirk, the British units abandoned tanks, field guns and transports. With the humiliating surrender of the French Government, the British army, and thousands of French troops travelling with it, now faced annihilation. Churchill had an agonizing choice: to go on fighting for France, or to save the British army. He compromised, but British troops under Lord Gort fell back on the port of Dunkirk and three nearby beaches, Malo-les-Bains, Bray-Dunes and De Panne.

Ramsay's evacuation began painfully slowly, and called for endurance, as well as Henry V's 'stiffened sinews'. For a week, it was blessed by good weather and a millpond-flat sea, enabling warships to take thousands of troops directly off the east mole in Dunkirk harbour, despite coming under attack from Stuka bombers. Though the RAF flew sorties over the beaches to keep Goering's Luftwaffe at bay, many ships were sunk as their precious cargo of exhausted troops desperately tried to escape the slaughter. When it became impossible to continue the evacuation from the mole, Ramsay called up an extraordinary 'armada of small boats', from Thames pleasure cruisers to paddle steamers such as the *Waverley*, to pluck more troops from the beaches, where the sea was too shallow for warships.

The evacuation continued from 26 May to 2 June. When it was over, it was hailed as a 'miracle'. The life-and-death struggle was brutally real for British soldiers slogging to the beachhead. They faced the confusion of refugees on the roads and strafing fire from German fighters; men were ordered by Churchill to fight to the last in a rearguard action so that others could live. Around forty thousand French and British troops were listed as captured when the evacuation was over.

Dunkirk was not the only embarkation zone. Troops cut off from Dunkirk had to find their way across the Somme to Saint-Nazaire, on the Atlantic coast. They included the father of John Prescott, later to become Labour's Deputy Prime Minister under Tony Blair, but for many, the march was in vain. The twenty-thousand-tonne liner *Lancastria* was bombed as it left Saint-Nazaire's harbour. The Cunard liner went down with over four thousand men on board – at least double its official capacity and the biggest loss of life in a single sinking in British history.

It could have been much worse, however, had the German Panzer divisions attacked in force. For four days, from 24 until 27 May, the German troops halted on the outskirts of Dunkirk. It infuriated some of von Rundstedt's Panzer officers, who knew the British were at their mercy.

There were good military reasons for calling a halt – after two weeks of relentless advances, the Panzers needed a rest to refit; they were vulnerable to a counter-attack; and Goering was boasting that the Luftwaffe could complete the job without the army. Churchill, in his history of the Second World War, attributed the delay to an error of judgement. He had access to von Rundstedt's headquarters diary, written at the time, which shows that von Rundstedt had pressed for the halt, and Hitler, who had visited the field headquarters on 24 May, had 'agreed entirely'. Churchill says a 'great opportunity' for the Führer 'was lost' with the order.

Churchill was the first to take on the task of writing a definitive history of the period, and, as they say, history is written by the victors. However, Professor Richard Overy of Exeter University insists Churchill was right: von Rundstedt made the decision and Hitler endorsed him.[4] Military historian Max Hastings also agrees, and describes the decision as an 'historic blunder' by Hitler.[5] The most illustrious dissenter, the late Roy Jenkins, was undecided on who had initiated the halt, and concluded that an answer to the mystery would 'probably always prove elusive'.[6]

Of course, Churchill had much to gain from the theory that Hitler simply blundered, and had not let the British escape. To allow that possibility would have been far too dangerous, implying that Hitler had a hidden, ulterior motive. The Führer's officers suspected a higher, political reason for calling the halt. Hitler, they believed, wanted to avoid the humiliation of Britain because he wanted conciliation and a peace treaty with the nation's leaders, who would join him to focus on the real enemy to Europe – communist Russia.

One who was there, Günther Blumentritt, von Rundstedt's operational planner, gave weight to the conspiracy theory: 'Hitler astonished us by speaking with admiration of the British Empire, of the necessity for its existence, and of the civilization that Britain had brought into the world... He said that all he wanted from Britain was that she should acknowledge Germany's position on the Continent.'[7] It is not surprising that none of that was included in von Rundstedt's headquarters diary.

B.H. Liddell Hart, the soldier and military historian who interviewed Blumentritt and other high-ranking German officers after the war, supported the Dunkirk conspiracy theory. He said the strategy Hitler laid out in this crucial conference with von Rundstedt was consistent with the views expressed in *Mein Kampf* ('My Struggle'), his 1925 political manifesto. 'There were elements in his make-up which suggest that he had a mixed love–hate feeling towards Britain,' said Hart.[8]

There is further circumstantial evidence to support the conspiracy theorists who believe that Hitler allowed the British forces to escape total destruction. Joachim von Ribbentrop, the German ambassador before the war, had secretly communicated the Führer's ambivalence about a war against Britain to sympathetic members of the British establishment. These included the Duke of Windsor, formerly King Edward VIII, and the American divorcee for whom he had abdicated the throne, Wallis Simpson (who was said to number von Ribbentrop among her former lovers). Both the Duke and the Duchess became notorious for their Nazi sympathies. FBI files later accused the Duchess of being in close contact with German agents during the war, once even asking the Gestapo for the return of her private things in Paris, after the couple fled for fascist Spain in 1940.

Wallis Simpson was not the only one to be seduced by the offer of peace with Hitler. As the desperate evacuation of Dunkirk continued, Churchill was going through a crisis of confidence with his own War Cabinet. These were the three days in May when, it is alleged, 'Winston wobbled'.

It was thought until relatively recently that the question of appeasement ended on 10 May, when Churchill replaced Chamberlain as Prime

Minister. Churchill omitted any mention of doubts from his own celebrated account of the war, but the later release of the Cabinet records showed that some doubts did arise. From 26 to 28 May, Churchill engaged in a behind-the-scenes struggle with Lord Halifax, the Foreign Secretary. Halifax proposed that Britain seek a negotiated peace with Hitler while Britain remained somewhat strong, rather than wait three months and seek peace from a position of weakness, on the verge of defeat.

The argument raged almost round the clock for those three days within the inner core of ministers – Churchill, Chamberlain, Halifax, Attlee and Arthur Greenwood for Labour. Churchill, puffing furious clouds of smoke from his cigars, pouring whiskies to sustain him, kept up an exhausting series of virtually back-to-back meetings with his War Cabinet, interspersing them with private hole-in-the-corner talks with one or two men, aiming to win their support. He even tried a cajoling chat with Halifax in the garden of Number Ten.*

Churchill had asked the chiefs of staff whether Britain could continue the war alone, if France capitulated. Their answer was presented to the War Cabinet in a top-secret military paper coyly entitled 'A Certain Eventuality'. The advisers had concluded that Britain could carry on single-handed, providing the RAF could deny the Germans the air superiority needed to mount an invasion. It was not entirely reassuring.

In the midst of the to and fro, on 26 May Halifax held tentative talks with the Italian ambassador, Giuseppe Bastianini, over the possibility that Italy's fascist leader Benito Mussolini might serve as a mediator for Britain and France in peace talks with Hitler. When Halifax gave a brief summary of their conversation to the War Cabinet, he reported that Bastianini had raised the question of whether the Government would consider it; Halifax had replied it seemed unlikely as long as hostilities continued. Bastianini's rejoinder: if talks started, 'war would be pointless'. The implication was clear – if Britain agreed to negotiate, the war could be ended. Halifax informed the War Cabinet that he had told the Italian ambassador that Britain was 'prepared to consider any proposals... provided our liberty and independence were assured'.

---

* The War Cabinet met at Admiralty House as well as Downing Street, because the Prime Minister refused to push the Chamberlains out of Number Ten. The disdain for the appeasers in the Churchill household extended as far down as the Downing Street cat; when the family finally moved to Number Ten a month later, Churchill's daughters brought with them Nelson, the Admiralty cat, and dubbed the Chamberlains' cat, the 'Munich Mouser'.

Churchill was unimpressed. He said he was opposed to any negotiations that 'might lead to a derogation of our rights and power'. The group broke for a time to allow the War Cabinet members to go to Westminster Abbey, where a national day of prayer for deliverance from Hitler's forces was being led. After the service, Churchill returned to Admiralty House for lunch with Paul Reynaud, the embattled French Prime Minister. Unilaterally, he told Reynaud that Britain would go on alone, if France was forced to sign an armistice. 'We would rather go down fighting than be enslaved to Germany.' This marked an open split with Halifax, who was still driving for a negotiated settlement with Hitler.

When the meeting of the War Cabinet reconvened, Halifax asked Churchill whether he would be prepared to begin discussions – assuming Britain's liberty and independence were assured. Churchill was now forced into a corner. He could not say 'no' at this stage. Chamberlain was wavering again. Without Chamberlain's backing, refusing to begin discussions over peace would have threatened the collapse of the Government. Churchill, ever the calculating politician, said he would be 'thankful to get out of our present difficulties on such terms, provided we retained the essentials and the elements of our vital strength, even at the cost of some territory'. He had in mind British control of Gibraltar, maybe Malta, perhaps some of the colonies in Africa, which were already coming free of the Crown. The meeting was dismissed.

Churchill then convened another meeting of the War Cabinet – the third that day. This time, no civil servants were present. The Cabinet minutes say: 'This record does not cover the first quarter of an hour of the discussion, during which the Secretary [Sir Edward Bridges] was not present.'[9]

Until the 'sofa government' of the Blair years, it was unheard of for important meetings to go unminuted by civil servants. The unprecedented secrecy surrounding this meeting suggests Churchill realized it was time to put his cards on the table. If he wobbled, it was then.

The drama surrounding Winston's 'wobble' was turned into a hit play in the West End in 2011 called *Three Days in May*. 'That is possibly the bit where Churchill had his wobble,' the author of the play, Ben Brown, told the *Daily Telegraph*. 'Churchill himself allowed Lord Halifax to draw up a draft proposal to go with the French and seek negotiation via Mussolini.'[10]

I disagree with Brown. I believe that is a misreading of the political dynamics of the time. Far from a personal wobble, all the evidence I gathered in conversations with those who knew the Prime Minister, as well as experts on his life, suggests he was determined to fight on, but he knew he had to hold together the national Coalition. It was the Conservatives, Chamberlain's supporters, not Labour, who were his biggest critics. They still could not put their trust in his judgement. He needed to give Halifax room to explore the options before closing him down. So Halifax was authorized by the Prime Minister to prepare a draft of his 'Suggested Approach to Italy'.

I share the view of Churchill's biographer, Roy Jenkins, who said: 'Churchill's resolution was not in doubt, but his political position was.'[11] The dilemma Churchill faced was also well documented by John Lukacs in his book *Five Days in London*. If Chamberlain had sided with Halifax, Lukacs argued, Churchill's position would have been untenable. Rather than wobbling and considering negotiating with Hitler, Churchill was quite clear – he would have resigned if he had lost the support of his party. In his absence, Chamberlain, as party leader, would probably have allowed Halifax to reach a settlement and Britain's independence would have been bartered away. As Churchill put it to his War Cabinet, Britain would have become a 'vassal state'.

I believe Churchill personally never wavered; far from it. Terry Charman of the Imperial War Museum agrees: 'I don't think that for a minute Churchill "wobbled" and the quote often used against him about "jumping" at a chance to make peace if it meant the surrender of a colony or two was just so much "hot air".' He adds: 'One has to remember that Churchill was not yet party leader or indeed the undisputed leader of Britain at this point in time and perhaps he felt that he had to appear somewhat conciliatory regarding Halifax's suggestions, which were at this stage supported, but not strongly, by Chamberlain, still party leader.'

Churchill had already warned President Roosevelt of the dangers of losing to the appeasers in the War Cabinet. In a telegram to the White House on 19 May, he appealed for military aid from the United States and laid bare his fears in the starkest terms: if he lost the support of his Cabinet, the appeasement camp would offer the British fleet as a bargaining counter to sue for the best peace deal from Hitler. Control of the fleet would make Germany powerful enough to challenge US trade routes. 'Excuse me, Mr President, putting this nightmare bluntly. Evidently, I could not answer for my successors who in utter despair and helplessness might well have to accommodate themselves to German will,' he wrote. He signed himself 'Former Naval Person', an amusing nom-de-plume he had adopted with the President during his days as head of the Admiralty.

Churchill knew he could count on support from one corner: Clement Attlee and Arthur Greenwood, the two Labour members of his War Cabinet. Labour may have been traditionally anti-war, but most were not pacifists. Many Labour supporters had volunteered for the Spanish Civil War to defeat General Francisco Franco and his fascists. Many were Marxists, whose sympathies were with Soviet Russia, not fascist Germany. The cynical 1939 Molotov–Ribbentrop non-aggression pact may have confused some Labour members until it was clarified by Operation Barbarossa, Hitler's invasion of Russia, in 1941.

Attlee and Greenwood would have been accused of betrayal if they had sided with Halifax. Within days of the crisis, an excoriating attack on the appeasers would be published by leading left-wing writers including Michael Foot, later the leader of the Labour Party, under the pen name of Cato. It was called *Guilty Men*. The 1940 copy that I have is faded and foxed, but it has lost none of its fire. As a sustained piece of polemic, it has few equals. It castigates fifteen politicians connected with appeasing the monster Hitler, starting with Chamberlain. The other 'villains' included the former Labour Prime Minister Ramsay MacDonald, who surrendered power to a coalition in the Great Depression, Chamberlain's chief cheerleaders Sir Samuel Hoare, Sir John Simon, Lord Halifax, the former Conservative Prime Minister Stanley Baldwin and the Government Chief Whip, Captain David Margesson, who was accused of acting as a fixer for the appeasers in the Commons.

The future of Britain now depended, once more, on which way Neville Chamberlain decided to jump. At the end of the three crucial days in May, Chamberlain sided with Churchill.

Chamberlain knew better than anyone else that Hitler would only respect force. He noted in his diary: 'The PM disliked any move towards Musso [Mussolini]. It was incredible that Hitler would consent to any terms that we could accept – though if we could get out of this jam by giving up Malta and Gibraltar and some African colonies he would jump at it. But the only safe way was to convince Hitler that he couldn't beat us. I supported this view.'

It is worth noting that Chamberlain was not ruling out a deal. He was giving Churchill qualified support to show Hitler that he could not defeat Britain. What happened next was open to question. But with this support in his pocket, Churchill was able to outfox the Holy Fox.

Halifax, a fellow of Oxford's All Souls College and a former Viceroy of India, was a remote figure at the best of times. With a seat in the House of Lords, he was cut off from Churchill's power base in the Commons. Churchill now showed his skill at political infighting, and routed the appeasers with a masterstroke.

At 6 p.m. on Tuesday, 28 May, the Prime Minister summoned members of the Cabinet who were not in the War Cabinet to a meeting, and briefed them in rough outline about the War Cabinet's discussions. It seemed innocent enough, but with Halifax absent, Churchill gave them a blood-curdling call to go down fighting rather than to do a deal with Germany. According to the account of the Labour Cabinet minister Hugh Dalton, Churchill told them that Hitler would demand Britain give up its fleet under the guise of 'disarmament'. 'We should become a slave state' if that were the case, Churchill told them, no better than a puppet government 'under Mosley', the British fascist leader, or 'somebody else' – presumably someone even worse than that.

Dalton wrote in the margin of his notes these lines from Churchill's brief: 'If this long island story of ours is to end at last, let it end only when each one of us lies choking in his own blood upon the ground.' Jenkins, in his biography of Churchill, said there is no knowing if this was Dalton's florid phrase or Churchill's[12], but I can say it certainly accords with Churchill's intentions. One of his first orders after becoming Prime Minister, I discovered, was for plans to be drawn up for the defence of Whitehall. A map was circulated around the Cabinet showing how pillboxes and machine-gun nests would be positioned around landmarks such as Downing Street, Admiralty Arch and Horse Guards. The civil service departments and Downing Street were to be the final battleground, a last bastion, and treated as 'the keep of a fortress', to be defended, street by street, room by room.

This was not an idle boast. Nicholas Soames, the Conservative MP and grandson of Churchill, told me the Prime Minister intended to go down fighting in his bunker under Whitehall (now the Cabinet War Rooms, and open to the public) if there had been an invasion. 'He would have died with a gun in his hand,' Soames told me. The late Walter Thompson, Churchill's bodyguard, recalled he had been ordered to keep a .45 Colt revolver fully loaded. 'He intended to use every bullet but one on the enemy. The last one he saved for himself.'

At the end of the meeting with the Cabinet, Churchill was given a show of overwhelming support, and some members came up and patted him on the back. From that moment, the case for a negotiated surrender was dead.

Churchill had passed the political crisis, but the threat of invasion remained.

Reporting to the Commons on 4 June, Churchill was at his most defiant. He declared: 'We shall fight on the beaches, we shall fight on the landing grounds, we shall fight in the fields and in the streets, we shall fight in the hills; we shall never surrender'.

The phrase which carried the most importance was a commitment to carry on fighting 'if necessary for years, if necessary alone'. Churchill, when he wrote his war memoir, said it was inserted 'not without design'. It was intended as a signal to the appeasers, to France, to the United States and to Hitler that, having defeated the appeasers at home, he now meant what he said: Britain would never surrender.[13]

Despite his fine words, there was organized panic in London. As early as 1939, the Foreign Office had made arrangements to decamp to Cheltenham; the Ministry of Labour had chosen to flee to Leamington Spa. The Air Ministry would move to Worcester, and the King and Queen would go to a country house nearby in the name of the French ambassador. Now private individuals were left to make their own arrangements to cope with invasion.

The writer Harold Nicolson, Parliamentary Secretary to the Ministry of Information, was sure his home at Sissinghurst, Kent, now famous for its National Trust garden, would be one of Germany's first targets. He wrote to his wife, exotic writer Vita Sackville-West: 'I think you really ought to have a "bare bodkin" [poison pill] handy so that you can take your quietus when necessary. I shall have one also. I am not in the least afraid of such a sudden and honourable death. What I dread is being tortured and humiliated.'

'Chips' Channon sent his young son, Paul – later to become a Tory Cabinet minister in the Thatcher Government – by liner to the safety of Canada. He asked his head gardener Mortimer to bury two tin boxes of valuables in the grounds of his mansion, to avoid his treasures falling into German hands when (not if) the invasion came. The larger box contained his celebrated diaries, which were full of society gossip, while the smaller tin had 'my best bibelots, watches, Fabergé objects'. Channon, a confirmed defeatist, confided to his diary: 'I wonder as I gaze out upon the grey and green Horse Guards Parade with the blue sky, the huge silver balloons like bowing elephants, the barbed-wire entanglements and soldiers about, is this really the end of England? Are we witnessing, as for so long I have feared, the decline, the decay and perhaps extinction, of this great island people?'

While keeping up an outward show of optimism, Churchill also secretly prepared for the worst. The King's wayward brother, Edward, Duke of Windsor, had been given a non-job in uniform as a liaison officer in France. But when Paris fell, the Windsors refused to return to Britain. They had instead gone to the South of France, then on to fascist Spain, then finally to Portugal, where they were mixing with fascists. Churchill heard of covert German plans to abduct them, with a view to making Edward a puppet king after an invasion of England.

The Duke was known for his loose talk with Germans, but what had infuriated Churchill was Edward's confidence to a German official that he believed continued bombing would force Britain into peace with Germany. Because of the Duke's increasingly dangerous and outspoken sympathies for the Germans and Hitler, Churchill packed the Windsors off to diplomatic exile. The Prime Minister telegrammed Edward in early August offering him the appointment as Governor of the Bahamas. He was not sure it would be the solution, and asked Max Beaverbrook: 'Do you think he will take it?'

'Sure he will, and he'll find it a great relief.'

'Not half as much as his brother will,' said Churchill.

The Prime Minister believed Edward and Wallis Simpson risked alienating the public from the monarchy. He also refused Edward permission to visit the United States because, he said, it would 'not be in the public interest'. He feared Edward would strengthen the isolationists in America who strongly opposed Roosevelt's aid to Britain because they claimed it compromised US neutrality.

Churchill's judgement was quickly proved correct. The Duke gave an interview in December 1940 to a popular American magazine, *Liberty*, which was close to treason, saying it would be 'a tragic thing for the world if Hitler were overthrown. Hitler is the right and logical leader of the

German people.' The article was heavily censored before publication, and he was never trusted with any public office again. The Windsors spent most of the rest of their lives in exile in Paris, and the Queen Mother took her enmity for Wallis Simpson to her grave in 2002.

On the side, Churchill made arrangements for the royal princesses, Elizabeth and Margaret, to leave London for the country, the mansion of Madresfield Court in Malvern, Worcestershire. I was advised by experts at the Imperial War Museum that, if the Germans had invaded, the whole Royal Family probably would have been shipped to Canada.

Churchill also despatched another supporter of appeasement, Sir Sam Hoare, to Madrid as Britain's ambassador to neutral Spain, which had become a hotbed of intrigue. On first becoming Prime Minister, Churchill had sacked Hoare, a leading supporter of Chamberlain, from the Cabinet. But Hoare had contacts with the fascists, and Churchill enlisted him to do his part to keep General Franco and Spain out of the war.

On 3 July, Churchill took an irrevocable decision that was utterly ruthless but proved a turning point: he ordered a British naval task force to sink French warships at Oran, on the coast of Algeria, to stop them falling into the hands of the Germans. It caused the deaths of 1297 French sailors, and outrage in France. As reports of the fighting with the French fleet came through, Churchill paced the carpet in Downing Street, muttering: 'Terrible… terrible.' It was a tragic decision, but it was highly popular. When he went into the Commons, Churchill was cheered to the rafters; MPs waved their order papers as if he had achieved a great victory.

President Roosevelt said Oran had convinced him that Britain would continue the fight for years, as Churchill had promised. Roosevelt had recently been receiving defeatist messages from Joseph Kennedy, the US ambassador in London, and needed persuading. Kennedy, the Irish-American father of the future US President Jack Kennedy, was reporting that Britain's surrender was 'inevitable'.

Oran encouraged the President to provide Churchill with the armaments Britain kept pleading for, particularly warships and planes, under a scheme called Lend-Lease. Churchill's biographer, Martin Gilbert, calls this one of the Prime Minister's key legacies of the war. Churchill's lasting legacy, however, was to hold out for Britain's freedom at a time when lesser leaders would have caved in. In a secret session of the Commons (held behind closed doors to avoid handing strategic information to the enemy), Churchill told MPs that he was playing for time until

Roosevelt was re-elected later that year. Roosevelt won, and the British aid programme was guaranteed.

Aid from the United States enabled Britain and the Commonwealth countries to go on alone in the war for another long, hard eighteen months. Roosevelt's support also consolidated Churchill's passionate belief in the special relationship with America – a belief he held all his life. But it came at a cost to the UK – companies such as Shell, Courtaulds, Lever Brothers, Dunlop and insurance firms were forced to sell off their US assets at 'fire sale' prices to reduce the debt in 1941. Britain owed a huge debt of gratitude to the US after the war, but the financial debt may have been greater, and was only finally paid off in 2006.

Colville noted, without a hint of criticism, that the old man seemed to enjoy war. Churchill was firing off minutes and memos, interfering in detail, running faster than younger men when he inspected the troops. He even found time to send a memo to the Admiralty asking for the 'dismal object' of a flag that was flying over its building to be replaced with a new one.

Hitler promoted Goering to *Reichsmarschall* of the Greater German Reich on 19 July 1940. This made Goering senior to all of Hitler's other generals, and thus signalled that he was Hitler's chosen successor. The same day, Hitler made a grand offer to Britain of a negotiated peace in a speech to the Reichstag. German bombers dropped leaflets over British streets carrying an English translation of the speech. The headline read: 'A last appeal to reason by Adolf Hitler'. Having been outmanoeuvred in the Cabinet by Churchill, it was left to Halifax to turn the Führer down.

There are many unanswered questions surrounding the events of 1940, and whether Britain seriously faced the threat of invasion is a key one. It was unclear even to Goering what exactly was in Hitler's mind, but there is evidence that the Führer was never completely serious about capping the defeat of France with an invasion of England. His generals say Hitler reluctantly ordered the drafting of invasion plans, codenamed Operation Sealion, as a last resort. His hesitancy was reflected in the wording of Directive 16, issued on 16 July 1940 from the Führer's HQ: 'As England, in spite of the hopelessness of her military position, has so far shown herself unwilling to come to any compromise, I have therefore decided to begin to prepare for, and *if necessary* carry out, an invasion of England.' The italics are mine, but the doubts clearly were Hitler's.

The Directive states that each of the fighting services should prepare plans based on a surprise crossing on a broad front extending from Ramsgate in Kent to a point to the west of the Isle of Wight. Their proposals had to be completed and submitted by the middle of August 1940 so that a final decision could be taken by the Führer. It was signed 'Hitler' and initialled by Field Marshal Wilhelm Keitel and Colonel General Alfred Jodl (who would later sign Germany's unconditional surrender).

One of the prerequisites for carrying out the plan, said Hitler, was that the RAF would have to be 'eliminated to such an extent that it would be incapable of putting up any substantial opposition to the invading troops'. Goering had already promised the Führer he would wring the RAF's neck. Churchill later recorded that the French also believed Britain would have its neck wrung like a chicken. 'Some chicken! Some neck!' said Churchill.[14]

The German invasion plan was for seaborne forces numbering about two hundred and fifty thousand troops with six hundred and fifty tanks to be transported in barges across the Channel. The spearhead would be commanded by Field Marshal Karl von Rundstedt, with General Ernst Busch on his right and General Adolf Strauss on his left. Von Rundstedt would land between Folkestone and Brighton with orders to strike towards the capital. An airborne division would capture the beaches from Dover to Folkestone. Ten German divisions would be landed in a first wave over four days to establish a wide bridgehead. Their objective would be securing ground from the Thames to Portsmouth within a week. A second thrust into the soft underbelly of England would be mounted by Field Marshal Walter von Reichenau. He would sail with his forces from Cherbourg to Lyme Bay to push northwards to the Severn estuary.

The German naval command had enormous doubts about Operation Sealion. They said it would require 155 transport craft, and these could not be assembled until mid-September. German generals were also apprehensive about the risks of reaching their landing points, given the supremacy of the Royal Navy, without overwhelming air cover. By 31 July, the head of the German navy, Admiral Erich Raeder, had persuaded Hitler to delay the invasion until after Goering had secured the air.

The Gestapo hurriedly threw together a guide for invading soldiers. The Black Book included a helpful list of 2820 people, including immigrants from Europe, journalists, politicians and Jews, who were to be rounded up, arrested and probably shot.

Field Marshal Walther von Brauchitsch, the army Commander-in-Chief, signed a directive stating that all able-bodied men aged between seventeen and forty-five were to be interned and despatched to the Continent. 'Not even in Poland had the Germans begun their occupation with such a brutal and drastic measure,' said Terry Charman of the Imperial War Museum. Anyone found posting placards hostile to the Germans would face immediate execution. Goering ordered Reinhard Heydrich, head of the Reich Central Security Office, to start the round-up as the invasion progressed 'in order to seize and combat effectively the numerous important organisations and societies in England which are hostile to Germany'.

This gave the lie to Halifax's naive hopes that Hitler had good intentions towards England. Those in the Black Book list included Beaverbrook, Claud Cockburn and Sefton Delmer of the *Daily Express*, H.G. Wells, Shirley Williams's mother Vera Brittain, Noël Coward, Rebecca West and J.B. Priestley – who did nightly broadcasts to America describing the plight of Britain. In one, on 5 June, Priestley described Dunkirk as 'another English epic… so typical of us – so absurd, yet so grand and gallant that you hardly know whether to laugh or cry'. West sent Coward a telegraph after the war when the list was first published, saying: 'My dear – the people we should have been seen dead with.' Churchill was also on the list, with his address conveniently printed for the SS to pick him up at Chartwell.

The Prime Minister believed that a German commando raid directed at him in his Whitehall bunker was more likely than a full-scale German invasion at the coast – a *coup de grâce*, like the plot of *The Eagle Has Landed*. It was not entirely fiction. Hitler believed the British would sue for peace, if Churchill could be removed. Charman, a Churchill expert, told me: 'Having seen what had happened in Holland on the invasion in May 1940, there was this great fear that the Government was more or less undefended against a parachute drop that might have taken them prisoner and paralysed the war effort.'

Though it was frighteningly real to most people, Churchill remained confident that the RAF and the Royal Navy could stop an invasion. Jock Colville's diaries show that the Prime Minister encouraged the 'invasion scare' for political reasons – it kept Britain on its toes and scotched talk of surrender. Colville admitted on 12 July that there was an element of sham in Churchill's invasion rhetoric:

> He [Churchill] emphasised that the great invasion scare (which we
> only ceased to deride six weeks ago) is serving a most useful purpose:
> it is well on the way to providing us with the finest offensive army we
> have ever possessed and it is keeping every man and woman tuned
> to a high pitch of readiness. He does not wish the scare to abate
> therefore, and although personally he doubts whether invasion is a
> serious menace, he intends to give that impression and to talk about
> long and dangerous vigils etc., when he broadcasts on Sunday[15]

Radio was the main means of communication in 1940. It was listened to
avidly in every household in the land. In his BBC broadcast on 14 July,
Churchill duly told the nation: 'We must show ourselves equally capable
of meeting a sudden violent shock or – what is perhaps a harder test – a
prolonged vigil.'

As usual, Churchill could not be sure that the threat he invoked would
be the one the nation would actually meet. General Bernard Paget and
Lieutenant General Claude Auchinleck thought the Germans might use
troop carriers, gliders and parachutists to seize a port as a bridgehead.
Churchill refused to spread his forces thinly across the beaches; he wanted
them held in reserve, in mobile formations, to counter-attack wherever
they were needed, if the Germans landed on British soil.

Newsreels kept up a ludicrously cheerful front for those facing the
grim reality of rationing and war on the doorstep. One showed the newly
mobile units being trained to combat the Führer's shock troops. The units
were mounted on motorcycles with sidecars, and riding over sand dunes,
preparing to meet 'Adolf if he drops in for a cup of tea and a bun'.

In addition to the militia of old men and young boys in the Home
Guard, hand-picked citizens, such as family doctors, who would have some
freedom of movement during an occupation, were recruited secretly into
a French-style British resistance. Weapons like something out of Heath
Robinson cartoons were imagined, and then produced. A makeshift tank
trap, consisting of petrol tanks that would be exploded over a Panzer
tank, was prepared for the main road from the coast at Shooters Hill to
London. Nearby, a command headquarters for the resistance movement
was established in the basement of a local house. All over England, road
signs and nameplates on station platforms were taken down to confuse the
enemy, an idea hatched in Whitehall by occult author Dennis Wheatley,
who was part of a 'black ops' deception team. It succeeded in confusing
everyone.

Churchill ordered that all the church bells throughout England be rung as a warning if the Germans landed, and a codeword was issued for the alert – 'Cromwell', after one of his heroes. Unfortunately, some overzealous officer issued the codeword by mistake, spreading a false alarm across the country.

Eagle Day, Goering's major assault on Britain's air defences, was delayed by bad weather until 13 August. The first raids were not as effective as the Luftwaffe surveillance officers claimed, but they quickly threatened the survival of the RAF as a fighting force, and without the RAF, the advisers said, Britain could not go it alone.

Britain was fortunate that Fighter Command was led by the resourceful Sir Hugh Dowding. Born in Moffat, Scotland, in 1882, Dowding was due to retire when war broke out, but stayed to oversee the Battle of Britain. Before Dunkirk, he jealously guarded his precious fighters, refusing to commit more to the defence of France as it fell, in order that he would have enough to defend Britain.

Many believe the Battle of Britain was an 'English show', but it was in fact a multinational effort. In addition to pilots from the colonies, including one Jamaican, there were one hundred and forty-five Polish airmen, eighty-eight Czechs, thirteen French and seven Americans – despite being banned from combat by their country's official stance of neutrality. In this and other covert ways, Cameron was partly right that Britain had a valuable ally in America in 1940.

The international contingent included 'Billy' Fiske, the rich son of a New England banker, and a double Olympic gold-medal winner on the US bobsled team. He had joined up with the 'Millionaires' 601 Squadron based at Tangmere, West Sussex, where Max Aitken, son of Lord Beaverbrook, was a squadron leader. Fiske showed great bravery against the German Stukas as they attacked the RAF. When the fuel tank of his Hurricane was hit by a dive-bomber during a raid on 16 August, he nursed his plane back to his airfield but as he did so, it burst into flames. He was rushed to hospital, with severe burns to his hands and ankles. The next day he was seen sitting up in bed, 'perky as hell', but later died of shock. He is buried in the village church at Boxgrove. A plaque to his memory is hung in the Crypt of St Paul's Cathedral. Its simple inscription reads: 'An American citizen, who died that England might live'.

During the Battle of Britain, Dowding lost over 540 fighter pilots, about one in six of those who fought, with many more injured. It has often been said that the RAF was winning the battle but its rate of attrition, particularly in pilots, was unsustainable. In fact, partly thanks to Beaverbrook's efforts to boost aircraft production, the RAF was keeping pace with its aircraft losses. The number of available RAF fighters fell from 714 to 645 during the first week of the battle, but by 21 August, it had risen again to 722. However, like Wellington's summary after Waterloo, it was a close-run thing, and Dowding was running out of pilots. While the battle was raging, on 20 August Churchill made one of his most memorable speeches to the House of Commons. He anticipated victory: 'Never in the field of human conflict was so much owed by so many to so few.' Churchill knew that Dowding had a secret weapon in his favour – radar. The invention enabled Fighter Command to gather planes in the air and target their attacks on incoming formations of German bombers with pinpoint accuracy. Churchill also had Ultra, the intercepted German signals using Enigma codes that had been deciphered by the code-breakers of Bletchley Park. Even so, Churchill's words seemed no more than defiant rhetoric. The outcome, despite the Prime Minister's brave phrases, was anything but certain. By 31 August, Fighter Command was on the verge of collapse because its airfields were being put out of action, and Dowding was wondering how long his fighters could hold out.

His answer came on 6 September when a mass formation of Heinkel bombers and supporting ME 109 fighters swept across the Channel. Fighter Command was ready for another pounding, but the Luftwaffe did not attack the airfields. They went instead to attack the port of London. It was a devastating daylight raid but for Dowding, the relief for his fighter squadrons was like an answer to a prayer. Churchill later wrote: 'If the enemy had persisted… the whole intricate organisation of Fighter Command might have broken down.'[16]

Somehow Fighter Command had survived. German fighters could only fly for ten minutes over British cities, leaving the bombers at the mercy of the RAF, so they quickly switched to night raids. The switch in Goering's tactics led to the Blitz on British cities, and the Blitz brought a new terrifying phase of the war, which increased the stoicism of the British people. But it also broke down barriers. One of the first lessons the besieged had to learn was that in war, the English reserve had to go. Everyone 'mucked in'. They had to get used to being crammed together. Now every street was in the front line.

~⟨∂~

In 1939, children from the cities – including my sisters – had been evacuated to the relative safety of houses and farms in the countryside. They pleaded in tearful letters to their parents to be allowed back home. And my sisters, like thousands of others not yet in their teens, did return home. They were reunited with my parents in Bootle, near the strategically important Liverpool docks, in the autumn of 1940, just as Goering's Blitz began. They recalled the terror of sitting in a basement, listening to the drone of enemy bombers overhead, the whine of the bombs as they fell and the crump of the explosions as they got nearer, never knowing whether the next one would fall on them. One night, an iron bar sealing the door to the cellar was blown across the room by a blast above. When they crawled out in the morning, they found a scene of utter devastation. The neighbour's house had received a direct hit and was gone; their own home – a flat above a chip shop in Marsh Lane – was laid bare, uninhabitable. My parents pulled my sisters through Liverpool on foot, past High Street shops that were still burning, and tramlines that had been torn up like toys, to Lime Street railway station, where they boarded a train for North Wales. They did not know where they were going. They were taken in as refugees by a farming family, the Wynns, in the Ffrith near Wrexham, where they thankfully spent the rest of the war in rural isolation. They were lucky.

Over the course of the Blitz, London was bombed on seventy-six successive nights and a total of forty thousand people lost their lives. In the first raid on London's civilian population, on 8 September, more than three hundred Londoners were killed and 1337 were seriously injured. Churchill visited the devastated area of the East End. He saw an air-raid shelter that had taken a direct hit, with the loss of forty lives. His Chief-of-Staff, General Ismay, noted that the survivors stormed Churchill as he got out of the car – but they showered him with messages of support. 'It was good of you to come, Winnie. We can take it. Give it 'em back,' they shouted.

The bombing was indiscriminate. During a raid on 14 October, Downing Street was damaged when the old Treasury building next door received a near-direct hit. Churchill could have been killed but he had a premonition, and unusually for him, had taken the precaution of having dinner served in the basement behind blast-proof doors. The Downing Street kitchen was wrecked and strewn with debris. Fortunately, Churchill had also ordered his cook, Mrs Landemare, his butler and his servants into the basement. Then he led his guests, three members of the Coalition Government, all wearing tin hats, onto the roof of the Downing Street bunker, also known as the 'Annexe'. There they watched London burning. They could see that the Reform Club had been hit. John Martin from Churchill's private office rang to find out how things were. The porter answered the phone: 'The Club is burning, sir.'

Buckingham Palace was hit too. This prompted the Queen to say: 'I am glad we have been bombed. It makes me feel I can look the East End in the face.'

High society continued to enjoy the swing of London nightlife, despite the blackout. Churchill's daughter, Mary, recalled going to Queen Charlotte's Ball during an air raid. When they emerged in the early hours, they saw the Café de Paris in Coventry Street had received a direct hit. 'Recalling it now, I am a little shocked that we headed off to find somewhere else to twirl away whatever was left of the night.'[17]

Churchill saw himself as one in a long line of leaders, including Elizabeth I and William Pitt, who had kept Britain free. In a broadcast on 11 September warning of the threat of invasion, Churchill said: 'It ranks with the days when the Spanish Armada was approaching the Channel, and Drake was finishing his game of bowls; or when Nelson stood between us and Napoleon's Grand Army in Boulogne.'

After the war, when he was honoured on the occasion of his eightieth birthday, Churchill said he had been given the privilege of uttering the Lion's roar. There was no better 'roar' than his speech to the Commons on 18 June 1940 when he offered the hope that if Britain stood up to Hitler, the whole of Europe would move to the 'broad, sunlit uplands'. He went on:

> But if we fail, then the whole world, including the United States, including all that we have known and cared for, will sink into the abyss of a new dark age made more sinister, and perhaps more protracted, by the lights of perverted science. Let us therefore brace ourselves to our duties, and so bear ourselves, that if the British Empire and its Commonwealth last for a thousand years, men will still say, 'This was their finest hour.'

Standing on Dover's White Cliffs, it is hard to argue with that.

NINE

1948

'New Jerusalem'

PARK HOSPITAL, TRAFFORD, MANCHESTER:
The birthplace of the National Health Service.

Vast crowds cheered as Sir Winston Churchill stepped onto the balcony of what had once been the Health Department, in Whitehall. It was 8 May 1945 – Victory in Europe (VE) Day. The masses cheered ever more lustily as the portly Prime Minister gazed down on the sea of adoring faces and made his famous 'V' sign. Here was created one of the enduring images to mark the end of the Second World War, though the balcony itself is now part of the HM Revenue and Customs building, and its daily view is mostly filled now with the stalled rush-hour traffic of Parliament Street. Churchill's balcony, if not the moment, is largely forgotten.

Churchill does not stand on the balcony alone. To one side, you can see Ernest Bevin, the thick-set Labour minister who had done more than anyone to mobilize the working class in support of the war effort;

elsewhere you find the minister for the home front, John Anderson, after whom the bomb shelters were named. Churchill had asked both men to take a more central place on the balcony, but Bevin had declined. 'This is your day,' he said.

One key minister from the War Cabinet was missing from the balcony: the dapper, mustachioed, pipe-smoking Labour leader, Clement Attlee. As the Deputy Prime Minister in the Coalition Government, 'Clem', as he was affectionately known, had served Churchill and the nation loyally. That was true on this day, as well. Attlee was then in San Francisco with Anthony Eden, the Conservative Foreign Secretary, at a conference to set up the United Nations.

The victory party had been going on for hours by the time Churchill walked out of the large, late-Victorian conference room and stepped onto the balcony. It was his third major speech of the day and officially it would be the last of the war. This was the moment when Britain's wartime history ended and its postwar history began.

Earlier, masses of people had swirled around Parliament, and as Big Ben struck 3 p.m. there was an extraordinary hush. Across the country, revellers stopped their celebrations to listen to the Prime Minister's broadcast from Number Ten. The address was relayed on speakers in Parliament Square, where vast crowds had gathered outside the Commons.

Churchill formally announced that at 2.41 a.m. the day before, an unconditional surrender had been signed by the chief of German high command General Alfred Jodl with Grand Admiral Dönitz, President of the Third Reich for a week, to the USA's General Eisenhower in Reims. In fact, news of the surrender was suppressed for twenty-four hours to allow a separate German surrender to the Russians to be staged for Stalin in Berlin, but it had leaked out.* The twenty-four-hour delay left many people feeling the official celebrations on 8 May were an anti-climax. Some stayed quietly in their homes, but many were thrilled just to be alive to hear the Prime Minister tell them what they already knew – the war (at least in Europe) was over, and they had won. Even so, there was a gasp from the crowd in Parliament Square at his phrase: 'The evil-doers are prostrate before us!'

Hitler had committed suicide in his Berlin bunker on 30 April, two days after the Italian dictator Mussolini had been strung up on a lamp-post

---

* The Associated Press reprimanded its reporter Edward Kennedy in 1945 for defying an official embargo and filing the story twenty-four hours early, one of the greatest scoops in its history. In May 2012, The Associated Press issued an apology to his family.

with his mistress by Italian partisans. Jodl was later tried by the Nuremberg war crimes tribunal for crimes against humanity for complicity in the Holocaust against the Jews, and executed; Dönitz was jailed in Spandau for ten years before being released. Churchill finished his speech with a cry for Britain to grasp the advantage of the peace: 'Advance Britannia!' Perhaps he suspected it would do, but without him as its leader.

After his broadcast Churchill was mobbed by the people as he drove the short distance to the Commons from the back of Downing Street in an open car. As they had done before, the MPs gave him a great cheer and waved their order papers when he entered the chamber. It was an emotional moment. He repeated the formal announcement of the German surrender that he had made in his broadcast, but added some personal words of thanks to Parliament for its support for him during the war. It reflected his love of the place, and the institution: 'We have all of us made our mistakes, but the strength of the Parliamentary institution has been shown to enable it at the same moment to preserve all the title-deeds of democracy while waging war in the most stern and protracted form.'

Churchill then moved for a motion following the precedent set by the Commons after the end of the First World War: that rather than have a debate, the MPs should go to the modest parish church across the road by the side of Westminster Abbey and thank God. Police forced a path through the crowds so Churchill and the Cabinet could walk to a short service of thanksgiving at St Margaret's Church. The Cabinet went on to Buckingham Palace to have their pictures taken, and thousands crowded into Pall Mall to cheer the King and the Royal Family when they appeared on the Palace balcony. The King also made a broadcast to the nation, and pointed to the difficulties ahead – the continuing war against Japan, and the challenges of Britain's postwar reconstruction. 'Much hard work awaits us both in the restoration of our own country after the ravages of war and in helping to restore peace and sanity to a shattered world,' said George VI.

Most people were not thinking about the trials of peace. Happy bands of people flocked around London's streets, or gathered around a bonfire on the beach at Dover, or danced a conga in Truro, or heard the 'All Clear' being sounded on a bugle in Sheffield. They had a right to celebrate the end of six years of worry, grief and hardship. In the capital, they joyfully marched along the Mall and spilled into Trafalgar Square wearing red, white and blue rosettes and hats and waving flags. The Board of Trade had suspended the need for ration coupons for bunting; Churchill that morning had made sure the pubs had sufficient supplies of beer. Jazz trumpeter Humphrey Lyttelton played 'Roll Out the Barrel' from the back of a handcart as he was pushed down the Mall. People broke into choruses of 'Knees Up Mother Brown' and linked arms with strangers to do the 'hokey-cokey'. The King's own daughters, the Princesses Elizabeth and Margaret, mingled incognito with the throng after midnight to share in the joy and relief.

After going to the Palace, the crowds marched back into Parliament Street to hear 'Winnie' one more time. 'My dear friends, this is your hour,' he said. 'This is not a victory of a party or of any class. It's a victory of the great British nation as a whole. God bless you all. This is your victory!'

The crowd roared back: 'No – it's yours!'

'In all our long history,' he said, 'we have never seen a greater day than this.' It was a claim with which few could disagree.

At night, Noël Coward walked down the Mall with the hoi polloi and was enchanted by the spectacle of the King and the Royal Family, who had once again come out onto the balcony of Buckingham Palace, and were now flood-lit. 'We cheered ourselves hoarse,' he recalled. 'After that I went to Chips Channon's "open house" party which wasn't up to much. Walked home with Ivor [Novello, the composer]. I suppose this was the greatest day in our history.'

Two months later, Winston Churchill, the great wartime leader, was dumped out of office, defeated by the democratic system he had fought to defend.

On the face of it, Churchill's defeat was the greatest upset in British political history. I go to meet Peter Hennessy, the author of *Never Again*, the definitive book on postwar Britain and a Whitehall expert, in the House of Lords.[1] He is an example of the upward mobility of those born in the postwar baby boom; he was born in 1947 in a council-requisitioned house in Finchley into a large Irish Catholic family which may never have expected to produce a peer of the realm. In 2010, he was awarded a life peerage as Baron Hennessy of Nympsfield, a patch of the Cotswolds where he spent his boyhood after the family moved out of London. He is a cross-bench (non-party) peer.

Sitting in the Strangers' Cafeteria in the House of Lords, Hennessy tells me that the Labour victory was the work of William Beveridge and his report. The Beveridge report ushered in a new age, the age of the welfare state. 'The NHS was not just the jewel in the crown,' says Hennessy. 'The NHS was the crown.' And while Churchill worried about affording the new tomorrow, Labour went full steam ahead. 'Labour was offering "Beveridge" without caveat,' he continues. 'Michael Young [then head of Labour's research department] wrote the 1945 Labour manifesto beautifully as only Michael Young could have done, but the choicest manifesto any political party could have had in this country was the Beveridge report. The *Picture Post* could pick it up.'

A former Whitehall correspondent, Hennessy is handsome, grey-haired and bespectacled, in a tweedy outfit that makes him look like he's auditioning for a mature sequel to *The History Man*. Lords staff say hello to him as we chat over tea and a piece of cake. He is at home here, and full of boyish enthusiasm for the story of the Attlee Government. Indeed, he is the Attlee Professor of Contemporary British History at Queen Mary, University of London. Many of the issues raised by Beveridge – specifically, around the cost of the welfare state – are still fresh today. From the Lords, Hennessy and several other peers are engaged in a rearguard action to protect the health service from some of the ills of the Government's NHS reforms.

It seems astonishing now that William Beveridge, a civil servant and academic, was commissioned by Churchill's Coalition War Cabinet to produce a report for the rebuilding of Britain while the nation was still standing alone against the Nazis in 1941. It is to the lasting credit of the Coalition Government that the blueprints for the NHS and other social reforms were drawn up at the blackest period of the war. But it is a myth to suppose, as many do, that the foundations of the welfare state were exclusively a Labour design – they were not. Beveridge became a Liberal; the 1944 Education Act – creating the grammar schools, the eleven-plus exam and secondary modern schools – was the product of a Conservative education minister, R.A. (Rab) Butler, who had been a leading Tory appeaser at the outbreak of the war. Butler's Education Act was introduced after the war by the first woman Education Secretary, the flame-haired, left-wing 'Red' Ellen Wilkinson. National Insurance, which was to pay for welfare benefits, was intended to be a contributory scheme based on the principle of self-help, which the Tories could embrace as easily as Labour, with its roots in friendly societies and workers' co-operatives.

Beveridge was sixty-two, donnish and difficult. He was also the outstanding expert on unemployment insurance in Whitehall. At the outbreak of war, Beveridge had been seconded to the Department of Labour after twenty years in academia, mostly at the London School of Economics with the last three years as Master of University College, Oxford. He was, however, a veteran of Whitehall, having cut his teeth as a civil servant advising Asquith's Liberal Government on the introduction of National Insurance in 1911. That administration, it is important to remember, included Winston Churchill.

The architect of the insurance scheme was the then Liberal Chancellor of the Exchequer David Lloyd George, a Welshman who loathed poverty just as much as Aneurin Bevan, the Labour minister who would later put his stamp on the welfare state. The Asquith Government used the money raised by employees' National Insurance contributions for a limited range of benefits. A deduction from wages of four shillings a week was taken in return for being put on a doctor's list, receiving hospital care (if your wages were low, what is called 'means-testing'), sickness pay and unemployment benefit (limited to certain industries). It was not comprehensive – Britain would have to wait for Beveridge for that – but it was better than the previous Dickensian system of workhouses, poor laws and parish charity.

The wartime Minister for Labour, Ernest Bevin, was happy to allow Beveridge to leave his department for what seemed like a dusty academic end to his career, chairing a committee on National Insurance. According to Hennessy, however, Beveridge had a secret weapon – Janet 'Jessy' Mair, who helped to inject the sweeping Cromwellian ideas and language into Beveridge's normally dull prose. Mair was then married to Beveridge's cousin, David, a mathematician, but when David died in 1942, she married Beveridge – just days after his report came out.

Inspired by Mair's language, Beveridge proposed tackling what he called the five 'Giant Evils' afflicting society: Want, Disease, Ignorance, Squalor and Idleness. He proposed improved state education, council housing, a comprehensive national health service and a range of benefits to lift people out of poverty, paid for from a new National Insurance scheme. He also proposed 'full employment', with a target of no more than three per cent unemployment (the level is now 8.4 per cent). This was not intended simply as an act of altruism; those who question the cost of the welfare state today should remember that Beveridge believed full employment was the vital component in delivering the taxes that would pay for his proposed social benefits.

Despite its less than snappy title, *Social Insurance and Allied Services* became a sensation when the staid HM Stationery Office published it in

December 1942. The Beveridge report sold one hundred thousand copies in a month; a special cheap edition was printed for the British forces. The sales figures were unprecedented and remain unequalled by the HMSO. In Nazi-occupied France, dog-eared copies of the Beveridge report were circulated and shared clandestinely by the Resistance. Beveridge was subversive because it provided a democratic rejoinder to fascist state socialism. In England, the report gave the people something else worth fighting for, in addition to their patch of island in the North Sea.

Churchill was reluctant to back the plan because he feared the cost would be unaffordable. The bill for putting Beveridge's proposals in place was then predicted to tally up to £100 million (about £3.3 billion at today's prices). The actual total today is £150 billion – and that is without accounting for the NHS. Diaries, written in a series of exercise books, by Norman Brook, the Cabinet Secretary, of secret conversations inside the War Cabinet reveal Churchill was furious with Beveridge, who wanted to do his own spinning of the report by briefing Parliamentary lobby journalists before its publication. Churchill rightly worried that Beveridge would bounce the War Cabinet into approving his report. The Prime Minister felt he could not allow that to happen.

The War Cabinet discussed Beveridge on 16 November 1942, after hearing reports on the allied bombing raids (Hamburg, 'bad weather'; Lübeck, 'half old town gutted'); weekly fighter sorties (2900 sorties, losses – twenty-two planes, eight pilots); and the ticklish issue of America insisting in the summer of 1942 on segregation for its black soldiers while they were in Britain (it was refused in public places for fear of upsetting Britain's black troops from the colonies). The War Cabinet also had to deal with the treatment of Rudolf Hess. Hitler's former deputy of the Nazi Party had crash-landed in Scotland, saying he was seeking to act as an intermediary for the Führer to negotiate peace with Britain.* Finally, after discussing neutral Spain and the rice supply in India, the War Cabinet turned to the question of how to present the Beveridge report to the public.

Brendan Bracken, the Minister for Information and a loyal ally of Churchill, explained to the Cabinet that Beveridge wanted to brief the press about his report two weeks before it was published officially. Even Labour members objected to that, as can be seen by reconstructing the discussion from Norman Brook's notebooks.

---

* Churchill wanted to declare Hess insane but was told it was not possible, because Hess was obviously not insane when he arrived. The former Nazi would spend the remainder of his life in Spandau prison, Berlin.

Bracken said Beveridge was working up a political campaign, 'to disclose not only contents of Report but his views on it'.[2] He suggested the Cabinet should give Beveridge no facilities, either at the Ministry of Information or the BBC.

Sir William Jowett, the Paymaster General, who had taken over responsibility for the report from Arthur Greenwood, said: 'I saw Beveridge tonight and told him it was improper to discuss the report before its presentation.' Churchill agreed: 'It would be a pity if such a comprehensive scheme failed to get a fair chance because of the propaganda of its author. The Cabinet will have to consider it in a small Cabinet committee. It will spoil it all if he pushes it; it will arouse opposition.'

Then, Sir Percy Grigg, a civil servant at the War Office drafted in as a minister by Churchill, suggested: 'Shouldn't we suspend publication of the report?'

The Prime Minister was firm. He suggested threatening Beveridge with a breach of Parliamentary Privilege if he leaked the report's contents. 'The report is Government property. Beveridge must be told he is not to expound on the Report and threaten him with Privilege. At the same time, we should be defining our attitude to it: do we like it or not like it, or haven't made up our minds about it?'

Ten days later, Churchill came under pressure to approve the Beveridge report in principle, but he continued to resist. This is a transcript from Brook's notebook:

CHURCHILL: Chancellor, what is the cost of all this?

SIR KINGSLEY WOOD, THE CHANCELLOR: £100 million, Prime Minister.

PM: Generally speaking I like the report but we must see how it fits into the postwar plan as a whole. Also we have to be mindful of our arrangements with the Americans. If we promise this level of largesse, far ahead of their standards, they may say we [they] have been asked to pay for this.

ATTLEE: But surely the Americans will be impressed by our boldness.

CHURCHILL: The most serious effect is on finance. There will be an effect on taxation.

Later, Churchill added: 'We will have a two-stage ending of war. While we finish off Japan, after the collapse of Hitler, there will be an interval during which the United Nations will go forward in companionship: and during that these plans can be matured.' To which Sir John Anderson, the Home Secretary, replied: 'When opinion crystallises, it would be a pity to let it appear that the Government was dragged reluctantly to support it. Could we not welcome it in principle?'[3]

In his minutes, Brook noted that Churchill and Kingsley Wood showed dissent. Churchill realized there would be widespread support for the Beveridge report, but he was keen to avoid being stampeded into a decision on its findings while the war raged on.

As the end of the war approached, his hesitancy caused a serious rift in the Cabinet. Attlee and his Labour colleagues were keen that Churchill not bind their hands over Beveridge, even if it meant bringing down the Coalition Government before the war was fully over. Churchill appealed to Attlee to postpone the election until at least the defeat of the Japanese, which might not happen until 1946. But, having taken soundings with other senior figures at the annual Labour conference in Blackpool Winter Gardens, Attlee refused. Beveridge's report therefore led to the General Election being called earlier than Churchill had wanted.

Even without the benefit of Norman Brook's secret Cabinet diaries, the public instinctively felt that Churchill was half-hearted about Beveridge, and they did not trust the Tories to implement it. Hennessy says Labour's role in the War Cabinet also helped Attlee win the election. It demonstrated Labour was a credible government-in-waiting; its ministers had come through the fire of war, and proved they were capable of running the country. The voters had become used to having Attlee, Bevin and Herbert Morrison, the former leader of the Greater London Council and grandfather of Peter Mandelson, in high office. Hennessy puts it this way: 'The key to 1945 [the election result] is that it was as if Labour had said, "We have seen the future and it works. It was the period 1940 to 1945".'

Polling day was on 5 July 1945, but there was a three-week wait for the votes of members of the armed services to be flown home and included in the counting.

Labour campaigned on the slogan 'Let us face the future'. The party manifesto explicitly called for the 'spirit of Dunkirk and of the Blitz' in its appeal to continue the socially minded patriotism that had been such a feature of the nation in the war. Attlee toured constituencies in a little car driven by his wife, Vi, and his message was what the people wanted to hear – Keynesian economics, nationally planned investment in essential industries, houses, schools, hospitals. He also promised civic centres would be built. While this last point may hardly seem like a vote-winner today, it reflected the municipal pride alive at the time, and the hidden hand of Morrison. Welfare benefits would be paid for via National Insurance; price controls would stop profiteering; and a new National Health Service, free at the point of delivery, would take the financial worry out of being ill.

The 1945 Labour manifesto went further, promising a massive programme of nationalization of the coal, gas, electricity, iron and steel industries. This was not part of the Beveridge report; it was not even part of Labour's original policy agenda. It was forced on the Labour leadership by left-wingers from the constituency parties at its conference in Westminster Central Hall in December 1944. It would put Red Socialist meat on the bones of Clause 4 of Labour's constitution, dating from 1918: 'To secure for the workers by hand or by brain the full fruits of their industry and the most equitable distribution thereof that may be possible upon the basis of the common ownership of the means of production, distribution and exchange, and the best obtainable system of popular administration and control of each industry or service.' Labour's 1945 manifesto could truly claim: 'The Labour Party is a Socialist party and proud of it'. It did so without a flicker of embarrassment. (That would come later with New Labour under Tony Blair, who rewrote the clause in 1995.)

The Conservatives campaigned under the slogan: 'Vote National – help him finish the job.' It was a nonsense – the voters were being asked to elect a Conservative rather than a 'National' government, and they saw through the sham.

The Conservative posters, depicting a hand putting an X in a box, urged the voters: 'Confirm your confidence in Churchill – put it there'. However, their message was confused: the Conservatives promised to carry out most of the Beveridge report, but Churchill's buccaneering Canadian friend, Lord Beaverbrook, owner of the *Daily Express*, spearheaded a scare campaign against Labour's proposed welfare state.

A twenty-year-old RAF pilot, Anthony Wedgwood Benn, was returning home on a troop ship after serving in Rhodesia and South Africa during the election campaign. Benn was then heir to the title Viscount Stansgate, but renounced it in 1963 and became better known as Tony Benn. He remembers the general derision that greeted Churchill's election campaign speech when it was broadcast over the ship's tannoy as it sailed towards England. Churchill warned that a socialist government would stamp on public dissent. 'They would have to fall back on some form of Gestapo.'

Even Churchill realized he was losing his touch, and the stance came to haunt him. It was born of a feeling, reinforced by Beaverbrook, that the experience of Britain 'pulling together' and 'mucking in' to win the war, mixed with a dash of spite among the millions of servicemen and -women who had had enough of taking orders from the officer classes, would seduce the British electorate into voting in the socialists.

There was some truth in that: war was a great social leveller. 'The most democratic thing was the ration book,' says Lord Hennessy. 'Even the King had one; name – HM King; address – Buckingham Palace, SW1. That was the badge of "we're all in it together".'

One of the first casualties of the war was that precious quality the British seemed to guard so jealously, personal space. Britons – whether bankers or cleaners – had to get used to the proximity of so much sweaty humanity, squeezing closer together, in queues, air-raid shelters and the London Underground, in a way that would have been thought indecent and un-British before the war.

Strangely, perhaps, when the Conservatives called on Churchill to ignite support by cashing in on his national prestige, he chose not to invoke the wartime spirit at all. He instead called for a 'spirit of independence' that he wanted to see reborn in postwar Britain – anticipating Margaret Thatcher's rallying call, nearly forty years later, to make entrepreneurs of us all. Churchill was engaging in a first skirmish in the postwar battle of ideas that was based, for the right wing, on the free-market philosophy of the Austrian Professor Friedrich von Hayek (*The Road to Serfdom*, 1944). Hayek's ideas were pitted against the Marxist theories (including socialist ownership of all means of production) advanced by Harold Laski, a professor at the London School of Economics (*Reflections on the Revolution of Our Time*, 1943). Churchill clearly sensed the general mood was swinging away from individual wealth creation; he warned Britain against becoming a nation of 'State serfs' through the nationalization of industries.

This was one battle in 1945 Churchill could not win. If the electorate heard his warnings, it fell on deaf ears. After two world wars, the voters did not want to go back to the austerity of the 1930s. Feeling was against the Tories, with the simplistic argument of 'never again'.

After polling day, Churchill left England and the elections far behind and flew to Germany for an historic international conference attended by the US President Harry S Truman (Roosevelt had died on 12 April) and the Soviet Premier Joseph Stalin. The 'Big Three' met in Babelsburg, an undamaged suburb on the south-western outskirts of Berlin near Potsdam, to complete the groundwork laid at the Yalta conference in February for carving up Germany and Eastern Europe between them. The mood after the defeat of Germany among the three big powers had changed. Now 'Uncle Joe' held most of the cards at the conference table; the Soviets had overrun most of Eastern Europe, including Poland, as Hitler's forces collapsed and the Potsdam conference, as it became known, presaged the coming Cold War and what Churchill memorably described as the 'Iron Curtain'.

The meeting was due to go on into August, but Churchill flew home for the election result to be declared on 26 July. Everyone expected Churchill to come back to the conference to work out the settlement with Stalin and Truman – Lord Moran, Churchill's personal physician, was so confident of a Conservative victory that he left his luggage at Potsdam. Stalin was among those stunned by Churchill's defeat, which meant that he had to deal with 'Little Clem' when the Potsdam conference resumed. 'It was as if the lion was replaced by a hamster,' Hennessy chuckles.

On the day before the results were declared Churchill told the King he was confident he had won with a majority of up to eighty seats. On the day of the count, Churchill, still unaware of how the country had turned against his party, donned his wartime 'siren' suit (like an adult romper suit with a zip up the middle). Then, almost out of habit, he went to the map room in the Cabinet underground bunker near St James's Park, which he had occupied throughout the war, to watch the results come in on a screen that had been rigged up. Mary Soames, his daughter, who had been with him at Potsdam, noted in her diary: 'Every minute brought news of more friends out – Randolph [Churchill], Bob [Boothby], Brendan [Bracken] out… We lunched in Stygian gloom'.[4]

Ironically, one of those who lost that day was William Beveridge. He lost the seat he had held for less than a year as the Liberal MP for Berwick-upon-Tweed. The canny voters did not entirely have faith that a technocrat from London could look after their interests, despite his fame. It had been a Liberal seat since 1935, but in 1945 they bucked the trend and voted Conservative.

Nobody was more surprised at Labour's victory than Attlee, the painfully shy Labour leader, who looked like a bank manager and was described by Churchill as a 'sheep in sheep's clothing'. He had been educated at Haileybury College, which turned out civil servants to run the British Raj;[5] now he had to run Britain. Three weeks later, Jock Colville, Churchill's private secretary who effortlessly slipped into the same civil service role for Attlee, recorded in his diary that Attlee had confided in him that, in his most optimistic dreams, he thought the Conservative majority might be reduced to forty seats.[6]

The 'Demob' vote – the postal votes of millions of men returning to Britain after the war – has often been blamed for the swing against the Conservatives. It was a unique factor in the 1945 election result, but its influence was not as great as many believed. Only one million of the total twenty-five million votes were postal votes – far higher than normal, but not enough by itself to change the result.

Labour took nearly twelve million votes, forty-nine per cent of the poll, and won 393 seats, producing an unassailable Commons majority of 146. The Tories won 202 seats, with over nine million votes and a thirty-nine per cent share of the vote. The Liberals won just twelve seats with nine per cent of the poll and two million votes. It was a Labour landslide.

Attlee found King George VI tongue-tied when he went to 'kiss hands' on taking office. Hennessy was told years later by the late Sir Robin Day, the BBC election anchorman, that Attlee broke the silence by informing His Majesty: 'I've won the election.' The King replied: 'I know. I heard it on the six o'clock news.' It may have been one of Day's neat jokes, but it accurately reflected the dismay at the result in the royal household. Queen Elizabeth, later the Queen Mother, blamed the overthrow of Churchill on the ignorance of the electorate – 'poor people, so many half educated and bemused'.

Wise politicians, unlike monarchs, never accuse the voters of being fools. The British electorate in 1945 rightly recognized that while Churchill had been one of the most outstanding wartime leaders in history, to stand alongside Elizabeth I and the Duke of Wellington, he was not the man to lead Britain through peace and reconstruction.

In truth, Churchill, aged seventy-one, was exhausted and out of touch, particularly on the postwar aspirations of the old British Empire and the demands of India for independence. Charles Moran later wrote in his diary that the blow of defeat hit the old man hard and brought on the bouts of depression that had afflicted the Churchills, and which Winston called 'Black Dog'. 'It's no use, Charles, pretending I'm not hard hit. I can't school myself to do nothing for the rest of my life. It would have been better to have been killed in an aeroplane or to have died like Roosevelt,' Churchill told Moran. 'I get fits of depression.' He was also to suffer the first of his strokes in August 1949, while holidaying in Monte Carlo.

Churchill, a product of the late Victorian age, was out of his time. He was a romantic, who looked backwards to the days of the Empire, refusing to accept that the sun was setting on Britain's powerful past. Historians of the Labour Party accuse Churchill of holding back the 'Overlord' landings in Northern France in 1942–3 to preserve Britain's imperial greatness with the 'Torch' invasion of North Africa.[7] A patrician Conservative, Churchill believed in his bones that the Empire had been a force for good, and did not want to see India plunged into chaos.

Attlee later wrote to India's first Prime Minister, Jawaharlal Nehru, that Churchill almost certainly would have won if Britain had been electing a president. Churchill was universally respected, even as he was hated in some pockets of the working class, such as in the Welsh Valleys, where they still accused him of sending in the troops to put down the miners' strike at Tonypandy in 1910. 'It is my private opinion that the PM is universally admired but little liked, which is sad,' 'Chips' Channon noted in his diary for 10 May.[8] Attlee credited a simpler equation for Labour's victory: 'We were looking towards the future. The Tories were looking towards the past.'

Though Attlee's Government was short-lived (it lost office in 1951), the socialist thrust of its 1945 manifesto, together with the recommendations of the Beveridge report, dominated the high ground in postwar British politics for at least two generations. Even the Tory writer and snob Harold Nicolson told a friend in 1947 he had become a socialist because 'socialism is inevitable'. The friend went on: 'He says the sad thing is that no one dislikes the lower orders more than he does.'

The battle of ideas between Labour and Conservatives settled into the postwar consensus known as 'Butskellism', merging the names of two leading voices at the time, Conservative Rab Butler and Labour leader Hugh Gaitskell, in a social democratic melange. Butskellism was not shaken until the arrival of Thatcher and her explosive programme of privatization for coal, steel, railways, gas, electricity and even water in the 1970s. She oversaw the undoing of all that the 1945 Government had achieved. People wondered what was left – privatization of the air?

Thatcher challenged the postwar orthodoxy that Beveridge and the welfare state were founded on social democratic principles and a 'good thing'. In 1984, I witnessed the clash in the Commons when a young frontbencher, Tony Blair, tackled her at Prime Minister's Question Time over the 1944 Employment White Paper, which, he said, put dealing with unemployment at the heart of economic policy. To everyone's astonishment, Mrs Thatcher grabbed her big black handbag from her seat, rummaged around in it and produced her own worn copy of the same 1944 White Paper, which she clearly carried around with her at all times. She read from the foreword, which she had underlined in red, highlighted in yellow and sidelined with a red asterisk and a red arrowed line: 'Employment cannot be created by Act of Parliament or Government action alone... Without a rising standard of industrial efficiency we cannot achieve a high level of employment combined with a rising standard of living.' It is now among the Thatcher papers at the Churchill Archive, Cambridge, along with that handbag.

In fact, a key part of the welfare state was built on a lie. Beveridge based his system on National Insurance Contributions (NICs), but universal state pensions were never funded by an insurance fund. State pensioners like to think they are getting back what they paid in over a lifetime of NICs; they have paid their insurance 'stamp' and are entitled to draw on the proceeds of their contributions in their old-age. It is a myth.

Beveridge described his new, universal state pension scheme as 'first and foremost a plan of insurance – of giving in return for contributions benefits up to subsistence levels, as of right and without means test, so individuals may build freely upon it'. He intended that NICs would gradually build up a pot to fund the old-age pension over twenty years. However, the Attlee Government knew that its supporters in 1946 would not wait until 1966 to get the pensions they had been promised after the war; the Government went ahead immediately, by raiding the contributions, without waiting for the fund to mature. That meant a key component of the welfare state, the state pension, was founded as a pay-as-you-go scheme rather than as Beveridge had outlined, as fully funded insurance.

Entitlement to state pensions requires NIC payments, but the state pension is in effect a massive, national Ponzi fraud.* Today's state pensioners are relying on the contributions of the people in work today; their own contributions have been spent on earlier generations of pensioners, and so today's state pensioners are taking their benefits from the pensioners of the future. No one has called in the fraud squad so far because the

---

* Charles Ponzi, an American fraudster in the 1920s, paid investors dividends from new investors, rather than from profits earned on stocks.

contributions have kept rolling in. No political party is brave enough – or stupid enough – to call a halt to this con trick. But with an ageing population, and a decreasing number of workers paying taxes to pay for their pensions, one day it may unravel.

The Labour MP appointed by Tony Blair to sort out the mess in the social security system, Frank Field, claims Blair and his Chancellor, Gordon Brown, broke the remaining link between insurance and other welfare benefits. Field argues in *The Purple Book*, a Labour think-tank publication, that they 'tore up' Beveridge's welfare contract by placing means-testing at the heart of party strategy.[9] Under New Labour, your right to claim benefits depends on how poor you are, not on how much you have put in; worse, the system offers active disincentives for getting out of poverty – earn just a bit more income and you lose your benefits. Field believes this change undermines the moral value of the contributory system envisaged by Beveridge.

Raising NICs is also a very sneaky way of increasing revenue without it appearing as income tax – the current top rate of income tax is quoted at forty-five pence in the pound, but to that you have to add NICs, an additional eleven pence. Tony Blair understood that clearly, and used it to his advantage. On a flight in his government jet from Dublin he gave me an exclusive for the *Independent*, disclosing that Gordon Brown was going to increase NICs by a penny to pay for an historic rise in spending on the NHS. It helped raise Britain's total spending on health up to the European average, and, because it was for the NHS (which most people support), it raised virtually no complaints. It is unlikely it would have got through Parliament if the money had been earmarked for social security benefits. Addressing the problem of Idleness requires taking from some and giving to others, unlike the NHS, for the most part.

Beveridge never intended the social service state to become a 'scroungers' charter' as it is characterized by critics today. Beveridge aimed to prevent poverty with a subsistence income rather than welfare that replaced former wage levels.[10] His aim was to ensure that those who contributed got higher benefits than those who did not. 'The state in organizing security should not stifle incentive, opportunity, responsibility,' he said.

~❡~

The alarm bells were already ringing by the time the foundation stones of 'New Jerusalem' were being laid in 1948. On the day that the new benefits system was introduced and the NHS was launched, *The Times* questioned whether it would be possible to reap the benefits of 'social service' (as Beveridge called it) without the 'perils of a Santa Claus state'. In the 1950 election, a young Tory candidate called Margaret Roberts in the constituency of Dartford, Kent ignored the cross-party consensus for Beveridge and primly told her supporters that Labour's policies for universal welfare benefits were 'pernicious' and 'nibble into our national character'. She lost that time, but later came back with a vengeance as Margaret Thatcher.

It could be argued that 1945 was a good election for the Conservatives to lose. Churchill knew that the country had been bankrupted by the war and was heavily in debt to the Americans for Lend-Lease. Not even the 'fire sale' of assets such as stocks in US industries had managed to pay it down much. Within months of Attlee taking office, just six days after VJ Day, America ended its Lend-Lease policy with Britain. The move plunged Attlee's Government into a deep financial crisis. The US saw no point in giving Britain soft loans when the war was won.

John Maynard Keynes, the economist whose *General Theory* had offered, through 'reflation', a way out of the Depression, privately said Britain now faced a 'financial Dunkirk'. He flew to America to plead for a bail-out from the US Federal Reserve Bank. Keynes had impeccable credentials among his American colleagues; during the negotiations for the Bretton Woods agreement, in 1944, he had helped to establish the World Bank and the International Monetary Fund. Yet Keynes had difficulty securing the necessary £3.57 billion loan. He might have begun to wonder why he had bothered with the trip, as his health was fading – the next year he would be dead. When Attlee sought Parliamentary approval for the rescue, it provoked a serious rebellion among Labour MPs and fuelled a mood of anti-Americanism at Westminster which persists today.

The party members accused Attlee and Bevin, the Foreign Secretary, of bowing to the US in the Cold War against the Soviet Union and raising the loan to pay for Britain's rearmament to please 'the Yanks'. The rebellion was not restricted to left-wingers such as Michael Foot and Barbara Castle. It included moderates such as James Callaghan, who later became Prime Minister. The loan went through and Attlee averted a collapse, but it made the need for postwar austerity even worse. It may have cost the Attlee Government the 1951 election, and it was not until 2006 that Britain's financial debt to America was finally paid off. There is a myth that Germany's rise from the ashes after the war was made easier because Britain was weighed down by debts to America while Germany's economy was fuelled by American aid. Historian Corelli Barnett argues that Britain gained more in Marshall Aid, named after US Secretary of State George Marshall, than Germany but wasted the money on pursuing a dream as a world leader, while Germany invested it in boosting industrial production.[11]

On the streets, the British bore austerity grudgingly. 'Being patient, waiting your turn, behaving with restraint, respecting the law... these remained formidable codes to break.'[12] That patience was tested to breaking point with rationing. It was a fairer system than first-come-first-served, and kept prices down but after the war, people wanted to see an end to it.

On 27 May 1945, three weeks after VE day, rations were actually reduced – the weekly allowance for bacon went down from four ounces to three ounces; cooking fat from two ounces to just one, and housewives – it was invariably women who had to look after the demobbed men – had to take part of their meat ration as half a shilling's worth of corned beef (the 'bully beef' that had become hated by many Tommies during the war). Worse was to follow when Labour came into office. Bread was never rationed during the war but – despite the loan from the Americans – it was put on the ration books in July 1946, where it remained for two years. Rationing of eggs and soap was only lifted in 1950, and it was not until 4 July 1954 that the wartime ration books were done away with by Churchill's second Government.

Mass Observation investigators were sent out to report back on what people were saying both during and after the war. The secret snoopers stood in the queues for rationed food, or sat in the pub and reported back on the comments they had overheard. It was all anonymized by age, social status and sex but it provides a fascinating insight into the people's mood. For instance, one Mass Observation agent reported the comments in a queue of about thirty people outside a baker's shop in London: 'I've been queuing ever since eight o'clock this morning, what with one thing and another,' said a woman in her forties from social group D, the working classes (categorized by the MO reporter as F40D). 'I'm about done for. I'd like to take that Attlee and all the rest of them and put them on top of a bonfire in Hyde Park and *burn* them.'

'And I'd 'elp yer,' agreed a working-class woman of about sixty-five (F65D). 'Same 'ere,' said several angry women, the reporter added.

No wonder the popular character of the period from *It's That Man Again*, a radio comedy show, was called Mona Lott. Her catchphrase was 'It's being so cheerful as keeps me going'.

The slow progress in building decent housing to replace the homes destroyed by the Luftwaffe was another cause of complaint. In a prequel of the current Occupy movement, forty thousand squatters invaded one thousand empty army camps. Others occupied vacant mansion blocks in London.

The task of reconstruction would have tested the competence of any government. Many city centres bore the scars of bombing long after the war. The striking thing about old black-and-white British films, such as the gritty drama *Tiger Bay* (shot in Cardiff in 1959), is the number of bombsites looming in the background. But even the slight escape of going to the pictures was cut back, along with supplies of petrol and food, as part of the austerity cuts of 1947. Yet another Mass Observation snooper overheard this conversation between two middle-aged working-class men on a bus in the City:

> 'Gor blimey Charlie – wot a bloody outlook etc. When are they going to stop cutting things I'd like to know. Still the people wanted 'em in, didn't they? Now they've got 'em they've found out a thing or two.'
>
> 'Worse than the war mate, ain't it?'
>
> 'At least you knew wot was 'appening then but yer don't know wot to expect now do you.'[13]

At least the creation of the NHS provided the Attlee Government with something everyone could cheer about… until it began to run out of money.

~෧~

Aneurin Bevan, MP for the famous Welsh mining seat of Ebbw Vale,* had long been a thorn in the side of the Labour leadership when he was put in charge of the health service by Attlee in 1945. Only the year before, he was almost thrown out of the party for attacking the Labour ministers in Churchill's Coalition Government. Bevan had accused Attlee, Herbert Morrison and Ernest Bevin of supporting what he called 'draconian measures' – the Emergency Powers Act and Defence Regulations – banning strikes. Bevan was a son of the Welsh Valleys, and imbued with the

---

* The seat would be held by another left-wing firebrand, Michael Foot, from 1960 until 1983.

mining tradition. He was also a fiery speaker, as gifted in oratory as a Welsh Evangelist, and became a darling of the Labour Left. By taking on Bevin, he was taking on the mainstream Labour movement.

Ernest Bevin, with his huge skull and heavy, black-rimmed spectacles, was head and shoulders above his colleagues; he was the physical embodiment of the pugnacious, common-sense working class he represented as leader of the Transport and General Workers' Union. He addressed workers at factories as 'mates' and called Labour voters 'our people'. That didn't keep Bevan from saying he was selling out on the workers by banning strikes during the war.

One of the best-kept secrets of the 1939–45 conflict is the number of strikes that took place while Britain was fighting the war. There were nine hundred strikes in the early months of the conflict, partly because communists in Britain refused to be bound by the calls for national unity until the Soviet Union allied with Britain in 1941. Bevin, a natural autocrat, responded by using emergency powers to ban strikes in the pits, in the factories and at the docks. He also upset Britain's miners by ordering one in ten of those conscripted to fight, to go down the pits instead. Known as the 'Bevin boys', these conscripts stirred resentment among regular miners, provoking still more strikes. Three union officials were imprisoned and over a thousand strikers fined in the Kent coalfield in 1942. The following year, twelve thousand bus drivers and conductors, and the dockers in Liverpool, went on strike – a considerable embarrassment for Bevin because they were largely members of the Transport and General Workers' Union.[14] In 1944, the strikes reached their peak, with over two thousand stoppages.

When Bevin introduced tougher anti-strike laws to settle the nation's wartime production, Bevan fired back with a Commons rebellion. The Minister for Labour, he said, had provoked the strikes through 'incompetence'. Immediately, Bevan was threatened; if he continued to criticize the anti-strike laws he would be kicked out of the party. He wisely avoided making himself a martyr. He was popular with the constituencies, and was running for a seat on Labour's National Executive, which would give him more influence. And he won. That meant Attlee had to come to terms with the Welsh rabble-rouser.

Bevan was buoyed by a wave of growing grassroots support in the constituencies against the compromises forced on Labour during its support for the National Government (mirroring the strains in the current Conservative–Liberal Democrat coalition). When Labour won the election, Attlee reluctantly had to put Bevan in his Cabinet. Giving him the Department of Health was potentially a bed of nails, but it seemed to be a position tailor-made for Bevan.

Bevan hit the Department of Health like a human tornado, and impressed his doubting civil servants with his drive. Within a few months, he had sorted out some of the most controversial aspects of the NHS reforms; within a year, in May 1946, the NHS Act was passed along with a National Insurance Act implementing the Beveridge proposals.

Hospitals had been run traditionally by a patchwork of charities, friendly societies and local authorities. Local councils controlled large health budgets, giving them power that they jealously guarded. A 1944 White Paper on the NHS by Henry Willink, the Tory Minister for Health, proposed keeping the hospitals under council control. Bevan had other ideas. He won a Cabinet battle against Herbert Morrison to bring the nation's hospitals all under the control of the Health Department. At a stroke, this single, centralizing move created a Leviathan with the biggest single workforce in Europe, after the Red Army.

Bevan said that if a bed pan dropped in the NHS, it should be heard by the Secretary of State. Though this may sound laughable today, he meant that the NHS 'buck' stopped with the Secretary of State for Health.

He had more difficulty with the doctors than with Ernie Bevin. Family doctors often charged for their services before the war, but Bevan was determined to ban them from extracting money from patients in 'his' NHS. Initially, he even refused to negotiate with them, which caused outrage among the leaders of the doctors' 'trade union', the British Medical Association. The doctors were convinced Bevan wanted to make them employees of the NHS and directly answerable to the Minister for Health when it came to the running of their surgeries. And there was some truth in this.

Bevan's ideas went back to his roots in the Welsh Valleys, and in particular to the Tredegar Medical Aid Society of his youth. In Tredegar – a name embedded in socialist legend, much like Ebbw Vale – steel workers and miners had banded together to provide health care for themselves in return for a deduction of three shillings in the pound from their wages; there was a higher subscription for others in the community, for instance teachers and shop workers. The contributions paid for a cottage hospital and a local health centre staffed by six salaried family doctors and set up in a corner shop, which is now part of a Bevan heritage trail in the town.

Socialist medical associations wanted similar health centres with salaried general practitioners across the country. But Britain's GPs wanted nothing to do with Comrade Bevan. One former chairman of the BMA, which represented thousands of family doctors, described the NHS Act as 'the first step to national socialism as practised in Germany. The medical service there was put under the dictatorship of a medical Führer. The Bill will establish the minister for health in that capacity.' Coming so soon after the war, this was incendiary language, but it accurately reflected the anger among doctors.

To present his case, Bevan met doctors' leaders secretly at an exclusive restaurant, the Café Royal in Regent Street, where Oscar Wilde had been a regular at the turn of the century, to thrash out a deal. 'We screwed our nerves – we might have been going to meet Adolf Hitler,' said Dr Roland Cockshot, one of the BMA leaders who attended. They noticed the Welsh class-warrior was wearing an expensive suit, and Cockshot joked: 'We were quite surprised to discover he talked English.' Despite these rather stiff pleasantries, Bevan's hopes of reaching a deal with the BMA failed.

Over the next two years, Bevan had running battles with the BMA as he pushed forward on the launch of the NHS. In the end, he conceded some ground to win them over: the general practitioners were allowed to keep their status as private contractors within the state health service, and were paid mainly according to the number of their patients, a scheme they still jealously guard today.

Bevan, realizing he could not take on too many vested interests at once, adopted a more conciliatory strategy with the surgeons, who wanted to keep their private income from operations. Curiously, at that time the president of their professional body, the Royal College of Physicians, was Lord Moran, Churchill's personal physician. It meant that the arch-socialist Bevan had to negotiate with Churchill's private doctor. Churchill detested Bevan, but he made it clear to Moran that he had to be free in his bargaining with him.

That did not stop Churchill having pangs of anguish about how it would all turn out, however. Moran wrote in his diary on 2 August 1945 that Churchill asked: 'If Aneurin Bevan becomes Minister of Health, will there be private practice? Will you be able to look after me?' Moran went on to note: 'He looked up at me like a puzzled child.'

Churchill need not have worried. Bevan bought the physicians off, as he described it, 'stuffing their mouths with gold'. He allowed them to keep their private practice, with pay beds in the NHS, much to the disgust of some socialists who accused him of selling out on his principles. In return, Moran clearly colluded with Bevan, proposing an amendment to the NHS Act to allay the doctors' fears of a full-time salary by ensuring it could only come about through new legislation. Some of the doctors' leaders accused Moran of double-crossing them, but it signalled the end of the GPs' resistance.

~ᅌ~

Finally, on a hot 5 July 1948, Bevan travelled to the leafy suburbs of Manchester to take charge of the keys to Park Hospital, Trafford, officially designated as the first hospital to be transferred into the NHS.

Nurses in starched white uniforms, red sashes and black capes formed a guard of honour around the floral gardens at the entrance to greet Bevan on his arrival. He stepped from a shining black Rolls-Royce, underlining that in the new age of socialism, there was nothing too good for the working class.

The Cabinet had considered putting off the 'Appointed Day' because of the row with the doctors, but Bevan refused to be knocked off course. It is likely the Health Department chose the hospital in Trafford for the ceremony because it was convenient for Bevan. The night before – the eve of one of the greatest days in Labour's history – he was due to address a Labour rally in Belle Vue, a stadium in Manchester often used for boxing; and in the afternoon he was scheduled to go on to Preston to make another speech.

At the Belle Vue rally, Bevan wound himself into a rage. He gave full vent to his anger against the Conservatives, blaming them for what he described as the 'bitter experiences of my youth'. No matter how the Tories might try to win him round, Bevan made it shockingly clear that he would not sup with them. He thundered: 'No amount of cajolery, and no attempts at ethical or social seduction, can eradicate from my heart a deep burning hatred of the Tory Party that inflicted those bitter experiences on me. So far as I am concerned, they are lower than vermin.'

His use of the 'V' word became as notorious as Churchill's claim that Labour would resort to 'Gestapo' tactics. The Tories hated him for it, and some Labour ministers argued it was a chief reason for the party's defeat in 1951. Still, Bevan's words accurately reflected a hatred held by a number of Labour left-wingers towards the Tories and all they stood for. Death duties brought in by the 1945 Labour Government directly attacked the inherited wealth of the aristocracy and the stately homes of England; Evelyn Waugh captured their demise in his novel, *Brideshead Revisited*, published that year. In 1946, Manny Shinwell, the socialist Minister of Fuel and Power, was accused of engaging in an act of class-war spite by sanctioning open-cast mining almost right up to the front door of one of the country's greatest stately homes, Wentworth Woodhouse, near Barnsley, South Yorkshire.

By the time he arrived at the Park Hospital, Bevan was in a more benign mood. It was just as well. His spin doctors had arranged for him to have a photo-opportunity with the 'first patient in the NHS', a young Manchester schoolgirl called Sylvia Beckingham. It had all the hallmarks of the slick presentation of later Labour Government propaganda concocted by Tony Blair, Peter Mandelson and Alastair Campbell, but like most photo-opportunities involving politicians with the health service, it did not go according to plan. An outbreak of measles on the children's Ward Five meant that Sylvia, suffering from a serious liver infection, had to be accommodated with adults in a glass-sided veranda close to the hospital's administrative entrance. That is why the historic photographs of Bevan attending the 'birth of the NHS' show him with the 'first patient' in what appears to be a greenhouse.

Sylvia wears a white ribbon in her hair and understandably looks intimidated by Bevan in his pinstripe suit and the formidable Matron Dolan, a Margaret Rutherford lookalike in a starched white cap and dark cape. Matron Dolan had wanted nothing to do with the event because she was against the state taking control of Park Hospital from the local council. The chairman of the hospital's management board noted in the hospital minutes: 'She did not want to be in the building when it was taken over. Happily, she changed her mind and was present at the big day.'

'Aneurin Bevan asked me if I understood the significance of the occasion and told me that it was a milestone in history – the most civilized step any country had ever taken, and a day I would remember for the rest of my life,' Sylvia later recalled. 'And, of course, he was right.'

For families like the Beckinghams, the NHS removed the worry of the cost of being sick. 'My dad earned five pounds a week and I remember whisperings about how much my treatment would cost. It should have cost seventeen pounds but my parents didn't pay a penny,' she said. Later, after growing up and getting married, Sylvia Diggory became a champion of the NHS; her son, Clive, became a GP in Malton, North Yorkshire.

*The 'first' NHS patient, Sylvia Beckingham,
with Aneurin Bevan and Matron Dolan.*

Trafford – the hospital was renamed on the fortieth anniversary of the NHS in July 1988 – is a microcosm of the pride in the NHS, and of its ills. The flowerbeds where the nurses applauded Bevan's arrival have long gone under the tarmac of service roads leading to a new Accident and Emergency unit. The veranda where Sylvia met Bevan has been pulled down, replaced by the hospital shop and offices. The administration block with its distinctive clock tower is still there, though the clock has been replaced with a bland, modern face. Sylvia Diggory was brought back to unveil a plaque in the entrance for the fortieth anniversary. Another plaque was unveiled to mark the NHS's fiftieth anniversary in 1998 by Frank Dobson, the first Secretary of State for Health in the Blair Government. As one mark of the progress the NHS has made over the decades, in 1948 the life expectancy for women was about sixty-three years; in Trafford, it had been raised to eighty by 2006, the year Sylvia Diggory died.

By 2012 the birthplace of the NHS, like many other hospitals, was in a financial crisis, as limited budgets tried to meet spiralling costs. Advances in medicine with their new, highly effective but often expensive treatments, accompanied by patient demands, seem to ensure the spiral will continue to rise exponentially in the NHS. Since Bevan's ceremony, the hospital has spread across the Trafford site like a vast factory, providing health care on an industrial scale. It has grown from fifty beds to five hundred and thirty beds, with over two thousand staff dealing with over twenty-four thousand in-patients each year. And though the total NHS budget now stands at £105 billion, that is still not enough to keep all hospitals like Trafford open. With the austerity programmes of the Coalition Government, £10 million has been cut from Trafford's budget; two wards and two operating theatres have been closed to stave off bankruptcy.

Sandra Howarth, who was born at the Park Hospital that day in 1948 when Bevan visited, said the cuts were a 'betrayal' of the NHS. Had her mother Winnie given birth the day before, she would have been charged one and sixpence – equivalent to her family's weekly shopping bill. 'The NHS was one of the best things to happen to this country,' said Howarth. 'People couldn't afford to pay for doctors and the NHS solved that. We are going backwards rather than forwards. Back to Victorian times.'[15]

One option for Trafford was for a private company to come in and run the hospital for the NHS. But headlines saying the Tories had 'flogged off the birthplace of the NHS' to the private sector would have been a propaganda disaster for David Cameron's Coalition Government, especially while it was in the throes of a bitter battle over plans to cut the cost of the NHS by injecting more competition into it. Instead, Bevan's hospital was taken over by the bigger Central Manchester University Hospitals NHS Foundation Trust.

I arrive at Bevan's hospital on the day before the takeover to find office staff dashing from one meeting to another in preparation for the Great Day, Mark 2. As I point my camera at the plaques unveiled by Sylvia Diggory and Frank Dobson, a hospital worker asks me: 'Is that the final photograph?' No, I say, the Tories could never let the birthplace of the NHS close now.

The Tory opposition under Churchill voted against the second and third readings of the NHS Act in 1946. I believe that was a major strategic blunder by Churchill. The party has been trying to repair the political damage ever since. It not only enabled Aneurin Bevan to take possession of the NHS as his own creation; it allowed future generations of Labour politicians to accuse the Tories of trying to strangle the NHS at birth – an allegation that is being made to this day. The former Tory Chancellor Lord Lawson said the NHS was 'the closest thing the English have to a religion'. Opposing it was like casting the Conservatives as the party of NHS heretics.

And there was no greater heretic than Margaret Thatcher. In the run-up to the 1987 General Election, she tried to reassure the public that the 'NHS is safe in our hands'. However, when she needed treatment for a claw-finger disorder, she relied on privately funded care. I was present when my late *Independent* colleague, Tony Bevins, the son of a Tory minister, Reg Bevins, asked her at a Tory election press conference, if the NHS was safe in her hands, why did Mrs Thatcher not use it? Mrs Thatcher replied: 'I, along with something like five million other people, insure to enable me to go into hospital on the day I want; at the time I want; and with a doctor I want.'

The honesty of her remarks caused a stunned silence. They appeared to confirm her critics' suspicions that she was not committed to the NHS at all. They did not change the outcome of the election, however, which the Tories won. The NHS is loved, but the 1987 election, like most others after the blip of 1945, was decided on the economy.

Yet Churchill was right about one thing – the cost of implementing the welfare state, particularly the NHS, would prove Labour's undoing. None of the Government splits was more destructive for Labour than the row over financing the creation of the NHS.

In December 1948, Bevan was already warning Cabinet colleagues that he would need an extra £50 million to maintain the NHS as a comprehensive and entirely free service – on top of its budget of £176 million for the first year. By 1951, Bevan, disenchanted with the Atlanticist direction of the Attlee–Bevin Government, was at the end of his tether. At a meeting of the social services committee of the Cabinet on 15 March, he discovered his successor, Hilary Marquand, had agreed with the Chancellor, Hugh Gaitskell, to introduce charges for dental care and spectacles. Bevan was no longer Health Secretary, having moved to the Ministry of Labour, but he took this news almost as a personal breach of faith between himself and his party. It meant that for the first time the health service, which he called 'my NHS', would no longer be free.

Worse, the change was to help pay for an increase in the defence budget, which Bevan took to mean British rearmament in the Cold War, to please the Americans. Gaitskell was a lofty, right-wing Wykehamist, an Old Boy of Winchester College, a combination guaranteed to rile Bevan. Bevan was incensed. Gaitskell stuck to his guns, supported by Herbert Morrison, the former Chancellor Hugh Dalton and ultimately Attlee, who had to go into hospital at the height of the crisis with an ulcer.

While the Prime Minister received the best treatment the NHS could offer, Bevin did his best to restrain the Welsh rebel but Bevin, too, was ill and would die in April. Bevan described the sum involved – about £13 million – as 'paltry' but said the principle was fundamental. He warned he would rally support among fellow left-wingers, and the Labour leaders would not get the change through without the backing of the Tories.

Harold Wilson, the Minister for the Board of Trade, supported Bevan, but many others did not. Dalton dismissed Wilson as Bevan's 'dog', undercutting the endorsement, and Manny Shinwell, now Minister for Defence, pronounced the hope of an entirely free NHS to be a 'pipedream'. In the end, the Cabinet backed Gaitskell and Bevan decided to go public. He told an angry meeting of dockers in Bermondsey that he would 'not be a member of a government which imposes charges on the patient'.

Gaitskell responded. He said he would be obliged to resign, if he lost the backing of the Cabinet. The Cabinet stood by the Chancellor's side, pointing out that in 1949, Bevan had agreed in principle to prescription charges. Bevan argued it did not count, as they were never introduced.

Bevan acted like a prima donna, threatening resignation and being persuaded to carry on until the Chancellor delivered the budget. It was a masterful performance by Gaitskell – he coupled the health charges with increases in old-age pensions – and there was hardly a murmur of dissent from the Labour side. The one exception came from Bevan's wife, the MP Jennie Lee, who – standing next to Bevan by the Speaker's chair – shouted 'Shame!'

Despite his petulant eruptions of anger, Bevan appeared to have been persuaded to stay in the Government. Then, the 20 April issue of *Tribune*, the left-wing political weekly, came out. It included a lacerating critique of the budget, accusing Gaitskell of rearmament at the expense of charges on dentistry and spectacles. Everyone knew it was written by Michael Foot, but the words were those used in private by Bevan. It brought 'Bevanism' out into the open, and left Bevan with no option: he had to resign to stand up for what he believed in. In his letter to the Prime Minister, Bevan wrote that the budget was 'wrong because it is the beginning of the destruction of those social services in which Labour has taken a special pride and which were giving Britain the moral leadership of the world'.

Bevan widened the rift in his subsequent resignation speech in the Commons, raising the betrayal of the working class in 1931, when a Labour Prime Minister, Ramsay MacDonald, surrendered power to a National Coalition Government to deal with the Depression. 'There is only one hope for mankind – and that is democratic Socialism. There is only one party in Great Britain which can do it and that is the Labour Party. But I ask them carefully to consider how far they are polluting the stream.'

His fellow Labour MPs did not take kindly to being accused of 'polluting the stream' of socialism for going along with charges for dental care and spectacles. His overblown rhetoric failed to win Bevan any friends, and the next day, 24 April, he compounded the error. At a packed meeting of the Parliamentary Labour Party, Bevan lost his temper. 'He was sweating and shouting and seemed on the edge of a nervous breakdown,' according to Dalton. Gaitskell said: 'He almost screamed at the platform. At one point, he said, "I won't have it. I won't have it". And this, of course, was greeted with derision. "You won't have it?".'

Bevan's biographer, John Campbell, compares his resignation to the tragedy of Othello or Antony: 'the Labour Party riven in two, doomed to waste itself in fractious opposition for half a generation, until both the principal protagonists were dead. Bevan's defeat was scarcely Gaitskell's victory. Between them they practically destroyed the thing that in their different ways they loved.'[16]

Bevan's resignation so close to the election appeared to many of his colleagues to be an act of destructive vanity, but they knew it was coming. In the 1950 General Election, the landslide majority that Labour had won in 1945 was slashed to just six seats, despite piling up over 1.5 million more votes than the Tories in its heartlands. The once-proud Labour Government was living precariously. By splitting the party at this moment, Bevan's critics argued he was sabotaging Labour's hope of keeping power when the election came.

On 26 October 1951, the divided Labour Government was thrown out of office. Churchill, nearly seventy-seven years old, an almost extinct volcano having suffered at least one stroke, was returned to office. He had a majority of just eighteen seats but it was enough; the Conservatives remained in power – through spy scandals and sex scandals – until 1964, when Bevan's 'dog', Harold Wilson, succeeded the aristocratic, affable but ineffectual Alec Douglas-Home as Prime Minister.

The historic split in the Labour Party between the Bevanites and the Gaitskellites that was started by the welfare state continued into the 1980s between the Bennites and the Blairites and is not over, even now. A natural Bevanite behind his bushy beard, Frank Dobson, the former Labour Health Secretary, told me he would have backed Bevan in the row over prescriptions: 'It has always been a trivial sum compared to the cost of the NHS.' In 2012, prescription charges were raised to £7.65 per item. 'Personally I would have no prescription charges,' he said.

As Health Secretary, Dobson had to pop over from his office at Richmond House to Downing Street on a regular basis to see the Prime Minister. He was Bevanite in his refusal to bring in the private sector to the health service. 'I did a lot of things they didn't approve of,' he said. 'Blair's officials would contact my officials afterwards and say the Prime Minister had raised with the Secretary of State the possibility of the private sector involvement in the NHS. They would say, "What are we doing about it?" I would say, "Nothing". Because he hadn't actually raised it with me.'

Alternatives to the NHS have been tried, and rejected. Even Thatcher drew the line at privatizing the NHS. She commissioned a review of an insurance-based system, like that in America, but it was found to be too expensive. In the United States, millions of people cannot afford the insurance premiums, and have no health cover – a problem that will not entirely go away with the recent American reforms. Barack Obama, the US President, has pushed to emulate portions of the NHS by extending public health rights to poorer people. The NHS may not be perfect, but it is the envy of most of the rest of the world.

Despite all its faults, Hennessy maintains, 'the NHS was and remains one of the finest institutions ever built by anybody anywhere'.

As a nation, we are right to be proud of that.

TEN

1982

*'Just rejoice at the news and congratulate our forces
and the marines… Rejoice!'*

SOUTH ATLANTIC OCEAN, 2 MAY 1982:
The General Belgrano sinking.

I stood in the red-carpeted Ways and Means corridor leading to the Members' Lobby of the House of Commons, looking for MPs. It was after 11 p.m. on Wednesday, 31 March 1982, and the House was deserted.

It was my usual haunt as a lobby journalist at Westminster where I could do trade with the MPs as they passed; it felt a bit like being a King's Cross hooker looking for some action; you could never tell who was going to come up to you for a chat. However, this was the fag end of the day, when most MPs had gone home. MPs had been discussing the Oil and Gas Enterprise Bill and were shortly to start the adjournment. The Mother of Parliaments seemed as dead as last week's news.

I turned to go back up the three flights of stairs to the press gallery when the avuncular Sir Spencer le Marchant came padding round the corner from the library corridor.

Spencer was an assistant Government whip, a great gossip and famous for his love of champagne. He was six feet four inches tall, ran the annual MPs' slimming club (at which he failed miserably each year), and his job was to tour the bars, picking up advance warning of plotting among his own backbenchers against 'Mother' (Margaret Thatcher). He was usually full of bonhomie and the Speaker's vintage champagne.

Tonight, Spencer's face was as pink as a cherub but his countenance was creased with concern.

I asked him what was going on. 'Oh,' he said, drawing close to me, 'it's all blowing up in the South Atlantic, old boy. You want to get onto it.'

I knew there was a bit of local difficulty with a bunch of scrap-metal dealers who had landed on a rock that Britain regarded as its own property, called South Georgia, and there had been some diplomatic wrangling with Argentina. The day before, Richard Luce, a languid Foreign Office minister, had run into flak from his own side when he gave a statement to the Commons on the ongoing row. He had said 'the situation... is potentially serious' and spoke vaguely of 'precautionary measures'.

Sir Bernard Braine was one of the veteran knights of the shires who were spluttering with rage at the effrontery of the 'Argies'. 'This comic opera' should never have arisen, he said. Denis Healey, Labour's Shadow Foreign Secretary, said he was forced for once to agree with the Tory-supporting *Daily Telegraph* – the Government's response was 'foolish and spineless'.

Earlier in the day, Margaret Thatcher had given a typically robust statement about the European Council she had attended, and there had been Foreign Office questions, but not a single enquiry about the Falkland Islands or its dependencies, the islands of South Georgia.

I was baffled. I asked Spencer: 'What do you mean?'

'I don't know, but we've all been called to a meeting.'

At that point, the Government Chief Whip Michael Jopling caught sight of us from the Members' Lobby. Jopling had the face of a basset hound. He did not need to say anything – the look with one of his big rheumy eyes was enough. Spencer made an intake of breath as if he had been hit in the solar plexus.

'Oh, he's seen me talking to you. Got to go, sorry,' he said, and scampered off in Jopling's direction. They disappeared, deep in conversation.

There was no one else around. It was clearly important, so I decided to tell my news desk at the *Guardian*.

I told them all I knew – something big was blowing up in the South Atlantic, and a whips' meeting had been called at Westminster. I suggested that whatever they already had on the subject from their foreign correspondents should be promoted to the front page. This was obviously important. Then, pleased that we would be ahead of the news, I went home.

The next day, nothing appeared on the front page, and for another day, 1 April, no one outside the small circle around Thatcher was let into the secret.

All hell broke loose at Westminster on Friday, 2 April, when the secret could be contained no more.

What I did not know on Wednesday night – nor did any other Fleet Street journalist – was that the Prime Minister had just finished a hastily assembled four-hour crisis meeting in her oak-panelled room in the suite of Victorian offices located in the House of Commons at the back of the Speaker's chair. The attendees included her most senior colleagues in the Cabinet and her chiefs of defence and intelligence. She had called the meeting after John Nott, the Secretary of State for Defence, had come to her with some worrying reports from the South Atlantic. He told her that it looked like the Argentinians were preparing to invade the Falkland Islands.

Nott had intercepts of coded military messages from Argentina. They had been passed on by GCHQ, the Government's authorized telecommunications hacking centre in Cheltenham, Gloucestershire. The signals showed an Argentine submarine, *Santa Fe*, had been sent to Port Stanley, the capital of the Falklands; the Argentine navy was assembling in a formation that could mount an invasion; an army commander had embarked on a merchant vessel, possibly to head up an amphibious attack force; and the Argentine navy had been ordered to destroy all documents. It was raw material, but the MOD intelligence chiefs felt it left little doubt that the Argentine junta planned an invasion of the Falklands for the morning of Friday, 2 April. Copies were passed to the Prime Minister's private office at Downing Street and Sir Robert Armstrong, the Cabinet Secretary.

Thatcher was furious.

The crisis meeting had started in total secrecy and high tension at about 7 p.m. The Prime Minister demanded to know what they could do to stop the Argentinians. The answer was: nothing.

Britain had a force of fewer than seventy Royal Marines in and around Port Stanley, eleven Royal Navy personnel and the Arctic survey ship, *Endurance*. That was all. The Marine contingent was actually twice the normal number due to a handover in progress with the force, but it was still far too few to hold Port Stanley for long. Britain had no serious military force in the South Atlantic with which it could deter or repel an invasion of the Falklands. The islands were practically defenceless.

Those ranged around the Prime Minister's dark oak table included the Foreign Ministers Richard Luce and the pleasant but plodding Sir Humphrey Atkins. Both were fully paid-up members of the so-called wets' club, and distrusted by the Thatcherites.* They were joined by Sir Antony Acland, head of the Joint Intelligence Committee; Clive Whitmore, the Prime Minister's private secretary; Ian Gow, her loyal Parliamentary private secretary (one of the most amusing men at Westminster, he was later murdered by the IRA with a car bomb); and Sir Frank Cooper, permanent secretary from the MOD, who had been summoned from a private dinner.

Peter Carrington, the Sixth Baron of Carrington and the Foreign Secretary, and the Chief of the Defence Staff, Admiral Sir Terence Lewin, were absent. Lord Carrington was in Tel Aviv; Lewin was in New Zealand. The invasion had caught the Government on the hop. The meeting was so rushed, many of Thatcher's most senior Cabinet ministers, including Home Secretary William 'Willie' Whitelaw, Conservative Party Chairman Cecil Parkinson and Francis Pym, the Leader of the House, who would form the core of the War Cabinet, were not there, despite being in the country.

After the meeting started, Nott was told that the Chief of the Navy Staff, Sir Henry Leach, was outside. Nott immediately asked for him to join the meeting. Leach, dressed in full uniform, had flown by helicopter from Portsmouth to London and, finding a flap on, had decided to intervene, believing Nott was about to sell the navy short again.

Thatcher – always impressed by a uniform – asked Leach for his counsel. He was quiet, calm and poised when he answered. 'I can put together a task force of destroyers, frigates, landing craft, support vessels.

---

* The term, of course, came from public-school slang – belittling the feeble and 'soppy' – and had been adopted by the Thatcher crowd for those Tories who were weak on her proposed monetary policies. When the dissenters retaliated by calling the Thatcherites 'dry', it lacked some rhetorical punch. But the names stuck.

It will be led by the aircraft carriers HMS *Hermes* and HMS *Invincible*. It can be ready to leave in forty-eight hours.' He believed that such a force could retake the islands; all he needed was the Prime Minister's authority to begin assembling it. Doubly impressed by Leach now, she granted her approval on the spot, though reserved the decision to send the Task Force to war to the full Cabinet.

'If they are invaded, we have got to get them back,' she said.

They were astonished and impressed by Leach's assurance. But unlike the politicians, the Royal Navy team at the Ministry of Defence had secretly prepared for just such an eventuality.

There was one dissenter in the room. Despite being on the verge of war, Nott lacked Thatcher's obvious trust in his First Sea Lord. 'I did not have such confidence – there had been a full year of misunderstanding between us. So I expressed my qualms to Margaret Thatcher about the viability of such an operation.'[1] The cause of their 'misunderstanding' had been the spending cuts ordered by Nott in the budget for the Royal Navy. Nott reasoned that set-piece naval warfare was largely a thing of the past and proposed, with Thatcher's backing, to slash the navy budget by scrapping two assault ships, the *Fearless* and the *Intrepid*; cutting the number of frigates and destroyers by twenty to a total of forty; and also scrapping the aircraft carrier *Hermes*, and selling a second, *Invincible*, to Australia. That would leave the UK with just one ageing carrier, *Illustrious*. Had Argentina's General Galtieri waited a few months, he would have found Britain without a carrier fleet to send to the South Atlantic.

Leach had made no secret of his conviction that Nott was cutting too deeply, and had been engaged in a running battle with the Defence Secretary before the crisis over the Falklands had blown up. Now he saw the Falklands War as a heaven-sent opportunity to rescue the Royal Navy from Nott's axe.

Nott, a former merchant banker and Treasury minister, had won Thatcher's support as one of the 'dries' on the economy in the great battle over the need to reduce public spending in 1981. She had put him into the Ministry of Defence in January that year to conduct a hard-headed review of defence, and cut the budget. He had some defence experience; he had served for six years as a regular soldier in the Gurkha Rifles, stationed in Singapore. But his passions were his family, his farm in the West Country where he grew daffodils, fly fishing and politics – not protecting the traditions of the Royal Navy. His value to Thatcher was that he was judged to be 'one of us' against the wets.

In the rough-and-tumble world at Westminster, he seemed a remote, cerebral character, brittle and on edge, unsuited, in the view of some of his colleagues, to the pressures of high office. Nott said of himself: 'I am an excitable person by nature, though normally I get excitable about little and unimportant things.'[2] He claimed in his memoirs that when it came to big things, he was overcome by calm. That is not how he seemed to me at the time. He gave the impression of not suffering fools gladly. With a thin face, balding hair, beady bespectacled eyes and a staccato voice, he came across as a typical public-school Tory.

He sometimes showed contempt for modern media techniques, and seemed to have little time for interviewers. Not long after the Falklands war, Nott committed the cardinal media sin of tearing off his microphone and walking out of a live BBC television interview with the grandee of political broadcasters, the late Sir Robin Day. Day was a household name, so famous in his trademark polka-dot bow tie and heavy horn-rimmed spectacles that he had become one of the staples for the impersonator Mike Yarwood. The revered Day politely put it to Nott that the First Sea Lord believed the navy cuts had gone too deep. The public, he continued, might believe Sir Henry Leach rather than Nott, a 'here today, gone tomorrow politician'. Nott was enraged at this contemptuous line of questioning. He stood up and said: 'I'm sorry. I'm fed up with this interview.' Then he removed his lapel mic, threw it down on Day's desk and left the studio, live on air. That was six months after the Falklands War, and the following year he walked out of politics altogether. He returned to being a merchant banker. (Nott subsequently showed some humility by using Day's phrase as the title for his memoirs.)

The media was not the only group in his bad books. Nott also held a barely concealed contempt for the 'feeble' Foreign Office and 'its demeaning role as a spokesman for foreign interests that rankles so deeply with Tories like myself'.[3]

He was clearly on a short fuse, but now he was also at the centre of the greatest firestorm of his political career. He needed sure media skills and close liaison with the Foreign Office. It was going to be a difficult time.

After the crisis meeting, Thatcher privately told him: 'I suppose you realize, John, that this is going to be the worst week of our lives.' He replied: 'Well, that may be so, but I imagine that each successive week will be worse than the last.'

He was right.

~ℓ~

Devoid of any substantial defence assets in the South Atlantic, the only action that Thatcher could take was to appeal to her ally in the White House for help. She sent a cable to President Ronald Reagan that night, and ordered Sir Nicholas Henderson, the British ambassador to Washington, to contact Alexander Haig, the US Secretary of State. Henderson was charged with asking the Americans to intervene with Argentina's three-man military junta led by General Galtieri. When Henderson showed Haig the British intelligence, Haig angrily wanted to know why the CIA had been unaware of it.

The next morning, Thursday, 1 April 1982, James Rentschler, the White House special adviser to President Reagan, noted in his diary his disbelief that the Brits were preparing to go to war over some rocks in the South Atlantic that he had never heard of before. It had a Gilbert and Sullivan ring to it:

> Never heard of them, right? Me neither – at least not until last evening when the Prime Minister Margaret Thatcher sent an urgent message through the Cabinet Line requesting the President to intercede with the Argies.
>
> Eighteen-hundred British-origin sheepherders, pursuing a peaceful life on some wind-blown specks of rock in the South Atlantic, now targeted by Argentine amphibious assault units – which, in turn, may soon be attacked by the largest naval armada ever to steam out of British ports since Suez? Yes indeed, the thing certainly does sound like Gilbert and Sullivan as told to Anthony Trollope by Alistair Cooke.
>
> But what started out as a comic opera now looks to have become not only quite serious, but exceptionally nasty.[4]

Rentschler made his diary entry in the West Wing as the President was 'eloquently pleading' on the long-distance phone line to Buenos Aires for Galtieri to call off his country's invasion of the Falklands. Listening in to the conversation, Rentschler noted that Galtieri sounded like 'a thug', speaking 'in broken Mafioso-type English'. The Argentine 'strongman' had miscalculated and misjudged the British temper.

Rentschler wrote a note on the President's conversation with Galtieri for a cable to be sent to Thatcher. It was not good news. President Reagan told her: 'He left me with the clear impression that he has embarked on a course of armed conflict.' Significantly, the President added: 'While we have a policy of neutrality on the sovereignty issue, we will not be neutral on the issue involving Argentine use of military force.' US intercepts of Argentine messages suggested that the junta would indeed press ahead with their invasion by early the next morning.

Reagan, the most right-wing President of the United States in more than a generation, was a natural Conservative ally of Margaret Thatcher. He had quickly established a very warm relationship with her, a mutual respect bordering on devotion. He was determined to give Thatcher his nation's support.

The President's duplicitous policy on the Falklands gave Reagan the cover to assist Thatcher in her hour of need but it caused a rift with the US State Department, which had been developing a strong pro-Argentina policy. Regardless of Argentina's status as a military dictatorship, Haig and his neo-Con advisers saw the country as a potential ally against the revolutionary left-wing juntas taking power in other parts of their South American backyard. They did not want one of their key foreign policy objectives to be wrecked on some 'wind-blown specks of rock' in the South Atlantic.

Jeanne Kirkpatrick, the US ambassador to the UN, was the leading pro-Argentine hawk. She insisted on the US remaining neutral in the conflict. As if to underline the point in bright red marker, on the day that Argentine soldiers fought a running battle in Port Stanley with British Marines for control of the Falklands, Kirkpatrick went forward with a dinner given in her honour by the Argentine ambassador to the US. She was accompanied by Haig's deputy, Walter Stoessel, and Tom Enders, Assistant Secretary for Latin American Affairs.

In London, I quickly discovered the wisdom of that old journalists' dictum, 'truth is the first victim of war'. In common with other lobby journalists, who were asking what Richard Luce had meant by 'precautionary measures', I was told that a nuclear submarine, *Superb*, was in the South Atlantic. This was intended to give the Argentine junta pause for thought, but it backfired. It encouraged Galtieri to accelerate his plans for invasion, which had been scheduled for the milder summer months of June and July.

In fact, *Superb* was heading towards its nuclear base in Faslane, West Scotland. A former Cabinet minister told me later it was ordered to stay on the seabed for a couple of days to maintain the fiction that it was in the South Atlantic. Only one of Britain's fleet of nuclear submarines, *Spartan*, could leave Gibraltar immediately for the south. Not until 1 April would *Splendid* sail from Faslane, with *Conqueror* following on 3 April. It would be 12 April before the first sub arrived near Port Stanley – far too late to be of any deterrent effect. This failure to prepare for a possible invasion was to be the central issue of a later inquiry into the debacle by a committee chaired by Lord Franks, former British ambassador to the UN.

One who was in the eye of the storm was Cecil Parkinson, the Conservative Party Chairman. Nott wanted Parkinson in the War Cabinet as a fellow Thatcher loyalist who would back him and the Prime Minister in the war. Parkinson, Nott believed, would be a useful voice against possible backsliding from Willie Whitelaw and Francis Pym. As events unfolded, Whitelaw – who had seen active service as a tank commander after the Normandy landings in June 1944 – was one of Thatcher's staunchest supporters for the war. Pym shared Nott's misgivings about the viability of the operation, while Parkinson says he found himself siding with an unlikely ally, Whitelaw, in backing up the Prime Minister.

These days, Parkinson is a Tory peer in a kind of living Valhalla in the House of Lords of the 1979–90 Thatcher Government. We chat in the Royal Gallery, sitting at a table in the shadow of the grand mural of another great British victory, the Battle of Waterloo. He still looks sleek, thirty years on, with his jutting jawline and his hair neatly parted; this was the look that made blue-rinse Tory ladies go weak at the knees on the rubber chicken circuit, when 'Cecil' was the dashing Party Chairman. He was never a toff; he was the son of a Lancashire railway worker and a grammar school boy but he was always a star who could turn heads, including Margaret Thatcher's.

He has brilliant recall, resurrecting names from events that have now passed into history. He remembers the day of the Argentine invasion of the Falklands, Friday, 2 April 1982, vividly, a day described by Thatcher the next day in the Falklands debate as one of 'rumour and counter-rumour'.

Even though the Cabinet had clear warning as early as Wednesday night, Cabinet ministers as senior as Parkinson were kept completely in the dark. That Friday, in blissful ignorance, he was on a round of speaking engagements in the Eastern region as Party Chairman. When he got to Cambridge for one of them, he was told to ring Number Ten. He was informed that the Prime Minister had called an emergency Cabinet meeting at 6 p.m. and would like him to attend.

Like everyone else, he was taken completely by surprise by the growing crisis in the Falklands. He remembers travelling back to London by car, listening to the news on the radio with growing disbelief – the simmering diplomatic row with Argentina was suddenly escalating into war. 'There was this extraordinary business of a radio ham – whom I subsequently met – who was saying, "Argentinian troop carriers are rumbling past my door full of troops",' he remembers. 'Then we switched to the House of Commons, where poor old Humphrey Atkins [the Foreign Minister] was saying, "We have no information and we cannot confirm the Argentinians have landed because we are waiting for the Governor [Sir Rex Hunt]." He was a prisoner of the Argentinians, though we didn't know that at the time.'

The night before, the Tories had taken a huge lead in the opinion polls, rising from twenty-four per cent to thirty-three per cent; the Liberals and the Social Democratic Party had fallen back; Labour under Michael Foot was trailing a poor third. Parkinson says the polling results show that Thatcher was on course to win the subsequent General Election in 1983 without the aid of the 'Falklands Factor', but he does not doubt that if Britain had been defeated, she would have lost it. 'I was really elated by this, and then I suddenly heard this terrible announcement. My reaction was the same as everybody else's – what on earth is going on?'

At the start of a special Saturday sitting on 3 April, Atkins was forced to apologize to the Commons for misinforming the House about Hunt and the situation on the islands. Atkins's unforced error at the Despatch Box confirmed the impression that the Government had been caught with its collective trousers down, and it raised worrying questions over whether it was competent to pull them up again.

Thursday was a 'lost' day. When Parkinson was recalled for a special Cabinet meeting on Friday, Thatcher and the Cabinet inner circle had known about the impending invasion for forty-eight hours but had been completely impotent to prevent it.

The Cabinet meeting that evening, Parkinson says, 'was a very dramatic occasion'. 'We had a presentation of the facts and Margaret went round the table. She asked every person, "Shall we despatch the fleet?" Everybody except dear old John Biffen said we should put the fleet to sea. John was honest enough to say it was a lost cause.'⁵ Trade Secretary John Biffen's Cabinet career was blighted from that moment on. He was clearly not 'one of us', as Thatcher liked to categorize the supporters on whom she could rely. He had been classed as a 'dry' on the economy; now he was cast out among the wets.

Even those who had spoken in favour of sending the fleet had their doubts about whether it could succeed. Parkinson and Michael Heseltine, having backed it to the hilt, slipped away to the Stafford hotel by Green Park to discuss their misgivings privately over dinner. 'We thought it had the potential for being a disaster for the Government,' says Parkinson. 'It was hugely ambitious – eight thousand five hundred miles away; no land-based air cover; the nearest land base (because we knew South America with the exception of Chile would be hostile) would be Ascension, four thousand miles from home; it was a colossal, chancy undertaking; that is how it seemed to us at the time.'

Few around the Cabinet table actually thought the crisis would end in fighting. A majority of the Cabinet, like many expert observers, believed it would end in a face-saving diplomatic deal with the Argentinians negoti-ated through Javier Pérez de Cuéllar, the Peruvian Secretary General of the United Nations.

Emergency debates were called the next day for the Lords and the Commons – the first Saturday sitting of Parliament since the Suez Crisis of 1956. The debates would give Thatcher the democratic mandate for the proposed Task Force to sail within forty-eight hours, but they could resolve nothing.

As one who was there, I remember the day was electrifying, but it was not a great debate; it was a walkover for Thatcher. The Prime Minister laid out the facts with quiet determination. Enoch Powell said it would test of 'what metal' the Iron Lady was made.

The day was made easy for her by Michael Foot, the veteran white-haired leader of the Opposition. He left the nagging questions of the Government's obvious failure to deter the Argentinians for a later inquiry (by the Franks commission). For now, he gave his wholehearted sup-port to the despatch of the Task Force. On the face of it, this seemed a remarkable transformation for Foot, who proudly described himself as a 'peacemonger', and was a key member of the CND's 'Ban the Bomb' marches of the 1960s. That may have been the image, but that was to mistake the man – Foot was not a pacifist. Indeed, he had been an anonym-ous co-author of the notorious book *The Guilty Men*, condemning Lord

Halifax, the Foreign Secretary, and other appeasers in 1940 for seeking an accommodation with Adolf Hitler (see Chapter Eight).

Foot was heavily influenced in his decision by the fact that Argentina was in the hands of General Galtieri, who had seized power after the death in 1974 of the elected president, Juan Perón, and the subsequent overthrow in 1976 of his popular widow, Eva, known as Evita. Foot saw the Falklands invasion as yet another fight between a fascist dictator and democracy. One of the last great orators in the House, he said that Britain had to 'ensure that foul and brutal aggression does not succeed in our world. If it does, there will be a danger not merely to the Falkland Islands, but to people all over this dangerous planet.'

'We had a stroke of luck in that Michael Foot, as the Leader of the Labour Party, was magnificent during the Falklands,' Lord Parkinson frankly admits. This astonishing compliment from one of Thatcher's most loyal lieutenants might embarrass Foot, were he still alive. And Parkinson's words reveal for the first time how much Thatcher was indebted to the Labour firebrand for backing her call to arms. Had Foot led Labour in opposing the retaking of the Falklands by military means, it would have shattered any chance for political unity at home around the Task Force, and potentially made it more difficult to reject the repeated offers of a negotiated settlement. Argentina would be left master of *Las Malvinas*.

Foot enforced unity down the line. Tam Dalyell and Andrew Faulds were sacked from the Opposition front bench for opposing his line on the war, and Tony Benn, backed by the unions, began a campaign against military intervention. 'I have wondered what it would have been like if it had been someone like Chávez [Hugo Chávez, leftist leader of Venezuela], but you speak as you find,' Parkinson says. He then repeats: 'Michael Foot was magnificent.'

On the morning of the debate, British newspapers were filled with evidence of Britain's humiliation. There were photographs of Marines lying face down in the mud after surrendering to the Argentine forces at Port Stanley – the pictures thoughtfully supplied to the press by the Argentine junta.

Tory MPs were livid, but largely kept their powder dry in the chamber. Nott, winding up the debate, badly misjudged the mood of the House, however. Having got Foot and Labour to back the war, he needlessly indulged in some party political point-scoring against Labour. Nott was stung by an intervention by David Owen, the former Labour Foreign Minister in the Callaghan Government.

Owen, who in 1981 left Labour to found the breakaway Social Democratic Party, had revealed that in similar circumstances in 1977 the Callaghan Government had ordered the fleet to take up a position just over the horizon from the islands to force the Argentine Government to back down. Nott retorted: 'He [Owen] added that it gave him confidence in his negotiations, whatever that means...' The rest was lost in uproar and Owen rose to his feet. Tory defence expert and diarist Alan Clark noted: 'The *coup de grâce* was delivered by David Owen... he forced Nott to give way and he told him that if he could not appreciate the need to back negotiations with force, he did not deserve to remain one minute as Secretary of State.'

Many Tory MPs agreed with Owen on that point. Clark himself had remarked: 'Poor old Notters was a disaster.' Nott's standing among his own MPs – never very high – sank lower. The debate ended in calls of 'Resign' as Nott fended off attacks. 'The debate was not a rip-roaring success from our point of view,' says Parkinson. 'Nott struck a very partisan note, and it just wasn't the right note.'

The Prime Minister swept out of the chamber immediately after the debate to her private room behind the Speaker's chair. Trailing behind her were Parkinson, Willie Whitelaw and Francis Pym. Nott and Lord Carrington were left on their own to face the flak from angry Tory MPs in a meeting of the 1922 Committee of Conservative backbenchers. In her room, Thatcher said she was dismayed by Nott's performance and, always circumspect, noted the debate had not been a great success. She was very impressed by the support from Michael Foot, however.

The scene in Committee Room Ten was quite different. MPs were crowded into the space, the largest on the committee corridor, with windows overlooking the Thames. As a peer, Lord Carrington was not allowed to speak in the Commons and his absence from the chamber was never more dangerous than now. He had been given an easy ride in a parallel debate in the Lords, but angry Tory MPs who had remained loyally silent in the chamber now wanted blood.

Carrington was also a true patrician aristocrat, humorous but aloof, out of touch with the rougher Tory MPs in the Commons. He began with a blunder. As they knew the facts, he said mildly, he would not bother making a speech, but he would answer any questions. His insouciance riled the already boiling MPs, who demanded to know why he and Nott had allowed Britain to be humiliated by the 'Argies'.

Carrington and Nott did their best to fend off the assault from their own MPs. Nott, who had been in the House since 1966, brushed off the criticism as coming from the 'usual suspects', but Carrington – regarded as a saint in the Lords – was not used to such aggressive treatment. He left the room visibly shaken.

Afterwards, Carrington confided in Nott that he was considering resigning.

On Sunday evening, Parkinson was at home when he was asked by Number Ten to telephone Thatcher. She reported: 'Peter Carrington wants to resign; he has agreed to wait until he sees the *Times* leader tomorrow. It seems extraordinary. What do you think?'

Carrington and Thatcher were unlikely bed-fellows politically. She liked toffs, but believed the aristocrats in her party were for the most part wet and lacked guts for a fight. The Tory peers in turn regarded her as an uncouth daughter of a tradesman, the sort who knew the price of everything and the value of nothing. Still, she did not want to lose her Foreign Secretary in the middle of a crisis when all his expertise would be most needed.

Parkinson had been impressed with Lord Carrington in the Cabinet and his readiness to stand up to Thatcher when necessary. Parkinson told her that Carrington would be a loss, but he felt it was right for him to go. Carrington's resignation would enable her to appoint a Foreign Secretary who was in the House of Commons at this critical time. It would also refocus the MPs' (and the public's) minds on supporting 'our boys' in the coming battle, rather than on the diplomatic debacle in the past. Thatcher decided to accept Carrington's resignation – if it was offered the next day. The fact that she did so may be seen as evidence that, ultimately, she knew already she did not need him, because she could not accept a diplomatic solution with Argentina.

The *Times* leader called for someone to pay with his (or her) head, and Lord Carrington fell on his sword along with the two other Foreign ministers in the Commons, Atkins and Luce. It was a remarkable triple resignation for honourable reasons that has never been repeated.

On Tuesday, 5 April, the Task Force sailed out of Portsmouth harbour, crowds cheering and tearful families waving at their loved ones as they departed. It was the biggest modern Armada since the Anglo-French invasion of the Suez Canal in 1956 – twenty-eight thousand men, average age nineteen, and two hundred civilian vessels, including the liners *Canberra*, requisitioned during a cruise of the Mediterranean, and the *QE2*, escorted by almost one hundred Royal Navy warships. Some of the ships were still carrying nuclear depth charges that could not be removed in time. It was an awesome sight, but they were sailing into uncertainty.

Denis Healey, the former Labour Chancellor, was one of many older MPs in the Commons at that time who had seen service in the Second World War. He had been a 'beachmaster' at the Anzio landings in Italy and adopted a tone that was far more hostile than Foot's. He warned that an opposed landing without overwhelming odds and air cover could end in a bloodbath. 'I tell the Prime Minister that the hard facts of military reality cannot be swept away by flabby rhetoric or misquotations from Queen Elizabeth I,' he protested on 7 April. 'Worst of all, an opposed landing would inflict intolerable casualties on the Falkland Islanders, whom it is our duty to protect. They are not asking for the peace of the cemetery.'[6]

Once the fleet had sailed, Britain was set on a remorseless course to war. For those on the sidelines in the US State Department, it was like watching a car crash in slow motion. Desperate efforts were made by Alexander Haig, Francis Pym and UN Secretary General Pérez de Cuéllar to find a peaceful resolution that would be acceptable on both sides.

On 8 April, Haig flew to London to try to avert the disaster personally. He found the Prime Minister implacable.

The day before – after a row in the War Cabinet with Pym, who was newly appointed as Foreign Secretary to replace Carrington – Nott had announced a two-hundred-mile Total Exclusion Zone around the Falklands. It was an effort to try to stop Argentina from resupplying its forces by sea. Pym was worried that Haig would feel the action sabotaged any peace efforts. But as their motorcade made its way to Downing Street, Haig and his entourage were more worried about their meeting with Mrs Thatcher.

She welcomed them in the drawing room adjoining the small dining room on the first floor of Number Ten. She wore a dark velvet two-piece suit with grosgrain piping, and James Rentschler noted her 'soft hairdo heightens her blond English colouring'. The Prime Minister showed them two portraits that had been recently hung on the walls of her refurbished state rooms and which she said were 'appropriate considering the subject on our minds'. One was of Nelson, the other of Wellington. They got the none-too-subtle message. They then moved to the small dining room to have supper of overcooked beef with Pym, Nott and the Admiral of the Fleet, Sir Terence Lewin. Nott and Lewin were both strongly supportive of the Prime Minister but Pym, the Americans noted, was not quite so implacably opposed to a negotiated settlement.

After supper, she got down to the 'nut-cutter nitty gritty' of business. The Americans had put forward a three-stage plan. First, Argentina would withdraw its troops; then an interim administration would be installed for the island; finally, there would be negotiations over sovereignty and self-determination.

High colour was in the Prime Minister's cheeks, and a note of rising indignation entered her voice as she replied to the proposal. She leaned across the polished table and flatly rejected the 'woolliness' of a multilateral body taking over the islands, even on an interim basis. She and her ministers, Nott and Pym, were pledged to the House of Commons to restore British administration, she said, her temper rising.

'I did not despatch a fleet to install some nebulous arrangement which would have no authority whatsoever,' she continued. 'Interim authority! To do *what*? I beg you, I beg you to remember that in 1938 Neville Chamberlain sat at this same table discussing an arrangement which sounds very much like the one you are asking me to accept; and were I to do so, I would be censured in the House of Commons – and properly so! We in Britain simply refuse to reward aggression – that is the lesson we have learned from 1938.'

This was the Iron Lady that her ministers had become accustomed to. Haig sat nervously tapping his leg and chain-smoking Merits while trying to keep his cool and reason with her.

The British side realized that Haig believed Britain could not win a war eight thousand miles away; he was trying to help his gallant ally to save face. Rentschler said Nott made 'gonadal noises' that the British fleet would be able to sustain operations in the South Atlantic despite the onset of winter, ice, snow and sixty-foot seas. Haig's team frankly found the claim incredible.

When they broke up, Haig went to Claridge's; the US Embassy residence was not available because the US ambassador to London was in America. When he slumped on a sofa, he asked one of his aides to fix him a stiff drink, then said: 'That's one hell of a tough lady.'

Haig told his staff not to worry about Nott. He said the Defence Secretary was 'showboating to convince the Cabinet that he is more royalist than the Queen'. The only reason Nott wasn't offloaded at the same time as Carrington, said Haig, was that it would make the Brits look too chaotic. Losing two high-level Cabinet ministers when the Brits were rushing to mobilize their Task Force would have been demoralizing.

In the meeting, Thatcher had insisted that Haig go to Buenos Aires with her demand for British administration to be restored to the islands. But Haig's aides worked on him overnight, and in the morning Cabinet ministers were told that he had changed his mind. He was not flying to Argentina; he wanted another meeting with the Prime Minister. He tried to persuade Thatcher to accept the US plan, but again she refused.

Haig had hoped to emulate Henry Kissinger with his shuttle diplomacy, but he flew to Buenos Aires knowing he was on mission impossible. War was now inevitable, barring a miracle.

In Buenos Aires, Haig was met with anti-British riots. Late one night, Galtieri levelled with Rentschler, saying that he would not last a week if he withdrew his forces and administrative presence. If the British attacked, he would have to accept the offer of full support made by the Cuban ambassador – implying that the Russians, who backed the Cubans, would secretly use one of their subs to sink a British carrier, potentially one with Prince Andrew, the Queen's second son and a helicopter pilot, on board.

As the Task Force sailed on, Pym, by now regarded by the Thatcher camp as semi-detached from her Government, patiently pursued peace talks, following the initiative of Pérez de Cuéllar.

Late on 26 April, amid the gloom, more startling information came out. At around 8.45 p.m., Margaret Thatcher appeared with John Nott outside the famous black door of Number Ten for an impromptu press conference, broadcast live on television. 'Ladies and gentlemen,' she began, 'the Secretary of State for Defence has just come over to give me some very good news and I think you'd like to have it at once.' It had been agreed that Nott would read out the news item, to avoid it looking too much like Thatcher's 'show'. The Prime Minister and her advisers had picked up a hint of resentment from the public that she was seen too much as Britannia. Her orders, for once, were to stay in a supporting role.

Nott nervously announced that the MOD had received a message: British troops had landed on South Georgia shortly after 4 p.m. London time. At about 6 p.m. London time, 'the white flag was hoisted in Grytviken beside the Argentine flag'.

It was a *coup de théâtre*, but the media were sceptical. Did this mean the war for the Falklands would be avoided? A journalist asked Nott: 'What happens next?'

Thatcher could not help herself. Before Nott could reply, she flashed a look of anger at the nit-picking journalist and said: 'Just rejoice at the news and congratulate our forces and the Marines.' Thatcher then turned towards the door to go back into Number Ten.

Someone in the media scrum shouted after her: 'Are we going to war with Argentina, Mrs Thatcher?'

She paused at the doorstep and uttered one defiant word at the cameras: 'Rejoice.' The moment inspired the title of books and plays, and became the leitmotif for Thatcher's conduct of the war.

In fact, as Nott says in his memoirs, the taking of South Georgia was a sideshow that very nearly ended in disaster, and had led to a great deal of debate before finally being sanctioned. The weather was atrocious and two helicopters carrying Special Air Service forces crashed in a white-out snowstorm. The men were brought off in an heroic rescue, suffering severe frostbite. However, Thatcher knew that the retaking of the islands where the crisis had erupted would focus minds across the world. It would show that she meant business.

A week later, on 2 May, Thatcher and the War Cabinet had to focus their own minds on the risks of ending the diplomatic process and going to war.

They were at Chequers when the Chief of the Defence Staff, Admiral Sir Terence Lewin, who had quickly gained the Prime Minister's confidence with his calm professionalism, reported on a signal received that day at Northwood, the military nerve centre in west London from where the Falklands War was being directed. It came from the skipper of the nuclear submarine *Conqueror*, Commander Chris Wreford-Brown, who said he had found the Argentine cruiser *General Belgrano*.

Lewin told the Prime Minister that the commander of *Conqueror* had the *Belgrano* in his sights. Did he have permission to sink it?

According to Lord Parkinson, 'We knew the *Belgrano* was out to sink a carrier. The fact that it was going one way or the other… it was manoeuvring to avoid a torpedo. We discussed the *Belgrano*, and what it was up to, *ad nauseam*. Then up comes the captain and says the *Belgrano* is going into shallower water and I can't follow it. These things are bloody enormous. Something as big as a nuclear submarine in shallow water was easy to hit. You couldn't allow that risk.'

The thirteen-thousand-tonne warship was outside the Total Exclusion Zone and steaming away from the Task Force. It was accompanied by an escort of two destroyers armed with sea-skimming Exocet missiles. The fact that it was not within the zone was politically highly controversial, but Thatcher and the War Cabinet were advised that it made little difference to the threat. The cruiser and its escorts could easily change direction again, but by then *Conqueror* may have lost its quarry. (A housewife from Cirencester, Diana Gould, later became an overnight celebrity after challenging Thatcher on British TV over the direction in which the *Belgrano* was sailing, asserting her point by quoting the map co-ordinates.)

Together with her War Cabinet, Thatcher gave the authority to sink the *Belgrano*. Now there could be no turning back.

The ship was formerly the USS *Phoenix*, which had survived the Japanese attack on Pearl Harbor. It was sunk by two vintage-style torpedoes. Of its crew of over one thousand men, 323 were lost. The grainy photograph of the stricken ship, listing heavily to port as sailors watched from life rafts, became one of the most potent images of the war.

Thatcher's former Cabinet ministers remain adamant that they were right to order the sinking of the *Belgrano*. They argue that, although it was sailing away, the ship was part of a pincer movement staged by the Argentine navy to try to destroy the two Royal Navy carriers, without which the invasion force would have had no air cover. They also quote Argentine Rear Admiral Jorge Allara, who after the conflict appeared to accept the decision to attack the ageing cruiser. 'We as professionals said it was just too bad we lost the *Belgrano*,' Allara said.

That was the military view but politically, it was a far more difficult call to make. It was alleged at the time that by sinking the *Belgrano*, Thatcher had also torpedoed the efforts of Haig, Pym and the Peruvians to negotiate a peaceful settlement. Tam Dalyell kept up a one-man Parliamentary campaign against Thatcher for sabotaging the Peruvian peace initiative.

In truth, no peace settlement, short of a total Argentine surrender, would have been acceptable to the Prime Minister. She wanted a military victory to restore British pride, in Nott's account. 'Margaret Thatcher had, I believe, made up her mind from the outset that the only way we could regain our national honour and prestige was by inflicting a military defeat on Argentina.'[7] In fact, it salvaged her own reputation.

The Falklands was Britain's first televised war. Film crews were censored, however, to avoid giving out information that could be useful to the enemy. Though reports sometimes sounded like propaganda, this was no idle threat from the 'media minders'. Reports back in London that the Argentine bombs were not going off were picked up in Buenos Aires and led to the fuses being reset with deadly results.[8]

Despite the censors, journalists captured memorable records of the war's conduct. The late BBC reporter Brian Hanrahan became famous after he announced on the *Hermes* that a number (he could not say how many) of Harrier Jump Jets had been in combat without loss. 'I counted them all out and I counted them all back,' he said in his broadcast. There were many others: the burning hole in the side of the Type 42 destroyer HMS *Sheffield* on 4 May caused by an Exocet missile; HMS *Coventry*, a Type 42 destroyer, wrecked and left burning by two bombs on 25 May; Argentine Air Force jets flashing low over British ships in San Carlos Water; the rescue of horribly burned Welsh Guardsmen including Simon Weston, still wearing their inflated red immersion suits, from the troop carriers *Sir Tristram* and *Sir Galahad* in Bluff Cove on 8 June; the Royal Marines marching across Moody Brook – the Marines and the Parachute Regiment covering fifty-six miles in three days carrying eighty-pound packs on their backs; and finally, the Argentine guns and helmets discarded on the ground after the surrender at Port Stanley. The relentless media coverage also brought a number of new words to the lexicon: *yomp* (Royal Marine slang for forced march carrying full kit, usually across boggy terrain, became common to describe any kind of walk, even one down to the shops); *tabbing* (tactical advance to battle, similar to yomping); *Exocet* (the deadly missiles fired by the Argentine jets that crippled HMS *Sheffield* and *Coventry* began to be used for any devastating attack, on anything, as in 'Everton's striker Andy Gray launched an Exocet at Manchester United'); *prof* (to steal); *Gotcha!* (the headline plastered across the *Sun* after the sinking of the *Belgrano*).

ON THE WAY TO PORT STANLEY, FALKLAND ISLANDS:
The iconic image of a column of Marines yomping.

But reporters' despatches from the war were very different, depend-ing on where they were allowed to go. Sir Max Hastings had a 'good war' – he famously claimed a world scoop by being the 'first to march into Port Stanley'. Others had a more difficult time, understandably causing frayed nerves among some of Fleet Street's finest. Gareth Parry of the *Guardian* was left, in effect, sitting on a floating bomb after being forced to stay on the ammunition ship *Resource* while it was under attack by Argentine planes in San Carlos Water. At one point, his ship was used as a shield for an aircraft carrier. He graph-ically described the day:

> Their technique was stunningly casual. Mirages and Skyhawks would fly low, weaving among the ships' masts, and flicking the bombs from below their wings. They scythed through the air, not above but alongside us, so close that we glimpsed the pilot's face and even the rivets on the duck-egg-blue undercarriage.
>
> Bombs miraculously dropped in the water between ships laden with ammunition and explosives. One man said to me, 'If they hit us,

they'll take out every fucking ship in the Atlantic. We've got about the explosive force of Hiroshima on board.'

HMS *Antelope* was not so lucky. It exploded in a shower of intense white light against the black night sky as a bomb disposal officer, Staff Sergeant Jim Prescott of the Royal Engineers, tried to withdraw the fuse. The moment of the explosion was caught by a still photographer, Martin Cleaver of the Press Association, who won an award for the image.

The SAS had been on the islands for twenty-six days, dug into the sodden peat on Beagle Ridge. They were wet and cold and camouflaged, watching the Argentine army at close quarters, reluctantly preparing for battle. They reported back to Westminster that morale was low among the Argentinians, many of whom had been conscripted. The members of the Parachute Regiment (known as the 'Paras'), the Guards, the Marines and the Gurkhas were professional, hard and dedicated soldiers, and they defeated General Galtieri's draftees.

It was no easy task. Seventeen Paras died, including their commanding officer Colonel 'H' Jones who, alone, charged an enemy machine-gun post at Goose Green on 27 May to carry the position that had been holding up his unit. He was posthumously awarded the Victoria Cross. The campaign involved bloody hand-to-hand fighting in trenches on Mount Tumbledown on the night of 13 June, before the way to Port Stanley was clear. The Argentine flag was run down on 14 June after the Argentine commander, Mario Menéndez, surrendered to Major General Jeremy Moore. Almost immediately, the inquests began.

The Franks report was published on 18 January 1983. It concluded that it 'would not be justified in attaching any criticism or blame to the present Government for the Argentine Junta's decision to commit its act of unprovoked aggression in the invasion of the Falkland Islands on 2 April 1982'. Few believed it, but the verdict got Thatcher off a nasty hook. It also set the pattern for later 'whitewash' reports on military adventures – such as the Hutton inquiry into the circumstances surrounding the death of Dr David Kelly, the expert on Saddam Hussein's weapons of mass destruction, and the Butler inquiry into intelligence mistakes surrounding the Iraq War.

~(~

The irony is that it all could have been avoided. The Falkland Islands had been a bone of contention between Britain and Argentina for over 150 years. Britain insisted it had exercised sovereignty over the Falklands since 1833 and its dependencies in South Georgia since 1775, when they were named by Captain James Cook in honour of George III. Though there was a continual British presence after 1833, Britain's legal claim for long periods amounted to little more than a flag stuck on a pole at an abandoned trading station. Its claim was challenged by the Spanish, who accused Britain of 'piracy'. The dispute had rumbled on inconclusively, with Argentina insisting it had inherited its claim from Spain.

Then, in December 1965, the declaration of unilateral independence from the British Empire by the white regime of Ian Smith in Rhodesia (now Zimbabwe) triggered renewed demands in the United Nations from Spain and Argentina. The collapsing colonial power, they said, should also shed Gibraltar and the Falkland Islands with South Georgia from its imperial grip. The next year, the territorial dispute over the Falklands hit the headlines when a gang of twenty Argentine nationalists hijacked an internal flight in Argentina and flew to Port Stanley to stake Argentina's claim. The amateurish 'coup' failed to gain the territory for Argentina, but it succeeded in raising the temperature.

In the following decade, the Falklands issue continued to simmer in Buenos Aires. Renewed efforts were made by Harold Wilson's Labour Government in the mid-1970s to reach an amicable accommodation between the settlers and the populist nationalist Argentine Government of Eva Perón.

Lord Shackleton, son of the Antarctic explorer Ernest Shackleton, offered some hope for the future with a report in 1975 on the economic development of the islands for fishing, tourism and oil. Crucially, it required a longer runway to be built at the airport. Successive governments did not take it up – including Thatcher's when it had the chance. Thatcher says it was not just the cost; building a longer runway would have sent a signal to Galtieri that Britain was not serious about talks. I do not find that very convincing, given that she was opposed to a compromise on sovereignty without the consent of the islanders. I remember the cost being the issue. Refusing to foot the bill for the runway was to prove even more costly.

~⟨⟩~

In the 1980s, Argentina became more belligerent as civil disorder at home increased. General Galtieri knew that nothing would gain him more popular support on the streets of Buenos Aires than to seize *Las Malvinas*. There were anti-government riots in Argentina days before Galtieri ordered the invasion.

He was gambling that the British Government would not be able to stop an invasion, if it were sprung as a surprise and presented as a *fait accompli*. It was a calculated risk, but the Thatcher Government had unintentionally sent a series of signals to the Argentine junta that it was no longer interested in defending its distant possession. As part of his savage cuts in the Royal Navy budget, John Nott had announced the intention to withdraw the *Endurance* to save £3 million a year from the defence accounts – a decision taken in the teeth of bitter opposition by Lord Carrington. The Government compounded this error by refusing to extend automatic rights of abode to the Falkland Islanders when the British Nationality Act was passed in 1981. (It would do so, however, a year after the Falklands conflict.) More importantly, the Government had actively sought a deal with Argentina for a 'lease-back' arrangement, which would have handed the Falklands to the Argentinians after the current population had died out.

This radical diplomatic solution had been proposed by a leading Thatcherite intellectual, Nicholas Ridley. He was a right-wing pragmatist, and had visited the islands on a fact-finding tour. To the chain-smoking Ridley, it seemed obvious that a lease-back plan – like the one that kept the Hong Kong colony British until it was handed back to China in 1997 – could relieve Britain of the ongoing cost of defending the Falklands against a possible attack, while keeping control of the islands for the foreseeable future, say, ninety years.

Ridley gained Thatcher's reluctant approval for the plan, but she could be two-faced when she wanted to be; she had a habit of distancing herself from her own Government's policies when she disapproved of them, and now she did it again. In her own memoirs, she writes: 'I disliked the proposal.'[9] Thatcher glosses over the truth in those pages, merely saying the House of Commons was 'noisily determined that the islanders' wishes should be respected'.

In fact, Tory MPs quickly found out that 'Mother' was opposed to the Ridley plan. Ridley went to the Commons to 'sell it' to MPs, making a statement to the House during which he was torn to shreds. The first to attack it as a sell-out to the wishes of the islanders was Labour's Shadow Foreign Secretary Peter Shore. Once he had opened the gates, the most reactionary Tory backwoodsmen piled in. Ridley was shattered, and so was his plan.

Years later I sat next to Shore at a *Spectator* awards lunch and playfully suggested to him that he had caused the Falklands War. He wondered how I came to that conclusion. I said: 'Because you shot down the Ridley lease-back plan.'

'I suppose I did,' he smiled, but I'm sure he was not convinced.

The failure of the lease-back deal was the last straw for the 'doves' in Argentina who had been pinning their hopes on a negotiated settlement.

Regardless of the view in Buenos Aires, when the Ridley plan was ditched the Government still steamed ahead with the proposed cuts in the islands' feeble line of defence, *Endurance*. Thatcher later had an attack of amnesia about the defence cuts. She made a speech after the war declaring: 'By not cutting our defence we were ready.' This was mendacity at its most brazen. *Endurance* was only still on station when the Falkland Islands were invaded because the cuts she approved had not yet taken effect.

Days before the invasion took place, Keith Speed, a former navy minister who had resigned over the defence cuts, ambushed Nott about *Endurance* during a debate on a decision to spend £8 billion on upgrading Britain's nuclear deterrent with Trident. 'How can we apparently afford £8000 million to meet a threat in thirteen years… when we cannot afford £3 million to keep HMS *Endurance* on patrol to meet a threat that is facing us today?' asked Speed. Nott brushed him aside, saying: 'I do not want to get involved in a debate about the Falklands now. These issues are too important to be diverted into a discussion on HMS *Endurance.*' Four days later, the Argentine Buzo Táctico commando forces invaded the islands.

The true stumbling block to a negotiated settlement was the long-standing commitment to the islanders that British sovereignty would not be conceded without their agreement, thus effectively giving them a veto over any deal with Argentina.

It seemed incredible to almost everyone I spoke to at the outbreak of hostilities – Cabinet ministers, defence chiefs and backbench MPs – that Britain would go to war over the Falklands. By the time the Task Force sailed, however, the vast majority were in favour of seeing the action through. John Major in his memoirs said that had Thatcher not sent the Task Force, she would not have survived as Prime Minister. Indeed, she emerged from the Falklands War immeasurably stronger.

Her victory – and at times her tenacity alone was all that prevented a humiliating capitulation – sent a message around the world that she would uphold the rule of law, with force if necessary. For a decade, it served notice on dictators that they would not be allowed to succeed if they attempted the same sort of smash-and-grab raid as Galtieri. The dying sun always seems to cast its strongest glow just before it goes down. To the rest of the world, the Falklands War must have seemed like a last effusion of light from the sun sinking over the British Empire.

Labour MPs attributed her subsequent 1983 General Election victory to the 'Falklands factor'. Defeating Galtieri certainly made Thatcher seem unassailable for nearly a decade, until she was stabbed in the back by her own Cabinet.

Argentina got rid of its hated junta. It became a South American democracy.

It is difficult, however, to argue that the Falklands War proved that in a war against dictatorships, democracies will prevail. Britain gained intelligence help from America, but that can be overstated. A myth has grown up that the balance was tipped in Britain's favour with the supply by the Reagan administration of spy-in-the-sky satellite images of the Argentine navy. In fact, these 'vital' US photographs of Argentine ships moored in their home port arrived in the British war rooms the day after the war ended.

Caspar Weinberger, the US Defense Secretary, secretly offered Britain a US carrier, but it was politely declined. The US certainly provided intelligence from its agents in the region. But the most important intelligence came from another source.

Britain's most valuable ally in winning the Falklands War against Argentina was Argentina's next-door neighbour, Chile, and its right-wing military dictator, General Augusto Pinochet, who rose to power through a coup. Chile and Argentina had been on the brink of war over the Beagle Channel, and it later emerged that Galtieri had ordered that these disputed islands in the channel should be seized – despite international law being on Chile's side – once the Falklands had been secured by Argentina. Pinochet had a vested interest in seeing Galtieri defeated.

It is known that Pinochet installed a long-range military radar to monitor Argentina's Comodoro Rivadavia air base; it beamed back minute-by-minute surveillance information of Argentine air force movements to the SAS headquarters satellite in Hertford for onward transmission to Northwood and later by VHF link direct to *Hermes* and the Task Force; this enabled the warships to prepare their defences against Exocet missile attacks and scramble Sea Harriers into the air to meet the attackers with what appeared to be uncanny precision. As a mark of the importance of the Chilean radar reports, the Argentine fighter-bombers were able to spring surprise attacks with heavy losses on board *Sir Galahad* and *Sir Tristram* on 8 June, a day when the surveillance system was down for maintenance.

What is not widely known, even now, is that Chile was passing raw intelligence material from Argentina directly to Britain even before hostilities began. There were reports that British intelligence was able to intercept Argentine messages from a base in Ascension. I think this was useful cover for the true source.

I have been informed that most of the vital 'sigint' – signals intelligence, the decoded intercepts of Argentine messages to its forces – came direct from Chile, not Ascension or the United States. This included the intercepted messages to Argentine commanders that alerted Thatcher and her ministers to the imminent threat of invasion at their first crisis meeting at Westminster that I stumbled across on the night of 31 March 1982. I can also reveal that it was Chile who provided the crucial 'sigint' information that enabled Britain to sink the *Belgrano*. This was confirmed by Lord Parkinson, who tells me: 'We had been discussing what would we do if we found it because we knew... because the Chileans were intercepting the orders. We knew the *Belgrano* was out to sink a carrier.'

An unpublished memorandum, written in 1982 for Thatcher by the head of the Chilean air force, General Fernando Matthei Aubel, confirms that Pinochet agreed to collaborate, but in complete secrecy. Diplomatic channels between the two countries were bypassed. Pinochet's sole proviso was that no SAS attacks on Argentina be mounted from Chilean soil.

In retrospect, the sinking of the ageing cruiser was a more pivotal moment in the war than Thatcher and her Cabinet realized. The US satellite pictures revealed that, after the sinking of the *Belgrano*, the Argentine navy retreated to port and ceased to be a threat to the Task Force. It ensured that once British troops had landed, the Falklands could be retaken.

Chile's assistance during the Falklands conflict helps to explain why Baroness Thatcher stood by General Pinochet when he was arrested in Britain on 16 October 1998 over charges lodged in Spain for allegedly being involved in over four thousand political murders during his rule. He had arrived in London for medical treatment for acute back pain at a local clinic. Robin Harris, a member of Thatcher's Number Ten Policy Unit, later said: 'Pinochet, who took every key decision, fully deserved Mrs Thatcher's gratitude... Margaret Thatcher would not have spoken up for him if she had believed him a monster.'[10]

At the end of the war, Thatcher invited more than fifty members of the 'winning team' involved in the Falklands campaign, including the senior staff from Northwood, to a victory dinner in the state dining room at Number Ten. They were all men, and they wore uniforms and their medals. Their wives, meanwhile, were hosted at a separate cocktail reception at the Prime Minister's residence. Parkinson recalls: 'After making a short, punchy little speech thanking everyone for what they had done for their country, she stood up and – she does have a sense of humour – she said, "Gentlemen, shall we join the ladies?"'

Looking back, thirty years on, the legacy of the adventure is mixed.

Margaret Thatcher described its impact as 'enormous'. 'We had come to be seen by both friends and enemies as a nation which lacked the will and the capability to defend its interests in peace, let alone in war,' she said. 'Victory in the Falklands changed that.'[11] Parkinson has no doubt she is right. 'We thought the alternative was even worse – to capitulate and let the Argentinians take the Falklands was just unacceptable. What could have been a disaster turned into a very proud year. She came out of the Falklands with a hugely enhanced reputation for leadership. It totally changed a lot of people's attitudes towards her.'

In total, 750 Argentine troops and 255 British servicemen died in the war. Many survivors lived with the physical and mental scars of the war long after hostilities ended. Britain also was forced to spend many millions of pounds maintaining a credible defence force in the South Atlantic: four Typhoon fighter planes, a Type 42 Destroyer, a Mine-sweeper, forces on the ground and regular visits by nuclear submarines. More millions were spent on extending the airfield at Port Stanley – the strip is now capable of landing bigger transport planes to reinforce the islands quickly in a crisis.

The population of the Falkland Islands is growing. Their future appears settled. The islanders are now trying to revive their fortunes by cashing in on the Falklands as a tourist destination. Where the *Canberra* and the *QE2* survived attempts to sink them, huge cruise liners dock in the peaceful bays. There is no evidence that Argentina would be foolish enough to repeat its attempt to seize the islands by force. Yet, these days I feel a strong sense of déjà vu.

The sabre rattling between Argentina and Britain is, if anything, intensifying.

Right-wing Tory MPs have once again begun to sound warnings against any attempt to weaken Britain's grip on the 'overseas territories' – code for the Falklands and Gibraltar. Take this exchange from Prime Minister's Question Time in November 2011:

> ROSINDELL (ROMFORD) (CON): The Prime Minister will be aware that there remain sixteen British overseas territories around the world where the Union flag still flies proudly. Will he pledge that Her Majesty's Government will protect, defend and cherish the loyal subjects of all those territories?

> THE PRIME MINISTER: I can happily give my hon. Friend that guarantee. Let me add that the overseas territories will remain British for as long as the people of those territories want to maintain their special relationship with us, and that the Union flag will continue to fly over the Governors' residences.'[12]

David Cameron, who was aged fifteen and at Eton when the war for the Falklands broke out, went on: 'We are increasing our assistance to overseas territories – my hon. Friend will be familiar with what we are doing in St Helena with the airport – and, of course, next year is the anniversary of the liberation of the Falkland Islands, which will be a moment for genuine celebration in all overseas territories.'

Just as in 1982, the growing belligerence in Buenos Aires was at first taken by Westminster as empty rhetoric. However, there were fears things might escalate for the thirtieth anniversary of the conflict in the spring and summer of 2012. The Argentinians objected to the announcement that Prince William, a helicopter pilot and the heir to the throne after the Prince of Wales, was due to serve in the Falklands that spring. In December 2011, the Mercosur bloc, an alliance of South American countries that includes Brazil, Paraguay, Uruguay and Argentina, announced that no ship bearing the Falklands flag would be allowed to dock in their ports.

Cameron responded by reissuing the commitment to the islanders on their power of a veto over any discussion about the sovereignty of the islands in his New Year message for 2012: 'We will never negotiate on the sovereignty of the Falkland Islands unless you, the Falkland Islanders, so wish. No democracy could ever do otherwise.' Cameron told the Commons: 'As long as the Falkland Islands want to be Sovereign British Territory, they should remain Sovereign British Territory. Full stop. End of story.'

Cristina Fernández de Kirchner, the Argentine President, described his remarks as 'arrogant – an expression of mediocrity and almost stupidity'. She accused Britain of being a 'crude colonial power in decline'. She insisted that Argentina would get back Las Malvinas but 'through international rights and through peace'. And once again, US foreign policy seemed to favour Argentina. She appears to have US Secretary of State Hillary Clinton on her side in seeking talks to resolve the Falklands dispute. In March 2010, the *Daily Mail* published photographs of the two women sharing a joke at a relaxed meeting, and reported Clinton as saying: 'We want very much to encourage both countries to sit down [to talks].'

Part of the cause of the renewed tension is the recent claims by oil companies that they have found recoverable oil reserves in the Falklands basin. Argentina has lodged angry protests against the British Government for allowing these companies to exploit 'its' oil in the disputed waters of the South Atlantic with their delicate ecological balance.

The Falklands, which served little purpose for the UK in 1982, may now have a strategic value to an energy-starved Britain.

I also have an eerie sense of déjà vu over Britain's defence budget. Once again a Treasury man, Philip Hammond, has been appointed as Defence Secretary with a brief to cut defence spending – just like Nott. In 2012, Hammond, who was Shadow Chief Secretary to the Treasury in charge of public expenditure when the Tories were in opposition, announced even deeper cuts than Nott dared: the army is to be slashed by twenty thousand regular soldiers by 2020; one of two new Queen Elizabeth-class aircraft carriers is to be 'mothballed'; there is doubt over when they will be brought into service, if ever.

It may be unintended, but the defence cuts send the same sort of messages to Buenos Aires that it picked up from London three decades ago. Argentina knows that Britain could never mount a 'Second Armada' to defend the Falkland Islands as it did in 1982; Britain simply does not have the carriers. Further, Britain has slashed its spending on the defence of the islands from £143 million a year in 2005–6 to £69 million for 2010–11. The former commander of the Task Force, Admiral Sandy Woodward, said: 'Without American support the Falklands… are now perilously close to being indefensible.' I have since learned that Argentine submarines appear to be testing the British defences by sailing close to the disputed territorial waters of the Falklands and the islands of South Georgia.

There is no evidence that Argentina would be foolish enough to repeat its attempt to seize the islands by force again. However, the Falklands adventure – perhaps the last great naval campaign we will ever see – and the subsequent conflicts in Iraq and Afghanistan raise a more fundamental question for Britain about our role in the world.

The latest cuts in British armed forces have led Conservative-supporting newspapers to question how long Britain might maintain the pretence of being a world power while it has slashed its defence budget. The day after the cuts were announced, the *Daily Telegraph* asked in its leader: 'When did we have a national debate about this country's decision to opt out of its role as a major player in global affairs?' Jim Murphy, Labour's Shadow Defence Secretary, said: 'This isn't just a smaller army, it's also a less powerful army in a less influential nation.' Britain retains a permanent seat on the UN Security Council alongside China, Russia, the US and France, and it is about to replace its ageing nuclear Trident weapons with a new nuclear system capable of destroying Moscow or Beijing, but it has yet to come to terms with its status as a post-imperial power living on reduced means. That process began with the retreat from Suez. We are in danger of resembling a grand old lady living in a Victorian mansion who cannot afford the council tax.

Victory over the Argentine junta undoubtedly reasserted the rule of international law, underpinned democracy in the region, raised Britain's standing in the world and secured Margaret Thatcher's place in history. As both sides marked the three decades that have passed since they went to war over the 'wind-blown specks of rock in the South Atlantic', one final question hangs over the Falklands conflict: have we learned anything from our past?

We are all Elizabethans now

I joined the cheering crowds on the banks of the River Thames on 3 June 2012 to watch the great waterborne pageant to celebrate Queen Elizabeth II's Diamond Jubilee, kicking off an extraordinary year of British pride and patriotism that would be capped with the London Olympics in the summer. Some had camped in the rain overnight, showing the same sort of stoicism that Henry V must have witnessed among his bedraggled army at Azincourt. The crowds with their Union Jacks were so dense, there was no room left on Westminster Bridge and so I retreated to the relative peace of the Palace of Westminster and a lofty turret room on the roof among the gargoyles, giving me a hawk's-eye view of the Thames. A multitude of craft came bobbing down the river, as if Canaletto's *The Thames on Lord Mayor's Day* had truly come to life, except this was Britain, and it was a typical British summer's day: grey and wet, with a freezing wind whipping off the river. On the top deck of a pleasure boat, converted for the day, the royal pensioners – the Queen, aged eighty-six, and Prince Philip, nearly ninety-one – shielded themselves from the cold blast off the river by standing behind two huge and tacky crimson thrones.

The star of the waterborne show for me was *Gloriana*, a reconstruction of a gilded royal barge powered by eighteen oarsmen. It sliced through the water – just as the Queen's barge must have done in August 1588 when the first Queen Elizabeth – England's Gloriana – was rowed downriver to Tilbury with her bodyguards and musicians to make her great Armada speech to her troops.

The Diamond Jubilee pageant was the greatest river extravaganza since the days of Charles II, who put on a show on the river because he needed a boost for his Queen consort, the Portuguese Catherine of Braganza, who was unpopular because she was a Catholic. Then, it failed to convince the public; this time, the magic of majesty seemed to cast its spell over the country, despite the rain. The whole nation seemed to lose its traditional reserve to celebrate the Second Elizabethan Age.

For many, it was simply a great escape from the austerity of our time. For some, it was a once-in-a-lifetime spectacle, to savour for history's sake. For the lucky thousands who later crammed into the Mall for a rock concert, it offered the chance to share the dusky evening with pop royalty, as well as the Windsors, against the backdrop of Buckingham Palace, transformed by a light show into a council house for 'Our House' by Madness.

Some historians saw the Diamond Jubilee as a reaffirmation of that elusive quality called 'Britishness'. 'We are the British of Shakespeare and Miss Marple, of Thomas Hardy and green pastures, with a whole-hearted contempt for political correctness and absurd health and safety regulations,' wrote Max Hastings wistfully in the *Daily Mail*.[1] He might have added the misty-eyed quotation from John Major in 1993[2]: 'Fifty years on from now, Britain will still be the country of long shadows on cricket grounds, warm beer, invincible green suburbs, dog lovers and pools fillers, and, as George Orwell said, "Old maids bicycling to holy communion through the morning mist".'*

Of course, Orwell could be forgiven for eulogizing the England of 'solid breakfasts and gloomy Sundays, smoky towns and winding roads, green fields and red pillar-boxes'. When he was writing, Britain was at war with Germany and the qualities he praised were facing an uncertain future. He opened his essay 'England Your England' in 1941 with the arresting line: 'As I write, highly civilized human beings are flying overhead, trying to kill me.' Orwell predicted that if Britain lost the war, and it was Russianized or Germanized, the enduring qualities of Britishness, its 'gentleness, the hypocrisy, the thoughtlessness, the reverence for law and the hatred of uniforms, will remain along with suet puddings and misty skies'.[3]

This harks back to the England of the Steam Age, and, to many who were born here in the second half of the Queen's long reign, a foreign country. Nostalgia surrounded the Diamond Jubilee like a London fog of the 1950s, the era when Elizabeth succeeded her father, George VI, a Union Jack was first planted on Everest (by a New Zealander, Sir Edmund Hillary), some people got their first television sets and Britain got the atomic bomb. The Queen was hailed as a sign of continuity in a changing world, a bulwark against the traumas of bank crashes, terrorism, street riots and, for many of her generation, the scary digital advances invading our lives such as the iPhone, Twitter and texting. It was no wonder

---

* Major misquoted Orwell's 'England Your England', in which he appreciated the 'old maids biking to Holy Communion through the mists of the autumn morning' as well as the 'rattle of pin-tables in the Soho pubs'.

that, in 2012, a wartime slogan became ever more popular: Keep Calm and Carry On.

The Diamond Jubilee was also a reminder of the enduring popularity of the second Queen Elizabeth (if not the institution of monarchy). During the Jubilee festivities, republicans were (not surprisingly) thin on the ground. Indeed, support for the Queen, often inspired by her own sense of duty, came from some unexpected quarters, including the über-modern artist Tracey Emin, who gained international fame for her unmade bed and a beach hut from Kent (how typically English can you get). 'I really love the Queen. Our figurehead of our country is a woman. This is a fantastic thing for our country,' she said in the run-up to the Jubilee parties. 'We haven't got a dictatorship. We haven't got a president that's going to go out in four years.'

The Jubilee celebrations, sometimes bordering on mass hysteria, were not a yearning for our long-dead past, nor a spin doctor's confection like Cool Britannia in the Blair era. They demonstrated how much Britain as a nation in the twenty-first century is changing. Emin declared: 'Our ideas of what the establishment was twenty years ago are very different. We live in a meritocracy; the establishment was class-based before. It's not now.'[4]

She, like so many others, is now proudly a member of the new Elizabethan establishment.

~૨~

Monarchy may have been a pillar of political stability in Britain for centuries, with just one or two exceptions (such as the excesses of the Prince Regent at the time of Waterloo).* But a study of our 'proudest' years shows the institution has survived because it was able to adapt. From the moment the seal was placed on Magna Carta by King John in 1215, the Divine Right of Kings has been open to challenge. The Great Charter laid the foundation stone for our constitutional monarchy giving the real power to an elected Parliament, which has helped to keep Britain stable while Europe has been repeatedly engulfed in revolution.

Those still calling for a republic in Britain either forget our history – or they ignore it: we tried it once and, after the death of Oliver Cromwell, the

---

* The House of Windsor is, of course, as German as Mercedes, and a recent invention – created by George V in 1917 to quell anti-German sentiment towards his family and its ties to the House of Saxe-Coburg-Gotha during the Great War. In that case, monarchy was stronger than history.

Lord Protector, we did not like it very much. A few hundred yards from the Victoria Embankment where the crowds riotously cheered Queen Elizabeth II, Charles I was beheaded in the name of the people, launching England on its brief experiment in republicanism. He stepped onto a scaffold outside the windows of the Banqueting House in Whitehall at 2 p.m. on 30 January 1649, to be executed on the orders of Cromwell and his Parliament. Eye-witnesses said there was an audible groan from the crowd when his head was cut off. The clock on Horse Guards still has the number '2' blacked out as a memorial to Charles's death.

The British flirtation with republicanism lasted just eleven years before the dead King's more accommodating son, Charles II, was brought back from the Netherlands and put on the throne. A jaunty equestrian statue of Charles I stands on a small island – these days ignored in a sea of traffic – looking down Whitehall to the spot where he was beheaded. It was placed there deliberately after the Restoration as an act of spite by monarchists. This was the site of the medieval Queen Eleanor's Cross which had been destroyed by Cromwell's men because of its royalist connections, and of the scaffold where some of the regicides who signed King Charles's death warrant were later hanged, drawn and quartered. They included Captain Cuttance, who, Samuel Pepys noted in his diary, died 'looking as cheerfully as any man could do in that condition'.[5] The English Republic anticipated the bloody French Revolution by 144 years, and pre-dated the regicide of the Romanov family in the Russian Revolution by 269 years.

Like it or not, the story of our proudest years is the story of our monarchy. It may be a typical British lash-up, a compromise, a live-and-let-live fix, but it works. The Queen is the head of state but has few real powers. Republicans complain that the royal prerogative gives the monarch authority to declare war and make or break governments. For instance, the 2010 Coalition could easily have created a constitutional crisis for the Crown, had the Queen become involved directly in the power-broking by deciding who should be called to 'kiss hands' as her next Prime Minister. In practice, however, she remained quarantined from the negotiations until they were over. These are mainly debating points. Would daily life be any better if these powers were vested in a president? I doubt it. And one glance at most of the world's republics (apart from Ireland) tells me that, were Elizabeth II or her heir Charles III brought to the block outside the Banqueting House one day for a ceremonial power cut, it would not be long before he or she were replaced by a president with a first lady (or first gentleman), living in an expensive grand palace with all the trappings of prestige and royalty. Even so, Prince Charles, having spent a lifetime in waiting, is unlikely to find the public so pro-monarchist when the Queen's long reign finally comes to an end. He will have to earn their respect. Perhaps one day we will show how much we have changed by allowing our Royals, even those in line for the throne, to earn a living outside the confines of the armed forces.

It may seem absurd in the twenty-first century to bend the knee to the housewife superstar who lives at the end of the Mall, but respect for the monarchy is one means of taking pride in our national identity. Our soldiers still go off to fight for 'Queen and Country'. It is striking how often our monarchs have supplied the unifying symbol – and often the rallying cry – for Britain at the times of our greatest peril, even if the words were supplied by others – Elizabeth I's Armada speech at Tilbury; the invocation of the lines from *Henry V* by Admiral Lord Nelson before the Battle of the Nile ('We band of brothers') and by Churchill in 1940 ('We few…'). Shakespeare provided the words, but the leadership of kings (and one queen) provided the inspiration for future generations to fight for their 'sceptred isle, set in a silver sea'.

More surprising to me was the discovery – or rediscovery – of how important the sea has been in our story. In the opening lines of *The Ecclesiastical History of the English People*, which he finished in 731, the Geordie priest we know as the Venerable Bede summed up Britain succinctly as 'an island in the ocean, formerly called Albion'. Thanks to the jet engine and the Channel Tunnel, we have forgotten we are still an island, and the sea defines much of who we are.

Investigating our past, I was repeatedly struck by how often the sea, particularly the English Channel, has been truly 'a moat defensive to a house, / Against the envy of less happier lands'. This narrow, twenty-one-mile strip of sea, which has protected and enriched Britain over the centuries, has also kept the nation insular. Having lost Calais in January 1558 during the reign of 'Bloody' Mary Tudor, we still appear to view the Continent – particularly the French – with an air of superior scorn: the popular British attitude over the current eurocrisis seems to be: 'We bailed them out in 1815 and 1940. Why should we bail them out again?' Despite its proximity, we remain reluctant Europeans, still arguing over whether we should be in or out of the EU.

This insularity has also earned Britons a reputation for treating foreigners with suspicion or condescension. We still have a tendency, when we travel abroad, to shout at foreigners when we want to be understood. University figures for 2012 show applications to European language courses are down by 11.2 per cent, and those to non-European languages are down by 21.5 per cent. The economist Will Hutton said that despite rising competition from India, China and the Middle East, we still expect the world to learn English and to 'pull up the drawbridge, make our welfare system as mean as possible and to balance our books' to repel the rest.[6]

It is extraordinary that a nation which, at the height of its Empire, governed one fifth of the surface of the world and one third of its population has been, until relatively recently, neither multi-racial nor multi-cultural. There were pockets of immigration – the French Huguenots in Whitechapel, the Chinese in Liverpool – but no large-scale immigration until after the war.

Over the centuries, Britain brought home the spoils of its Empire but not its people. We transported slaves to the Americas but not to Britain, partly, no doubt, because we knew that, if we had done so, they would be freed under the law. We preferred instead to 'civilize' through commerce, turning the spoils into goods to sell back to people in our colonies. We sold them cotton garments spun in wet Lancashire mills; steam engines and machined tools forged in Birmingham; silver and steel knives moulded in Sheffield and wool run through the looms of Yorkshire.

When it shared ideas about leadership and organization with far-flung peoples under its command, it exported the civil service bureaucracy invented in Whitehall (as well as Britain's other great civilizing export: public sewers and the sanitary ware of Thomas Crapper), but not the one-person, one-vote democracy made in Westminster. Britain preferred to run its Empire through governors rather than representation, until it was forced to change course after the Second World War.

As the flag was lowered in the imperial outposts, Britain had to concede independence to its former colonies – and grant them Parliamentary democracy, based on the Westminster model. With the start of the Second Elizabethan Age, people began to arrive from the Commonwealth of Nations. Large-scale immigration, including a significant influx of Afro-Caribbeans and Asians with an Islamic faith and culture, is continuing to change Britain. In the past decade, they have been followed since 2004 by an estimated seven hundred thousand migrants from the former Soviet bloc countries of Eastern Europe which are now members of the EU.

At the time of writing, the Coalition Government is proposing a new 'Britishness' test for immigrants wanting to settle, and there was speculation it would include key battles and their dates, as well as knowledge of historic figures such as the Duke of Wellington, Nelson and Emmeline Pankhurst.[7] Regardless of the tests they are set, I suspect the new arrivals will integrate into our cultural life with a peculiarly British twist. If our past is anything to go by, before long they will be drinking tea, standing in queues and complaining about the weather.

Britain is changing. It will be a very different Britain from the one in which Elizabeth II was crowned and in which I grew up. British-built cars are now reliable but our most famous marques (Rolls-Royce, Land Rover, Jaguar and Bentley) are all owned by foreign companies. Our Premier League football teams lead the world but are mostly owned by oligarchs or potentates or (most depressing of all) corporate raiders backed by hedge funds – the football bubblegum cards I used to swap in the schoolyard would carry few home-grown Premier league players today. And the reputation of our bank managers – pillars of the establishment at the start of Elizabeth's sixty-year reign – has joined our politicians (and journalists) in the gutter. But in a fundamental sense, I share Orwell's (and Major's) optimism – fundamentally, Britain will remain the same: self-deprecating, diffident, suspicious of authority (unless it comes dressed as a doctor), keen on fair play, jealous of our freedom of speech, generous in our support for the underdog and as bolshie as King John's barons. If Britain stands for anything, it is for evolution rather than revolution. We smother radicalism by embracing it, like playing the Sex Pistols' 'Anarchy in the UK' on BBC Radio 2, the easy listening channel.

The time cannot be far off when Britain will have its first Anglo-Asian or Anglo-Caribbean Prime Minister, but I suspect whoever replaces our current crop of leaders, he or she will follow in the tradition of Gladstone, Disraeli, Thatcher, Blair and Cameron – a leader who supports Parliamentary democracy despite its imperfections as well as those sometimes Gilbertian customs, such as slamming the door of the Commons in the face of Black Rod at the State Opening of Parliament – to reassert the primacy of the Commons over the Crown. These customs are maintained precisely to remind us of our past and our hard-won rights, including those derived from Magna Carta, which others sometimes value more highly than we do.

It seems to me this future Britannia is good reason to remember the most glorious years of our past, not as we hope they were, but as they really were.

APPENDIX

The Poll

In the summer of 2010, YouGov posed the following question:

> David Cameron has said that 1940 is the proudest year in British
> history. Which of these, if any, do you regard as the proudest year
> in British history?

Fieldwork was undertaken on 28 July and the survey was carried
out online. The total survey size was 693 adults, and the figures were
weighted to be representative of all adults aged eighteen and older
in Great Britain.

YEAR AND EVENT	OVERALL %
1215 – King John signs Magna Carta	3
1415 – Henry V wins the Battle of Azincourt	0
1588 – Sir Francis Drake defeats the Spanish Armada	1
1689 – Parliament adopts the Bill of Rights	1
1815 – Wellington defeats Napoleon at Waterloo	2
1833 – Britain finally abolishes slavery	13
1928 – Women get the vote on the same terms as men	12
1940 – Britain stands alone against Hitler	29
1948 – Birth of the National Health Service	24
1982 – Britain under Margaret Thatcher wins the Falklands War	3
Other	2
None	2
Don't know	8

BY AGE AND GENDER

YEAR	AGE				GENDER	
	18–29	30–39	40–59	60+	MALE	FEMALE
Weighted sample	167	95	238	193	336	357
Unweighted sample	144	99	225	225	323	370
	%	%	%	%	%	%
1215	3	0	4	3	3	3
1415	0	0	0	0	0	0
1588	0	0	1	2	1	0
1689	0	2	2	2	2	1
1815	4	2	2	2	5	0
1833	13	22	8	13	7	18
1928	10	9	9	18	3	20
1940	31	34	29	26	38	21
1948	23	18	26	26	25	23
1982	1	0	5	2	3	2
Other	3	0	3	2	4	1
None	0	0	3	2	1	2
Don't know	11	12	9	2	8	8

BY VOTING INTENTION AND SOCIAL GRADE

YEAR	VOTING INTENTION			SOCIAL GRADE	
	TORY	LABOUR	LIB DEM	MIDDLE CLASS (ABC1)	WORKING CLASS (C2DE)
Weighted sample				385	292
Unweighted sample	236	179	86	462	215
	%	%	%	%	%
1215	5	1	4	4	1
1415	0	0	0	0	0
1588	1	0	2	1	1
1689	2	1	0	2	1
1815	5	2	1	2	3
1833	11	12	13	13	12
1928	10	7	12	12	12
1940	39	26	24	32	26
1948	10	42	33	20	30
1982	5	1	2	3	3
Other	3	2	2	2	2
None	1	1	1	1	2
Don't know	8	7	5	7	8

BY REGION

YEAR	LONDON	REST OF SOUTH	MIDLANDS / WALES	NORTH	SCOTLAND
Weighted sample	89	230	146	168	61
Unweighted sample	96	247	133	145	72
	%	%	%	%	%
1215	3	2	3	3	3
1415	1	0	0	0	0
1588	2	1	0	1	0
1689	2	2	1	1	0
1815	4	2	4	1	2
1833	18	13	12	12	8
1928	8	12	15	4	28
1940	27	30	34	29	20
1948	25	22	24	28	23
1982	0	3	1	5	0
Other	1	3	1	3	1
None	0	1	0	3	5
Don't know	8	8	5	9	8

NOTES

Introduction: Ten Years

1. Interview, *Today*, BBC Radio 4, 28 July 2010.
2. Lord Moran, *Winston Churchill: The Struggle for Survival, 1940–65* (London: Constable (1966), p. 324.
3. Interview, *Newsnight*, BBC2, 28 July 2010.

One. 1215

1. Holt, James Clarke, 'King John's Disaster in the Wash', *Nottingham Medieval Studies, vol.5 (1961), 75–86*.
2. Hindley, Geoffrey, *A Brief History of the Magna Carta: The Story of the Origins of Liberty*, Robinson (2008), p. 11.
3. Warren, W.L., *King John*, Penguin (1966), p. 209.
4. Hewlett, Henry J. (ed.), 'Chronicles of Roger of Wendover', *Flores Historiarum*, Rolls Series (1886–9).
5. *Rotuli Litterarum Patentium in Turri Londonensi asservati, 1201–1216* (Patent Rolls of King John), Record Commission (1835), National Archives, London, series reference C66.
6. Howlett, R. (ed.), 'Chronicle of Richard of Devizes' in *Chronicles of the Reigns of Stephen, Henry II and Richard I*, Rolls Series (1884–90), p. 388.
7. Breay, Claire, *Magna Carta: Manuscripts and Myths*, British Library (2011), p. 15.
8. Hewlett, 'Chronicles of Roger of Wendover'.
9. Cathedral history, www.salisburycathedral.org.uk.
10. Breay, *Magna Carta*, p. 39.
11. Innocent III, Papal letter, Treasures Gallery, British Library.
12. Warren, *King John*, p. 274.
13. Ibid., p. 277.
14. Linebaugh, Peter, 'Secret history of the Magna Carta', *Boston Review* (Summer 2003), http://bostonreview.net/BR28.3/linebaugh.html.
15. Breay, *Magna Carta*, p. 7.
16. Warren, *King John*, p. 256.
17. Bingham, Tom, *The Rule of Law*, Allen Lane (2010), p. 12.

18. Interview, *Guardian* online, 23 November 2010,
    http://www.youtube.com/watch?v=5lFGQrBp_Mw.
19. Press Association, 'Ministers in row over human rights,' *Guardian*, 4 October
    2011, http://www.guardian.co.uk/uk/feedarticle/9878765.

Two. 1415

1. Shakespeare, William, *Henry V*, Act 4, Scene 3.
2. Fernández-Armesto, Felipe, 'The Myth of Henry V', BBC History, 17
   February 2011,
       http://www.bbc.co.uk/history/british/middle_ages/henry_v_01.shtml.
3. Shakespeare, *Henry V*, Act 4, Chorus.
4. Holmes, Richard, *The Complete War Walks: From Hastings to Normandy*, BBC
   Books (2003), p. 52.
5. Shakespeare, *Henry V*, Act 4, Scene 3.
6. Lyons, Bill, dir., *Battlefield Detectives: Agincourt's Dark Secrets*, Granada TV,
   30 July 2003.
7. Ibid.
8. Askew, Graham N., Federico Formenti, and Alberto E. Minetti, 'Limitations
   imposed by wearing armour on Medieval soldiers' locomotor performance',
   Proceedings of the Royal Society B 279 (1729, 2011): 640–4, doi: 10.1098/
   rspb.2011.0816.
9. Morelle, Rebecca, 'Treadmill shows medieval armour influenced battles',
   BBC News, 20 July 2011,
       http://www.bbc.co.uk/news/science-environment-14204717.
10. Barker, Juliet, *Agincourt: The King, the Campaign, the Battle*, Little Brown
    (2005), p. 297.
11. Holmes, *Complete War Walks*, p. 76.
12. Barker, *Agincourt*, p. xvi.
13. Curry, Anne, *Agincourt: A New History*, Tempus (2005).

Three. 1588

1. Hanson, Neil, *The Confident Hope of a Miracle: The True History of the Spanish
   Armada*, Random House (2004).
2. Frye, Susan, 'The Myth of Elizabeth at Tilbury', *Sixteenth Century Journal*
   23 (1, 1992): 95–114.
3. N.A., *Queen Elizabeth Slept Here*, Thurrock Local History Society (1988),
   p. 22.
4. Adams, Robert, 'Thamesis Descriptio' engraving 1738, British Library, ms.
   44839.
5. Leyin, Alan, 'Elizabeth's review of her troops: Tilbury 1588', Thurrock Local
   History Society *Panorama* 45 (2007): 5.
6. Adams, 'Thamesis Descriptio'.
7. Nolan, John S., *Sir John Norreys and the Elizabethan Military World*, University
   of Exeter Press (1997).

8. Bingley, Randal, 'The Armada camp: A locational report', Thurrock Local History Society *Panorama* 29 (1987): 30.
9. 'Order of Battle, Tilbury', National Archives, SP 12/215, no. 18, p. 48.
10. Brown, Colin, *Whitehall: The Street that Shaped a Nation*, Simon and Schuster (2009), p. 102.
11. Frye, 'The Myth of Elizabeth at Tilbury'.
12. Sharpe, Leonel, Text of Elizabeth's oration at Tilbury, 1623, British Library, BM Harleian ms. 6798, article 18.
13. Ibid.
14. Nolan, *Sir John Norreys and the Elizabethan Military World*.
15. Hawkins, John, Letter to Francis Walsingham, National Archives, SP 12/213, 21 July 1588.
16. Fenner, Thomas, Letter to Francis Walsingham, National Archives, 4 August 1588.
17. Handwritten note, Voyagers gallery, National Maritime Museum, Greenwich, London.
18. Interview with the author, 8 November 2011.

Four. 1688

1. Israel, Jonathan I., and Geoffrey Parker, 'Of Providence and Protestant Winds: The Spanish Armada of 1588 and the Dutch Armada of 1688', in Jonathan I. Israel, ed., *The Anglo-Dutch Moment: Essays on the Glorious Revolution and its world impact*, Cambridge University Press (1991).
2. Miller, John, *James II: A study in kingship*, Yale University Press (1978), p. xvi.
3. Thurley, Simon, *Whitehall Palace: The official illustrated history*, Historic Royal Palaces (2008), p. 98.
4. James II, Letter to William of Orange, National Archives SP 8/4 f. 72, 12 June 1688.
5. Ibid., f. 77.
6. Macaulay, Thomas Babington, *The History of England, from the Accession of James II*, Amazon Kindle (2011), location 15441.
7. Callow, John, *James II: The triumph and the tragedy*, John Callow, National Archives (2005), pp. 80–1.
8. Earl of Middleton, Letter to Lord Preston, National Archives, SP 44/97 f. 23, 24 November 1688.
9. Bentinck, Hans Willem, notation on campaign record, Bentinck Papers, Nottingham University, Pw. A 2235, November 1688.
10. Brown, Colin, *Whitehall: The Street that Shaped a Nation*, Simon and Schuster (2009), p. 143.
11. Barillon, Paul, Diary, 1/11 December 1688.
12. Evelyn, John, *Diary of John Evelyn*, London: Everyman's Library (2006 ed.), p. 891.
13. Maer, Lucinda, and Oonagh Gay, House of Commons Library Note to the Bill of Rights 1689, Parliament and Constitution Centre, SN/PC/0293, 5 October 2009.

14. Maer, Lucinda, House of Commons Library Note to the Act of Settlement and the Protestant Succession, Parliament and Constitution Centre, SN/PC/683, 24 January 2011.

Five. 1815

1. Holmes, Richard, *Wellington: The Iron Duke*, HarperCollins (2003), p. 236.
2. Siborne, H.T., *History of the Waterloo Campaign*, Leonaur (1848), p. 211.
3. Woodford, Lt-Gen. Sir Alexander, Letter to Coldstream Guards, in H.T. Siborne, *The Waterloo Letters: Accounts of the battle by British officers for its foremost historian*, Leonaur (2009).
4. Ibid., p. 170.
5. Gronow, Rees Howell, *The Reminiscences and Recollections of Captain Gronow: Being anecdotes of the camp, court and society 1810–1860*, The Bodley Head (1964), p. 190–1.
6. Powell, Capt. H.W., Letter to H.T. Siborne, in Siborne, *Waterloo Letters*.
7. Longford, Elizabeth, *Wellington: Pillar of State*, Weidenfeld & Nicolson (1972), p. 4.
8. Clare, John, 'The Fallen Elm', in *John Clare: Selected Poetry and Prose*, ed. by Merryn Williams and Raymond Williams, Routledge (1986), p. 212.
9. Hernon, Ian, *Riot!: Civil Insurrection from Peterloo to the Present Day*, Pluto Press (2006), p. 8.

Six. 1833

1. Wilberforce, Robert and Samuel, eds, *The Life of William Wilberforce*, five vols, John Murray (1838).
2. Mann, Charles, *1493: Uncovering the New World Columbus Created*, Random House (2011).
3. Hochschild, Adam, 'The idea that brought slavery to its knees', *Los Angeles Times*, 25 January 2005.
4. Lubbock, Tom, 'The great art series: The *Brookes*', *Independent*, 23 March 2007.
5. 'Plan and sections of a slave ship the *Brooks* (sometimes *Brookes*)', National Maritime Museum, Greenwich, London.
6. Pollock, John, *Wilberforce*, Lion Books (1986), p. 187.
7. Court record, Dominica, Leeward Islands, National Archives, London, CO 71/51, 15–16 January 1814.
8. Hansard, vol. 3, cc. 641–74, 28 February 1805.
9. 'The Atlantic: Slavery, trade, empire', Permanent Exhibition, National Maritime Museum, Greenwich, London.
10. Quoted in discussion of *The Empire Pays Back* (Channel 4 TV), BN Village, 3 August 2005, http://www.bnvillage.co.uk/f90/empire-pays-back-76518.html.
11. 'Couple jailed for "slave" treatment', Press Association, 12 July 2012.

Seven. 1928

1. Bunn, Frank, '1913 Derby: Transcript of the report of PS 4NR Frank Bunn relating the events at Epsom on Derby Day June 4 1913', Epsom and Ewell History Explorer,
www.epsomandewellhistoryexplorer.org.uk/Derby1913PoliceTranscript.pdf.
2. Colmore, Gertrude, *Suffragette Sally*, Pandora (1911, reissued 1986), p. 57.
3. 'Emily Davison: Muerte en el Derby de Epsom', enhanced video of Derby Day, Epsom, 4 June 1913,
www.youtube.com/watch?v=TH_r6-JpO9Q, uploaded 10 March 2008.
4. *The Times*, 11 June 1913, p. 15.
5. Byrne, Ashley, prod., 'The Lost World of the Suffragettes', BBC Radio 4, 12 February 2012.
6. Phillips, Melanie, *The Ascent of Woman: A History of the Suffragette Movement and the Ideas Behind It*, Abacus (2004), p. 201.
7. Morley, Ann with Liz Stanley, *The Life and Death of Emily Wilding Davison*, Women's Press (1988), p. 144.
8. Davison, Emily, essay, *The Suffragette*, 13 June 1913, p. 577.
9. Sleight, John, *One-way Ticket to Epsom: A journalist's enquiry into the heroic story of Emily Wilding Davison*, Bridge Studios, (1988), p. 9.
10. Morley with Stanley, *Life and Death*, p. 109.
11. Interview, 'Woman's Hour', BBC Radio 4, 24 June 2011.
12. Phillips, *The Ascent of Woman*, p.305.

Eight. 1940

1. Colville, John, *The Fringes of Power: Downing Street Diaries, 1935–55*, Hodder & Stoughton (1989), p. 150.
2. Shakespeare, *King Richard II*, Act 2, Scene 1.
3. Channon, Chips, *'Chips': The Diaries of Sir Henry Chips Channon*, ed. Robert Rhodes James, Phoenix (1996), p. 249.
4. Overy, Richard, *The Third Reich: A Chronicle*, Quercus (2010), p. 242.
5. Hastings, Max, *Finest Years: Churchill as Warlord 1940–45*, HarperPress (2010), p. 40.
6. Jenkins, Roy, *Churchill: A Biography*, Pan (2002), p. 598.
7. Liddell Hart, B.H., *History of the Second World War*, Cassell (1980), p. 83.
8. Ibid., p. 83.
9. War Cabinet minutes, National Archives, CAB 65/13, 1 May–30 June 1940.
10. Rees, Jasper, 'When Winston Churchill wobbled', *Daily Telegraph*, 25 October 2011.
11. Jenkins, *Churchill*, p. 599.
12. Ibid., p. 608.
13. Churchill, Winston, *Their Finest Hour*, Penguin Classics (2005), p. 197.
14. Holmes, Richard, *In the Footsteps of Churchill*, BBC Books (2005), p. 233.
15. Colville, *Fringes of Power*, p. 159.
16. Ibid., p. 292.

17. Soames, Mary, *A Daughter's Tale: The memoir of Winston and Clementine Churchill's youngest child*, Doubleday (2011), p. 191.

NINE. 1948

1.   Hennessy, Peter, *Never Again: Britain 1945–51*, Penguin (2006).
2.   Brook, Norman, First Notebook, Cabinet Minutes, 13 April–19 November 1942, National Archives, Kew, Richmond, Surrey, CAB 195/1.
3.   Brook, Norman, Second Notebook, Cabinet Minutes, 26 November 1942–14 July 1943, National Archives, Kew, Richmond, Surrey, CAB 195/2.
4.   Soames, Mary, *A Daughter's Tale: The memoir of Winston and Clementine Churchill's youngest child*, Doubleday (2011), p. 356.
5.   Brown, Derek, 'Labour and the creation of the welfare state', *Guardian*, 14 March 2001.
6.   Colville, John, *The Fringes of Power: Downing Street Diaries, 1935–55*, Hodder & Stoughton (1989), p. 576.
7.   Morgan, Kenneth O., *Britain Since 1945: The People's Peace*, Oxford University Press (2001), p. 12.
8.   Channon, Chips, *'Chips': The Diaries of Sir Henry Chips Channon*, ed. Robert Rhodes James, Phoenix (1996), p. 406.
9.   Field, Frank, 'Restoring Labour's moral economy: The role of National Insurance', in Robert Philpott, ed., *The Purple Book: A Progressive Future for Labour*, Biteback (2011), p. 159.
10. The Commons Select Committee on Social Security, fifth report.
11. Barnett, Corelli, 'The wasting of Britain's Marshall aid', BBC History, 3 March 2011, www.bbc.co.uk/history/british/modern/marshall_01.shtml.
12. Kynaston, David, *Austerity Britain: 1945–51*, Bloomsbury (2008), p. 123.
13. Ibid., p. 227.
14. Davis, Mary, 'The labour movement and World War Two', TUC History Online, n.d., www.unionhistory.info/timeline/1939_1945.php.
15. 'Tory cuts put first NHS hospital at death's door', *Daily Mirror*, 21 February 2011.
16. Campbell, John, *Nye Bevan: A biography*, Hodder & Stoughton (1994), p. 245.

TEN. 1982

1.   Nott, John, *Here Today, Gone Tomorrow: Recollections of an Errant Politician*, Politico's Publishing (2002), p. 258.
2.   Ibid., p. 267.
3.   Ibid, p. 263.
4.   Rentschler, James, diary entry, 1 April 1982, Margaret Thatcher Foundation, http://www.margaretthatcher.org/document/114319.
5.   Interviews with the author, November 2011.
6.   Hansard, House of Commons Debate, vol. 21, cc959–1052, 7 April 1982.
7.   Nott, *Here Today, Gone Tomorrow*, p 287.
8.   Parry, Gareth, 'The price of victory', *Guardian*, 25 February 2002.

9.   Thatcher, Margaret, *The Downing Street Years*, HarperCollins (1995), p. 175.
10. Harris, Robin, 'Thatcher always honoured Britain's debt to Pinochet', *Daily Telegraph*, 13 December 2006.
11. Thatcher, *Downing Street Years*, p. 173.
12. Hansard, vol. 536, Prime Minister's Questions, 30 November 2011.

POSTSCRIPT: WE ARE ALL ELIZABETHANS NOW

1.   Hastings, Max. 'Jubilee Fever', *Daily Mail*, 26 May 2012.
2.   Major, John, Speech to the Conservative Group for Europe, 22 April 1993.
3.   Orwell, George, *The Lion and the Unicorn: Socialism and the English Genius*, Secker & Warburg (1941).
4.   Interview, *Andrew Marr Show*, BBC1, 27 May 2012.
5.   Pepys, Samuel, *The Diary of Samuel Pepys*, 13 October 1660, http://www.pepysdiary.com/archive/1660/10/13/.
6.   *The Observer*, 5 February 2012.
7.   Doughty, Steve, 'Trafalgar, Nightingale and Brunel: What migrants will need to learn to live in UK', *Daily Mail*, 2 July 2012.

ACKNOWLEDGEMENTS

My thanks are due to Claire Breay, Curator of Medieval Manuscripts and expert on Magna Carta, British Library; Nigel Boden of the National Trust for a tour of Runnymede; Graeme Rimer of the Royal Armouries, Leeds, for laboratory tests on the longbow; Dr Andrea Clarke, Curator of Early Modern Historical Manuscripts, British Library; Thurrock Historical Society and Sam at the Library, Grays, Essex for invaluable research on Elizabeth I's Tilbury visit; the staff of the excellent Brixham Heritage Museum; 'Jimmy' and the Loyal Orange Lodge members who gave me an insight into their world; Alice Berkeley of Project Hougoumont; Michael Farrar, my guide at Waterloo; the staff of the Wilberforce House museum, Hull; Sonia Gomes at the Women's Library for access to the files on Emily Wilding Davison; Barbara Gorna, scriptwriter and owner of Davison's scarf, for her expertise on 'Emily'; Terry Charman, the outstanding expert on Churchill at the Imperial War Museum; the staff at the Secret Wartime Tunnels, Dover Castle; Lord Parkinson and Niki Stafford; Ross Lyndall of the *London Evening Standard* for help with the Jubilee barge; the team at YouGov including Peter Kellner; Colin Harris of the Bodleian Libraries; Andrew Grice, political editor of the *Independent* for his knowledge of European affairs, and Spurs; Melanie Unwin, Deputy Curator, Palace of Westminster collection; my tireless editor Robin Dennis for her commitment to this project; my copy-editor Tamsin Shelton for her unfailing attention to detail; and of course my wife, Amanda, for her company on this journey.

ILLUSTRATION CREDITS

Langham Pond, Runnymede: © Colin Brown

The Wash trackway map: Old Series, Ordnance Survey

Magna Carta: © The British Library Board Cotton Augustus 11.01.06

Rue Henri V, Azincourt: © Colin Brown

Henry V: Courtesy of the National Portrait Gallery, London

Armada off the coast of Dover: Courtesy of the National Maritime Museum, Greenwich, UK

Tilbury Fort causeway: © Colin Brown

Thamesis Descriptio engraving: © The British Library Board Maps Crace 18.17

Elizabeth Armada portrait: Courtesy of the National Portrait Gallery, London

Orange marchers, Brixham: © Colin Brown

William of Orange statue: © Colin Brown

Triumph of Peace and Liberty: © Nickmard Khoey

Hougoumont gatehouse: © Colin Brown

Lion Mound: © Colin Brown

Hougoumont farm: © Colin Brown

Wilberforce Oak: © Colin Brown

Brooks slave ship poster: © Wilberforce House, Hull City Museums and Art Galleries, UK/The Bridgeman Art Library

Emily Davison's rail tickets: Mary Evans Picture Library/The Women's Library, London

Davison's funeral procession: Mary Evans Picture Library/The Women's Library, London

Goering looking towards Dover: © Tempo. Courtesy of the Imperial War Museum, London

Churchill at Hellfire Corner: Crown copyright. Courtesy of the Imperial War Museum, London

Ramsay's window in the cliffs: © Colin Brown

Park Hospital, Trafford: © Colin Brown

Sylvia Beckingham and Aneurin Bevin: © Central Manchester University Hospitals NHS Foundation Trust

ARA *General Belgrano*: © PA (Press Association)

Port Stanley march: Crown copyright. Courtesy of the Imperial War Museum, London

INDEX

Page numbers in italic denote illustrations and an italicized n a footnote.